Violence and Belonging

Modernisation in Africa has created new problems as well as new freedoms. Multi-party democracy, resource privatisation and changing wealth relationships have not always created stable and prosperous communities, and violence continues to be endemic in many areas of African life – from civil war and political strife to violent clashes between genders, generations, classes and ethnic groups. *Violence and Belonging: The Quest for Identity in Post-colonial Africa* explores the crucial formative role of violence in shaping people's ideas about who they are in uncertain post-colonial contexts. As resources dwindle and wealth is contested, identities and ideas of belonging become a focal area of conflict and negotiation. Focusing on fieldwork from across the continent, case studies consider how everyday violence ties in with wider regional and political upheavals, and how individuals experience and legitimise violence in its different forms. The chapters also challenge the popular image of an African or 'ethnic' violence that is primordial, anarchic and 'primitive', arguing instead that violence, even in its most terrifying form, is integral to modern social, political and business interests. The Zimbabwean and Sudanese civil wars, Kenyan Kikuyu domestic conflicts, Rwandan massacres and South African Truth and Reconciliation processes are among the contexts explored.

Contributors: Jocelyn Alexander, Astrid Blystad, Vigdis Broch-Due, Harri Englund, John G. Galaty, Amrik Heyer, Sharon Elaine Hutchinson, Björn Lindgren, Jo Ann McGregor, Isak Niehaus, Johan Pottier, Fiona C. Ross and Kjetil Tronvoll.

Vigdis Broch-Due is Professor in International Poverty Research and Social Anthropology at the University of Bergen in Norway. She has held senior teaching and research positions at the universities of Washington, Oslo, Cambridge and London, and at Rutgers University. Her books include *Carved Flesh/Cast Selves: Gendered Symbols and Social Practices* (1993), *The Poor Are Not Us: Poverty and Pastoralism in Eastern Africa* (1999) and *Producing Poverty and Nature in Africa* (2000).

Violence and Belonging

The quest for identity in post-colonial Africa

Edited by Vigdis Broch-Due

Routledge
Taylor & Francis Group

LONDON AND NEW YORK

First published 2005
by Routledge
2 Park Square, Milton Park
Abingdon, Oxon OX14 4RN

Simultaneously published in the USA and Canada
by Routledge
270 Madison Ave, New York, NY 10016

Routledge is an imprint of the Taylor & Francis Group

Transferred to Digital Printing 2005

Selection and editorial material © 2005 Vigdis Broch-Due;
contributions © 2005 individual contributors

Typeset in Galliard by
Keystroke, Jacaranda Lodge, Wolverhampton

British Library Cataloguing in Publication Data
A catalogue record for this book is available from the British Library

Library of Congress Cataloging in Publication Data
Violence and belonging : the quest for identity in post-colonial Africa /
edited by Vigdis Broch-Due.
   p. cm.
   "Most of the chapters of this volume come from a larger collection of
papers produced for a conference held in 2000 under the auspices of the
Research Programme 'Poverty and Prosperity in Africa: Local and Global
Perspectives' at the Nordic Africa Institute, Uppsala, Sweden"—Pref.
   Includes bibliographical references and index.
   1. Political violence–Africa–Case studies–Congresses. 2. Poverty–Africa–
Congresses. 3. Africa–Politics and government–1960–Congresses.
I. Broch-Due, Vigdis.
   HN780.Z9V585 2005
   303.6'096–dc22   2004009258

ISBN 0–415–29006–6 (hbk)
ISBN 0–415–29007–4 (pbk)

Contents

Contributors

Jocelyn Alexander, Lecturer in Commonwealth Studies, University of Oxford, and **Jo Ann McGregor**, Lecturer in Human Geography, University of Reading, have researched and written on Zimbabwe for the past fifteen years. They are co-authors with Terence Ranger of *Violence and Memory: One Hundred Years in the 'Dark Forests' of Matabeleland* and of numerous other articles and chapters.

Astrid Blystad is Associate Professor at the Department of Public Health and Primary Health Care, University of Bergen. She heads the cross- disciplinary research programme entitled Gender, Generation and Communication in Times of AIDS: The Potential of 'Modern' and 'Traditional' Institutions. She has published several articles on the Barabaig/Datoga of Tanzania.

Vigdis Broch-Due is Professor at the Department of Social Anthropology, University of Bergen. She also holds the Professoriate in International Poverty Research in the Faculty of Social Science. Her books include *Carved Flesh/Cast Selves: Gendered Symbols and Social Practices; The Poor Are Not Us: Poverty and Pastoralism in Eastern Africa; Producing Poverty and Nature in Africa.* She has published numerous articles on many aspects of life among Turkana, Kenya.

Harri Englund is Lecturer in African Anthropology at the University of Cambridge. He is the author of *From War to Peace on the Mozambique–Malawi Borderland*, the editor of *A Democracy of Chameleons: Politics and Culture in the New Malawi*, and the co-editor (with Francis Nyamnjoh) of *Rights and the Politics of Recognition in Africa.*

John G. Galaty is Professor in the Anthropology Department, McGill University. His books include *World of Pastoralism: Herding Systems in a Comparative Perspective; Herders, Warriors, and Traders: Pastoralism in Africa;* and *Power and Poverty: Development and Development Projects in the Third World.*

Amrik Heyer is a social anthropologist and development consultant working on Africa and India. She is currently developing a new research project on middle-level traders, markets and states in Kenya and Africa. Previous work includes research on gender and processes of formalisation/informalisation in Kenya's

Central Province and conflicts between entrepreneurs, pastoralists and the state over control of territory, labour and markets in Northern Kenya.

Sharon Elaine Hutchinson is Professor of Anthropology and African Studies at the University of Wisconsin-Madison. She is the author of *Nuer Dilemmas: Coping with Money, War and the State*. She continues to carry out field research in war-torn Sudan, and acted as an official monitor on the Civilian Protection Monitoring Team – Sudan during early 2003.

Björn Lindgren has a Ph.D. in Cultural Anthropology from Uppsala University. He has a background in journalism which he studied at Stockholm University. Lindgren has published several articles on politics, ethnicity and gender in Zimbabwe. He is currently working on issues of local governance.

Jo Ann McGregor, see Jocelyn Alexander.

Isak Niehaus is Professor in the Department of Anthropology and Archaeology at the University of Pretoria in South Africa. His research interests are cosmology, gender and sexuality in South African rural areas. He is the author of *Witchcraft, Power and Politics: Exploring the Occult in the South African Lowveld*.

Johan Pottier is Professor in the Department of Anthropology and Sociology at SOAS, University of London. His books include *Anthropology of Food: The Social Dynamics of Food Security; Practising Development: Social Science Perspective; Migrants No More: Settlement and Survival in Mambwe Villages, Zambia.*

Fiona C. Ross lectures in Social Anthropology at the University of Cape Town, South Africa. Her recent research on women and violence appears in *Bearing Witness: Women and the Truth and Reconciliation Commission in South Africa*. She is currently engaged in research on the meanings of home among poor residents of an informal settlement in Cape Town.

Kjetil Tronvoll is Senior Research Fellow in African Studies at the Norwegian Centre for Human Rights, University of Oslo. He is author of *Mai Weini: A Highland Village in Eritrea*, co-author of *Brothers at War: Making Sense of the Eritrean–Ethiopian War* and *The Culture of Power in Contemporary Ethiopian Political Life*, and is co-editor of *Ethiopia Since the Derg: A Decade of Democratic Pretension and Performance.*

Preface

Most of the chapters of this volume come from a larger collection of papers produced for a conference held in 2000 under the auspices of the Research Programme Poverty and Prosperity in Africa: Local and Global Perspectives at the Nordic Africa Institute, Uppsala, Sweden. This was the third and final conference organised by this five-year programme, headed by Vigdis Broch-Due. Entitled Conflict's Fruit, it focused on the interplay between poverty, violence and the politics of identity in the African post-colony. To explore these vexed issues, we invited leading specialists on these topics from Scandinavia, Europe, USA and Africa.

The impetus for the conference and this volume came from research co-operation between the Poverty and Prosperity Programme at NAI and the Gender Institute at the LSE. The convenors, Henrietta L. Moore and Vigdis Broch-Due, had collected a group of researchers and graduate students from Scandinavia and Britain to get fresh research data on the intersection of gender, conflict and impoverishment in selected field locations in Kenya, Zambia, Ethiopia and Eritrea. The research co-operation was the result of a growing unease shared by the convenors that despite the frequent occurrence and ubiquitous nature of conflicts in Africa, their complex causes and widespread effects were little understood.

Conflicts occur in different arenas of social life and on widely different scales: from region-wide upheavals to factional disputes, but also in clashes of identity politics, between genders, generations, classes and ethnicities. When resources are scarce, disputes flourish and social identities become the arena of conflict and negotiations. Our research and the subsequent conference focused on how conflict in all its forms profoundly affects peoples' access to resources and all the modalities of exchange, both material and symbolic. Conflicts disrupt livelihood strategies, thus reconfiguring the social topography of poverty and prosperity. This gives rise to hegemonic struggles erupting into violence, transforming the social arena with its own particular logic of sexual, racial and ethnic 'othering'.

This volume contains case studies ranging from war and genocide to recurrent conflicts producing changes in the wider political economy – those associated with globalisation, commodification, large-scale movement of populations and diverse forms of resource extraction, coercion and constraint. The images of brutal anarchy that dominate the mass media's representation of conflicts in Africa are countered by detailed studies, highlighting the views and experiences of both victims and perpetrators. This volume provides an analytical window into the formation and deployment of violence in such contexts as ritual, sorcery and the domestic domain. It also scrutinises efforts to go beyond violence to forms of healing and reconciliation.

Much of the material has been considerably changed since the original conference. I am grateful to the authors who have been so willing to rewrite and reorganise their papers along the theoretical lines suggested. I would also like to acknowledge the vital contributions to the discussions at the conference by those participants who for various reasons could not be represented by a separate chapter in this book. From this list I am particular grateful to James Ferguson, Henrietta L. Moore, Karen Tranberg Hansen, Ann Whitehead and Richard Werbner, who all served as excellent discussants. Mekonnen Berhane, Michael Barrett, Pamela Kea, Todd Sanders and Mats Utas actively participated in the discussions and, together with the discussants, helped to develop the theorisation of the volume.

Thanks are also due to all those at NAI who worked so tirelessly to make the conference a success. Ellen Selvik, who so efficiently co-ordinated all the practicalities involved in the conference, and Abraham Bariamikael, my supportive programme assistant, each deserves a special mention. Last, but not least, the editor would like to acknowledge the financial support to the original conference by the Nordic Africa Institute and, by extension, the Foreign Affairs Ministries of Denmark, Finland, Norway and Sweden who jointly funded the activities of the above-mentioned research programme. The editor is particularly grateful to the Research Council of Norway in general, and its section of Environment and Development in particular, whose generous funding enabled me to explore issues of violence and belonging in my more recent research and, thus, produce this volume.

I am also grateful to Henrietta L. Moore for placing the ethics of theory so firmly on the agenda of our workshop; to James Ferguson for elaborating on the point that scholarly ethics is significantly linked to our ability to captivate the imagination of larger audiences; to Sharon E. Hutchinson for suggesting some key comparative issues concerning conflicts; and to Graham Townsley for his constructive reading of my own chapter.

Vigdis Broch-Due

Chapter I

Violence and belonging

Analytical reflections

Vigdis Broch-Due

> Violence enacted is but a small part of violence lived.
>
> (Nordstrom and Martin 1992: 8)

This volume brings together a number of original chapters which collectively set out to chart the disturbing landscape of identity conflicts in contemporary Africa. It represents some of the latest empirical work on recent and ongoing conflicts in the area and takes a fresh look at theories of violence and boundary maintenance in anthropology and related social sciences (Marx 1976, Riches 1986, Barth 1969, 1994, Bloch 1992). It includes new work on identities and updated analytical positions relevant to post-colonial realities (Cohen 2000, Vermulen and Govers 1994). The picture which emerges challenges the popular image of an African or even 'ethnic' violence that is primordial, anarchic or 'primitive'. Writing against the grain of generic interpretations of violence as the 'anti-social' par excellence – the absence of society, the residues of primordial impulses or genes, suppressed desires, the rupture of the social – all our authors insist that violence, even in its most terrifying form, is not only integral to the social but is intrinsically part of the modern, translocal arenas of state bureaucracies and business interests.

We now understand clearly that the effect of multi-party democracy, privatisation and structural adjustment has not been the creation of more stable and prosperous communities across the continent. All too often, it has been attempts at 'development' and 'modernisation' that have led to violence and upheaval. In fact, routinised violence has become an inevitable part of the modernising state. Analysing these forms of routinised violence in their contexts of production and interpretation, the volume raises important questions about the tensions between actors' intentions and real choices, and how these relate to overarching frameworks of cultural values and understandings.

The dramatic reconfiguration of want and wealth, so characteristic of the post-colonial landscape, has produced extreme levels of uncertainty about the legitimacy of established identities, rights and claims. As this volume shows, violence is often deployed as part of a futile quest to produce certainty, a means to reinforce essentialised ideas about identity and belonging. It also shows something surprising and perhaps unsuspected: the effect of violence is usually the reverse, reinforcing diversity in identity rather than eliminating it. From the Sudan to South Africa, our case studies show how, as resources dwindle and relations of wealth are reconfigured in the wake of violence, identities and ideas of belonging – whether to a gender, generation, class or ethnic group – become the focal arenas of conflict and negotiation.

There is a novel contribution to social theory in this volume too and it lies in its exploration of the precise linkages between wider regional upheavals and the routinised forms of violence in everyday life: how violence infiltrates not just public, political arenas but the most intimate spaces of the personal also. Thus contributors concentrate on how individuals experience and account for violence, using history and memory to make claims about its legitimacy or illegitimacy. From the troubling narratives and testimonies of violence collected here, we discover how violence is formative of people's perceptions of who they are and what values they adhere to.

The individual chapters speak eloquently for themselves so what I can hope to do in my introduction is to paint aspects of the wider landscape of social and political upheaval in Africa which forms the backdrop against which all local examples take place. In doing so, I will inevitably call on some of my own work and experiences in Turkanaland, Kenya. What I also hope to do is explore some of the extreme ambiguities which make violence such a vital and troubling part of what it means to be human, ambiguities explored to the full in the ritual worlds of the Turkana and many other African societies too. This volume seeks to cast violence as a force for social (re)construction far beyond the confines of cosmologies and local warfare, into the working of the post-colonial state and its international relations, seeing violence as a 'force that achieves its repetitive and expanding energy simply because it is such a force' (Kapferer 2001: 63).

The larger, perhaps more unfamiliar, point I want to establish in the context of this volume is this: if we think of violence as an aspect of power in a double valence of subordinating and producing, of destroying and creating, it becomes easier to explore the possible interconnections between different modalities of violence – structural, symbolic, physical – as they play themselves out in social relationships (Bourdieu 1977, Nagenast 1994). And if we expand the conceptual horizon of the social processes contributing to the formation of violence, it becomes easier to reframe the analysis of identity politics away from the reification of ethnicity as the only beast loose on the streets in the post-colony.

This over-reliance on ethnic identity in studies of violence at the expense of other identities has roundly and rightly been criticised in recent scholarship in Anthropology. Yet the typical response is to expand the list including additional identities formed around gender, generation, region, nation and so on. While this empirical strategy produces more ethnography, it does not necessarily produce more theoretical clarity. The problem with a lot of identity thinking is the 'thing-like' and bounded character of its conceptual parameter, as if the construction of gender and ethnicity, for example, belongs to separate fields of experience, rather than being embedded in each other (Moore 1994). This entanglement of relations with their ensuing identity projects constitutes forces within highly disparate and fluid social and political fields. At particular heated moments during the historical formation of nationalist or sectarian sentiment or during class struggles, a chain reaction of energy within these entangled identities can be unleashed into vicious cycles of violent action.

We have all worked hard on *Violence and Belonging* and believe it is an innovative attempt to explore the emergent and elusive matrix of violence and identity politics in modern Africa.

Disconnection and the shrinking African state

This volume addresses violence and sociality in at least two senses that are interrelated. First, we are concerned with large-scale war scenarios in which the distinctions between civilians and combatants are collapsing, causing the greatest casualties to be among women, children and the elderly rather than soldiers. Second, we are concerned with a range of conflicts born of radical impoverishment, contested resources and their attendant flux of identities. From one perspective, all these forms of violence can be viewed as the bitter fruit of transformations in the meaning of citizenship as they have worked themselves out during the last decades in post-colonial Africa.

The broader canvas for this change in the contours of citizenship is bound up with the inability of African states after independence to live up to the expectations of their subjects to provide welfare, security and prosperity. Grand schemes to develop public services have been nipped in the bud by the combined effects of homebred corruption and the push toward privatisation imposed by the global banking and development conglomerate. This has lead to a breakdown of the redistributive function of the state and its ability to provide welfare, education, health and service to its citizens This is not simply a quantitative shift, a decrease in the resources flowing from the state to its citizens but, more significantly, it is also a qualitative shift. Many of the vital obligations the state has towards its citizenry are being erased, some taken over by NGOs and private institutions while others are simply left in the hands of the citizens themselves (Comaroff and Comaroff 1997).

The transformation of the meaning of citizenship throughout most of the continent is itself born out of the changing position of the post-colonial nation state on the world arena. Stripped of most statecraft functions but for their sovereignty, contemporary African states are increasingly in the pocket of business corporations, NGOs and international aid bureaucracies. These translocal organisations have usurped many state functions but without any legitimacy from African constituencies, making their plans and decisions in Western capitals and being very distant, geographically and conceptually, from the local arenas where their investments subsequently are set to work. Under the banner of 'liberalism' this consortium of private and public capital has pushed through the implementation of devastating 'structural adjustment' policies engineered by IMF and the World Bank to ease the flow of capital, goods and labour, a process now called 'globalisation'. Yet this new, celebrated form of 'connectivity' has been very selective in who the engineers of these policies find promising and profitable enough to connect. While most commoners have experienced that the flow of capital and concern have passed them by to settle on the elite, the destructive forces of globalisation have turned in on them with a vengeance as the 'glorification of the gun' is rapidly spreading alongside destitution (Hutchinson 1996, Broch-Due and Schroeder 2000).

Clearly this reconfiguration in the relationship between the state and citizen has opened up new divides between wealth and want. In the absence of accountable democracy or any clear comprehension of the dynamics at play, many ordinary Africans feel caught up in a maelstrom of mysterious forces forever beyond their control. Called 'structural adjustment' or 'tariffs', these forces are as intangible and inescapable as witchcraft and, like witchcraft, are seen to be powered from afar, inflicting damage on the fragile heart of people's existence, not just on their material well-being but on their very soul, and leaving the afflicted with little hope of redress. Overt violence is but an inevitable accompaniment to the growing chorus of despairing voices raised against the economic and political failures of post-colonial states in Africa, and their corrosive effects on everyday relationships (Berry 1993, Geshiere 1998, Anderson and Broch-Due 1999).

This is what James Ferguson in *Expectations of Modernity* (1999) so succinctly has called 'the feeling of abjection and sense of having become second class'. The profundity of the sense of marginalisation expressed by his Zambian informants is dramatically evident to visitors in any African capital city nowadays. During my last trip to Nairobi, for example, I was struck by the decay of many of the high-rise buildings down-town. Once the pride of a modern nation-in-the making, these skyscrapers have become symbols of pervasive disrepair and neglect into which the post-colonial state has fallen: decay and corrosion are steadily creeping up their stairs, from one dusty floor to another, eating into the very foundation of the buildings.

Flying in the face of the connectivity trumpeted by enthusiasts of globalisation, urban Kenyans share with the Zambian informants of Ferguson the experience of disconnection and exclusion. Where they once felt included in an imagined modern world and its 'progress', they now feel utterly excluded. When, on this same recent trip, educated Kenyans talked to me about their material poverty they not only spoke of having lost the measure of material prosperity they once possessed but also expressed their sense of exclusion from the world 'out there'. They too were not simply lamenting a lack of connection, but articulating a specific experience of 'disconnection'. Thus the African 'middle-class-in-the-(un)making' share an experience of their new-found poverty not simply as a lack, but as a loss.

As I once again drove along the dusty highway from Nairobi to Lodwar, crossing the district boundaries, I was amazed by the almost total absence of traffic. The tarmac road, finished two decades ago, was once a busy thoroughfare. Now it stretched out in a straight, silent line through the vast, empty landscape, traversed only by herds of livestock. It was deserted: a striking contrast to the busy state of affairs a decade ago. The mid-eighties were the heyday of high-spending by NORAD (the major aid agency) – a time when Lodwar even got a roundabout and the town was permanently veiled in the fumes and noises of lorries and Landrovers. This boom in town life and 'development' corresponded with a bust in livestock holdings and a loss of pastoralist control of their pasture land.

By the mid-1990s, the situation had completely turned around. NORAD had been forced to close down all activities and stop all funding of projects in the wake of the breakdown in diplomatic relations between Kenya and Norway. Other donors had left Lodwar too, rushing up north to the border with the Sudan. Here a tiny Turkana village had been turned into the headquarters for the huge UN co-operation called 'operation life-line'. This corresponded not just to the seriousness of the civil war in the Sudan but also to the changing fashion in development philosophy in which the figure of 'the pastoralist' had been replaced with the figure of 'the refugee' as the prime recipient of aid and concern.

Turkana suddenly found themselves on the wrong side of two boundaries, one a national frontier, the other a definitional one: they were not in Sudan and they were not refugees. While their pastoral neighbours, the Toposa, luckily located on the 'right side' of both these boundaries, received free rations of food and veterinary services, local Turkana received nothing but for the bullets from the revitalised Toposa warriors. They were abandoned in what was once again a dusty hinterland, now even drier because of a rapidly dwindling water supply caused by the excessive water consumption of UN personnel and refugees. Back in Lodwar, a few NGOs and the Catholic Mission were left with limited resources to buttress the devastating effects of the recently implemented World Bank structural adjustment programmes.

In the space of fifteen years, modernity had come and gone in the most surreal and paradoxical way. On the sites of closed-down irrigation and fishing facilities animals once again wandered, but now amongst the rusting machines of the old development projects. Herders were clearly in the process of claiming back the old paths and pastures from which they had been expelled by 'modernisation'. While contentment and prosperity seemed to have returned to most pastoral camps on the plains, the situation amongst most town people had become one of desperate poverty. Ethnic clashes on a national scale, orchestrated by the rulers, had the effect of ending all external marketing of small stock, simply because the traders were not willing to take the risk of transporting live animals on trucks through these troubled zones. This loss of a significant source of cash, coming on top of the regular restrictions placed on cattle sales from Turkanaland, had spreading effects that curtailed other types of local trading. Among those who were settled all this contributed to severe economic depression. While the pastoralists could subsist directly from the nurturing powers of their milk herds, few townspeople had any cash left to spend on food and even less to cover the increased fees for schooling and hospital treatment (Broch-Due 1999).

This regional crisis had percolated into the most intimate spheres of personal life and all too often its expression was violent. I noticed it on my first night there, which was a deeply unsettling one. The soundscape of Lodwar, once that of a booming frontier town filled with the noise of engines and raucous entertainment, was now eerily empty, punctuated only by the furious shouting of men and the screams of women as they were beaten or mourned their dead children. It was a tragic reminder of the way the personal becomes a barometer of wider social conditions. It is precisely this complex interconnectedness of different social arenas which many of the studies of violence in this volume illustrate.

The idiom of blood revisited

In popular descriptions of African violence, one idiom is privileged above all others: ethnicity. This is not just the creation of foreign journalists, for ethnic opposition frames extensively the explanations of the perpetrators and victims themselves. Yet the tendency to privilege ethnicity in the storyline of violent encounters by participants and spectators alike should not blind us to the fact that ethnicity is not some isolated social fact of African existence. It is deeply embedded in other social relationships and identities formed around gender, generation, locality, class, religion and nationality. Indeed ethnicity typically gains its momentum in conflicts by tapping into the structure and content of these underlying sets of relations with which it is so deeply enmeshed (Werbner and Ranger 1996, Wilmsen and McAllister 1996) Collectively, the chapters demonstrate very clearly that the quest for identity and belonging in post-colonial Africa is a process of struggle fought out at every level of existence.

If it is the case that many Africans currently embroiled in conflicts and warfare share the social experience of economic contraction and impoverishment, why is it that ethnicity features so prominently in the reporting of violent events both by the media and those directly involved? Why are class interests, or the role of the state, or the international community virtually absent in popular accounts of violence? Indeed, as demonstrated by Johan Pottier in his chapter dealing with the genocide in Rwanda, even scholars will resort to reductive and simplified frames of ancient, tribal hatred if asked by a journalist for an 'expert' opinion on the terrible and traumatic events they have witnessed.

Ethnicity, then, has become a sort of universal shorthand that masks a host of much more complex issues of identity and difference (Hayden 1996). It is often foregrounded precisely in times of war when finer shades of distinction have been forgotten, to define an 'other' who is the enemy. In his chapter on violence in Eritrea, Kjetil Tronvoll shows exactly how this wartime foregrounding of ethnicity has been fed back into anthropological theory as if it were an essential, ever-present reality. If one re-frames the picture taking 'grassroots' identities and processes as points of departure, as Tronvoll does in his chapter exploring the effects of violence on everyday life in the war-torn Horn of Africa, it is easy to see how refractory and distorted a picture of empirical processes such macro-oriented 'ethnic' models yield.

We can understand more about why ethnicity features figures so prominently in the formation and representation of contemporary violence in Africa if we look at some of the historical processes which fed into the formation of the colonial state (Mbembe 1992, Comaroff and Comaroff 1992) From the beginning, the implantation of the European idea of the nation state faced serious obstacles in Africa. It was not the existence of 'tribes' which created the problem, rather the sheer number of them. In fact the nineteenth-century nationalism which fed into colonial ideas of the nation state was heavily indebted to the idea of the 'tribe'. Romantic nationalism throughout Europe pictured an ideal state built around a 'nation' with its roots in some tribal grouping of European prehistory (Britons, Magyars, Germans, Norse, etc.). The true nation state would be one in which geographical frontiers coincided with linguistic and ethnic ones within which everybody would be united by blood, language, tradition, in short, ethnicity. This ideology was the motor of much nineteenth-century history and even resulted in a number of nations states which approached the ideal.

There was not even the remotest possibility of such a thing occurring in Africa. With such a plethora of 'tribes' it was clearly impossible that each tribe would have its state, but colonialists nevertheless thought that they could make tribes the administrative building blocks of the new colonial states-to-be. The entire concept of 'indirect rule' was based on this idea that indigenous political categories should be preserved and pressed into the service of the colony. The 'tribe' was thus written into the bureaucratic and constitutional framework of the colonial administration and, later, formed the basis for power block building within the post-colonial African states. Rights to land, the demarcation of administrative provinces, taxation structures and many other features of the state all became dependent on ethnic criteria. The effect was to give ethnic boundaries a solidity and administrative reality that they had never in the past possessed (Cooper and Stoler 1997).

Gender identity was similarly turned into a bureaucratic category for the purposes of taxation, ownership and other legal matters. While the gender bias built into the colonial state was just a replica of European patterns of the time in that they excluded women as citizens in their own right, the specific bureaucratic blend of gender and ethnicity as the basis for rights granted or withheld continues, in transmuted form, to play powerfully into the operation of the post-colonial state in Africa as a dimension of structural violence (Linke 1997, Olujic 1998).

The creation of the white settler colony in Kenya, which I have dealt with in more detail elsewhere (Broch-Due 2000a) can serve as an apt exemplification of the ambiguity surrounding the bureaucratisation of ethnicity. The history of Turkanaland during the last century unfolds against a background of nation-building. Located on the contested ground where the British Empire intersected with the Ethiopian Empire, boundary-making was of paramount colonial concern in a very tangible sense. This international concern combined with the country's 'mosaic' of Europeans, Africans and Asians of necessity foregrounded a certain self-consciousness about the *constructedness* of nationhood, more so in colonial discourses than elsewhere.

In the ambivalent process of imagining the Kenyan settler colony, *placelessness* was a threat. The desire to put everybody and everything 'in place' became the defining feature of the colonial regime in words and in deeds. European ideas of nationalism were drawn upon in the colonial place-making process (Ashcroft *et al.* 1995). The juxtaposition of identity, landscape and jurisdiction was reproduced, not only in the singular, large-scale form of a nation, but in smaller versions, the tribal territories, each imagined as a nation in miniature, each solidified in reality through a string of bureaucratic decrees, acts and interventions.

From this perspective those most 'out of place' were the nomads of the Northern Province. The colonial discourse of tribes, territories and fixity was the result of a sedentary vision bound to a very European idea of nature. In this vision, 'nature' is essentially predictable, controllable and highly amenable to stable boundaries and identities. This 'pastoral' European vision was totally opposed to the Turkana vision and that of the other nomadic communities.

These true pastoralists have a vision of nature and identity which is in every way more fluid (Broch-Due and Schroeder 2000), presuming a constant flux of people and in the distribution of grasslands and water on which the growth of calves, children and communities depends. On the basis of their experience of an unpredictable nature, the Turkana social is shaped into flexible networks of crosscutting 'identities on the move'. This was bound to come into conflict with the new colonial vision. As the colonial regime attempted to control the pastoral communities in the Northern Province, it did so by expropriating huge herds for its own food provision (Lamphere 1992). On account of the fact that every peripheral jurisdiction had to pay its own way, the creation of a civil administration reinforced this predatory behaviour through the taxation of goats used as food and as a currency that through export sales could cover the cost of governing. The colonial regime literally 'ate' its way into the Turkana economy.

In a matter of five decades, the colonial project of boundary-making had turned a fluid network of communities into something much more solidly bounded, an ethnic group, no longer an 'imagined community' (Anderson 1983) but, in the words of Appadurai, an 'enumerated and essentialised' one (Appadurai 1990), complete with a delimited territory. Towards the end of the colonial period the whole population along with its livestock had been classified, counted, taxed and issued with special passports to prevent 'trespassing' across district boundaries.

This bureaucratic logic of building smaller self-generating constituencies of taxpayers out of the larger canvas of fluid nomadic communities was the overriding colonial concern in the region. The rationale behind establishing tribal grazing-zone boundaries, for instance, reflected no environmental considerations but only administrative ones. Although zoning was presented to pastoralists as a way to 'protect' from foreign raiding parties, the records shows that seasonal and spatial zoning in Turkanaland was a means, first, to ease access by tax collectors to their subjects and, second, to prevent the movements of tax-evaders across the boundaries to other districts and thus the potential loss of local revenues.

This forging of clear-cut tribal identities was not always easy. In cases of ambiguity of membership in the eyes of an officer the plaintiff had to demonstrate his/her indignity in an European idiom of kinship based on genes and narrow pedigrees. Those who failed the test risked dislocation. During the 1940s and 1950s, for example, thousands of Turkana who had lived for generations in other districts were forcefully evicted and escorted back to 'their' tribal territory where they faced marginalisation and impoverishment – an action labelled 'repatriation' (Broch-Due 2000a).

The response of people like the Turkana to this regime was, of course, when direct opposition failed, to try to manipulate it to their own advantage. Most interestingly, by reading between the lines of many colonial records one can deduce the ways in which 'protection', 'repatriation' and other essentialist notions/ identities in the colonial vocabulary were subverted and strategically deployed by Turkana as discursive resources against the administration. In particular, these notions seem to have been exploited to press (unrealistic) claims of compensation for raiding and unlicensed grazing against other 'tribes'. These, in turn, returned similar claims against *the* Turkana. British officers on each side of the border acted as the representative of their tribal 'constituency'. Indeed this 'taking sides' led to conflicts within the colonial corps of officers, as is evident in the records of complaints put to Provincial Officers.

Most significantly for our purpose, the identity politics set in play by the colonial state itself rebounded back on other social distinctions, for example by reinforcing the divide between poor and prosperous, those with and without cattle. It clearly had a gendered core. Officers would only press claims by 'head of household' (males) and insisted, in contrast to local valuation, that the worth of a wife was but half of a man (an estimate they had imported from the Somali, a Muslim group completely different from Nilotic peoples in terms of kinship and gender) .

Cases like these are perfect for understanding the key issue raised by most of the papers in this volume: the ways in which ethnicity is a *social production* of cultural difference. Based on very detailed archival material from different locations in Africa these chapters also allow us to address the related issue of the role of the state as an influential third player in the process of boundary constructions between groups. This is an exciting line of enquiry pushed forward through the focus on the 'policy-making core' of the *specific* state regimes in operation over the last century (Barth 1969, 1994).

Although ethnic boundaries were clearly solidified by being inscribed as official identities by the colonial state, I am not proposing that they did not exist before, in pre-colonial times. On the contrary shared identities clearly existed even among unruly nomads in spite of mobility and fluidity (Waller 1985). The significant point here is that what it means to be 'Turkana', 'Barabaig', 'Nuer' or 'Dinka' has changed considerably throughout the century, and the way global and local arenas have articulated and mutually informed one another in this larger modern context has given rise to complex and unpredictable results.

The picture emerging from my own historical research in Northern Kenya is that the colonial state exacerbated, and in some instances actually created, the very conditions of civil unrest, warfare and cycles of poverty which the colonial administration was supposedly attempting to eliminate or contain. When administrators were few, for instance, and failed to collect taxes or conscript the necessary local labour to do so, colonial forces repeatedly confiscated thousands of cattle. Early reports suggest that administrators saw these as punitive raids that would 'teach' the Turkana the power of the colonial authorities. These government raids were also supposed to stop inter-tribal raiding in the area, as they often targeted cattle-wealthy sections that were notorious for raiding others (Broch-Due and Sanders 2000).

Unfortunately, the colonial policy had a somewhat different effect. It seems, first, to account in part for the enormous amount of active and passive resistance put up by most Turkana: their refusal to pay taxes at all or to have anything else to do with the administration. Second, such government raids led to the immediate and irrevocable impoverishment of Turkana raid victims who lost thousands of head of livestock. As the Turkana were entirely dependent on their animals for survival, these government tactics led to further Turkana raids on their neighbours in order to replenish their herds.

Over the course of the colonial period, as Turkana and their neighbours were increasingly drawn into labour markets and commodity exchange, life for the locals appears to have become increasingly difficult. Many were caught in 'poverty traps' from which, given the prevailing structural conditions, it was virtually impossible to escape. Even so, this was not a unilinear movement from a pastoral lifestyle to a sedentary sector organised around a rudimentary colonial market economy. Rather there have been a number of boom and bust cycles since the turn of the century that allowed some to prosper in certain years while others lost everything (Broch-Due 1999).

These types of unintended consequences of imposed policies are rampant in the contemporary scenario also. Commodification of land and labour in Turkanaland was accelerated dramatically in the 1980s, fuelled by large-scale aid projects and the development of a stronger market economy. In the 1990s a different economic climate prevails, with a revival in the strength of the local livestock economy, a decline in the availability of cash and a dramatic slump in the market economy as the major Norwegian donor was forced to leave. The collapse of the aid-based economy not only caused destitution among the clients of development, but also left in its wake waves of raiding and violence throughout the region. All these upheavals and uncertainties have solidified the identity of being 'Turkana', renewing respect for local modes of knowledge, rituals and practices. It has also fuelled the mistrust against external intervention and state policies. Blystad's chapter on the Barabaig violence moves against a similar canvas of dramatic destitution, displacement and erosion of trust.

As many of the chapters in this volume remind us, the processes through which ethnic identity is produced and reproduced by social, economic and political forces mobilise deeply rooted issues of being, belief and desire to belong. Individuals and groups call on cultural and historical narratives, arguments and ideologies, to challenge established parameters and reinforce their claims to legitimacy. Through the activation of ideologies and norms, the production of ethnicity becomes a 'tournament' (Barth 1994), where individual 'performances' are gauged in relation to larger ontological and cultural frames that transcend the importance of ethnicity itself (Heyer, this volume). Just as the 'structure' of ethnicity, its capacity to order and hierarchialise internal and external difference, is vital to its conflict-producing potential, so too is its 'content'. The richness of 'content', the economic, political, cultural and ontological grounding of ethnicity, gives it its experiential relevance and power (Cohen 1994, Kapferer 1997).

When such deep-seated beliefs are mobilised, ethnic boundaries and conflicts can fast come to appear as absolutes. However, with a shift in circumstances, everything can change and a frontier that once seemed so solid can begin to fade. Isak Niehaus in his fascinating chapter, 'Violence and the boundaries of belonging: comparing two border disputes in the South African lowveld', examines the historical development of an ethnic conflict which in 1985 seemed intractable. A confrontation between the Northern Sotho Moletele chiefdom and the Shangaan Mnisi chiefdom over land led to an absolute entrenchment of the ethnic boundary and, finally, a bloodbath. Ten years later, however, the two chiefdoms had united against the new post-Apartheid state and that same boundary was becoming porous.

All the chapters in the volume remind us of the complex ways the intricate and shifting tissue of ethnicity has been woven into the fabric of the African state, and of the repercussions this has throughout society. A wonderful example is provided by Amrik Heyer's chapter, 'Nowadays they can even kill you for that which they feel is theirs: gender and the production of ethnic identity in Kikuyu-speaking central Kenya'. In it she demonstrates how the original inscription of the Kikuyu as the dominant ethnic group in the Kenyan state, and their subsequent fall from grace, has unleashed a wave of interfamilial conflict and violence, particularly between brothers and sisters who come into conflict over inheritance. Ultimately, however, these conflicts are expressions of the central contradictions of state and capitalist development in Kenya. Their viciousness is a product of the unusual synonomy of the Kikuyu community with state and capitalist processes, such that the latter are directly realised through relationships between Kikuyu men and women.

It is yet another reminder of the ways in which the post-colonial state's relation to the global economy and to the flexible deployment of capital has a direct effect on people's intimate relations. While scholarly convention has tended to direct us towards conjugal relations as the 'natural' site for analysing the interface between economy and family, it can equally be other relations such as those between siblings, parents and children, grandparents and grandchildren. All of these can provide promising sites from which to look at the historical transformations in the relationship between the household, community and the state (Schmidt 1990,

Mutongi 1999). Here we can observe a growing trend in African kinship systems through which the significance of sibling relations is growing over that of conjugal relations, thus creating a drive towards matri-focal households. We also see the contours of a different configuration of the urban–rural interface. Whilst the evolutionary logic that underpins modernisation theories has taken it for granted that the movement is one-directional – from rural ('traditional') to urban ('modern') – we see the contour of the reverse process across our papers, a contemporary move from urban to rural. The crisis in the formal economy of many African states brought forth by the global restructuring of private capital is clearly a decisive factor. However, this is not a new phenomenon. The historical depths of the case studies in this volume clearly show that crises pushing people from rural to urban only to pull them back again are repeated over the colonial and post-colonial landscapes. They are linked to a wider reconfiguration of identities, rights and resources. Indeed the urban and rural are embedded in one another, linked by a perpetual exchange of savings, concern, capital and people within extensive networks of kinship, partnership and ethnicity (Geshiere and Gugler 1998, Ferguson 1999).

Yet another example of how the household and intimate kin relations become the arena for wider gendered and ethnic struggles appears in the chapter by Jocelyn Alexander and Jo Ann McGregor, 'Hunger, violence and the moral economy of war in Zimbabwe', which explores perceptions of violence and debates over the allocation of household resources in Zimbabwe's post-independence war. It does so from a particular perspective – that of the insurgents in this war, the so-called dissidents, and the civilians accused by Zimbabwe's ruling party of sustaining them. It is a fascinating study of the way violence reconfigures fundamental questions of gender, familiarity and morality.

The perfect counterpart to this case is provided by Bjørn Lindgren in his chapter, 'The politics of identity and the remembrance of violence and gender at the installation of a female chief in Zimbabwe'. Lindgren discovers reasons for the unheard-of creation of a female chief among the Ndebele in the ferocious violence of the mid-1980s in Zimbabwe. He goes on to carefully analyse the grand reconfiguration of ethnic and gendered identities of which the installation was both product and cause.

Even more troubling is Sharon Hutchinson's report on the ongoing violence in the Sudan, '"Food itself is fighting with us": a comparative analysis of the impact of Sudan's civil war on south Sudanese civilian populations located in the north and the south'. Sudan is, as the author reminds us 'a laboratory of social pathologies common to many of the world's most intractable sectarian conflicts, from Northern Ireland to Rwanda to the blood-stained hills of Kosovo'. She shows how northern politics of Islamic purity have been played out primarily on the bodies and lives of south Sudanese women. She also shows how an ethnically divided southern military elite has transformed women from 'mobile assets' into 'military targets'.

All the above chapters remind us of the importance not just of understanding the dynamics of ethnicity but also the dynamics of the state in understanding the deployment of violence. All too often this has been ignored by anthropologists who assume that, like the European state, the post-colonial state is a more stable bureaucratic entity which exists at a remove from the complex machinations of society. In his work on state violence in Sri Lanka, Bruce Kapferer (2001) argues that models of state and bureaucracies in current circulation within the social sciences – whether they follow in the tracks of Weber, Hobbes or Marx – tend to operate with an abstracted, ahistorical and top-down template in which 'the state' and 'society' are seen as separate entities. Much recent theorising about the re-emergence of ethnic conflicts and nationalist movements around the globe is born out of specific Euro-American, historical experiences of the growth of nation states and modernity. They often forget that the North American and European state, through the homogenising effects of mass culture and consumerism, has been able to streamline social memory and produce a sort of functional conformity which has rendered the old ethnic-nationalist ideas more or less obsolete. This modern Western state is indeed a legalistic entity that largely ignores ethnic distinctions which, correspondingly, tend to become less marked officially (although not necessarily so in popular discourses). This 'domestication of ethnicity', as the above discussions make clear, has not been achieved by the post-colonial state in Africa. On the contrary, state bureaucracies and elites in the post-colony are actively playing the ethnic card for what it is worth in an effort to conceal increasing social inequality, class differentiation and capital formation.

The ways in which the local exercise of power and meaning through agencies of the state shape forms of action and interpretation in communities is the topic for John Galaty's chapter, 'Double-voiced violence in Kenya'. Examining episodes of local conflict in East Africa, specifically among pastoral communities, during colonial and post-colonial periods, the chapter explores the ways in which political 'scale' influences the occurrence, nature, and course of conflict. Notwithstanding that it is acts and their outcomes that are ultimately violent, this chapter enquires as to the extent to which violence often represents an enduring relation, among individuals, within groups, or between groups and the state, that is rarely exclusive of other types of social relations.

Towards a comparative framework of states and conflicts

When it comes to putting the state back on the anthropological agenda to scrutinise its role in orchestrating violence, we should remind ourselves that all states have complex institutional structures, with specific ideological, economic and political histories. We should not start out by making universal generalisations about the nature of states, nor should we see each state as a single entity, capable of acting as an organic unit. We cannot simply 'add' the state atop of the other entities we study, like the person, household, ethnic group, class or whatever. This is because state policies shape and are shaped by all other kinds of discourses and practices, global, national and local ones. As many of our chapters show, the social effects of state policies percolate down into everyday life, and they do so in complex and contradictory ways.

The point is that these complex intersections are specific and will therefore require empirical analysis on two interrelated fronts. First, we will have to examine how gender, ethnicity, class, religion and education affect the ways in which women and men enter into relations with the state. Bearing in mind that the state has a role not just in regulating people's lives, but in defining their identities, we have a second front. We will have to examine how state ideologies themselves produce or reproduce all these other categories. For example, through administrative procedures and family policy, states participate in defining gender ideologies, conceptions of 'femininity' and 'masculinity'. The state apparatus determines ideas about what sorts of persons women and men should be. And when the state has classified its citizens along such lines, this will determine each category's influence on state actions and access to state resources (Moore 1994). These fronts combined are vital for exploring the complex ways in which violence seeps into the state–citizen relationship.

Many anthropologists who have contributed to this volume are working with these and related issues. They do so well aware that in the welfare and development aspects of states-in-networks, 'needs' talk has been institutionalised as a major vocabulary of political discourse and dissent (Fraser 1989, Broch-Due 1995). The contemporary study of the state–citizen relation is framed by the questions of the basic 'needs' of the population. 'Needs' talk, however, is not always consonant with 'rights' talk and 'interest' talk. For example, aid agencies do not only want to reach the poor, but the poorest among the poor which by a slippage of terms in international slogans has come to mean women in general and ethnic groups on the margins who are not fully integrated into the market or nation state. However, when anthropologists and others focus on the politics of needs, rights and interests they tend to concern themselves with whether or not the state satisfies these basic conditions. Over and above these issues, we need to ask new questions like: Why has needs talk become so prominent in the political culture of state-to-state interaction? What does the emergence of the need idiom imply about the shifts in the political, economic and domestic or personal spheres of life? What are the major types of needs talk and how do they interact polemically with one another?

Needs talk seems unproblematic as long as it stays at the level of 'thin' needs such as food, clean water and medical care. Most people will agree that governments have a responsibility to provide for this need. However, as soon as we go to a lesser level of generality, needs claims become far more controversial, and turn into 'thick' need claims, wrapped in the specificities of real, lived, social worlds. It is here, of course, that conflict emerges and it is at this level that fruitful analyses such as those evidenced in this volume must pitch themselves.

When we focus on the *effects* of the state, as they work themselves out in discursive fields and practices, we can refocus the question into one concerning the politics of the interpretation of needs, rights and interests (Moore 1994). We have to look at the implication of need claims, right claims and interest claims in contested networks. We have to ask: 'Who interprets the needs in question and from what perspective and in the light of what interests?' The struggle to establish authoritative thick definitions of people's needs, rights and interests is the struggle for political power itself (Fraser 1989: 164). As we move towards an understanding of how the power/knowledge regime of states is itself produced and reproduced, we also move closer to an understanding of the deployment of violence itself, and how different modalities of violence – structural, symbolic, political, sexual – are heavily implicated in one another.

The central proposition of this volume is that violence is forged in social relationships. The volume as a whole could thus be seen as taking its lead from Harri Englund's sophisticated theorising in the chapter 'Conflicts in context: political violence and anthropological puzzles'. By moving the sociality of conflicts to the core of theorising, Englund argues, we avoid the temptation to simplistically locate violence in some bounded context, whether geographical (the 'local') or conceptual ('culture of violence', 'warscape'). Ideas of the 'local' and 'culture' demand the contextualisation that only the 'thick' descriptions of anthropologists can provide. Re-focusing the analysis to a concern with social relationships also enables us to avoid the counter pitfall: the temptation of looking at violence as a *radical rupture* with the attendant risk of turning violence into its own context with its predictable cast of perpetrators, victims and facile distinctions. This produces the 'thin' description which, with its simpler cast and narrative, may appeal to a wider readership, but usually ends up creating much more confusion than the thicker descriptions of which it is intended to be a sort of layman's synopsis. A genuine contextualisation, however, makes it possible to grasp how translocal forces flow through particular relationships and crises. It also allows us to find the pre-existing fault lines in wider social landscape of contested identities, institutions and resources along which social relationships began to fragment and break down.

Being faithful to the values of 'thick' description does not, as some might argue, mean an end to large-scale comparison of different wars and conflict situations. It simply means a different way to tackle them. From the cases in this volume, we can easily tease out a few variables which could generate such a variation-centred model of the social transformation relevant for analysing conflict. The following does not aim to be an exhaustive list but is intended to give an impression of the variety of potential axes for comparison.

The time dimension of wars is a crucial comparative tool. Wars that last a few months reverberate very differently through the biographies, trajectories and social memory of those involved than wars that last decades. In most cases, the longer the war, the more completely it reconfigures the social and cultural universe (Feldman 1991, Taussig 1987, Nordstrom 1997).

In addition to the duration of wars, the *density* of wars is a crucial axis for comparison. The 'density' of war is a matter of both topography and intimacy. War topography determines whether there are pockets of safety where some notion of normality in terms of production and everyday relationships can persevere, or whether people have to move away to become refugees in foreign places. The intimacy of war concerns the social distance between combatants. The relative closeness or distance in terms of kinship, ethnicity and history of relationships between perpetrator and victim on the killing fields is bound to shape social memory in specific ways. Whether a community is faced with a protracted war or finds itself in a post-war reconstruction period, the troublesome issue of social intimacy will shape particular modalities of remembering and forgetting in the narratives constructed. We would expect the intimacy of war to be revealed in the degrees of bitterness, shame or silence and to shape subsequent regimes of hatred and particular technologies of revenge (Warren 1993, Nordstrom and Robben 1995, Das 1997).

As well as the duration and density of wars, the ways in which localised war scenarios become embedded in translocal forces and flows are also extremely significant. One of the most important of these is clearly the international arms trade, but along with it (and usually given much less analytical attention) is the flow of military manuals and training ideologies across international borders and the effects of these on the behaviour of local conscripts. Recipes for warfare made in those countries with the most advanced military powers or, alternatively coming out of regimes of terror and other long-term sectarian hotspots, are imported into warscapes in Africa, Asia and South America where they often have unforeseen results. These blueprints for action and conquest are clearly gendered, inculcating the narrowest and most brutal models of masculinity (White 1990, Campbell 1992, Kesby 1996, Blom Hansen 1996, Breckenridge 1998).

Another significant vector of global scale affecting local wars is the humanitarian relief industry and its organisation. A crucial line of analysis would be to trace the long-term effects of imported food aid for the viability of local food production, marketing and consumption. In other words, what are the economic ramification in war zones of dumping surplus grain from the US and EU that is already heavily subsidised domestically and gratis at the distribution points? The politics of food is of course always focal in war situations not only in terms of the civilian population but also the provisioning of the combats. Where the food is produced, how it is distributed and processed, whether it is freely given, fought over or simply forcefully appropriated, are all factors which influence not only the survival rates of civilians versus combatants, but also the future of post-war communities.

Yet another translocal object of comparative analysis should be media representations of warfare: who controls them and how they manipulate international response to any particular war. War seems to trail with it a universe of stock meanings, emotions and images which the media tend to recycle *ad nauseam*. Yet one of the central contentions of this volume is that we should resist the tendency to imagine that there is such a thing as a 'culture or war' or 'cosmology of war'. Violence is embedded in already existing cultures and cosmologies and, through extensive social networks, interacts with the ideas and practices of all those involved, insiders and outsiders (Green 1994, Malkki 1995, Krohn-Hansen 1997). The task of analyses is to see how these shape and are shaped by violence. It is here that we meet many of the 'ethnic' issues treated by this volume, the processes of polarisation by which a 'we' is coached to believe in some catastrophic threat from a 'they'.

As our volume repeatedly shows, the plethora of consequences that wars trail in their wake everywhere penetrates the most intimate spheres of the domestic and personal. The identities and bonds of family, marriage and gender are reconfigured. So too is the subjective space of the individual. The repercussions of war on the personal often appear as drug abuse, alcoholism and an increase in domestic and sexualised violence (Liddle 1996, Olujic 1998).

The purchase of violence on the psychology and inner worlds of those affected by it is a something that we are only just beginning to understand (Daniel 1996, Stoller 1995, Kleinman *et al.* 1997). In the sections to come I want to consider this lived, existential dimension of violence and the troubling ways it communicates with other arenas of personal life, apparently not directly within the domain of war and upheaval.

Transformative violence

Violence is an unruly, upsetting and unsettling topic. It appears as the very anti-thesis to our sense of belonging, so destructive of identity, relationship and life-world that the vocabulary of the social seems completely out of place. And yet as we shall explore in this section, violence weaves itself into our tangled ideas of belonging and identity in powerfully social ways. Predictably, perpetrators deploy violence as a political weapon to force through their own desire to belong by destroying similar claims of belonging by the victims. Perhaps less predictably, certainly less obviously, violence works an undercurrent of desire to produce tangible, embodied effects in the emotional economy of social selves. In both modalities, physical or psychic, often entwined, violence fragments old structures and fabricates new ones.

Let us begin this look at the strange psychic life of violence by considering its ubiquity in our lives. Those of us distant in our everyday life from real violence enacted are nevertheless constantly cast as spectators to virtual forms of violence in the imagery that bombards us from wars, action films and forensic crime scenes. We may be academics but we are all also the captive audience of virtual violence. To revisit these scenes yet again but now in a context for scholarly dissection and discussion is neither easy nor pleasurable but it is important. The shock and terror created by violence, whether virtual or real, seems to be an uncomplicated and natural reaction to it but there are other residues of violence which are less immediate and more ambiguous, an uncanny sensation in which fear is mixed with fascination, perhaps even pleasure. This uncanny quality of violence directs us to pay attention to the recesses of our awareness where an embodied, existential violence, unconscious and transmuted, reverberates through the formation of our psychic life, subject positions and sociality. This is the space of a violence that is integral to the human condition. The ability of virtual violence to penetrate deeply into the emotional structure of the spectator is, as many have observed, dependent on this space. Thus violence is potentially a very powerful device for theorising not only the intersection of the buried and the explicit, but also the intersection of the generic and the specific in human experience.

Despite this intrinsic capacity for conceptualisation and comparison, violence invites fine-grained analysis only with difficulty; more often than not violence puts an end to it. In *Charred Lullabies*, E. Valentine Daniel (1996) summons what so many victims of violence can attest to but never adequately recount: a silence that threatens humanity, a world in which 'there is no future but only a present that [serves] as the repository of a deadening past'. Other studies too confirm how the experience of violence – torture, rape, chronic pain – produces voids, border zones and amorphous aches in those subjected that are difficult to overcome let alone express in words (Scarry 1985, Das 1997). When perpetrators carve their signatures into the flesh of victims, or the signs of the flesh break into language, such as when the tortured finally find a poetic form to inscribe and contain the pain they have lived through, we are at the border between the unconscious and the conscious, dealing with symbols that transfer the inchoate into social form.

Conversely, suffering that once had found a social expression may slip back into the inchoate. In *Death Without Weeping: The Violence of Everyday Life in Brazil* (1992) Nancy Scheper-Hughes shows how the realities of 'structural violence', social inequality and poverty are camouflaged by a social discourse organised around a physical syndrome, '*nervios*':

> The transition from a popular discourse on hunger to one of sickness is subtle but essential in the perception of the body and its needs. A hungry body needs food. A sick and 'nervous' body needs medications. A hungry body exists as a potent critique of the society in which it exists. A sick body implicates no one.
>
> (1992: 174)

Thus these poor people come to embody a new twist in which the discourse of poverty becomes one of individual pathology. The interior of their bodies turned into the battlefield. They blamed themselves for their fate, endlessly complaining about dizziness and lack of sleep, turning up at the health-centre with their screaming and suffering babies, not to get food but medication. This move in the social construction of poverty from 'hunger' to 'nerves' as the site of suffering is a stark example of the connection between structural violence and intimacy. It also reminds us that violence contains an explosive potential that those in power are usually keen to diffuse, and the search for official euphemisms is one way to do that. Whether emerging into speech and consciousness or disappearing from them, the uncanny quality of violence exists at the limit of the sensory domain that structures our bodily experience.

The difficulty of giving a scholarly anthropological voice to violence, it seems to me, is that we are so accustomed to think about violence in its overt destructive form, the force that presses on the subject from the outside, that subjugates, subordinates, degrades and destroys both subjects and social relationships. We neglect the uncanny quality of violence that connects it to the core of human and social existence.

Violence is vital to our quest for identity, not only as a matter of categorical grouping but as a *process* of identification and differentiation. These processes are engaged for all of us, in different ways, with the desire to belong, to be part of some community, to pass through life in ways that become part of a biography properly enacted. Belonging invokes the desire to be located but, as Henrietta Moore reminds us, all 'locations are provisional, held in abeyance. One is never truly anywhere and if locations or positions are to be specified, they will always be in the plural' (1994: 2).

The crisis of location at the heart of the yearning to belong is a productive one because it propels the process of identity formation – a project in which a certain modality of violence plays a necessary part. To really understand this uncanny connection of violence and belonging we need to remind ourselves that violence is an aspect of that Foucauldian power which forms the subject, which is 'is not simply what we oppose but also, in a strong sense, what we depend on for our existence and what we harbour and preserve in the beings that we are' (Butler 1997: 1). Judith Butler's statement on power does not, of course, concern itself with physical violence but with the ontology of being and becoming. I have taken liberty with her words out of context because it helps us to reframe the problem of violence and create an avenue into more familiar anthropological terrain. What I want to tease out of Butler's exposition is that while the power that 'enacts the subject into being' in the transitive sense by structuring the trajectories of desire is not necessarily violent in any physical sense, it draws violent imagery around itself of suppressed rage, unhappiness and loss. At defining moments it is these violent emotions which can be enacted in the real world.

Whilst anthropology has focused less on the psychic form of power than on the social forms power take, it is certainly not unfamiliar with the formative power of violence in domains of experience that focus on transitions, be it in terms of the biographies of individuals, the social life cycle of communities or the construction of cosmologies. Thus classical theories about taboos, rites of transition and sacrifice are closer to psychoanalytic approaches to subject formation than has commonly been acknowledged.

Physical violence figures prominently on these ritual occasions that most anthropologists label merely 'symbolic'. It is inflicted on the subjects' bodies in immediate, somatic and often extremely painful form. Specific agents are ritually authorised and empowered by the social collective to perform the transformation visually and viscerally in human flesh. The technologies of violence employed range from etching scars and tattoos on the skin surface of the initiand, or penetrating deeply into genitals that are cut and reshaped. In the comparative ledger of initiation customs from Africa and elsewhere there is a long list of similar ordeals that novices are forced to suffer while in the liminal phase. They are deprived of food, sleep and company, they are forced to do strenuous tasks or endure uncomfortable body postures. While the severity of suffering inflicted on the subjects of ritual initiation varies greatly, the violent form it takes almost everywhere is clearly significant for shaping the experience of those subjected and the spectators alike. For out of the bodily pain and ordeals endured during the liminal phase, the novice is reborn at the end of the ritual a different person, formed by the ritual experience and equipped with a new status, knowledge and roles.

Rites of passage – birth, initiation, marriage and death – are occasions on which the biography of individuals is woven together with that of the community. At the same time each rite of passage is thus an occasion where people 'perform operations on their identities' to paraphrase Marylyn Strathern (1988). Rites of passage are therefore about a complex interweaving of persons, relationships (and sometimes objects) that are partial signs for one another, as they are also partial signs for the social relationships they produce and reproduce, and which produce and reproduce them.

Rituals stimulate people to speculate on the mysteries of cosmos and serve as spotlights on their social lives. The specific spatial design and scripted performances of the ritual in question aim at revealing to the world the relations, substances and spaces of which the person is composed. They are heightened moments of belonging – in its double sense of positionality and place-making. Rites of passage are an expression of the community's desire to put everybody and everything in place. They work on the novice's deep-seated desire to reach a new, perhaps more empowered, status, they are about positioning and repositioning and the urge to place oneself within the whole.

In other words, during the different stages of a rite of passage, 'power' not only acts on the subject, it *enacts* the person into a new subject position within the larger repertoire of such positions that exist within the social collective in question. The force brought to bear on the subject's body and mind grows and reconstructs the social person. It creates a new order by reordering relationships and identities. Events like rites of passage and sacrifice constitute perfect examples of the generative effects of violence, and help us to comprehend more generally the dual aspects of violence, as both repressive and formative (Foucault 1979).

The distinction between 'the psychic life of power' (Butler 1997) and the social life of power reminds us that violent transformation is the crucial dynamic in creation stories around the world. In these stories, the originary moment – of the subject, society and universe alike – is commonly imagined in violent and visceral terms, not by the subjects of anthropology but by the models of the natural and social sciences too. Thus physicists imagine the birth of the universe in the 'Big Bang' and Freudian analysts imagine the birth of culture in patricide. Indeed the ur-paradigm of psychoanalysis was the Greek myth of Oedipus who, unaware, committed the sin of sleeping with his mother and killed his father. This visceral tragedy constructed around the male child's fear of castration, was imaged as a model for the process of gaining a separate identity which is premised on relinquishing his desire for his mother to attain the patriarchal rights promised by his father. The violent core of this transition is further elaborated in Lacanean strands of post-structuralism as the move from the symbiotic and unmediated domain (the 'maternal', 'unconscious', 'bios') to the symbolic domain mediated by language (the 'paternal', 'conscious', 'logos'). These and other stories embed the violent birth of self and sociality in intimate relationships between kindred, evoking ideas of primordial tension between parents and children, between siblings and between in-laws. Such personal, embodied ties have been exhaustively drawn upon as a great metaphoric resource in the European discourses of more large-scale, public identity projects of ethnic groups and nations. It is what 'Imagined Communities' are built upon as elaborated in the popular work of Benedict Anderson on contemporary nationalism (1983).

Although the cast, crime and story-line clearly vary cross-culturally, violent tensions permeating close relationships are the stuff of which cosmologies typically are spun, whether projected on to the domains of spirits or the nation state. The problem with much popular theorising of myths and the imaginary, including that of Benedict Anderson, is the notion that these are purely abstract forms, belonging to the realm of ideas and not deeds. Even when enacted in rituals, they appear in a scripted, dramaturgical and bounded form that keeps the distance between image and referent in place. Yet, as Marilyn Strathern so succinctly reminds us, what appear as 'symbolic constructs' from the analyst's point of view may be 'recipes for social action' from the native point of view (Strathern 1988: 271).

For all their projective force and for all their cryptic projects, myths, imaginaries and rituals are deeply embedded in everyday experience and everyday relationships. As part of social practice symbols produce their own effects in the world and they are often violent. While the distance between image and referent remains fixed in most situations and in most people's mind, so that a compelling story remains within its fictive universe, the image and referent may move so close to one another that they collapse into a tangled experiential entity. Thus at certain heightened moments, the fictive violence of myth which captured the imagination and rapt attention of its audience, or the violent drama enacted on the ritual stage, can erupt into an all too terrifying reality. Freed of its fictive bonds, it runs amok and wreaks its furious energies on real bodies.

In order to grasp this dynamic interconnection between the symbolic and physical modalities of violence we have to deconstruct the predominance of abstract metaphoricity in European thought and create a central space for the metonymic. In my work I have pushed open the operational scope of metaphor and metonymy, deploying these terms not only as tropes employed by thought, talk and texts, but also as practical and perceptual techniques employed in the everyday actions and experiments of an active engagement with the world (Broch-Due 1990, 1993).

In *Prey into Hunter* (1992) Maurice Bloch argues that symbolic violence is part of the generating force of ritual as a social phenomenon, whatever the specificities of place and time. Herein lies the explanation for the often-noted, but poorly theorised, observation that the spiritual domain of religion and cosmology so easily furnishes and fabricates a legitimisation for actual political violence. Let us briefly review how ritual politics revolve around Bloch's 'idiom of rebounding conquest', a radical reworking of the classical insights of Van Gennep.

Bloch starts from the premise that rites of passage are performances where people play with core problems of living: notably how to transcend the physical and perishable flux of earthly life and, for a moment, reach for an eternal life. To move beyond process and become part of permanence, performers must be rid of the signs of ordinary inner vitality. But this poses the problem that if the loss of vitality is too absolute it means death, so ritual actors must take on vitality from outside; a vitality conquered from other beings, be they animals, plants or other people. This exchange of an internal vitality for an external one momentarily allows humans to move beyond this life and still be vital.

Sacrifice, the moment of ritual violence par excellence, is the perfect example for the ways in which such excessive energy is generated and embodied in the participants. In his reanalysis of Dinka sacrifice as rebounding conquest, Bloch draws our attention to one aspect of sacrifice which tends to be overlooked, notably how the sacred invocation surrounding the spearing of the animal victim is soon followed by a profane feasting on the flesh by the participants. The meat is simply turned into food that energises the bodies of sacrificers. Indeed, the self-sacrifice in the guise of a gift to divinity, and the shift to the entirely secular consumption of the slaughter, are inseparable. It is precisely the combination of the two that makes sacrifice so vital a mode of communication (Bloch 1992).

Despite a few surface differences in the ways that sacrifice is performed among Dinka and Turkana (Broch-Due 1990), in both cases sacrifice ritually orchestrates a specific mode of violence which then reverberates through the lives of all concerned. The logic of it begins with an analogy between community and animal. When this metaphoric bridge has been established, people begin to play with the association, moving image and referent closer so that at a given moment they collapse into each other and the sacrificial beast is turned into a metonym for the people. As they inflict death on the animal, the sacrificers simultaneously and symbolically 'kill' a part of themselves. The rite, however, deconstructs the body of the victim into two aspects: A 'sacred' and vital animal part, which is banished and a 'secular' and vital meat part, which is consumed by the sacrificer. The meal that follows significantly changes the mood of the participants. The animal victim has lost its analogy with people and is now treated as a regular slaughter to be sliced up and eaten. The meat ceases to be human flesh and its consumption restores the vitality destroyed in the first part of the ritual. Yet, and this is the significant point, the incorporation of the meat is clearly not only a recovery: it represents an *excess* of bodily energy which fuels the drive for an outwardly directed conquest against other people. Among many Nilotic pastoralists, including the Turkana, sacrificial feasting is often a pre-stage for cattle raiding and warfare.

Again, by re-framing the analysis of ritual to include the acts that typically follow it but are usually excluded from the analysis, we see how modalities of violence, ritual and real, flow into one another in the social experience of the participants.

From this point follows the next: the *positive valuation* of the 'other', the foreign cattle or wives that are the traditional targets for organised raiding among Nilotic warriors. The vitality ritually conquered in Bloch's terms is a good, generative vitality that nourishes the conquering community. It is its very reproductive locus. This is in stark contrast to the *negative valuation* of 'the other' characteristic of the warfare orchestrated by modern states and other militarised agencies whose violence is merely instrumental. Unlike Turkana or Dinka raiding, state-sponsored wars in Africa are shot through with the rhetoric of demonisation and annihilation of the enemy. The genocide in Rwanda and the civil war in Sudan are cases in point (Pottier, Hutchinson, this volume).

Astrid Blystad's insightful chapter traces the historical transformation from one mode of violence to the other among the Barabaig. She shows how the cosmology of this pastoralist people of Tanzania, once moulded by the idiom of rebounding conquest with its enormous valuation placed on the quality of the desired 'prey', has been transformed and replaced by the idiom of total destruction. Provoked by the demolition by Canadian aid workers of Barabaig sacred grave mounds (shaped, grown and nourished as pregnant wombs of the dead), the more controlled ritual killing of the past has escalated into a frenzy of murders not, interestingly, against the foreign culprits but against neighbouring groups. These neighbours, mostly agriculturalists, with whom Barabaig coexisted for decades, albeit on tense terms, have been tragically redefined as emissaries of the 'state', 'development' and 'modernisation', the very forces that threaten Barabaig communities with destruction and obliteration. Blystad compellingly demonstrates that violent action must be understood as a set of cultural practices and forms whose meanings can only be made sense of through an understanding of the wider political and economic context of the society within which violence appears, evolves and achieves effect.

A recurrent scenario throughout our chapters concerns the extreme levels of uncertainties not only about identities and resource flows but also about the very survival of self and community in the face of escalating state violence and sectarian struggle. Cursed with what has become the world's longest surviving and most lethal of civil wars, South Sudanese populations, in particular, have experienced depths of poverty and destruction unimaginable to most of us. In her powerful chapter, Hutchinson compares and contrasts evolving patterns of poverty and political violence penetrating into the most intimate core of Nuer populations located both deep within the southern war zone as well as in shanty towns on the outskirts of Khartoum. Whilst women, children and cattle once were perceived as the embryonic core of cosmology and community so that earlier forms of 'rebounding conquest' focused on acquiring and cultivating these vital assets, here too modern violence has crushed such positive valuation. During this endless war, peoples like Nuer and Dinka have, in increasing numbers, subscribed to translocal religious movement, adopting a demonising rhetoric from Christianity which opposes itself to a similar rhetoric directed against them from the Muslim North. Thus unarmed Nuer women and children suffer not only economic destitution but gross physical and sexual abuse at the hands of both the national Islamic state government in the North and an ethnically polarised military elite in the South. Indeed women's bodies have become the corporeal site upon which the vicious identity politics of Sudan's long-standing civil war inscribe themselves.

The intense focus on the physical, intimate and sensory qualities of human bodies in violent encounters is not simply because physical violence is directed at embodied victims, but because of the plasticity of corporeality itself. The immense variability and changeability of body morphology make up a visceral symbolic resource, frequently mobilised for carving terrifying messages aimed at the larger community involved in the conflict. The testimony of Beatrice, a survivor of the genocide in Rwanda whom we meet in Pottier's chapter, contains many graphic references to the confused, culturally specific meanings assigned to body shape. Certain physical characteristics could easily become a death sentence.

Thus in the most horrifying atrocities, killing was not enough but had to be accompanied by specific mutilations. The fact that violence often follows this grotesque cultural logic is evident not only in chapters of this volume but also in the works of Veena Das (1994), Allen Feldman (1991) Liisa Malkki (1995) and Michael Taussig (1987). In his seminal article 'Dead certainty: ethnic violence in the era of globalisation', Arjun Appadurai underscores the violent obsession with body fragments in contemporary warscapes in the post-colony:

> Wherever the testimony is sufficiently graphic . . . it becomes clear that even the worst acts of degradation – involving faeces, urine, body parts; beheading, impaling, gutting, sawing, raping, burning, hanging and suffocating – have macabre forms of cultural design and violent predictability.
>
> (1998: 229)

As indicated by his title, the author places this grisly bodily theatre within a much broader context of social transformations and structural violence. Inspired by the classical works of Durkheim and Simmel, Appadurai develops an approach to ethnic violence that focuses on doubt, uncertainty and indeterminacy as the fruit of the growing multiplicity and fungibility of identities in the modern world. Whilst violence and uncertainty underlay the contours of colonialism too, there has been a growing sense of radical uncertainty about people, situations, events, norms and even cosmologies in the post-colony. This has been exacerbated by weakened states, refugees, economic deregulation, systematic forms of pauperisation and criminalisation, and the intervention of transnational aid bureaucracies. Many uncertainties are the product of 'state simplifications' (Scott 1998) and the techniques of legibility that characterise modern statecraft. Uncertainty, for instance, can flow from a national census (how many are 'they' relative to 'us'), or the standardisation of international intervention according to new generic identities (the 'poor', the 'women', the 'refugee') and sectors ('forestry', 'fishery', 'rural') that reconfigure the social by dividing the population up into arbitrary segments that cut across communities. Likewise, uncertainty flows from the erosion of local cosmologies by the large-scale faith-based identities of world religions.

All these forms of uncertainty about identity and belonging create anxiety about access to resources where, in a situation of increasing scarcity, entitlements are frequently directly tied to who 'you' are, and thus to who 'they' are. In the fear-filled atmosphere of large-scale displacements and the erosion of existing networks of social knowledge by rumour and terror, violence can lead to a macabre form of creativity. Rather than producing abstract tokens of ethnicity out of the flesh of real bodies, as Feldman and Malkki argue, ethnic violence, in Appadurai's terms, becomes a grotesque inversion of 'life-cycle' rituals in which the perpetrators construct 'real persons' out of the violated, mutilated and fragmented corpses of their victims.

The techniques of violence which target special body parts are an effort to stabilise the morphology of the ethnic body by eliminating all its variability, thereby forging categorical certainty through death and dismemberment. This drive to 'purify' or 'essentialise' is, of course, fruitless and leads only to more frustration, rage and fear among potential victims of future killings, who themselves may embark on a killing spree in an effort to prevent fresh rounds of attacks. Thus when violence turn into a 'symbol that stands for itself' in Roy Wagner's terms (1986) perpetrator and victim are constantly exchanging position, blurring not only the social memory about the historicity of the conflict itself but also about the periods of peaceful cohabitation.

We must resist, however, this capacity of violence to create the appearance that it is its own meaning and remember that it is always specific, produced in certain political/economic situations and draws upon certain cosmologies (Worby 1998). What is so striking in the 'death-cycle' rituals of ethnic violence conjured by Appadurai is that they become a means of constructing 'the other' through bodily revelations, precisely by *enacting* the dead into a new subject position, as it were. Like a rite of passage seemingly gone horribly awry there is, beneath the surface of grotesque excess, a cultural logic throbbing with the echoes of funerary rites practised among many African peoples, and beyond.

In the funeral rites of both Turkana and Barabaig, for example, corpses and foetuses become associated beings. Mourners shape corpses so that they lie curled in the same position as a foetus, enveloped in analogous containers, embraced and (re)produced by feminine acts of cooking and feeding; archetypal Turkana and Barabaig techniques of transformation (Broch-Due 1993). The pregnancy imagery of funerary rites is explicitly elaborated and extended to contain birth, death and rebirth as the elements of one powerful equation. It is not hard to see how a cultural logic that blurs the boundaries between corpse and foetus, implying that death is a source of life, is one that may be prone to violence. This is the darker side of the rebirth scenario. The positive side is the reassertion of sociality and a renewal of life and creative power. Turkana and Barabaig share these dilemmas of the fertile death with many other cosmologies and religions but give them a particular twist which helps us to ask novel questions about the role of violence in both subject formation and sociality (Broch-Due 1990, Blystad this volume).

While rites of passage such as funerary rites employ violence as a regenerative technique aimed at social reproduction, there is also a subversive side to ritual practices which finds its expression in the spectacle of sorcery and witchcraft (Kapferer 1997). This darker force becomes an aspect of 'the obscenity of power' (Mbembe 1992). The brutality of contemporary political violence clearly nourishes itself from this source as well. In his work on West Africa, Geshire (1998) evokes contemporary scenarios in which witchcraft and sorcery, far from being static cultural forms, are highly flexible moral discourses responding to new wealth, inequality and power. They both feed, and are fed by, mass media, national politics, global flows of commodities, and rumours of the illegitimate flows of people, goods and body parts (White 1997).

Thriving in a social climate of gossip, deception and uncertainty, these discourses inscribe large-scale political and economic uncertainties on to maps of kinship, ethnicity and gender, weaving these transnational realities into the local debates about equality and morality played out in households across the region. The 'politics of the belly' (Bayart 1993) has become the shared ground of state and home in the post-colony, juxtaposing eating and power in the most visceral ways. Across the chapters of this volume, food or the lack of it, is the stuff of much dissent. Food is foregrounded in times of crisis, not only because it may be a matter of life and death, but also because food has a metonymic relation to maternal nurture, thus profoundly symbolising sociality. Elaborating on the classical insights of Marcel Mauss in *The Gift* (1967), Marshall Sahlins has stressed the metaphoric power of food sharing to outline the orbits of sociability:

> Food dealings are a delicate barometer, a ritual statement as it were, of social relations, and food is thus employed instrumentally as a starting, a sustaining, or a destroying mechanism of sociability . . . Food offered in a generalised way, notably as hospitality, is good relations. . . . Food not offered on the suitable occasion or not taken is bad relations. . . . In these principles of instrumental food exchange there seems little variation between peoples.
>
> (1972: 215–216)

Alexander and McGregor discuss a perfect case of food politics concerning the deep misgivings aroused when former Zipra guerrillas returned to arms and renewed their claims to be catered for by the community. Facing a formidable enemy in the shape of the security forces of the new Zimbabwean state, but having only minimal military resources at their disposal, the dissidents were regarded by civilians no longer as freedom fighters and protectors, but as security risks and parasites. While moral distinctions and evaluations shaped by sociality were central to civilians' understandings, survival and a desperate attempt to retain their liberation war identity as professional fighters were central to the dissidents' perceptions. At the heart of the debate was food-sharing and violence. Dissidents were popularly nicknamed *silambe over*, a metaphor playing on their taste for meat and prodigious demands for food. They stood accused of abuses of women, and of a lack of respect for elder men which manifested itself in the use of violence. These debates waged through the idiom of food were central to the nature of war in this region of Zimbabwe, and to the complex search for healing in its aftermath. The postscript of the story is a stark reminder of the ways in which the post-colonial state deploys hunger as an instrument of rule. The Zimbabwean state refused local communities supporting the opposition access to famine food aid provided by international donors.

Several chapters underscore the importance of political and military identities and wartime moral economies in understanding the ways in which people interpret the use of violence and give meaning to basic resource struggles. Indeed, by reading across the chapters, one is very struck with the similarity of the signifying economies which surround violence and warfare. Elaborate, refined and specific cultural repertoires are stripped down to a concern with the bare essentials of existence: food and reproductive sources as both material and symbolic assets. Perhaps not so surprising but still very striking are the ways in which the basic dilemmas surrounding life and death are moved to the fore of social consciousness and everyday struggles. Violence lends force to primordial symbols that are instantly and intuitively apprehended at the most intimate level of embodied experiences. Food is a major fault line along which so much violence erupts but also focal for the re-establishment of new parameters of sociality.

In a more transient sense, food is a mediator between the inchoate domain of individual consciousness where the unspeakable effects of violence reside, and the discursive domain in which the social and intersubjective can be articulated. Ricoeur's (1978) analytical distinction between metaphor – belonging to the 'logos' – and 'symbol', which resides on the dividing line between 'bios and logos', is pertinent here. In other words, metaphorisation is seen as a traffic between semantic domains, while symbolisation extends beyond any pre-established structure of meaning, to the pre-linguistic and pre-logical. The implications of the distinction between metaphor and symbol are worth exploring further in the hope of throwing some light on how processes of symbolisation contribute to creating meaning out of violent experience. There is a parallel in the psychoanalytic view of symbols as the instant expressions of something unspeakable and often deeply idiosyncratic. The symbolic expression is formed 'in bios', but the process of analysis, as a joint venture between psychiatrist and patient, strives to bring it into 'logos'. My own venture in the context of exploring different dimensions of violence is an analogous one; I draw my material from 'muted' areas of violent scenarios and sub-texts in the chapters of this volume. There is thus a parallelism between my project here and the project of Judith Butler inspired by psychoanalytic and post-structural approaches. I would hope that through both analyses a field of meaning is gradually gaining its contours. This parallel can be extended further, to the situation which is most common in anthropological practice: the one in which the anthropologist tries to break through a communicative barrier to an alien culture and, for example, look into both violence enacted and lived.

Violence seems always to return us to the body and what is embodied. In its various modalities and with various effects, violence works on the 'body morphology' (Irigaray 1985, in Burke *et al.* 1994), retracing and reshaping the surface of the material body by a series of social signs (see Gatens 1991, Broch-Due and Rudie 1993) As structural violence, it starves the body into skin and bones. In its political manifestation, violence seeks to arrest or obliterate altogether the textured but transient structure of dress, make-up and physiognomy of the ethnic other. In rites of transition, violence touches the permanent skin layers with scars and tattoos, even surgery directed towards specific body parts. All these corporeal technologies of violence that open some surfaces and orifices to signification and close down others effectively reinscribe bodies and selves into new cultural categories. This is what Mary Douglas (1970) meant when she wrote, 'What is carved in human flesh is an image of society'.

Douglas suggests that what constitutes the confines of the body is never merely material, but that the surface, the skin, is systematically used to signify other boundaries invoked by social taboos and anticipated transgressions. Whether the boundaries are stable ones, as presumed by Douglas, or more permeable, as this volume suggests, the 'matter out of place' is the uncanny stuff that the desire of belonging is spun from as is the violence driving the quest for identity.

This uncanny site, synonymous with the contours of the 'polluted' (Douglas 1966) and 'the abject' in Julia Kristevas terms,

> lies outside, beyond the set, and does not seem to agree to the rules of the game. And yet, from its place of abandishment, the abject does not cease to challenge its master. Without a sign it beseeches a discharge, a convulsion, a crying out.
>
> (Kristeva 1982: 8, in Moi 1986)

Whilst the 'abject' (embedded in the 'Semiotic', or 'bios') precedes and exceeds the 'Symbolic'(or 'logos'), overflowing and confounding its boundaries, it is the Symbolic that provides this turbulent suppressed with a voice and a mode of representation, however partial and provisional. And it is to violence narrated we now turn in order to round out the introduction to this volume.

Narrating violence

Experience can certainly not be accessed directly through narration, but it can be moulded by it. Giving voice to violation is in itself an interpretative act, translating 'knowing into telling', in the words of White (1987: 1).Through the act of narration a whole series of non-explicit dispositions and orientations evoked by violent events are shaped and made comprehensible. Thus a whole range of idiosyncratic and social experiences become framed, formed and filtered through structures of meaning that follow specific narrative conventions that are culturally specific and socially conditioned. These structures of meaning are shaped by *metaphors* that carry the capacity of coupling the said and unsaid, text and context. Occurring at some distance from the formative experience itself, narration is necessarily a process of remembrance and, by the same token, a process of forgetting (Werbner 1991, Schmidt 1997, Broch-Due 1999). The editing of experiences is desire's attempt to keep ineffable psychic forces at bay, but also undesirable social memories. Narration as a technique of memory-making, active in biographical and social projects alike, works against a moral economy of guilt, blame and the politics of truth-telling in emotionally wrought encounters (Harri Englund, this volume). The stories people tell themselves about themselves (and others) as social selves, whether scripted as history or cosmology, constitute an extremely valuable source not only for the narrators and their intended audiences, but for anthropologists too.

A narrative is typically composed of 'a story *(histoire)*, the content or chain of events (actions, happenings), plus what may be called the existents (characters, items of setting); and a discourse *(discours)*, that is, the expression, the means by which the content is communicated' (Chatman 1978). Any given narrative moves against the real in different ways and with different levels of opacity. In this volume we encounter narratives in the form of interviews, testimonies, cosmologies, rumours, gossip and the generic stories of mass media, all nested into our own anthropological accounts. In the same way that narratives clearly belong to different genres, so narrators are also not created equal either. I am not only referring to the degree of experiential distance from the narrated events and the differences in the vocabularies of telling, but to the positionality of the narrator within a wider web of 'intertextuality' (Kristeva 1980) specific to the social formation in question. Metaphor enlarges local actors' understanding of their world, but actors are equipped with unequal discursive resources with which to discover and negotiate their subject positions within that world. Again we are back to the politics of identities: your gender, age, ethnicity and class clearly shape your voice and the reception of your utterances in public consciousness. This contested nature means that narratives must be compared and juxtaposed; there is simply no single privileged standpoint from which to studying social processes.

In order to sketch out the force of voice in violence and the formation of identity it may be useful to play around with the vital elements; the story is the *what* in a narrative that is depicted, discourse the *how*, and subject position the *who*. Let us start with the contents of the stories offered by those implicated in violence enacted or endured, whether they are victims, perpetrators or occupy the permeable border zone between.

What emerges powerfully from the ethnography portrayed in the chapters dealing with the social effects of violence in regions embroiled in fighting over generations is the deep mistrust many people display for simplistic slogans and arguments cast in the 'idiom of blood', ethnic or national. Voices from Mozambique and Ethiopia speak from social locations where tremendous variations in historical experiences contribute to complex mosaics of extreme turmoil and shifting political loyalties. Despite these fractious circumstances our informants refused to turn warfare into a context for everything else. The villagers in Tronvoll's and Englund's chapters certainly endured the exhaustive cycles of war as a predicament in the social lives of themselves, their children and of their community. And yet, just because there was war they did not cease to be specific, recognisable human beings in particular relationships, with all the interests, compassion and contradiction that social life everywhere involves. Above all, social life entails a differentiation of experience, produced by the different subject positions open to people in specific places, but also by the vagaries of real life events and the idiosyncratic responses of individuals. Voices evoked in this volume contradict one another, even themselves, in subtle and sometimes more direct ways; events take place conjuring unwanted memories or occasion the politics of impression management. Most profoundly we get a sense of how the interlocutors actively tried to modify their circumstances to the best of their ability, sometimes with debilitating outcomes for others. Based on their own words, but also through their omissions and evasions, we can infer that many shift their allegiances as events unfold, complicating not only the idea that persons caught up in a war are essentially 'innocent' victims, but also the gendering of victimisation. A Tigrean woman interviewed by Tronvoll, for instance, was central in the orchestration of the fighting. A former combatant turned middle-aged and thus dislodged from the army, she was now active conscripting local youth to military service against Eritrea, including her only son. Yet other female (and male) voices, speaking from different stages in the life cycle and drawing on different life histories, bitterly resisted the conscription and the nationalistic project inscribed in the fresh round of combat facing their war-torn community.

The dissonance of African voices across our chapters demonstrates how dissent eats into any fixed ethnic idiom. What our interlocutors do share, however, is a profound sense of the formative power of violence, albeit not necessarily its fruit. Time and again, we are told how violence forms and reforms perceptions of identity and belonging, an ongoing process that forges social identities but fragments individual experiences. While violence is commonly deployed to solidify boundaries its unintended consequence is the opposite: an increased fluidity of boundaries, both personal and social. Doubts, rumours and uncertainty thrive in the border zones but also hope, compassion and affirmation of a human commonality. This point is compellingly brought home in Johan Pottier's chapter 'Escape from genocide: the politics of identity in Rwanda's massacres'. Using material from a recorded interview with Beatrice, a Tutsi survivor, the author details her 'escape route' in terms of the strategy and logic she deployed to pass through the numerous *interahamwe* checkpoints. She travelled with her two young children and was accompanied by a Tutsi friend and her baby. The friend and baby were killed during their escape. Beatrice's story highlights various social realities that are often overlooked in discussions of the Rwanda genocide: the importance of cross-ethnic solidarity (in this case facilitated by the sharing of a religious identity, Islam); the class basis to the desire to humiliate and kill; the power of money; how national identity (in this case being Zairoise) could be used to dispel the killers' 'concern' about one's ethnic identity (though money too might be needed); and the role of the RPF assault on Kigali in opening up the escape route.

The moving testimony of Beatrice reminds us how friendships, generosity and compassion are enduring features in the face of ethnic hatred. The successful manner in which she managed to draw on past experiences in her survival project helps us grasp how social identity and notion of self weave themselves from a myriad of overlapping and conflicting subject positions. However, we also sense that the social repertoire at play at this vexed moment, and the discursive resources at her disposal, were circumscribed by Beatrice's being an attractive woman of some means. In other words, the subject position open to her in the toxic negotiation process with the militias was rather singular and rotated around discriminatory notions of femininity, foreignness and finances – which she skilfully managed to twist to her own advantage, saving her own life and those of her children.

The limited and highly sexualised subject position open to women in public discourse on violence and violation is the topic of our penultimate chapter too, entitled 'Women and the politics of identity: Voices in the South African Truth and Reconciliation Commission'. In a sensitive and subtle analysis, Fiona Ross scrutinises testimony to the South African Truth and Reconciliation Commission, which was set up to elucidate retrospectively violence committed during the apartheid era. It identified subjects in their thousands as victims of 'gross violations of human rights', a substantial number of whom were invited to testify in public hearings. For the most part, testifiers were poor and black: a reflection of the intersection of apartheid's racial classification, class structures and the deployment of violence by the state. While women would join the male voices and testify about violations committed against husbands, brothers and sons, they kept quiet about their own violent experiences. Thus the Commission came to consider women to be 'secondary victims'. However, after intervention from feminist activists, claiming that the framing of questioning served to mute the specific sexualised violence targeting women, the reports from the hearings began to include 'violations of rights to bodily integrity' in order to highlight particular facets of personal experience. The women embraced by this clause clearly used their testimonies to make sense of the physical harm they had suffered by placing the traumatic event in a larger biographical trajectory of subject positions, socially formed around the decisive events of impoverishment, political activism and tensions permeating close relationships. In the most poignant way, underscoring the purpose of this volume, they wove together various modalities of violence – structural, political and sexual – in an entangled web of life experiences, telling themselves and their audience how one unfortunate circumstance seemed to produce another.

Despite these contextual and complex accounts, what subsequently appeared on the page was heavily edited: reduced and shaped into stories of rape and sexual abuse. As the author shows, one effect of the strategy was to erase women's political agency from the Commission's historical record and to replace it with representations of women as passive victims in the face of injury. In contrast, the Commission did not interrogate men about possible sexual abuse. Sadly, as an unintended effect, the female witnesses, pressured into testifying in public about sexual violence, an experience that was so raw that most had difficulty forcing the pain into words, were doubly violated by the official discourse. Traumatic experiences that they had kept secret even from their own family and friends were published in the newspaper reports from the hearing, tremendously increasing these women's feeling of shame and violation. Through this kind of careful reading of testimonies, Ross traces the South African women's placement of self within the stories of harm they told at the public hearings, providing a compelling critique of simplistic notions of political agency, violation and gendered identity.

The larger point is that the agency of the many different male and female voices who clamour for our attention in the context of this volume is largely conditioned by the narrative resources and positions available to them within the discourse horizon of the social collective, its actual configuration being subject to substantial variation cross-culturally. In terms of gender identity, for example, we see how the conceptual space of 'woman' expands and contracts across the chapters relative to the gender relations at work in the specific setting under scrutiny. Moreover, we also see that the placing of the trope 'woman' within these social narratives sets the cultural parameters within which or outside of which real women speak (Kristeva 1980, 1981). Within each social collective, we see how class, race and ethnicity differentiate the identities of women and thus their subject positions within public discourses. By theorising identities, agency and selfhood in terms of *positionality* rather than essence, we are able to accommodate both the pluralism that acknowledges the vast differences between the lived experiences of individual women (and men), and the specificity of social contexts delineating those experiences that are shared (Moi 1986).

This point leads to the next: the configuration of conceptual space where men and women can place and articulate their lived experiences is also a matter of narrative genre. Friendly chatting between neighbours, open-ended field interviews, police interrogation, public testimonies, newspaper reports and virtual media represent different modalities of narrative. Moreover, this sequence of narratives, roughly in the order mentioned, also represents a conceptual move from 'thick' to 'thin' descriptions (Geertz 1974) and, by extension, a streamlining of subject positions from life-stories to blueprints. Thus the play of metaphor significantly changes across narrative modalities. Whilst metaphorisation is a process of switching from one domain to another in order to accomplish a 'creative transcendence' (Fernandez 1982), at the 'thin' end of templates metaphors rapidly lose their creative spark and 'wear out', conjuring only conventionalised meanings. The way that women's rich experience from the political struggles in South Africa was narrowed down to a singular concern with sexualised violation in the post-apartheid hearings is precisely the effect of the persistent work of metaphors in reproducing a taken-for-granted meaning. For metaphors are not only bridges between the conscious and unconscious domains of the human psyche, they are basic to cultural understanding. Metaphors signify and reflect an underlying system of meanings that reaffirm and constitute that cultural configuration (Lakoff and Johnson 1980, Fernandez 1982).

Given that metaphors are located within historically specific horizons of social understanding, they do not always travel with ease across cultures, genre and time. While the story, the *what* in a narrative, appears to be more accessible across languages than discourse, the *how*, the sub-texts and subject positions at play are structured by symbolising devices that need more context-sensitive deconstructive work in order to be deciphered. The symbols at work at these deeper, less accessible, areas of discourse may be poetic, philosophical or, as Pierre Bourdieu (1977) reminded us, practical too.

The ease and certainty with which the generic war story of western mass media inserts itself between event and reception violates the complexities and subtleties involved in the local narratives which it abstracts for its own purpose. In the 'idiom of blood' that structures the generic report, all atrocities are created equal: the dead are flawless, the perpetrators sinister and the surrounding politics insane or non-existent. While specific labels of geography and groups serve as signpost to authenticity, it reads like the same story from everywhere: a tribe in power butchers a disenfranchised tribe, another round in those ancient hatreds; the more things change the more they stay the same; and so on. The violence conjured is 'endemic', 'epidemic', and 'ethnic', and the extremities of it all erase any appeal to think about the single instance (Gourevitch 1998). The reporting of the genocide in Rwanda followed this template. Its inadequacy as explanatory tool is roundly critiqued in the chapter by Pottier.

As with any story, a template weaves itself from the world on different scales and with different scopes. Which narrative gets picked up, whose voice is authorised, which truth claims are conveyed and which genre of evidence is evoked depends largely on its location in the wider political economy. Templates are built by drawing on the techniques of storytelling, being equipped with a narrative structure that is comprehensible within the horizons of experience and expectations of the target readerships. Certain templates and blueprints have long been at work in European representations of Africa, not only as technical devices for storytelling, but also as filters selecting certain kinds of stories and not others (Roe 1991, Broch-Due 2000b).

There is a profound desire shared by vast numbers of social actors – from civilians and politicians caught up in the maelstrom of conflict, to media journalists and their audiences – for accounts that would allow us to tell stories about these awful situations cast with 'good guys' and 'bad guys'. The world would appear more reassuring if fixed in binary equations such as 'Tutsi are good' and 'Hutu are bad', that the men are exploiting and the women are exploited, the militarists are wicked and violent and the civilians are pure and innocent. There seems to be a powerful need to distil social complexity into moral simplicity. In many warscapes religion plays an important role precisely because of the desire to situate horrific material events in a cosmological framework that renders them meaningful. Conspiracy stories are similarly constructed as distillates that allow some sort of legibility to replace opacity (Galaty, this volume). Time and again we hear those caught up in severe conflict and suffering castigating themselves over the state of affairs. Somewhere along the way sociality, as the afflicted know it, has broken down. Punishment has befallen because people have become selfish, uncaring, withholding food and whatever other severe shortcomings stipulated by the particular 'moral book' in place. Among those living in the troubled zones there is a profound sense that there are 'evil things' afoot and, thus, there must also be 'evil-doers'. Indeed we are writing at a time in history when a rhetoric of 'evil-doers' and 'evil-deeds' is bandied about as the dominant cosmology of global diplomacy.

This is not to deny that there are plenty of evil-doers in the African post-colony and from this volume alone we could easily draw up a Rogue's Gallery from the hot spots it represents. However, we have sought actively to resist the temptation to join the moralising tendency in so much contemporary cultural criticism. Ascribing blame and punishment to individual culprits is a matter for courts and judicial systems. To put matters this starkly implies the existence of an essential opposition between complexity and what is morally significant. On the contrary, this volume exemplifies that it is possible, indeed desirable, to develop an ethics of complexity, a scholarly project that seeks to grasp how violence and poverty are socially produced, upheld or reduced. Our shared suspicion for the simplified story, particularly the ones projected by powerful templates that reach large audiences through virtual technologies, is thus not simply because anthropologists take a particular pleasure in complex and contextualising accounts. It is because we firmly believe that to have better and more adequate understanding is necessary for making more proper responses.

The simplifying stories our authors are objecting to simply 'obliterate relationship', as was the effect of the human rights framing of the Truth and Reconciliation Commission discussed earlier. This volume seeks to take the study of violence and poverty away from an overriding concern with categorisations and definitions (for example, whether we are dealing with 'ethnic violence', 'sexualised violence' or 'structural violence') towards foregrounding the question of *social relationship*. This is because violence and poverty imply a relationship; they both have to be analysed in relation to wider sets of issues concerning the edges of the membership categories of the unequal world that we all live in. By embedding its dynamic in the vast and differential field of social inequality, our reframing of violence is also an effort to think relationally at a large scale. The analytical strategy of focusing on the interaction between modalities of violence engages the question not only of the 'local', but of global capitalism and how it constitutes its social and geographical categories of membership.

Most profoundly, this volume seeks to respond ethically to the realities of connectivity. In other words we take seriously the fact that the socio-cultural life in the many African locations conjured across the chapters entail a set of implicit gestures towards membership in a larger world (Gupta and Ferguson 1997). These gestures of a relational sort make a claim on us as academics, as subjects often leading privileged lives at a comfortable distance from the troubled locations of our informants. Thus the question of where we belong as anthropologists in relation to the topic of violence clearly engages the 'ethics' of theory. Our quest is not for a morality of theory, or a moralising theory, but precisely a perspective based in ethics.

In order to demonstrate this finer point let us finally revisit the concept of 'structural violence'. It reminds us that, for instance, poverty is a form of violence that is incredibly powerful and incredibly destructive, but difficult to actually pinpoint in terms of agents and evil-doers. The extreme social inequality, for example, that manifested itself in a medical disguise in the symptom of '*nervios*' in the hungry bodies of the pauperised women earlier conjured, was the end product of political and economic forces at work in multiple, differential fields. At its core were the social constructions of gender difference – and the structuring role of gender relations in social, economic and political processes. 'Gender' is itself a contextual and complex concept. It associates a diverse range of qualities and practices, both enabling and disabling, to its definitions. In this case, as in similar cases across our chapters, we are concerned with those marginalised within the post-colonial regimes of wealth and values, partly orchestrated by the state. The overall gendering of suffering occurs through gender discriminations applied differentially over a host of processes and social fields (Broch-Due 1995). On the surface these effects may not be obviously linked to 'sex' or 'gender' at all. This means that many aspects of gendering (like legislation) cannot be simply measured and counted, but must still be accounted for as powerful movers in the social drama of poverty and violence. We could make similar arguments in terms of how other decisive identities, often prescribed by the state, are implicit in the scenario of structural violence up to and including ethnic cleansing.

The pervasive nature of structural violence leaves people with a tremendous sense of helplessness in the face of it. For example, when the exchange rates of local currencies are falling, leaving empty pockets behind, those affected feel devastated by mysterious forces emanating from afar in the intricate world of international money markets, forever beyond their control. We are less accustomed to view the production of physical violence through the same lenses as those applied to the production of poverty. In contrast to creeping marginalisation, violence enacted clearly has immediate actors, perpetrators and victims. The term 'structural violence' seems inappropriate to describe people being cut open with bayonets. And yet, when we listen carefully to the testimonies of victims and perpetrators alike, what comes through is an overwhelming sense of people being sucked into processes of intensification and production of violence in a way that leaves them feeling very much like the victims of poverty feel, that all of this has happened to them for reasons they do not comprehend. It is possible to take seriously these voices declaring a feeling of having been pulled into a maelstrom of violence against their will, without discarding the idea of accountability and responsibility in the hands of the culprits involved in single instances of atrocity.

All the contributors to this volume believe that producing complex and relationship-centred contextual accounts is a matter not only of thick ethnography, but relates powerfully to the ethics of theory. The ethics of theory is centrally about developing further anthropology as a comparative instrument. In order to avoid the infinite regression into an ever-thickening ethnographic terrain of unique scenarios of violence and belonging, I outlined previously a few components of a 'variation-centred model' (Gould 1996) which could keep large-scale comparison on track.

However, we cannot ignore the fact that the complex and contextualised accounts we produce in dialogue with our interlocutors, even if they are placed within a larger framework and firmly grounded in comparison, fare badly outside the seminar room. We are simply writing against the grain of widespread yearnings for cosmologies of simplicity, purity and order, which can put violence in its proper place. The problem here is that we cannot dislodge simplistic stories simply by arguing that they are factually 'wrong' or in want of the necessary complexity. To dislodge a story we must provide a better story: more convincing and more compelling. Thus the question of the ethics of theory is in part a question of the pragmatics of how do you tell a better story? In addition to addressing large-scale phenomena, focusing on social relationship and putting back a comparative frame, telling a better story entails a certain self-consciousness about the fact that we are narrators in addition to being researchers (Glifford 1988). Doing effective storytelling means that we should try to captivate the imagination of larger audiences with the vexed relations that exist between violence and belonging. Replacing simplified generic stories with more compelling and sensitive ones may itself be a Utopian project, but it is one that can organise useful scholarship. The contributions to this volume are all part of this collective endeavour.

References

Anderson, B.R. 1983. *Imagined Communities: Reflections on the Origin and Spread of Nationalism*, New York and London: Verso.

Anderson, D.M. and Broch-Due, V. (eds) 1999. *The Poor Are Not Us: Poverty and Pastoralism in Eastern Africa*, Oxford: James Curry.

Appadurai, A. 1990. 'Disjuncture and difference in the global cultural economy', *Public Culture* 2: 1–24.

—— 1998. 'Dead certainty: ethnic violence in the era of globalisation', *Public Culture* 10(2): 225–247.

Ashcroft, B., Griffiths, G. and Tiffin, H. 1995. *The Post-colonial Studies Reader*, London and New York: Routledge.

Barth, F. (ed.) 1969. *Ethnic Groups and Boundaries: The Social Organization of Cultural Difference*, Oslo: Universitetsforlaget.

—— 1994. 'Boundaries and connections', in A.P. Cohen (ed.) *Signifying Identities. Anthropological Perspectives on Boundaries and Contested Values*, London and New York: Routledge.

Bayart, J.F. 1993. *The State in Africa: The Politics of the Belly*, New York: Longman.

Berry, S. 1993. *No Condition is Permanent: Social Dynamics of Agrarian Change in Sub-Saharan Africa*, Madison, Wisc.: University of Wisconsin Press.

Bloch, M. 1992. *Prey into Hunter: The Politics of Religious Experience*, Cambridge: Cambridge University Press.

Blom Hansen, T. 1996. 'Recuperating masculinity: Hindu nationalism, violence and the exorcism of the Muslim "Other"', *Critique of Anthropology* 16(2): 137–172.

Bourdieu, P. 1977. *Outline of a Theory of Practice*, Cambridge: Cambridge University Press.

Breckenridge, K 1998. 'The allure of violence: men, race and masculinity on the South African goldmines, 1900–1950', *Journal of Southern African Studies*, 24(4): 669–693.

Broch-Due, V. 1990. 'The bodies within the body: journeys in Turkana thought and practice', Ph.D. thesis, University of Bergen.

—— 1993. 'Making meaning out of matter: Turkana perceptions about gendered bodies', in V. Broch-Due, I. Rudie and T. Bleie (eds) *Carved Flesh/Cast Selves: Gendered Symbols and Social Practices*, Oxford and Providence, R.I.: Berg Press.

—— 1995. 'Poverty paradoxes: the economy of engendered needs', *Poverty and Prosperity Occasional Paper Series*, no. 4, Uppsala: Nordiska Afrikainstitutet Uppsala.

—— 1999. 'Remembered cattle, forgotten people: the morality of exchange and the exclusion of the Turkana poor', in D.M. Anderson and V. Broch-Due (eds.) *The Poor Are Not Us: Poverty and Pastoralism in Eastern Africa*, Oxford: James Curry.

—— 2000a. 'A proper cultivation of peoples: the colonial reconfiguration of pastoral tribes and places in Kenya', in V. Broch-Due and R. Schroeder *Producing Nature and Poverty in Africa*, Uppsala and New Brunswick: NAI and Transaction Press.

—— 2000b. 'Producing poverty and nature: an introduction', in V. Broch-Due and R. Schroeder *Producing Nature and Poverty in Africa*, Uppsala and New Brunswick: NAI and Transaction Press.

Broch-Due, V. and Rudie, I. 1993. 'Carved flesh – cast selves: an introduction', in V. Broch-Due, I. Rudie and T. Bleie (eds.) *Carved Flesh/Cast Selves: Gendered Symbols and Social Practices*, Oxford and Providence, R.I.: Berg Press.

Broch-Due, V. and Sanders, T. 2000. 'Rich man, poor man, administrator, beast: the politics of impoverishment in Turkana, Kenya, 1890–1990', in E. Fratkin and T. McCabe (eds) *Nomadic Peoples*, special edition: 'Social Change in Eastern Africa'.

Broch-Due, V. and Schroeder, R. 2000. *Producing Nature and Poverty in Africa*, Uppsala and New Brunswick: NAI and Transaction Press.

Burke, C., Schor, N. and Whitford, M. 1994. *Engaging with Irigaray*, New York: Columbia University Press.

Butler, J. 1997. *The Psychic Life of Power*, Stanford, Calif.: Stanford University Press.

Campbell, C. 1992. 'Learning to kill? Masculinity, the family and violence in Natal', *Journal of Southern African Studies* 18(3): 614–628.

Chatman, S. 1978. *Story and Discourse: Narrative Structures in Fiction and Film*, Ithaca, N.Y.: Cornell University Press.

Cohen, A.P. 1994. *Self Consciousness: An Alternative Anthropology of Identity*, London and New York: Routledge.

—— (ed.) 2000. *Signifying Identities: Anthropological Perspectives on Boundaries and Contested Values*, London and New York: Routledge.

Comaroff, J. and Comaroff J.F. 1992. *Ethnography and the Historical Imagination*, Boulder, Colo.: Westview Press.

—— 1997. 'Postcolonial politics and discourses of democracy in Southern Africa: an anthropological reflection on African political modernities', *Journal of Anthropological Research* 53(2): 123–146.

Cooper, F. and Stoler, A.L. 1997. *Tensions of Empire: Colonial Cultures in a Bourgeois World*, Berkeley, Calif.: University of California Press.

Daniel, E.V. 1996. *Charred Lullabies: Chapters in an Anthropography of Violence*, Princeton, N.J.: Princeton University Press.

Das, V. 1994. 'Our work to cry, your work to listen', in Veena Das (ed.) *Mirrors of Violence: Communities, Riots and Survivors in South Asia*, Delhi: Oxford University Press, pp. 345–398.

—— 1997. 'Language and body: transactions in the construction of pain'. *Daedelus* 125(1): 67–92.

Douglas, M. 1966. *Purity and Danger. An Analysis of the Concepts of Pollution and Taboo*, London: Routledge and Kegan Paul.

—— 1970. *Natural Symbols*, London: Barry and Rockcliff.

Feldman, A. 1991. *Formations of Violence: The Narrative of the Body and Political Terror in Northern Ireland*, Chicago, Ill. and London: University of Chicago Press.

Ferguson, J. 1999. *Expectations of Modernity: Myths and Meanings of Urban Life on the Zambian Copperbelt*, Berkeley, Calif.: University of California Press.

Fernandez, J. 1982. *Bwiti: An Ethnography of the Religious Imagination in Africa*, Princeton, N.J.: Princeton University Press.

Foucault, M. 1979. *Discipline and Punishment: The Birth of the Prison*, London: Allen Lane.

Fraser, N. 1989. *Unruly Practices: Power, Discourse and Gender in Contemporary Social Theory*, Minneapolis, Minn.: University of Minnesota Press.

Gatens, M. 1991. *Feminism and Philosophy: Perspectives on Difference and Equality*, Bloomington, Ind.: Indiana University Press.

Geertz, C. 1974. *The Interpretation of Cultures*, New York: Basic Books.

Geschiere, P. 1998. Globalization and the power of indeterminate meaning: witchcraft and spirit cults in Africa and east Asia, *Development and Change* 29(4): 811–837.

Geschiere, P. and Gugler, J. 1998. The urban–rural connection: changing issues of belonging and identification, *Africa* 68(3): 309–319.

Glifford, J. 1988. *The Predicament of Culture*, Cambridge, Mass.: Harvard University Press.

Gould, S.J. 1996. *Full House: The Spread of Excellence from Plato to Darwin*, New York: Harmony House.

Gourevitch, P. 1998. *We Wish to Inform You that Tomorrow We Will Be Killed with Our Families: Stories from Rwanda*, New York: Picador.

Green, L. 1994. 'Fear as a way of life', *Cultural Anthropology* 9(2): 227–256.

Gupta, A. and Ferguson, J. (eds) 1997. *Anthropological Locations: Boundaries and Grounds of a Field Science*, Berkeley, Calif.: University of California Press.

Hayden, R: 1996. 'Imagined communities and real victims: self-determination and ethnic cleansing in Yugoslavia', *American Ethnologist* 23(4): 783–801.

Hutchinson, S. 1996. *Nuer Dilemmas: Coping with Money, War and the State*, Berkeley, Calif.: University of California Press.

Irigaray, L. 1985. *This Sex Which is Not One*, Ithaca, N.Y.: Cornell University Press.

Kapferer, B. 1997. *The Feast of the Sorcerer: Practices of Consciousness and Power*, Chicago, Ill.: University of Chicago Press.

—— 2001. 'Globalization, the state and civil violence in Sri Lanka', *Bulletin of the Royal Institute for Inter-faith Studies* 3(2): 55–111.

Kesby, M. 1996. 'Arenas for control, terrains of gender contestation: guerrilla struggle and counter-insurgency warfare in Zimbabwe 1972–1980', *Journal of Southern African Studies* 22(4): 561–584.

Kleinman, A., Das, V. and Lock, M. (eds) 1997. *Social Suffering*, Berkeley, Calif.: University of California Press.

Kristera, J. 1980. 'Desire', in L.S. Roudiez (ed.) *Language: A Semiotic Approach to Literature and Art*, Oxford and New York: Blackwell.

—— 1981. 'Women's time', *Signs* 1: 13–35.

—— 1982. 'L'abjet d'amour', *Tel Quel* 91 (Spring): 17–32.

Krohn-Hansen, C. 1997. 'The anthropology and ethnography of political violence', *Journal of Peace Research* 34(2): 233–240.

Lakoff, G. and Johnson, M. 1980. *Metaphors We Live By*, Chicago, Ill.: University of Chicago Press.

Lamphere, J. 1992. *The Scattering Time: Turkana Responses to Colonial Rule*, Oxford: Clarendon Press.

Liddle, A.M. 1996. 'State, masculinities and law – some comments on gender and English state-formation', *British Journal of Criminology* 36(3): 361–380.

Linke, U. 1997. 'Gendered difference, violent imagination: blood, race, nation', *American Anthropologist* 99(3): 559–573.

Malkki, L. 1995. *Purity and Exile: Violence, Memory and National Cosmology among Hutu Refugees in Tanzania*, Chicago, Ill.: University of Chicago Press.

Marx, E. 1976. *The Social Context of Violent Behaviour*, London: Routledge and Kegan Paul.

Mauss, M. 1967. *The Gift. Forms and Functions of Exchange in Archaic Societies*, New York: Norton.

Mbembe, A. 1992. 'Provisional notes on the postcolony', *Africa* 62(1) 3–37.

Mbembe, A. and Roitman, J. 1995. 'Figures of the subject in times of crisis', *Public Culture* 7: 323–352.

Moi, T. 1986. *The Kristeva Reader*, New York: Columbia University Press.

Moore, H.L. 1994. *A Passion for Difference*, Cambridge: Polity Press.

Mutongi, K. 1999. '"Worries of the heart": widowed mothers, daughters and masculinities in Maragoli, Western Kenya, 1940–60'. *Journal of African History* 40(1): 67–86.

Nagenast, C. 1994. 'Violence, terror, and the crisis of the state', *Annual Review of Anthropology* 23: 109–136.

Nordstrom, C. 1997. *A Different Kind of War Story*, Philadelphia, Penn.: University of Pennsylvania Press.

Nordstrom, C. and Martin, J. 1992. 'The culture of conflict: field reality and theory', in *The Paths to Domination, Resistance and Terror*, Berkeley, Calif.: University of California Press.

Nordstrom, C. and Robben, A.C.G.M. (eds) 1995. *Fieldwork Under Fire. Contemporary Studies of Violence and Survival*, Berkeley, Calif.: University of California Press.

Olujic , M. 1998. 'Embodiment of terror: gendered violence in peacetime and wartime in Croatia and Bosnia-Herzegovina', *Medical Anthropological Quarterly* 12(1): 9–31.

Riches, D. (ed.) 1986. *The Social Anthropology of Violence*, Oxford: Basil Blackwell, pp. 1–32.

Ricoeur, P. 1978. *The Rule of Metaphor: Multi-Disciplinary Studies of the Creation of Meaning in Language*, London: Routledge and Kegan Paul.

Roe, E. 1991. '"Development narratives" or making the best of blueprint development', *World Development* 19(4): 287–300).

Sahlins, M. 1972. *Stone Age Economics*, Hawthorne, N.Y.: Aldine.

Scarry, Elaine 1985. *The Body in Pain: The Making and Unmaking of the World*, New York: Oxford University Press.

Scheper-Hughes, N. 1992. *Death Without Weeping: The Violence of Everyday Life in Brazil*, Berkeley, Calif.: University of California Press.

Schmidt, E. 1990. 'Negotiated spaces and contested terrain: men, women, and the law in colonial Zimbabwe, 1890–1939', *Journal of Southern African Studies* 16(4): 622–648.

Schmidt, H. 1997. 'Healing the wounds of war: memories of violence and the making of history in Zimbabwe's most recent past', *Journal of Southern African Studies* 23(2): 301–310.

Scott, J.C. 1998. *Seeing Like a State: How Certain Schemes to Improve the Human Condition Have Failed*, New Haven and London: Yale University Press.

Stoller, P. 1995. *Embodying Colonial Memories: Spirit Possession, Power and the Hauka in West Africa*, New York: Routledge.

Strathern, M. 1988. *The Gender of the Gift: Problems with Women and Problems with Society in Melanesia*, Berkeley, Calif.: University of California Press.

—— (ed.) 1995. *Shifting Contexts: Transformations of Anthropological Knowledge*, London and New York: Routledge.

Taussig M.T. 1987. *Shamanism, Colonialism, and the Wild Man: A Study in Terror and Healing*, Chicago, Ill.: University of Chicago Press.

Vermulen, H. and Govers, C. (eds.) 1994. *The Anthropology of Ethnicity: Beyond 'Ethnic Groups and Boundaries'*, Amsterdam: Het Spinhuis.

Wagner, R. 1981. *The Invention of Culture*. Chicago, Ill.: University of Chicago Press.

—— 1986. *Symbols that Stand for Themselves*, Chicago, Ill.: University of Chicago Press.

Waller, Richard D. 1985. 'Ecology, migration and expansion in East Africa', *African Affairs* 84(336): 347–370.

Warren, K.B. 1993. (ed.): *The Violence Within: Cultural and Political Opposition in Divided Nations*, Boulder, Colo.: Westview Press.

Werbner, R. 1991. *Tears of the Dead: The Social Biography of an African Family*, Edinburgh: Edinburgh University Press.

—— 1998. (ed.) *Memory and the Postcolony: African Anthropology and the Critique of Power*, London: Zed Books.

Werbner, R. and Ranger, T. 1996. *Post Colonial Identity in Africa*, London: Zed Books.

White, H. 1987. *The Content of the Form*, Baltimore, Md.: Johns Hopkins University Press.

White, L. 1990. 'Separating the men from the boys: constructions of gender, sexuality, and terrorism in Central Kenya, 1939–1959', *International Journal of African Historical Studies* 23(1): 1–25.

White, L. 1997. 'The traffic in heads: bodies, borders and the articulation of regional histories', *Journal of Southern African Studies* 23(2): 325–338.

Wilmsen, E.N. and McAllister, P. (eds) 1996. *The Politics of Difference: Ethnic Premises in a World of Power*, Chicago, Ill.: University of Chicago Press.

Worby, E. 1998. 'Tyranny, parody, and ethnic polarity: ritual engagements with the state in Northwestern Zimbabwe', *Journal of Southern African Studies* 24(3) 561–578.

Chapter 2

'Nowadays they can even kill you for that which they feel is theirs'

Gender and the production of ethnic identity in Kikuyu-speaking Central Kenya

Amrik Heyer

Introduction

The violent mobilisation of ethnic and other forms of identity is highly visible on our television screens and newspapers. This often leaves unquestioned the processes through which identities themselves are produced, and the manner in which they achieve their potency. This chapter explores the role of conflict in the production of identity in Central Kenya.

The chapter investigates the significance of the *nyumba*, the 'home', in the construction of Kikuyu ethnicity. Since the early decades of colonialism, the *nyumba* has played a crucial role as a repository for the investment of wealth and the construction of Kikuyu political identity in relation to the state and state-controlled economy. During this process, the *nyumba* has been transformed from its nineteenth-century significance as the embodiment of 'female clan', into a twentieth-century site of male wealth and power. The last two decades of the twentieth century have shown a weakening of Kikuyu control over the state along with fluctuations in the global and national economy. The construction of the *nyumba* in terms of a dominant masculinity is now challenged by returning single-mother 'sisters', and its expression of Kikuyu collectivity is being subtly transformed.

The *nyumba* is particularly potent as a symbol of ethnic identity because of its genealogical construction in terms of origin, blood and descent (Roosens 1994). The essentiality of these idioms makes relationships to the *nyumba* appear inviolable. In reality, however, they are notoriously unstable, and must continually be legitimated in relation to the construct of the *nyumba* itself. The boundaries of the *nyumba* are equally volatile. What is 'within' and what is 'without' is re-workable, and may encompass much larger spheres of identification. The porous nature of the *nyumba* makes it a potent site of social transformation. Its mutability allows for the simultaneous expression of difference and unity, where the conflicts engendered by social divisions become resonant with an experience of the 'whole'.

As a site of production and division of labour, the *nyumba* is located in a global field of political and economic relations. The production of identity in the context of the *nyumba* is thus a process of material, social and existential struggle, which is fundamentally political. The chapter examines the nature of this process in Central Kenya through the relationship between gender and ethnicity. Gender becomes the axis of difference through which individuals compete to legitimate themselves in relation to the *nyumba*, and through which they define the *nyumba* in terms of their own material and political interests. Through the (gendered) contestation of political and economic relationships, difference becomes hierarchialised in relation to the collective. Ethnic identity thus encodes an expression of power which reinforces the dominance of certain groups over others.

The processes through which ethnic identity is produced and reproduced mobilise deeply rooted cultural and ontological understandings. Individuals and groups call on cultural and historical narratives, arguments and ideologies in order to challenge established parameters and reinforce their legitimacy in relation to the collective. Through the activation of ideologies and norms, the production of ethnicity becomes a 'tournament' (Barth 1994), where individual 'performances' are gauged in relation to larger ontological and cultural frames that transcend the importance of ethnicity itself.

In Central Kenya, relationships to the *nyumba* are assessed against a social morality of fertility and 'wealth', which is historically and culturally grounded (Berman and Lonsdale 1992: Vol. 2). To achieve legitimacy in relation to the *nyumba*, men and women must demonstrate their ability to command the wealth which renders the *nyumba* productive, as well as their ability to ensure its continuity by bringing children into the home. Collective identification is thus experienced through the agency of individuals, and through the depth and power of the cultures and histories they invoke.

Just as the 'structure' of ethnicity, its capacity to order and hierarchialise internal and external difference, is vital to its conflictual potential, so too is its 'content'. The richness of 'content', the economic, political, cultural and ontological grounding of ethnicity, gives it its experiential relevance and power (Cohen 1994, Kapferer 1988). The embeddedness of ethnic identity is crucial to the manner in which ethnicity is instrumentalised in violent or other interactions, and in the effects of this instrumentalisation on the individuals and relationships it inscribes. The chapter investigates both the 'content' and 'structure' of ethnic identification through relationships between men and women in twentieth-century Kenya.

Female nyumba: matrifocality and the ethnic shadow

The rifts between brothers and their single-mother sisters over the *nyumba*, the 'home', are some of the most vicious schisms which cleave rural households in Central Kenya in the present day. For many single mothers, relationships with their homes are full of ambiguity and tension. Close bonds which often exist with parents and brothers are strained by the threat that single mothers now pose to the relationships and resources of their rural homes. The contest over the *nyumba* and its resources, particularly land, is a product of shifting relationships to state and global capital in the present day. However at the heart of these conflicts is a more long-term concern, involving the restructuring of a relationship between wealth and identity which has shaped rural societies across time and space.

Single motherhood has become a widespread phenomenon in Kikuyu-speaking communities since the 1970s. This is seen in part as a response to the legacies of the independence war of the 1950s. During the war, the incarceration of large numbers of Kikuyu men left Kikuyu women to manage their households alone. The daughters of the independence war were to become the single mothers of the 1970s by which time 'women [had] learnt from their mothers that they can't trust men and must rely on themselves' (Muni[1] interview: Murang'a town 1994).

Anne Njoki became a single mother in the 1970s. At that time, she said, women who bore children out of wedlock were cast out of their homes and excommunicated from their churches. Since the 1970s however, single motherhood has become increasingly prevalent such that nowadays, according to Muthoni Wainaina, 'ladies have become accustomed to stay single'. Correspondingly, attitudes are beginning to change.

One of the symptoms of the new legitimacy which women are acquiring in relation to their natal homes is a government bill passed in the early 1990s. The bill stipulates that single women must inherit land equally with their brothers. Despite this legal sanction, many women will not press their claims to land; either they value their relationships with their families too much, or they fear the reprisals.

Nyina wa Martha is one of many single mothers whose conflicts with her brothers over the resources of her home, particularly land, have torn through the bonds that united the family since childhood.

Nyina wa Martha became a single mother when she was just about to finish school. Because of this her parents rejected her, and she left home to give birth to her baby and find work in the nearby town of Nyeri. It was only after her second child was born that her parents asked her to come back. She spent her maternity leave at home, and once again established a close relationship with both parents, particularly with her mother to whom she had not been close since she was a child.

Nyina wa Martha had to move continuously in the early years to look for work, so her parents asked her to leave the children with them. She did this for a few years, but eventually decided that she did not want to live without her two daughters. As is the experience of so many single mothers, her parents refused to let her take the children back. Nyina wa Martha finally gained their compliance, saying that the girls' education would suffer in the rural areas.

While her daughters were staying there, Nyina wa Martha took on the role of caring for her parents, traditionally the role of sons. 'If my mother runs out of cooking fat it is I who must buy her some more,' she said. She still continues to contribute to her home, even though her daughters are no longer staying there. Her support extends to her youngest brother who has not got a job, and who lives at home working half-heartedly on his parents' land. In this he is typical of many young men who cannot find jobs and thus remain at home. Nyina wa Martha has also helped her younger sisters one of whom has also become a single mother. In contrast to their brother, neither Nyina wa Martha nor her sisters can remain in their natal home despite the fact that their children may reside there. As Wanjiku put it, 'You do not feel good staying at home with your parents and your brothers.'

Unlike Nyina wa Martha, her other brothers were able to finish their education and, with the exception of the youngest, they are now very well off. Nyina wa Martha continued to maintain close relationships with all her brothers after they got married, but already the strains were beginning to show. While she was nursing her sister-in-law, Nyina wa Martha found a letter that one of her brothers had written to the other saying that Nyina wa Martha was 'sucking our parents home dry' because her daughters were being looked after there. Nyina wa Martha's brothers also blamed her for the fact that another of their sisters had become a single mother, accusing her of setting a bad example. Gradually the rifts between Nyina wa Martha and her brothers, buried deep under their close relationships, were beginning to emerge. However it was land which finally broke these bonds apart.

When the time came for their father to divide his land, he said he would divide it between Nyina wa Martha and her brothers. They all went to the land office but the officials refused to ratify the division due to the fact that no provision had been made for the younger sisters who were as yet unmarried. Nyina wa Martha's father had assumed that, out of the goodness of her heart, Nyina wa Martha would give her younger sisters some of her land if they did not get married. The brothers and her father were now furious with Nyina wa Martha, accusing her of having been to the District Office behind their backs on behalf of her other sisters.

The conflict between Nyina wa Martha and her brothers had begun to fracture the whole household along lines of gender. During the land case Nyina wa Martha's father chose to side with her brothers against her. This was despite the fact that it was Nyina wa Martha's children, not those of her brothers, who were being brought up in the family home. In addition, it was not the brothers but Nyina wa Martha who was supporting the parents in their old age. Thus it seemed odd that her father would choose to side with his sons who have not kept up their traditional obligations.

Furthermore, Nyina wa Martha's father had had an exceptionally close relationship with her since childhood. Her mother had left home for a number of years when Nyina wa Martha was young. As the eldest daughter, Nyina wa Martha brought up her younger siblings almost as a surrogate mother. During this time she was very close to her father and saw him as the rock of the family when her mother abandoned them. Since the land case however, Nyina wa Martha has become almost estranged from her father. In contrast, her closeness to her mother has grown, despite the bitterness she felt towards her mother's abandonment of herself and her family since childhood.

Nyina wa Martha's relationships with her family bring to the fore the tensions which surround rural households in the present day. The attachment of the older brothers to the family land is striking, given that they are extremely well off and have little need of the small portion of land that they would inherit from their father. Their attitude is particularly questionable given that their sisters are struggling and have a much greater need of the resources of their natal homes. The tenacity of the brothers is partly explained by the threat which returning daughters pose to the foundations of male wealth, power and even personhood in the context of contemporary societies.

Similarly, the behaviour of Nyina wa Martha's father expresses the tension between his role as a parent/grandparent, whose closeness to his daughter was strengthened by the presence of her children in his home, and his masculine identity which is now threatened by female claims to the resources of the *nyumba*. To trace the root of these conflicts, it is important to understand the significance of the *nyumba* itself in contemporary Kikuyu communities.

By the end of the nineteenth century in Kikuyu-speaking areas, the *nyumba* referred to the self-contained unit of hut and land which was given to a wife on marriage. A man could marry many wives, but each wife was given her own *nyumba* (hut) and *migunda* (pl) (farm, pieces of land) from which to rear and nurture her family. The *nyumba* and its associated farmland expressed the 'female' aspect of clan: matrifocal, self-contained, creative, and oriented to sustenance and cyclical time rather than social, linear time and the creation of wealth. (The 'female' aspect of clan must not be confused with those aspects with which women were associated. Women were equally important in the social relationships between clans that countered the individualism and matrifocality of the *nyumba*. This was particularly true in the context of marriage and trade.)

The land associated with the *nyumba*, given originally to wives on marriage, was also divided through wives as inheritance. If a man had many wives, each wife would have a specific portion of land and, irrespective of how many sons she had, her land would be divided equally among them. Thus, despite sharing the same father, half-brothers might gain access to very different portions of land. The conditionality of male relationships to land-as-a-resource reliant upon the persons of wives or mothers was a consequence of the essential relationship between women and production.

In the nineteenth century, the farmsteads of the women were widely dispersed and were associated with the individuals who farmed them. In this they contrasted with the land of the *mbari* (sub-clan) on which the clan members resided. This was communally owned and associated with the territorial aspect of identity. Whilst the *nyumba* expressed 'female' clan, the *mbari* expressed 'male' clan.

At the eve of the colonial encounter, exogamous ties between individual *mbari* were central to the Kikuyu social economy. In this was maintained a particular definition of the relationship between sociality and wealth whereby movement and inter-clan relationships were dominant over individualism and intra-clan relationships. In its association with both individualism and 'female' clan, the *nyumba* expressed the shadow side of nineteenth-century Kikuyu ethnicity. However, from the turn of the century with the incorporation of capitalist and state processes, the *nyumba* was to achieve a new and radical significance.

Male nyumba: ethnic identity and the state

By the end of the nineteenth century, the majority of land was given over to grazing, reflecting the precedence of livestock as wealth over agriculture as sustenance, and of the male expression of clan over the female. From the first decades of the twentieth century, however, in response to the opportunities and markets opened up by the colonial state, agriculture became highly profitable. The development of a white-settler economy created a new infrastructure, access to global markets, and a wage labouring force which greatly expanded the domestic market for agricultural goods. By the 1930s in areas like Murang'a, there was a large amount of agricultural output surplus to household use and available to the market. Much of this resulted from the intensification of women's labour (Kitching 1980: 20).

The unit of the *nyumba/mugunda* had begun to move from the realm of sustenance into the realm of wealth. Simultaneously the *nyumba* was becoming a focus for competing claims. These were variously harnessed to the interests of the state, as the basis for the reproduction of labour and controlled agricultural enterprise: the Asians, as the basis for new commercial ventures; Kikuyu men and Kikuyu women as the basis for new forms of profit.

Men like Guka wa Njeri started buying grain from Kikuyu women and transporting it by donkey to sell in nearby shopping centres. As Marris and Somerset record, the efforts of Kikuyu men to harness the output of Kikuyu women were challenged by the newly established Asian traders (Marris and Somerset 1971: 48). The latter had much greater resources, and would come to the rural areas with lorries and pickups and buy grain in bulk. In addition, women themselves began to market their own produce, making trips to Nairobi to sell the output of their farms, and even to buy and sell from the farms of others. Nyina wa Wanjiku for instance, started business taking oranges and avocados to Nairobi to sell in the 1930s. These trips were often challenged by husbands although the latter, working away from home, could not altogether prevent the enterprise of their wives. The state also colluded with men in the curtailing of women's independent enterprise, again with only partial success (Berman and Lonsdale 1992).

Whilst women maintained some independence as wives, this was increasingly diminished as the *nyumba* and its resources became a new site of male wealth and power. Men who initially invested their wages in livestock for bridewealth now began to invest in land. Working men needed rural wives to look after their land and assets and to bring up their children. Bridewealth, paid increasingly in cash, was directly linked to the new value of wives as agricultural producers whose labour was controlled by men. In an inversion of the nineteenth-century scenario, wives had become the 'guardians' of their husbands' land and assets, rather than producers of female clans in their own right. Labour, marriage and land were becoming increasingly commoditised, and with them the *nyumba* itself.

In the rural areas, the significance of the *nyumba's* link to the investment and creation of wealth was now bolstered by its significance in the construction of political identities. In the context of nationalism, the *nyumba* had become crucial as the social, biological and territorial manifestation of 'tribal' identity. The individualism which the *nyumba* had always embodied, accorded well with the autonomous concept of 'tribe' as an inversion of the fluid ethnic identities of the nineteenth century.

Tribalism achieved its primary importance as a political tool in the bid for control over the state. Its centrality hinged on a particular relation between state and capital, fostered during the colonial period and developed in the post-independence era under the Kikuyu presidency of Jomo Kenyatta. In this context, individual relationships to wealth were underwritten by control over the state defined through collective identity. In the colonial period this was achieved through the construct of white racism which protected the interests of European settlers. Under the Kenyatta presidency, it was achieved through Kikuyu chauvinism, by means of which control over the state was consolidated in the hands of one ethnic group.

By Independence in 1963, Kikuyu-speaking peoples were privileged over other ethnic groups to such an extent that they came to dominate the country's professional, political and economic institutions. Under Kenyatta's government, land and clan become key metaphors through which the Kikuyu consolidated their supremacy. Although much of the wealth of the Kikuyu was gleaned through the urban arenas of formal sector and state, it was always invested back 'home'. This was explicitly encouraged by Kenyatta, who would stress that wherever one may go abroad or within the country, one must always bring one's wealth back 'home'. The *nyumba*, the home, became the site of Kikuyu wealth, and the linchpin of 'tribal' identity through which state power was preserved in the hands of one ethnic group.

Kikuyu today refer to themselves as *andu a nyumba*, people of one *nyumba*, or as the *Mbari ya Mumbi*, the sub-clan of Mumbi, the creator/mother of the Kikuyu. Both emphasise the importance of female clan in the construction of contemporary ethnic identities. Far from being associated with women, however, this 'feminised' 'individualised' expression of ethnicity came to be defined through men. In effect, the *nyumba* became the new locus of male economic and political power through which the Kikuyu as a whole came to dominate the post-independence nation state.

In Kikuyu-speaking communities, the relationship between male identity, agricultural wealth and political power has been cemented through land inheritance. Male inheritance of land is legitimated through recourse to the 'traditional' *mbari* where 'the 'ownership' of the land passes from father to son' (Guka wa Kibaru). In the nineteenth century, the *mbari* was a particular definition of clan through male descent and territory. It did not relate to the control over land as a resource, which was explicitly associated with women as part of the unit of the *nyumba*. However in contemporary definitions of 'tradition', land as territory and land as resource have been amalgamated in the reconstruction of the *nyumba* as a new expression of male political and economic power.

For Kikuyu men, the importance of land as the territorial expression of the *nyumba* cannot be over-stressed. The inheritance of ancestral land has become a crucial expression of masculinity and an embodiment of collective identity, in relation to the contemporary nation state. This has led to a situation where even wealthy, urban men will fight tooth and nail for a tiny portion of their ancestral land which can be of little economic consequence to them. 'Whatever you have it is enough,' said Guka wa Kibaru, 'even if you have ten sons and only one acre.'

In the shifts that occurred from an economy defined through moveable wealth to one defined by the investment and accumulation of capital, the *nyumba* came to be central to a new relationship between wealth and identity in Kikuyu-speaking communities. At the same the contradictions embodied in the colonial state's relation to capital entailed the splitting of the *nyumba* into male and female: one based in the rural areas under the 'guardianship' of wives, and the other based in the cities under the control of female household heads. It was the latter which was to become the social and economic base for the new wave of single mothers which increased rapidly from the 1970s onwards.

During the colonial period, the state's inability to control the reproduction of labour, particularly in the cities, spawned the beginnings of a dual economy. One sector was associated with the extraction of capital though organs of state. This was heavily reliant on protectionism, particularly of agriculture in the hands of

European settlers, and on the exploitation of resources of African labour and land. The other was based on urban property, trades such as building and carpentry, and other forms of entrepreneurship connected with the sustenance of the male wage labour through provision of food, 'companionship' and housing (White 1990, Nelson 1977, Robertson 1999). Much of this urban-based economy operated outside state control.

David Anderson (1996) argues that the 'illegitimate' face of the urban economy stemmed from the rivalry between Asians and Europeans for control over the state as an organ for the extraction of surplus and resources. By the early 1930s, the Asians had lost out in their bid to gain power in the institutions of the state. In contrast to the 'legitimate' means of surplus extraction employed by the colonial state through taxation, Asians were forced to capitalise on their businesses through illegal channels, thereby engendering a counter-state economy based on 'corruption'. In the early decades of the twentieth century, the second economy owed more allegiance to Islam than to Christianity. Its links with the African community lay not so much with men, as with women. Through various liaisons, the latter exploited the increasingly corrupt 'underbelly' of the state to their own ends, investing their profits in urban property and enterprise. Kikuyu women were particularly successful, and it was here that the *nyumba* acquired its other face.

In colonial times, the urban *nyumba* came to represent the 'underbelly' of the state, crucial to its control over the economy, yet unfettered by its extractive powers and its protectionist relationship to global enterprise. In the hands of urban (Kikuyu) women, the *nyumba* embodied more closely the female clans of old: self-sufficient, matrilineal and now creative of wealth through the commoditisation of their productivity. In the post-independence era, the legacies of the urban 'informal economy' and the female *nyumba* were to become both a challenge to, and the salvation of, a new relationship between wealth and socio-political identity: a relationship which currently hinged on a more fragile connection between state and capital defined through the persons of men and their wives.

Challenge to the Nyumba: ethnic identity revised?

In post-independence Kenya, relationships to the state turned out to be a precarious tool through which to forge a link between wealth and social identity in Kikuyu-speaking communities. Not only was control over the state insecure and the state itself unstable in its links with the world market, the state was also highly partisan. It strengthened the position of men vis-à-vis women; it strengthened the position of a wealthy 'bourgeoisie' over the Kikuyu as a whole; it strengthened the position of Kikuyu from certain areas over others. These tensions were to become increasingly apparent after Kenyatta's death in 1978, when the Kikuyu lost their control over the government. At the same time the country as a whole began to suffer from an economic downturn which severely affected the economic base of Kikuyu men. (Among other things, the fluctuations of coffee on the world market dealt a major blow to Kikuyu farmers.) Just as gender had been crucial to the structuring of relationships between state and economy since colonial times, so it was to be the fault line along which these relationships fragmented.

The precarious control of the state over capital was making it increasingly difficult for men to sustain their rural resources and earn enough money to marry; to 'serve their wives' as one man put it. In addition, the number of divorces was becoming increasingly high because of the tensions induced by men's separate existence in the cities, from where they offered little support to rural wives living in their husbands' clans. Rural wives and rural land were the basis for 'tribal' identity and the investment of wealth through which control over the state and the economy was effected. The breakdown of rural marriages threatened men's economic base and social power. It was also a threat to their very personhood. As Rosemary Wangari explained: 'Women can have children even if they do not get married. Men must get married otherwise their names will be lost forever.'

The institution of marriage was equally threatened by independent urban women. Single mothers are referred to as 'housebreakers'. As girlfriends they break up men's marriages, siphoning off men's wealth for their own *nyumbas* rather than those of the men themselves. Furthermore, as sisters they not only fail to bring in bridewealth which their brothers may then use to get married, they are also now in competition with their brothers over the resources of the clan.

These conflicts are apparent in relation to single mothers and wives. Wives maintain a definition of community in terms of 'tribe': a definition which is increasingly threatened by its dependence on the state-controlled economy, and by the rival wealth and security which single mothers can command through alternative channels. Elizabeth who is a single mother, told me; 'Wives are terrible; they think because they are wives they are better than us. They think we are nothing.' There was a time when Elizabeth came to physical blows with her sister-in-law and the two had to be separated by her father.

It was partly the breakdown of men's relationships to the state-controlled economy and to global markets which opened the way for the ostracised urban female *nyumbas* to reintegrate themselves into rural communities. Independence from the state as well as the reliance on indigenous rather than export markets has allowed single urban women to weather the economic and political weakening of Kikuyu communities better than men. This is beginning to make single motherhood appear in an increasingly favourable light. The single mothers of today are beginning to come back home, with far-reaching implications for the relationship between wealth and identity in their rural communities.

Initially, the connections between single mothers and their homes took the form of (grand)parental childcare. Mothers working in the cities would leave their children to be at least partly brought up by their own parents in the rural areas. In return, single women were expected to make contributions to their natal homes. The contributions made by the single daughters of rural homes are seen to be partly in *lieu* of bridewealth. In this they continue an association between women and wealth which was the linchpin of the nineteenth-century system of exogamy. Where sons are now failing to bring wealth into their rural homes, the role of daughters in this respect is beginning to assume a new significance. Guka wa Maina has a daughter who is a single mother. 'With Kikuyu, single mothers are no problem,' he said. 'In the end girls are preferred because a girl must always bring something with her when she visits her parents, whilst a boy can come just carrying a newspaper! Now land is given to girls.'

Today the connections between single mothers and their homes through children and financial contributions have begun to take on a more formal dimension. Nyina wa Kamau is a single mother. Even though she does not intend to get married, Nyina wa Kamau is planning to perform her own *gurario*, bride-wealth ceremony, by slaughtering a goat for her clan. This decision has come about partly because her younger sister has recently been married, and her husband cannot in theory complete his *gurario* until the older sisters have also been 'slaughtered for'. Nyina wa Kamau's failure to complete her ritual dues threatens her sister's marriage with bad luck. As a single mother she thus jeopardises not only her own position in relation to her clan but also that of her whole family.

Nyina wa Kamau also has another motive for legitimising her position within the clan. At the moment it looks very unlikely, as a single mother, that she will be given land along with her brothers. She does not want to press the issue because she does not want to jeopardise her relationship with her family and particularly her brothers, which she values so much. She knows that if she stakes her claim to clan land, her brothers' wives will say; 'Wanjiru didn't marry because she wanted this land,' and, said Nyina wa Kamau, 'the children [of the brothers and their wives] can even kill you because of that which they feel is theirs . . .' However if she performs her '*gurario*', they will not be able to refuse her request; 'they must give me land because I am to do everything else.' Nyina wa Kamau is not wealthy, and thus the substantial investment which her *gurario* would entail is not simply a matter of legitimising her clan identity. In that it may give her access to land, it is also a matter of life and death, of the survival of her children.

Women like Nyina wa Kamau who pay their ritual dues to their clan without getting married can be seen to be re-feminising the *nyumba* in terms of women's traditional relationship to clan as 'bringers of wealth'. In the past women brought wealth to their natal clans through the bridewealth which accompanied their marriage. Only after this could a woman set up her own *nyumba*, not in her own clan, but in the clan of her husband. Today however, women are in a position to bring wealth to their clans without getting married. In performing the *gurario*, the thanksgiving feast which accompanies the giving of bridewealth, women affirm their role as daughters, as 'bringers of wealth' into their natal clans, and thus legitimise their single status.

In formally legitimising their status in relation to their homes and clans, women are also complying with a definition of social identity in which single motherhood is seen as illegitimate. This contrasts with their brothers who maintain social legitimacy within their clans even if they do not get married. While challenging their ostracisation from their natal homes, women who perform their own *gurario* are thus sustaining a cultural construct which has de-legitimised their single status in the first place.

The phenomenon of single women performing their *gurario* or bridewealth ceremony has become institutionalised among certain groups. There is a body of Thika businesswomen who have formed a group called 'Home Again'. The members of the group, all wealthy businesswomen, make regular contributions involving substantial sums of money to finance a 'visit' to each member's home. As with the traditional marriage ceremony, a feast is arranged for the woman's clan at the house of the woman whose turn it is. Her parents will be given money to cover the expenses. However, in a slight twist of the traditional ceremony, instead of the bulk of the money being given to the clan as bridewealth, it is kept by the woman herself. ('These Thika women are very cunning!' said Nyina wa Wanjiku.)

In the past, bridewealth compensated the clan of the bride for the loss of her labour and fertility. The wedding feast, the *gurario*, was a thanksgiving feast by the clan of the groom to the clan of the bride for the gift of a daughter. Home Again is similarly a *gurario* for the woman's clan in thanks for her upbringing. Rather than being performed by the groom and his clan, the *gurario* is given by the daughter herself and her contemporaries, to whose group she now owes her allegiance.

In that she brings in children and contributes financially to her home, neither the fertility nor labour of the Home Again daughter is lost to her clan. In the Home Again ceremony, the fact that the woman herself keeps the majority of the 'bridewealth' is an acknowledgement of her independent agency in contributing her labour and fertility to the clan. In this she demonstrates her status as both insider and outsider of her natal clan within whose orbits, as a single mother, she will continue to remain.

The growing acceptance of single women in rural communities is demonstrated in their prominence in high-profile community events. Lucy, a successful single urban woman, was one of four 'guests' invited to the fund-raising event of her (rural) parish church. Despite her single status, Lucy was perceived as a prominent local personage who was expected to contribute a sizeable amount of money using her own wealth and influence in the wider community. Even more than the clan, the church has become the local embodiment of community identity. Of the four guests invited to the fund-raising, three were women, thus demonstrating the significance of single women and women in general in relation to wealth and prestige in contemporary rural areas.

With the demise of Kikuyu relationships to the state and the decline since the 1980s of the Kenyan economy, relationships between male and female claims to the *nyumba* have become intense. This tension is illustrated through the relationship between grandparents and grandchildren. This relationship now straddles the contradictions embodied in the relationships between men, single women and wives, such that grandparents more than wives become 'guardians' of the *nyumba*.

Grandchildren are named after their grandparents and are in some ways seen as their reincarnations. Grandparents become immortalised through alternate generations, thus immortalising the clans. In the nineteenth century the clans were perpetuated through the son and his wife whose children remained in the clan of their fathers. This situation has altered due to the significance of the *nyumba*.

The contemporary *nyumba* is defined principally through control over property, in which context descent rather than alliance is the dominant principal relating to the creation and preservation of wealth. In theory the clans can perpetuate themselves matrilineally or patrilineally. Unmarried daughters can also produce descendants within their clans. In the present day, independent women not only produce descendants for their natal clans through their biological motherhood. They are also in a position to bring in wealth, particularly through their links with small-scale entrepreneurship. Given the current inability of men to bring in wealth and to maintain their rights over children, it is becoming unclear whether the interests of grandparents now lie with their daughters or with their sons. Grandparents in effect became the arbiters of the relative capabilities of male and female capital to realise social regeneration and to nurture rural homes.

In the late twentieth century, sons and single mother daughters have to fight not only for access to resources embodied in land, but also for legitimacy within the *nyumba* itself. At the same time both sons and single mothers must operate outside the *nyumba* to generate the capital which will render the *nyumba* productive. Whilst single mothers were always excluded from the *nyumba*, the peripheralisation of men in relation to the *nyumba* was previously amended through their wives. Today, however, men must also struggle to legitimise their position in relation to their rural homes. The return of single women is now dangerously threatening to their brothers for whom the *nyumba* and its resources are increasingly the source of survival itself.

The story of Elizabeth brings to the fore conflicts between siblings which emerge in the tension between male and female claims to the home. Through these struggles, the *nyumba* itself is transformed, with far reaching implications for relationships between wealth and identity in the wider community.

Guka wa Maina has a sympathetic relationship with his single-mother daughter. However his relationship with his sister Elizabeth has been full of tension. Elizabeth is a single mother working as a housemaid in urban Nairobi. Despite working in Nairobi, Elizabeth maintains close links with her rural home, high up in the hills towards the Aberdare mountains. She is especially close to her mother and was also close to her father before he died. It was her parents who brought up her own children while she worked in the city.

Whilst Elizabeth has a close relationship to her parents, her relationship with her brothers is one of bitter struggle. Elizabeth's brothers live on their own portions of land surrounding that of their parents. In this sense the family is typical, with the brothers based on the family land and the sisters living away from home. Before he died, Elizabeth's father insisted that Elizabeth should inherit land along with her brothers. 'But they could not give me a single cent from my father's land,' she said. Instead the brothers eventually clubbed together and bought her some land in the Rift Valley. It seemed they would rather buy her land out of their own pockets than forgo even a small portion of their father's land which they viewed as their right, and theirs alone.

The rifts between Elizabeth and her brothers over issues such as land have recently come to a head in relation to the *nyumba* itself, their mother's home. Recently the sons, who are wealthy tea farmers, decided they must build their mother a stone house to replace the mud and wattle one which she has occupied until now. Her mother's homestead will go to Elizabeth after her mother dies and thus Elizabeth, despite her meagre income, was also asked to contribute to the building of the house which she would eventually inherit. She did this through a loan from her employers.

The first dispute arose after their mother moved in. The brothers had designed the building of the house without a back door for the kitchen. 'So there is nowhere to pour water,' said Elizabeth, 'and if my mother wants to bring in firewood she has to carry it through the living room!' In actual fact many women in the rural areas do not like to cook in a stone kitchen, which is very impractical compared to a mud and wattle kitchen that is especially suited to rural conditions. Elizabeth says that she is going to make her mother an outside kitchen using some of the materials from the mud and wattle house in which her mother used to live. The brothers won't hear of it and say they will build their mother a drainage channel in the new house where she can pour water. Elizabeth says she is going to build that kitchen even if it means she doesn't speak to them for a year.

The kitchen is the heart of the *nyumba* and the most important place in the homestead for women. Not only is it the centre of their activities it is also the place where they socialise as opposed to the living room or the compound which is reserved for men and for visitors. Men are thus peripheralised in relation to the *nyumba* from the outset even when they live in the rural areas. Equally single mothers are peripheralised in relation to the *nyumba* because, as daughters they are supposed to leave home and get married.

Elizabeth's desire to build her mother a kitchen outside the house that her brothers have built is a bid to reassert her own control over the *nyumba* from which she, as a single mother, has been marginalised. She defends her position partly on the grounds of gender. She insists that it is unthinkable for a woman to operate in a kitchen such as her brothers have built for their mother, thereby stressing the legitimacy of her voice as a woman over theirs. For Elizabeth's brothers, it is important that their mother continues to operate from the kitchen in the house they have built where, as sons, they will sit and talk with her when they come to visit. In this way they too appear to be seeking to strengthen their connection with their mother's *nyumba*, a link which in the past would have been beyond question.

Elizabeth's problems with her brothers have continued. They have finally given her the title deed to her land in the Rift Valley, and have even added another acre. For this, they want her to give them the house and its plot belonging to her mother which she is supposed to inherit after her mother's death. She has refused to do this. To add to the tension, one of Elizabeth's daughters who now has children of her own is currently living in Elizabeth's mother's home. Elizabeth's brothers have been constantly chiding both Elizabeth and their mother, saying that Elizabeth herself may occupy the house until she dies, but her descendants have no rights there and should not be living there. Elizabeth's daughters have lived in their grandmother's house since they were born, and their grandmother is very attached to them.

Recently Elizabeth's mother started suffering from pains in her belly and had to be taken to hospital. At the same time, Elizabeth herself was taken ill with the same symptoms. Her mother refused medicine, saying the pains had come about because of the brothers' behaviour. They were overcome with mortification and have since stopped trying to harass Elizabeth over the issue of land and over the fact that one of her daughters has gone back to stay in her grandmother's home.

Elizabeth's constant battle with her brothers to legitimise her status and that of her children in relation to her natal home has recently taken a new turn. Her long-term boyfriend, with whom she has been for over twenty years, recently told her that she was living in a state of disharmony with her family and that she must 'do right' by them. He had been listening to a programme on the radio where the speaker was extolling the importance and value of 'traditions'. On the basis of this, he told Elizabeth that she should perform her ritual dues to her clan, her *gurario*, or thanksgiving.

She knew that her family, being Christians, would not agree to let her perform this ceremony. So she told them she wanted to have a family gathering and to slaughter a goat, at which they were very happy. She asked her boyfriend to give her at least part of the money to pay for the feast (11,000 Ksh, equivalent to roughly £100.00). He said that it was 'her work', but that he would contribute 1,000Ksh. In the event he gave her 6,000Ksh, over half of the expenses of the *gurario*.

With her boyfriend's help, Elizabeth has now legitimised her position and that of her descendants in relation to her clan, at least in the eyes of the ancestors. This will be recognised by the family even if it cannot be openly admitted that she has performed her *gurario*. When her mother dies, she will inherit her mother's house. In addition to this she has acquired a plot of land nearby with a loan from her employers. Thus when she retires she will be able to move back to her family home and, unless the friction with her brothers finds a new vent, it looks as though her re-integration into the *nyumba* will be complete.

Conclusion

This chapter examines the relationship between identity and violence in Central Kenya, through the transformation of the *nyumba* as a symbol of Kikuyu ethnicity. At the beginning of the century, the *nyumba* was the site of female productivity, organised around matrifocal household units, geared towards sustenance and bounded within the framework of inter-clan relationships. By the time of Independence in 1963, the *nyumba* had expanded to become a site of collective social and political identity, and a locus of wealth in the context of capitalist markets and the state.

In the early stages of this process, the *nyumba* was the focus for competing claims by the colonial state, Asians, Kikuyu men and Kikuyu women. The forces of Asian capital and female entrepreneurship were overridden by an association between the state and male wage labour/agricultural investment, which reached its apotheosis in the time of Kenyatta when the Kikuyu took control of the government. As a site of agricultural production and 'tribal' identity, the rural *nyumba* became vital to Kikuyu control over the state. Through its reconstruction in terms of the 'traditional' *mbari*, 'where the ownership of the land passes from father to son', the female *nyumba* became the new locus of male wealth and power, and the lynchpin of twentieth-century ethnic identity.

At the same time the *nyumba* came to embody a contradiction in the colonial state's relation to capital, such that it was expressed separately in the urban areas through independent women, and in rural areas through men and their wives. In the urban areas, an association between Asian/Muslim capital and female entrepreneurship re-established the *nyumba* as a site of matrifocality, matrilineality and female productivity. This was also creative of wealth through its mobilisation in the context of small-scale entrepreneurship outside the orbits of state control. In contrast to rural *nyumbas* however, urban *nyumbas* have been conceived of as 'illegitimate' in relation to the state and rural communities. In the decades since Independence, the failure of the state (and the world market) in the consolidation and augmentation of Kikuyu wealth has brought these two *nyumbas* on to the same ground and into conflict.

In recent decades, women's economic significance is beginning to strengthen their position in relation to the *nyumba*. The importance of descent as opposed to alliance in the consolidation of wealth and property re-evaluates women's position as biological mothers and social members of their clans. In addition, their role in production and trade is increasingly crucial to rural economies. The channels opened by female entrepreneurship are creating new links between rural and urban, between agricultural production and indigenous as well as export markets. These markets operate relatively independently of the state, and go some way towards mitigating the economic crisis which rural communities currently face. In the case of today's 'daughters', their labour and fertility need not be lost to their clans, as it was in the nineteenth century, when wealth was generated through inter-clan relationships formed through exogamous marriage.

Returning single-mother sisters violate the boundaries of the rural *nyumba* constructed by men over the course of the century. In so doing, they redefine its parameters in ways that draw on its pre-colonial as well as post-colonial significance. Just as the institution of the *mbari* was invoked to legitimate male claims over the *nyumba*, so women make use of the 'traditional' *gurario*, marriage feast, to affirm their position as daughters and bringers of wealth to their clans. In addition, women like Elizabeth and Nyina wa Martha reinforce cross-generational and gender ties particularly with their mothers, to challenge their brothers' exclusivity in relation to their homes. The efforts of single-mother sisters to reintegrate themselves into their rural homes have been aided by a new government bill which legitimises female claims to land. These challenges are transforming the parameters of ethnicity itself, and creating new ways of 'being Kikuyu'.

Through an investigation of male and female claims to the *nyumba*, the chapter explores the interaction between macro-level economic and political forces, individual agency and the production of collective identity. It shows how ethnicity embodies relationships of dominance and exclusion in terms of its construction through the hierarchialisation of difference. In this case, gender is the axis of difference through which economic and political dynamics are mobilised to create a hierarchy of power, experienced through the *nyumba* as a symbol of the 'whole'.

In the context of ethnic identification, relations of dominance and subordination are continually contested and re-ordered through the agency of individuals and groups, who tap into deeply rooted cultural and historical narratives in their quest for belonging and empowerment. In this process, ethnicity is reproduced and transformed in such a manner that it becomes individually internalised as a core aspect of existence, resonant with material, cultural and political realities. The reworking of ethnic identity in relation to the *nyumba* is made even more potent by the dynamism and emotional rawness of relationships between brothers and sisters, between lovers, fathers, mothers, children, spouses. The experiential power inherent in the production of ethnicity is latent in the potential force which ethnic identity can acquire in acts of violence and war. Both destructive and creative, conflict is integral to the production of ethnicity, where its creative power and its cruellest metal come to the fore.

Notes

1 In cases where sensitive or personal information is discussed, I have changed the name of the interviewee to protect his or her identity.

Glossary

Gurario: Feast of thanksgiving by the clan of the groom for the clan of the bride for the gift of a daughter. The *gurario* initiates a relationship between the two clans which will last 'for the lifetime of the couple and beyond'. Its fruits include the bridewealth (cattle) paid to the bride's clan, and rights over the labour and fertility of the bride which will benefit the groom's clan. It also includes mutual gifts which continue to pass between clans, and are symbolic of the principle of fertility and 'increase' embodied by the marriage.

Mbari: Sub-clan. This is a territorially and ancestrally defined unit. It locates in time and space the nine metaphysical clans of the Kikuyu. Sub-clans normally resided on the ridges between the valleys which make up Kikuyuland. The territory associated with the *mbari* was the physical manifestation of *mbari* identity, rather than being a form of property in the modern sense. It was differentiated from the gardens of the women which were widely dispersed. The *mbari* comprised the descendents of a particular ancestor. It was expected that enterprising young sons would go off to found their own *mbari* and colonise new tracts of land. Unlike the clan, the unit of the *mbari* was thus always temporary and historically contingent.

Nyumba: In the nineteenth century, in a polygamous system, this referred to the household of a wife and her children.

References

Anderson, D. 1996. 'Corruption at City Hall? Nairobi 1944–63', paper given at Centre for African Studies conference *Africa's Urban Past*, 19–21 June, SOAS, University of London (unpublished).

Barth, F. 1994. 'Enduring and emerging issues in the analysis of ethnicity', in H. Vermeulen and C. Grovers (eds) *The Anthropology of Ethnicity: Beyond 'Ethnic Groups and Boundaries'*, Amsterdam: Het Spinhuis.

Berman, B. and Lonsdale, J. 1992. *Unhappy Valley: Conflict in Kenya and Africa*, Vols 1 and 2, London: James Currey, Nairobi: Heinemann Kenya.

Cohen, A. 1994. 'Boundaries of consciousness, consciousness of boundaries: critical questions for anthropology', in H. Vermeulen and C. Grovers (eds) *The Anthropology of Ethnicity: Beyond 'Ethnic Groups and Boundaries'*, Amsterdam: Het Spinhuis.

Kapferer, B. 1988. *Legends of People, Myths of State: Violence, Intolerance and Political Culture in Sri Lanka and Australia*, Washington and London: Smithsonian Institution Press.

Kitching, G. 1980. *Class and Economic Change in Kenya: The Making of an African Petite Bourgeoisie 1905–1970*, New Haven and London: Yale University Press.

Marris, P. and Somerset, T. 1971. *African Businessmen: A Study of Entrepreneurship and Development in Kenya*, London: Routledge and Kegan Paul.

Nelson, N. 1978. 'Dependence and independence: female household heads in Mathare Valley, a squatter community in Nairobi, Kenya', Ph.D. thesis: University of London.

Robertson, C. 1997. *Trouble Showed the Way: Women, Men and Trade in the Nairobi Area 1890–1990*, Bloomington, Ind.: Indiana University Press.

Roosens, E. 1994. 'The primordial nature of origins in migrant ethnicity', in H. Vermeulen and C. Grovers (eds) *The Anthropology of Ethnicity: Beyond 'Ethnic Groups and Boundaries'*, Amsterdam: Het Spinhuis.

White, L. 1990. *The Comforts of Home: Prostitution in Colonial Nairobi*, Chicago, Ill.: University of Chicago Press.

Chapter 3

Conflicts in context

Political violence and anthropological puzzles

Harri Englund

Contextualisation may be taken to define all production of knowledge if it is understood to effect a 'transformation of already existing awareness' (Strathern 1995a: 6). New knowledge grows out of old, not by a simple procedure of refutation, but by re-framing existing perceptions. The impetus to such a re-framing comes from diverse sources. The empirically minded generally put their faith in the feedback effects of 'the world' on their perceptions, while others stress a myriad historical and cultural reasons for what passes for knowledge and its transformations.

Common to both views is the understanding that contextualisation is beyond the control of the subject. Contexts impose themselves on the observer, and contextualisation as an active intervention in knowledge production always appears compromised by its dependence on existing framings. Anthropology's special claim to contextualisation as a mode of knowledge-production is the topic of increased reflection (see e.g. Blommaert 2001, Dilley 1999, Duranti and Goodwin 1992, Englund and Leach 2000, Howard-Malverde 1997, Strathern 1995b). Whether the unfamiliar is made familiar, or the familiar is de-familiarised, explicit re-framing often assumes pride of place in the anthropological strategies to produce new knowledge. In current anthropology, at issue is less the functionalist criticism of ethnographic representations made 'out of context' (Strathern 1987) than the multiplicity of the contexts which the anthropologist may summon up for any given sociocultural phenomenon.

Consider, for example, well-known cases of re-framing the social processes that underlie economic life. By contextualising productive relations as relations of kinship in some societies, anthropologists have paved the way for further insights into how both 'economy' and 'kinship' might be understood (Strathern 1985). But it also becomes difficult to consider one context as more 'basic' or 'primary' than another. Contexts multiply themselves without an identifiable point of origin, despite the utility of assuming such a point in both life and analysis (Wagner 1981: 41).

Re-framings are illuminating, and political violence is another domain in which anthropologists have deployed them to a good effect. More knowledge about 'tribal warfare' has been made available by drawing attention to the processes of state formation and the transnational regimes of extraction and exploitation (Ferguson 1990). A particularly radical re-framing has been achieved by those ethnographies which unsettle the assumption that violence, and even the annihilation of human lives, are universally pathological conditions (see e.g. Harrison 1993 and 1995). While, in the world-view of most readers of anthropological studies, physical violence signifies the absence or the end of a relationship, Melanesian ethnography discloses situations in which warfare occurs between persons who are already in social relationships. This Melanesian understanding presupposes existing relationships not only with tribal neighbours but also with white strangers.

This anthropological re-framing appears disturbing, even dangerous, to those who are familiar with the devastation and brutality of much twentieth-century warfare. Anthropologists run the risk of subverting the ethics of their profession by making the familiar look too unfamiliar. Political violence, after all, marks the unfortunate collapse of diplomacy and popular peace-making, with civilians, particularly women and children, often bearing the brunt of their leaders' inability to negotiate. In this view, the context of civilians' suffering and resistance would seem to be so obvious that the anthropological re-framing would become a dubious intellectual venture. Should the anthropological contribution to the study of political violence confine itself to documenting the horrors of political violence and the forms of popular resistance against it, utilising the discipline's tradition of intensive fieldwork?

I focus in this chapter on the war in post-colonial Mozambique so as to demonstrate not only the need for alternative re-framings of political violence, but also the effect which these contextualisations have on anthropological knowledge. The academic and popular debates on the war in Mozambique are suggestive for the way in which contextualisation has been a major concern throughout their 'paradigm shifts' (cf. Clarence-Smith 1989). The attention of the participants in these debates has been drawn to the effects of scale on explaining and understanding the war. 'Local' studies of the war appear to diminish scale and increase complexity. Against that, some argue that the 'local' itself owes its specificity to translocal events and movements. By taking as my standpoint an engagement with a recent anthropological attempt to re-frame the 'local' in the debate on the Mozambican war, I question the spatial contours of the 'local' as a notion, and outline other ways of understanding specificity and context in this war. I have offered the ethnographic justification for my argument in detail elsewhere (Englund 2002), and I explore here wider issues of scale and complexity.

Many wars in one?

Waged for most of the years of Mozambique's short history as an independent nation, the war between the forces of the Frelimo government and Renamo rebels witnessed such brutality and caused such displacement that no re-framing can justifiably alter its nature as one of the grimmest post-colonial wars. A more contentious issue is the origin of the war. From the first rebel attacks in the late

1970s until the signing of the peace treaty in 1992, many Mozambican and foreign observers put the blame on Renamo as a puppet movement which the Rhodesian minority government designed and the South African military trained and equipped to destabilise the young socialist state (see e.g. Fauvet 1984, Metz 1986, Cammack 1988). The other external enemies of independent Mozambique included right-wing sympathisers in Europe and the United States.

The 'paradigm shift' that began in the late 1980s had to acknowledge that Renamo was able to gain some local support in certain parts of Mozambique, and that the Frelimo government itself had to take some of the blame for the war. While to define the war as a civil war continues to evoke passionate arguments, the Frelimo government's unpopular villagisation programmes and antagonism to religion and 'traditional' authorities have been widely cited as flawed policies which paved the way for Renamo's advance (see e.g. Geffray 1990, Hall 1990: 59, Young 1990, Vines 1991: 93, Simpson 1993: 323–331). This observation has invited a host of case studies which highlight the complexity of the war according to its phase and to the locality where it was waged. Such complexity has ensured that the war can no longer be understood by re-framing it into distinct sets of 'external' and 'internal' causes.

One consequence of these case studies is the difficulty of arriving at plausible generalisations about the war. One observation always seems to be contradicted by another from elsewhere in Mozambique. Depending on the locality and region, it is as true to say that a local Frelimo secretary and a 'traditional' chief were in a bitter conflict with one another, as it is true to say that they could co-operate, or indeed be one person (Alexander 1994: 44 and 1997, Wilson 1992a: 5). In some parts of Mozambique, Renamo was seen as an 'Ndau political project' (Roesch 1992: 469), while elsewhere ethnicity played little role in the conflict. Other allegiances could be equally surprising from a generalising viewpoint. For example, despite Renamo's opposition to the Marxist-Leninist Frelimo, the mercantile elite in certain areas supported the government military in order to safeguard its local prominence (Wilson with Nunes 1994: 211). Even more disturbing for any attempts at generalisation is the observation that political affiliations could change in the course of the war, the divide between being Renamo and not being Renamo appearing less clear-cut than an overview of the war would have suggested (see e.g. Englund 2002, McGregor 1998).

Beyond the well-documented origins of Renamo in the hostility of neighbouring minority governments against Frelimo, and the facts of brutality and displacement during the war, the case studies would seem to leave little space for a general pattern in which variations would confirm a rule. Each local study, in other words, seems to re-frame existing knowledge about the war in ways that defy attempts at a coherent overall picture. There is, however, at least one recent anthropological study which boldly refuses to contribute to this proliferation of local studies. Carolyn Nordstrom's *A Different Kind of War Story*, whilst acknowledging a measure of uniqueness in each armed conflict, emphasises 'a shared experience of coeval political violence' which 'span cultural divisions based on national and ethnic identities' (1997: 6). The approach would appear as no less anthropological than the one which highlights cultural and historical specificity: Nordstrom's study belongs to the grand anthropological tradition of seeking to understand a common human condition. She arrived in Mozambique after studying political violence in Sri Lanka, and finds in one conflict much that resonates with another, as they do with the experiences of violence beyond these two settings. What is the effect of re-framing the Mozambican war in such a manner?

A shared culture of violence?

In so far as the case studies of the war in Mozambique are presented as 'local' studies, they expose themselves to a well-established anthropological critique. I return to this critique below, but, briefly put, it is a critique of the discipline's alleged 'obsession' (van Binsbergen 1998: 874) with the local, most often the village. The critique stresses the provisional nature of any bounded unit of study, and shows the translocal underpinnings of apparently local and personal phenomena. One instance is given in Arjun Appadurai's concept of 'ethnoscapes' (1991), intended to capture the reconstruction of histories and ethnic identities by diasporic migrant communities. Nordstrom endorses this theoretical concern, and is clear about the accompanying demands for contextualisation: 'Even the most circumscribed of locales is set within a *larger* context of international influences, indelibly changing both the character of the local and the translocal' (1997: 37, italics added).[1] Nordstrom's response to such analytical challenges is the concept of 'war-scapes'. It refers to the many groups and persons who act and interact in the local and transnational construction of conflict.

No sooner has Nordstrom introduced this effort to grasp the 'larger' context of the war than she feels obliged to comment on its effects on understanding anything in particular: 'This concept of war-scapes . . . makes it possible to transcend individual expressions of the war in particular locales, to understand the creation of a culture of war throughout Mozambique' (1997: 38). A host of 'disparate but equally powerful realities' (p. 10) maintain, nevertheless, an uneasy presence throughout the study. They include 'individual' (p. 10) and 'personal' (p. 123) realities, linguistic and cultural diversity within the vast country (p. 147), the local variations in the war noted by earlier scholarship (pp. 104–106), not to mention the diversity entailed by such variables as age and gender (p. 22). Nordstrom acknowledges the need to study all these issues, but insists on a shared 'culture of violence' (e.g. p. 123) which emerges through 'war-scapes' as a dynamic reality.

The simple equivalence between a culture and a locality thus erased, one is led to investigate whether the concept of culture actually surpasses certain obsolete conceptualisations of culture in cultural anthropology (cf. Kuper 1999). There is a recurring epithet in *A Different Kind of War Story* which one would have expected to have disappeared from ethnographic accounts. Nordstrom's interlocutors are 'average people' (p. 12), 'average Mozambicans' (p. 143), 'average citizens'

(p. 220) and 'average civilians' (p. 206 and *passim*). *Average*, presumably, is the most the ethnographer can say about these interlocutors when their concerns and experiences are contextualised as tokens of a shared culture. It is the same concept of culture which makes Nordstrom emphasise the possibility of 'a true spark of creativity' (p. 198) under desperate circumstances. It is creativity that provides civilians with a means of resistance against dehumanising violence. Nordstrom juxtaposes creativity with the processes of transformation that build upon the old to achieve something newer. Although the abject conditions of war account for such 'sparks of creativity', they only appear as such against the established repertoires of a shared culture.

The war in Mozambique, in other words, is contextualised in terms of a shared culture of violence, not through the culture of any particular group within Mozambique. Because the concept of 'war-scapes' covers a whole range of subjects in a conflict, who are likely to have disparate interests, the shared culture Nordstrom writes about presupposes a sufficient degree of commonality in experience. Her focus is on civilians, understood, importantly, to carry undeserved guilt and responsibility for the tragedy of the war (p. 162). They are, *tout court*, victims. Their lot is to offer 'creative resistance' against the calamity they have been thrown into. Examples include certain counter-violence movements led by spirit mediums and healers. According to Nordstrom, they 'championed traditional African power and culture', and thereby posed a threat to both 'the scientific-Marxist government of Frelimo' (p. 150) and the Renamo rebels.

The effect of this re-framing becomes clear when it is observed, first, that the Marxism-Leninism promised in Frelimo's early rhetoric hardly reached many areas in Mozambique's countryside, and that Frelimo itself had given it up by the 1990s (see Hall and Young 1997). Second, 'African power and culture' were not the prerogatives of civilian 'victims', but the use of mediums and healers has been documented for both Frelimo and Renamo combatants (see Wilson 1992b). These observations, together with the ones above on shifting political affiliations, question the analytical benefit that can be derived from contextualising civilians as separate from combatants, and associating the victims with a particular 'culture of violence'. Other contextualisations simply appear to produce more ethnography.

A subtle discussion of 'violence' as a notion and as a lived experience is one of the strongest contributions of Nordstrom's book (see pp. 114–132). 'To essentialise violence theoretically', she observes, 'is to reify it' (p. 116). The discrepancy between violence as a notion and as an experience appears here as a major problem for anthropological understanding, but it is the 'ontological experience of violence' (p. 117) that gives rise to a shared culture amenable to anthropological investigation. This contextualisation, however, is the origin of the difficulty of taking the complexities of the war into account. The difficulty is not the emphasis on the ontological force of violence; there are ethnographies which show how integral violence can be to social dynamics (see e.g. Bloch 1986, Kapferer 1997). In Nordstrom's account, political violence in Mozambique becomes, rather, a context in itself instead of demanding a context. How this re-framing, together with the 'shared culture' that accompanies it, circumvents 'reifying' violence is not clear, unless any contextualisation of violence is regarded as its 'theoretical taming' (pp. 16–19). And yet, if the price of such an approach is a focus on the 'average' people – a sociological fiction par excellence – one may well ask what is missing in this contextualisation. Missing are the *social relationships* that constitute persons as the subjects and objects of war. They are, moreover, enmeshed in social relationships which have histories beyond the dramatic incidents of political violence.

What is the 'local'?

My discussion is not intended to deny the fact that in any war there may be intolerable numbers of pure victims, persons caught up in a tragedy without any error of judgement on their own part. Nor do I deny the importance of contextualising even the most personal experiences of the Mozambican war through the transnational regimes of extraction and exploitation that have long shaped Mozambican realities. The challenge is to devise a perspective in which one re-framing does not immediately call for revisions to another, thereby creating a haunting sense of inadequacy. I have in mind Nordstrom's re-framing of the Mozambican war in which a 'shared culture' requires a comment on 'individual' experiences, and 'tradition' must be complemented by 'true sparks of creativity'. My focus here is not on the familiar dichotomies which may give rise to such analytical quandaries, such as culture versus individual, or tradition versus innovation. I propose to question the validity of 'political violence' as a self-evident topic of anthropological inquiry.

By highlighting historical and local specificity, ethnography is often able to unsettle the self-evident nature of any topic or domain. Current anthropology, however, casts a shadow of doubt over certain conventional contextualisations by which the appearance of specificity is achieved in ethnographies. This critique, as mentioned above, is particularly attentive to the way in which spatial metaphors often displace the questions of scale in the ethnographic representation of sociocultural and historical specificity (see e.g. Fog Olwig and Hastrup 1997, Gupta and Ferguson 1997). Specificity has too often been understood as a property of the 'local' that is encompassed by a hierarchy of regional, national, transnational and global contexts. The 'local' presupposes the 'translocal' or the 'non-local', and the analytical error has been to view the 'local' as a context rather than as requiring a context for understanding its own emergence.

No less problematic is the analytical strategy which situates the different contexts on distinct and abstract levels. A consequence is the need to contemplate how one level relates to another; whether, for instance, the local level is determined by the global level. Such analytical problems are sustained by the belief that analysis involves discovering a context which is more primary than others.

Although the belief in a primary context may arise from no more than a fiction, analysis can hardly proceed without some version of it. The task is to modify this fiction so that it captures, however incompletely, contextualisation as an ongoing dynamic. The multiplication of contexts should be the point of departure for ethnographic analysis, not uncomfortable noise to be explained away. If the subject-matter is social relationships, the fiction of a primary context can be retained, while analysis shows the ongoing dynamic of those relationships. By focusing on particular relationships, ethnography can demonstrate how the many histories that impinge on them become one process in the lives as lived. In other words, the transnational and even global histories of extraction and exploitation which have long shaped Mozambican lives do not become abstract levels which must somehow be related to the specific histories of villages, families and persons. The multiplication of contexts is evident in the subject-matter itself.

Such an approach to contextualisation has a displacing effect on political violence as a context for sociocultural phenomena. Anthropologists may expect this effect to invite consternation. It is a truism to say that the public demand for relevance, not least through the vagaries of research funding, influences the questions that anthropologists find worth asking. Such phenomena as political violence and refugee crises seem to require little explanation as worthy topics of study, and anthropologists imperil the relevance of their discipline by ignoring them. Although I concur with this line of thinking, it is precisely anthropology's special sensitivity to contextualisation that makes it difficult to take any topic for granted. The anthropologist may choose a particular crisis as his or her topic of study, but the reflexive long-term fieldwork which is expected to characterise his or her engagement with this topic frequently produces insights which displace the assumptions which led to this topic in the first place.

A brief autobiographical note may clarify my position. An interest in a particular human predicament preceded my interest in any particular country or ethnographic site. I was interested in famines when I found the book, which had been recently published, by Megan Vaughan (1987) on a famine in colonial Malawi. Written by a social historian, this book made extensive use of ethnographies about Malawi, and was able to present a fine-grained account in which victims did not appear as an undifferentiated population, but as social persons enmeshed in relationships which were under stress. By the time I had the chance to conduct my first fieldwork in Malawi and Mozambique in 1992–1993, this book had inspired me to read more widely about Malawi's history and ethnography. I was becoming, in short, a 'Malawianist', and, after learning about a huge influx of refugees, a 'Mozambicanist' in order to understand the background to this crisis. Again I was moved in my anthropology by a desire to study, and perhaps alleviate, human suffering; now the crises were war and displacement. But on the eve of my fieldwork, it was clear to me that I was going to encounter people who carried relationships with them from beyond the crisis where I was going to find them.

At least three ambitions, therefore, guided my research among Malawian villagers and Mozambican refugees during this first fieldwork. The first was to contribute to the general anthropological debate on personhood and social organisation; the second was the desire to enrich the existing ethnographic record on Malawi and Mozambique; and the third was to engage with popular and multidisciplinary debates on refugees and political violence. Crucially, one objective did not override the other, but all were supposed to contribute to a better understanding of a historically specific human predicament. There was a moral undercurrent to my interest in famines, displacement and political violence; but there was an equal interest in appreciating the lives and times of my interlocutors in their infinite richness and complexity, in their historical specificity.

Was my study, therefore, a 'local study', one that Nordstrom's contribution complements as a qualitatively different enterprise altogether? Although my fieldwork was certainly localised, I would stress the methodological point of having relationships rather than a locality in focus. Not only was this an odd locality, a borderland on the periphery of two countries, and yet a setting for many key historical events in the region: more importantly, my own relative immobility during fieldwork was irrelevant to my will to appreciate the translocal currents that flow through the social relationships I defined as the subjects of my research. Oral histories, archival research and existing academic, government and missionary publications were all available to complement fieldwork. Complexity and indeterminacy came to nuance my theoretical interest in social organisation under such crises as displacement and political violence.

In order to represent this complexity in ethnography, the obvious solution was a focus on particular, named persons. This focus was not a response to the analytical quandary which Nordstrom's notions of 'war-scapes' and a 'shared culture' seem to occasion – the starting-point was not an encompassing culture which would make one contemplate individual variations. Accordingly, the conviction that ethnography should devote itself to representing irreducibly individual experiences – a conviction that still receives a moral content among some anthropologists (see e.g. Abu-Lughod 1993, Rapport 1997) – was wholly inappropriate. The focus on the complexity of social relationships entailed a notion of subjectivity in which persons were constituted by their relationships with one another. These relationships could undergo highly variable transformations during specific historical events.

This contextualisation placed great demands on the method of ethnographic representation. The method I chose may not be the only or the best method for solving the kinds of analytical problems I have outlined, but it has enabled me to focus on complexity and process in a way that more conventional ethnography would not. It is the extended-case method, first developed by anthropologists associated with the Rhodes-Livingstone Institute some fifty years ago in what is now Zambia. The most successful pioneer in using this method was Victor Turner (1957), whose approach challenged the orthodoxies of his time. It was a period when, for example, A.R. Radcliffe-Brown regarded what he called 'the actual relations of Tom, Dick and Harry' (1952: 192) as mere raw material which filled fieldnotes, whereas the aim of social anthropology was the abstraction of general laws and principles. For the anthropologists who launched the extended-case method, personal relationships were not illustrations of the abstract principles of structural-functional anthropology. Personal relationships were social forces that had the capacity to generate surprising and original twists in the process that was social life.

In Turner's monograph *Schism and Continuity in an African Society* (1957), the *form* of residential instability occurring in *many* villages did not simply disclose the *process* of growth and dispersal in a *single* village. The underlying contradiction between maternal descent and virilocal residence brought regularity to village fission, but it alone could not disclose how actual social groups came to be objectified and mobilised in practice. Important also were the wider politico-economic fields in which Ndembu villages were embedded. By following a whole sequence of events involving the same persons, Turner was able to show how the social process was not a matter of maintaining a system in abstract structural time, but a process in which people could, sometimes despite themselves, transform the very conditions of their relationships.

I should emphasise that I see Turner as a pioneer in using this method, not as someone whose particular use of it should be followed in every respect. It must be remembered that the anthropologists who first introduced the extended-case method did not share a coherent theory as to how the negotiation of meaning and norms took place (Kapferer 1976, Werbner 1984). At one end lurked the shortcoming of many transactional models which represented social life as an idealised market place – unconstrained individuals interacting as equals. As Pierre Bourdieu (1977: 26) has noted, Jaap van Velsen's (1964) study of the politics of kinship among the Lakeside Tonga of Malawi came particularly close to representing social manipulation in utilitarian and individualistic terms. Against that, as already mentioned, social relationships are intrinsic to human being, both constraints and motives of social action. Persons, in other words, are *constituted* by those relationships rather than being autonomous individuals. This revision to the extended-case method makes explicit the assumption that the very distinction between society or culture versus individuals does not have to arise in ethnographic analysis.

Another criticism that can be levelled at the extended-case method is its relatively scant attention to the narrative forms of people's own accounts. Whatever air of authenticity it creates, however, the direct reproduction of informants' 'voices' is no less informed by the ethnographer's selection and intervention than the definition of an 'event' in the seamless flow of social life. Richard Werbner's (1991, 1995) studies of life-historical narratives, moreover, have shown the continuing importance of keeping ineffable social forces in the analytical grasp. Both the said and the unsaid must belong to the purview of ethnographic analysis. Here Nordstrom's reminder is pertinent – a narrative does not provide unmediated access to the experience that is being narrated. As she goes on to say, when the ethnographer is dealing with the sensitive issues of war and displacement, 'something is always wrong with the facts one is given' (1997: 43). To me this suggests that there is no one narrative that would give a privileged standpoint to studying social processes – narratives must be compared and juxtaposed, persons, including the ethnographer, must be seen as situated actors in a complex process.

Was there a 'localised' war?

At first sight, the way in which the war reached the village I know best in the Angónia District in Tete Province in northern Mozambique along the Malawian border would not seem to need extended cases at all in order to be understood. The headman of that village, who had been deposed by the Frelimo government's campaign against traditional authorities in 1975, went, in 1985, to a Renamo base in the interior of Angónia District before the guerrillas had reached the frontier area. He had made a simple request; the guerrillas should proceed to his village and end the Frelimo rule. According to those who had contributed to this plot, he had given the guerrillas a substantial sum of money and had claimed that the people in his village were really behind Renamo. The guerrillas had, however, been reluctant to move into an area which they thought was part of Malawi. They had urged the ex-headman to collect more money in order to show that the villagers really supported Renamo. After the ex-headman's second visit, when he had handed over more money, the war did reach this village.

Given what we know, or think we know, about the history of Mozambique, this headman's action would seem to be rather unproblematic, even natural, and if I add that the Frelimo secretary in the village who had effectively taken over the village leadership from him was his own full brother, we then would seem to have a particularly uninteresting case of inevitable rivalry which led to involvement in a guerrilla war. However, the fact that other studies have shown how traditional authorities and party officials were not in any necessary conflict in other settings demands that one sees even such a prototypical case as problematic. My extended case of this village's path to war shows how the rivalry between the two brothers itself was an outcome of a process, a process that could have taken a very different course in other circumstances.

In the history of this part of Angónia District in Tete Province the resettlement schemes that created discontent in some other parts of Mozambique were avoided, because both colonial and post-colonial authorities have considered the area to have such compact settlements and high population density that no resettlement was thought to be necessary. Nor have major agricultural estates been established near the research area. Instead, the area was for a long time, from the turn of the century until the 1970s, a labour reserve for plantations elsewhere in northern and central Mozambique and, above all, for gold mines in South Africa. For the last two decades before independence in 1975, this area was also important in what some have called 'Portuguese shopkeeper colonialism' (Hanlon 1984: 188). Portuguese settlers lived in the countryside and engaged in small-scale commercial farming and trading in or near villages.

These aspects of district history, which, in turn, of course, were shaped by regional and even global histories, played a role in the emergence of the village in the 1930s and the eventual rivalry between the two brothers, the rivalry that was seen to bring the postcolonial war to the village. These histories did not *cause* the rivalry, but were aspects of their relationships which provided the specific context for the war in the village. Rather than going through the process by which the ex-headman came to visit the Renamo base (see Englund 2002: 59–74), more can be said about the question of guilt in a war, a question which Nordstrom's study raises so clearly.

Villagers in the Angónia borderland were certain about who bore the responsibility for the war reaching their area. They were less concerned about the Frelimo government than about culprits amongst themselves, and, sadly, quite unaware of South African and Rhodesian involvement in the war. It is crucial, however, to realise that there were, and are, those who think that the war was justified and that other villagers should be blamed for the conditions which made them support the guerrillas. Above all, as mentioned, many people shifted their allegiances as events unfolded, and the real challenge for ethnographic analysis in this case is to demonstrate how the remembered guilt focuses on a small number of actors, while in fact many more shared the sentiments that would by no means suggest that they were victims of a war. They were, instead, persons who actively tried to modify their circumstances under specific, though not necessarily 'localised', historical conditions.

Although the Frelimo government did not carry out some of its most unpopular policies in the area, and was represented in the local setting by its officials who themselves were villagers, the area had plunged into economic decline by the mid-1980s which made alternatives to Frelimo interesting. It should be recalled that the majority of men had been labour migrants to South Africa before both Malawi and Mozambique ended it in the mid-1970s. The end of wage labour in South Africa was, and continues to be, a major source of discontent in the area, because smallholder agriculture has proved to be a poor compensation, and most villagers have been unable to maintain the standard of living they had when labour migration was at its peak. Another issue which caused resentment in this part of Mozambique was the exodus of Portuguese settlers after independence. Their farms and shops had provided work and wealth to villagers, who had in most cases established real rapport with them.

When the guerrillas arrived in the village, therefore, some villagers, especially those men who were not active in the local Frelimo hierarchy and even some of those who were, had ample reason to feel curious about the newcomers. Renamo did not come to burn houses and rape women as some studies would lead one to expect, but it first organised meetings in the bush for those who were interested. Its message was loud and clear, however – the Frelimo government had to be destroyed so that the whites could return and true prosperity begin. When the guerrillas began to appear in the villages, they did harass local Frelimo leaders, but they also left with many villagers to their base and only after several months became more violent, in the end so violent and unpredictable that most villagers fled to Malawi, including the ex-headman, and only a handful remained with Renamo.

After the event, few villagers admit that they were interested in Renamo to the extent that they followed the guerrillas to their base. Almost everybody swears to have been abducted, forcibly made to act as porters and later as combatants for the guerrillas. Putting their lives at great risk, they eventually escaped from Renamo. Long-term fieldwork and a method which is sensitive to variation and diverse social positions can disclose more complexity behind the assertions of innocence. People contradict one another, or even themselves, in subtle and sometimes more direct ways, and events take place which occasion undesirable memories, such as that someone was a Renamo collaborator. The ethnographer can focus on the uses of social memory of political violence, but the conflicts, quarrels and stories that arise long after the war can also provide insights for reconstructing the war in particular relationships.

Crucial to such an ethnographic undertaking is to resist abstracting the period of political violence from the flow of social life as if it were a context for everything else. Villagers in my area of study certainly endured the war as perhaps the most dramatic crisis in their lives, but just because there was war they did not cease to be specific, recognisable human beings in particular relationships, with all the interests, compassion and contradiction that social life everywhere involves. Political violence, if anything, must be contextualised, if we are to give justice to the complexity of our interlocutors' lives.

Questions of guilt and context

The idea that persons caught up in a war are victims hinges on the notion that political violence is the context which defines their predicament. Deeply cultural preconceptions may underlie this contextualisation. Nordstrom's (1997) account, for example, is essentially a success story, a moving image in which the good are oppressed by the bad, but eventually get the upper hand with their 'creative resistance'. But rebels, dissidents and combatants also have their own perspectives on wars, and their omission from studies may distort our understanding (see e.g. Alexander 1998, Peters and Richards 1998).

Particularly for those studies that are based on research after political violence has abated, the obvious methodological problem is to reach beyond discourse in the present in order to discern the histories that made persons the subjects and objects of political violence. The problem is closely linked to the instability, if not crisis, of social memory. But it would be too simplistic to view social memory as a projection of present interests into the past. Past atrocities do have a moral force in the present that is beyond the control of any particular subject (cf. Werbner 1998, Alexander *et al.* 2000).

I have argued for a perspective in which ethnographic enquiry resists the inevitable temptation to see in political violence a radical rupture. The ethics of ethnography may require a documentation of atrocities in their full brutality, but another ethnographic task is to represent persons enmeshed in those atrocities as human beings in relationships. If there is an irreducible, 'primary' context for ethnographic enquiry, it can only build upon a theoretically informed view of what human being entails. Political violence may bring unliveable ruptures, but it is only through the disruption of their constitutive relationships that persons experience those ruptures as unliveable. Contextualisation in life and in analysis, therefore, resemble one another when both are shown to be dynamic processes of re-framing existing knowledge. I have sought a new context for the ethnographic analysis of the war in Mozambique. The result has been a re-framing, one that has been possible only after questioning the 'local' in local studies and, equally importantly, the notion of a 'shared culture of violence' in a study which seeks to move beyond the 'local'.

Notes

1   The 'character' of the local refers, presumably, to the preoccupations of earlier anthropological writing, not to the world, because, in this view, there can hardly be a locale whose 'character' has not already been set within the 'larger' context.

References

Abu-Lughod, L. 1993. *Writing Women's Worlds: Bedouin Stories*, Berkeley, Calif.: University of California Press.

Alexander, J. 1994. 'Land and political authority in post-war Mozambique: a view from Manica Province', unpublished ms, University of Oxford.

—— 1997. 'The local state in post-war Mozambique: political practice and ideas about authority', *Africa* 67: 1–26.

—— 1998. 'Dissident perspectives on Zimbabwe's post-independence war', *Africa* 68: 151–182.

Alexander, J., McGregor, J. and Ranger, T. 2000. *Violence and Memory: One Hundred Years in the Dark Forests of Matabeleland*. Oxford: James Currey.

Appadurai, A. 1991. 'Global ethnoscapes', in R.G. Fox (ed.) *Recapturing Anthropology*, Santa Fe, N.Mex.: School of American Universities Press.

Bloch, M. 1986. *From Blessing to Violence: History and Ideology in the Circumcision Ritual Among the Merina of Madagascar*, Cambridge: Cambridge University Press.

Blommaert, J. 2001. 'Context is/as critique', *Critique of Anthropology* 21: 13–32.

Bourdieu, P. 1977. *Outline of a Theory of Practice*, Cambridge: Cambridge University Press.

Cammack, D. 1988. 'The "human face" of destabilization: the war in Mozambique', *Review of African Political Economy* 40: 65–75.

Clarence-Smith, G. 1989. 'The roots of Mozambican counter-revolution', *Southern African Review of Books* 4: 7–10.

Dilley, R.M. (ed.) 1999. *The Problem of Context: Perspectives from Social Anthropology and Elsewhere*, Oxford: Berghahn.

Duranti, A. and Goodwin, C. (eds) 1992. *Rethinking Context: Language as an Interactive Phenomenon*, Cambridge: Cambridge University Press.

Englund, H. 2002. *From War to Peace on the Mozambique–Malawi Borderland*, Edinburgh: Edinburgh University Press for the International African Institute.

Englund, H. and Leach, J. 2000. 'Ethnography and the meta-narratives of modernity', *Current Anthropology* 41: 225–248.

Fauvet, P. 1984. 'Roots of counter-revolution: the Mozambique national resistance', *Review of African Political Economy* 29: 108–121.

Ferguson, B. 1990. 'Explaining war', in J. Haas (ed.) *The Anthropology of War*, Cambridge: Cambridge University Press.

Fog Olwig, K. and Hastrup, K. (eds) 1997. *Siting Culture: The Shifting Anthropological Object*, London and New York: Routledge.

Geffray, C. 1990. *La Cause des Armes au Mozambique: Anthropologie d'une Guerre Civile*, Paris: Karthala.

Gupta, A. and Ferguson, J. (eds) 1997. *Anthropological Locations: Boundaries and Grounds of a Field Science*, Berkeley, Calif.: University of California Press.

Hall, M. 1990. 'The Mozambican National Resistance Movement (RENAMO): a study in the destruction of an African country', *Africa* 60: 39–45.

Hall, M. and Young, T. 1997. *Confronting the Leviathan: Mozambique since Independence*, London: Hurst.

Hanlon, J. 1984. *Mozambique: The Revolution under Fire*, London: Zed Books.

Harrison, S. 1993. *The Masks of War: Violence, Ritual and the Self in Melanesia*, Manchester: Manchester University Press.

—— 1995. 'Transformations of identity in Sepik warfare', in M. Strathern (ed.) *Shifting Contexts: Transformations in Anthropological Knowledge*, New York and London: Routledge.

Howard-Malverde, R. (ed.) 1997. *Creating Context in Andean Cultures*, Oxford: Oxford University Press.

Kapferer, B. 1976. 'Introduction: transactional models reconsidered', in B. Kapferer (ed.) *Transaction and Meaning: Directions in the Anthropology of Exchange and Symbolic Behaviour*, Philadelphia, Penn.: Institute for the Study of Human Issues.

—— 1997. *The Feast of the Sorcerer: Practices of Consciousness and Power*, Chicago, Ill.: University of Chicago Press.

Kuper, A. 1999. *Culture: An Anthropologist's Account*, Cambridge, Mass.: Harvard University Press.

McGregor, J. 1998. 'Violence and social change in a border economy: war in the Maputo hinterland, 1984–1992', *Journal of Southern African Studies* 24: 37–60.

Metz, S. 1986. 'The Mozambique National Resistance and South African foreign policy', *African Affairs* 85: 491–507.

Nordstrom, C. 1997. *A Different Kind of War Story*, Philadelphia, Penn.: University of Pennsylvania Press.

Peters, K. and Richards, P. 1998. '"Why we fight": voices of youth combatants in Sierra Leone', *Africa* 68: 183–210.

Radcliffe-Brown, A.R. 1952. *Structure and Function in Primitive Society*, London: Routledge and Kegan Paul.

Rapport, N. 1997. *Transcendent Individual: Towards a Literary and Liberal Anthropology*, London and New York: Routledge.

Roesch, O. 1992. 'Renamo and the peasantry in Southern Mozambique: a view from the Gaza Province', *Canadian Journal of African Studies* 26: 462–484.

Simpson, M. 1993. 'Foreign and domestic factors in the transformation of Frelimo', *Journal of Modern African Studies* 31: 309–337.

Strathern, M. 1985. 'Kinship and economy: constitutive orders of a provisional kind', *American Ethnologist* 12: 191–209.

—— 1987. 'Out of context: the persuasive fictions of anthropology', *Current Anthropology* 28: 251–281.

—— 1995a. 'Foreword: shifting contexts', in M. Strathern (ed.) *Shifting Contexts: Transformations of Anthropological Knowledge*, London and New York: Routledge.

—— 1995b. (ed.) *Shifting Contexts: Transformations of Anthropological Knowledge*, London and New York: Routledge.

Turner, V. 1957. *Schism and Continuity in an African Society*, Manchester: Manchester University Press.

van Binsbergen, W. 1998. 'Globalization and virtuality: analytical problems posed by the contemporary transformation of African societies', *Development and Change* 29: 873–903.

van Velsen, J. 1964. *The Politics of Kinship: A Study in Social Manipulation Among the Lakeside Tonga of Malawi*, Manchester: Manchester University Press.

Vaughan, M. 1987. *The Story of an African Famine: Gender and Famine in Twentieth-century Malawi*, Cambridge: Cambridge University Press.

Vines, A. 1991. *Renamo: Terrorism in Mozambique*, London: James Currey.

Wagner, R. 1981. *The Invention of Culture*, Chicago, Ill.: University of Chicago Press.

Werbner, R.P. 1984. 'The Manchester school in south-central Africa', *Annual Review of Anthropology* 13: 157–185.

—— 1991. *Tears of the Dead: The Social Biography of an African Family*, Edinburgh: Edinburgh University Press for the International African Institute.

—— 1995. 'Human rights and moral knowledge: arguments of accountability in Zimbabwe', in M. Strathern (ed.) *Shifting Contexts: Transformations of Anthropological Knowledge*, London and New York: Routledge.

—— 1998. 'Beyond oblivion: confronting memory crisis', in R. Werbner (ed.) *Memory and the Postcolony: African Anthropology and the Critique of Power*, London: Zed Books.

Wilson, K.B. 1992a. 'The socio-economic impact of war and flight in Posto Derre, Morrumbala District, Zambezia, unpublished ms, University of Oxford.

—— 1992b. 'Cults of violence and counter-violence in Mozambique', *Journal of Southern African Studies* 18: 527–582.

Wilson, K.B. with J. Nunes 1994. 'Repatriation to Mozambique: refugee initiative and agency planning in Milange District, 1988–1991', in T. Allen and H. Morsink (eds) *When Refugees Go Home*, London: James Currey.

Young, T. 1990. 'The MNR/Renamo: external and internal dynamics', *African Affairs* 89: 491–509.

Chapter 4

Hunger, violence and the moral economy of war in Zimbabwe[1]

Jocelyn Alexander and Jo Ann McGregor

Introduction

This chapter explores perceptions of violence and debates over the allocation of household resources in Zimbabwe's post-independence war. It does so from a particular perspective – that of the insurgents in this war, the so-called dissidents, and the civilians accused by Zimbabwe's ruling party of sustaining them with material and political support. We argue that understandings of violence are shaped by the elaboration and defence of rules of conduct, and notions of the moral economy of war. These ideas must be explored historically; they are rooted in past wars, and linked to the political and military goals and identities forged within them. In this case, the liberation war that immediately preceded the post-colonial war provided the benchmark for assessment of the behaviour of dissidents by civilians, and for dissidents' own self-perceptions. In the aftermath of war, the search for healing and for material well-being was shaped by this same history.

The chapter draws on research conducted as part of a collaborative project on the history of the Shangani region of Matabeleland North Province, Zimbabwe. As part of this research, extended interviews were conducted with over twenty-five former dissidents, as well as with over 150 civilians, many of whom were involved in political activity. Sections of the paper draw on this wider research (see Alexander *et al.* 2000a), and on earlier work on dissidents (Alexander 1998). Below, we begin with a discussion of the dynamics of the liberation war before turning to Zimbabwe's post-independence conflict and its aftermath.

The liberation war

Accounts from both civilians and dissidents of the post-independence war were rooted in their memories of the liberation war. This was a prolonged and bitter struggle, fought predominantly in the country's rural areas. It began with sporadic attacks in the mid-1960s, and escalated dramatically from the mid-1970s onwards, eventually leading to Zimbabwe's negotiated independence in 1980. Unlike other guerrilla wars in Africa, Zimbabwe's two guerrilla armies did not create formal 'liberated zones'. Nonetheless, and particularly in the final years of the war, guerrillas lived for prolonged periods in rural communities. The relationship between guerrillas and the communities who supplied them with shelter, food, clothing and intelligence stood at the heart of military and political strategy. The centrality of this relationship is underlined in the rich literature on the liberation war, though interpretations of the roles and agendas of guerrillas and civilians have differed markedly (Kriger 1992, Ranger 1985, Lan 1985, Bhebhe and Ranger 1996, Bhebe 1999, Maxwell 1999).

Most of this research took place in regions where the guerrilla army Zanla (the Zimbabwe African National Liberation Army), the armed wing of the now ruling Zanu-PF (Zimbabwe African National Union-Patriotic Front), predominated. Our own research, in contrast, focused on an area where Zipra (the Zimbabwe People's Revolutionary Army), the armed wing of Zapu (the Zimbabwe African People's Union), operated throughout the war.[2] Our findings with regard to the interactions of guerrillas and civilians differed significantly from those of researchers who worked in Zanla areas.

Perhaps the most significant difference lay in the history of Zapu's nationalism in the Shangani. In contrast to areas where Zanla and Zanu came to predominate, there was an unbroken history of rural nationalist organisation in the Shangani, dating back to the 1960s and even earlier in some instances. The same individuals had often held party posts for over a decade when guerrillas first arrived. These men and women had developed a powerful nationalist ideology over the course of many years of confrontation with the colonial state. This process was by no means always an amicable one: there were tensions across divides based on religion, education, class and ethnicity, and tensions between members of the different waves of migration that had settled the area. While these sources of division were never fully overcome, the nationalist party in the Shangani elaborated an increasingly inclusive ethic as the war spread. Few households were left untouched.

The longevity and intensity of local political organisation in this region meant that the arrival of Zipra guerrillas was greeted quite differently than elsewhere. In other parts of the country civilians demanded that the young men with guns prove their humanity. In a story that has achieved almost mythical status, they asked guerrillas to show them that they did not have tails. In the Shangani, civilians instead demanded evidence of the guerrillas' party credentials, and guerrillas often already knew the names of key party activists. Zapu leaders already had a political agenda when guerrillas arrived; they already had a history of specifically nationalist struggle, a sense of belonging to a wider political movement whose programme had been adapted, however contentiously, to their own experiences. As a result, the interaction with guerrillas took place within a shared and explicitly political framework, if one that was constantly being challenged and reworked.

Out of this shared political agenda there emerged a set of moral precepts and rules of behaviour which guerrillas were expected to observe. Guerrillas did not, of course, always accept these rules, and even where they did accept them, they did not always follow them. But a powerful aspect of the memory of the liberation war in the accounts of party leaders is their effort to enforce rules in the context of wartime, their shame and sense of failure where they failed, and their pride where they succeeded. We have explored these questions at length in our book; here, we provide a brief summary. There were several areas in which civilian leaders sought to regulate guerrilla behaviour. One related to the demands which guerrillas placed on civilian households for food and other material support such as clothes and cigarettes. Party leaders developed a system by which demands were spread across households and those with particular access to resources – migrant labourers, bus drivers, shop keepers – were drawn into action. Guerrillas divided themselves into small groups so that no one household had to feed too many at once; guerrillas were expected to eat what civilians ate and not to demand meat or other special treatment. Rotas were established for the supply of cigarettes and other goods. Those with jobs in town were called upon to acquire those items not easily available in the rural areas. This was, in contrast to Zanla operational areas (Kriger 1992), one of the least contentious arenas of guerrilla interaction with civilians.

A second field of concern related to sexual relations between guerrillas and young women who were often involved in feeding or otherwise helping the guerrillas. Many Zapu chairmen struggled to control these interactions, and guerrilla commanders supported them in this so far as rape was concerned. Rape did occur, but it received harsh condemnation from both civilians and guerrilla commanders. Relationships that did not involve coercion were more difficult to regulate. Guerrillas considered relationships in which they 'proposed love' as acceptable, though these were often vehemently objected to by elder party leaders as an infringement of their familial authority.

Civilians also sought to stop guerrillas (and often also party youth) from destroying infrastructure and services, particularly schools, which they argued would be needed in an independent Zimbabwe. They sought to stop guerrillas from attacking the buses and bridges on which they relied for transportation. In such cases they were often successful, convincing guerrillas to attack only those buses operated by drivers and conductors who refused to conceal goods intended for guerrillas, and persuading guerrillas to merely shut down rather than destroy schools. Civilians were less successful, however, in preventing guerrillas from attacking mission churches, and in suppressing Christian worship.

Perhaps the most contentious arena of negotiation and conflict had to do with the use of violence by guerrillas against those accused of being sellouts or witches.[3] These two categories are often treated as one in analyses of Zimbabwe's liberation war. But many party chairmen in the Shangani made a clear distinction between the two. In the case of sellouts, party leaders and guerrillas debated the proper form of punishment, as well as the definition of a sellout, at great length. Party leaders tried to prevent the execution of those who had once, or even continued, to work in the civil service; they sought to prevent cruel methods of execution, and to argue for a careful weighing of evidence before a judgement was reached. But both guerrillas and party chairmen agreed that once identified as a sellout, a sellout had to be punished, if not killed.

Witches were different, and before discussing wartime violence against them, it is necessary briefly to spell out the variety of means by which witches were dealt with before the war, none of which involved physical violence (see McGregor 1999). *Sangoma* spirit mediums, who were associated with the Ndebele, dealt with witches with herbs, blood sacrifices and other ritual acts of therapy and 'enacted a counter-aggression to attacks by sorcery by dancing, costumed as warriors and brandishing spears' (Werbner 1991: 201). Chiefs for their part had been prevented from dealing with witches under the Witchcraft Suppression Ordinance of 1999, though there is evidence that their courts continued (illegally) to deal with cases of witchcraft through a combination of divination and compensation. Famous itinerant witch eradicators also moved through the Shangani, the most important of which were often outsiders of Malawian or Zambian origin. They 'cured' witches by confiscating their magical paraphernalia and reincorporating the accused within the community. Zionist churches had also grown in influence and were associated with powers against witches. The means of identifying witches during the war drew on these pre-war practices: community leaders and guerrillas called upon those with expertise against witches such as *sangoma* mediums and Zionist prophets. But in a wartime context, ridding a community of witches could result in these individuals being killed, rather than cured, cleansed and reincorporated into society, due to the dangers they were deemed to pose to the struggle at large and to guerrillas individually.

To try to control such killings, party leaders sought to draw on their under-standing of nationalism as a secular, rights-based movement. They argued that the war was not being fought against witches, that they were irrelevant to the nationalist project, that they had always been present and always would be present, and that they were a matter for other authorities to deal with. Guerrillas – along with some party leaders – were not always convinced by this line of argument. Some guerrillas saw witches as a military threat, or interpreted their own role as encompassing the combating of evil as represented by witches. Guerrillas often claimed, and were often accorded, a privileged position of authority, giving them the right to pass judgement, often in conjunction with civilian specialists, on people accused of witchcraft. However, many party leaders, and eventually the guerrilla command, sought to prevent guerrillas from assuming this role. The deaths of those accused of witchcraft were nonetheless numerous, and few other arenas of wartime debate are seen as having produced so many failures in the party's efforts to exert control (for further, see McGregor 1999).

It is perhaps particularly relevant to the discussion here that the worst witch hunts of the war years were the product of Rhodesian counter-insurgency measures that involved infiltrating guerrilla supply lines with poisoned clothing and food, using chemicals such as thallium and warfarin (in food and drink) as well as a type of organophosphate known as parathian (absorbed through the body from doctored clothing). This was a deliberate attempt to exploit the popular association between poisoning and witchcraft and thus break the crucial relationship between rural communities and guerrillas on which successful guerrilla war depended (Brickhill 1992–1993, McGregor 1999). In many instances, political and military leaders managed to locate the source of the poisoned goods and to change supply routes. But where infiltration went undetected, the deaths of poisoned guerrillas provoked devastating reprisals against civilians, and caused the most profound ruptures of the ideal moral economy of war desired by party and military leaders. The centrality of food to the political relationship between guerrillas and civilians could not have been more gruesomely underlined.

Of course, the elaboration of a wartime morality was not applied simply to guerrillas: government forces were similarly judged, and ranked according to their behaviour and motives. The greatest vilification was reserved for the operations of the paramilitary forces, a range of units that were often hastily recruited and usually militarily less than competent. Guerrillas remembered these units with humour or even pity – they were easy targets. But for civilians, they were the worst contravenors of wartime morality. In the case of some units, this was because they were recruited from amongst local people, and they turned their knowledge of political allegiances and their petty hatreds against their neighbours. But all such units were hated above all for their wanton looting, conspicuous consumption in a time of dearth, and extreme use of violence against unarmed civilians. While the 'professional' soldiers of the Rhodesian army certainly committed many atrocities, they were seen to be doing so in the course of fighting the guerrillas; the paramilitaries were not. Their attacks were seen as motivated by greed, jealousy, revenge and a desire for status. Such motives were, in party leaders' eyes, utterly illegitimate, and their self-enrichment and uses of violence during the war were as a result vividly remembered and roundly condemned. As one party leader remarked: 'They enjoyed eating free food, to be seen eating canned beef and baked beans. They took delight in insulting us. They were proud of their good food and gun.'[4]

If the record of enforcement of rules of conduct and a moral economy of supply was a chequered one, the existence of this record is one of the key memories of the liberation war. It set a benchmark for the way in which guerrillas were meant to act; it set a precedent for the authority that civilians were meant to have; and it served to delineate the goals of nationalism all the more clearly. If the liberation war was fought by a guerrilla army, reliant on a nationalist party, and seeking to achieve a clear set of goals, the post-independence war was very different. There were efforts to revive aspects of the liberation war relationships, but these largely failed. Instead, the liberation war was used as a means of questioning the conduct and purpose of the post-independence war.

Dissidents and civilians

The bulk of the armed dissidents of the post-independence period were drawn from Zipra's ranks. In a context of increasing political conflict between the two nationalist parties, Zapu and Zanu-PF, they took up arms again in the early 1980s, for the most part due to fear of, or actual, persecution. The former Zipra guerrillas' return to arms was met with deep misgivings by the civilian party members who had supported them during the liberation war. Dissidents also faced a far more formidable enemy in the shape of the security forces of the new Zimbabwean state, and themselves had only the most minimal of military resources at their disposal. In this context, their relations with civilians changed dramatically from those of the liberation war.

Party leaders were placed in an unenviable position. Many of them had felt that Zapu's loss to Zanu-PF in the elections of 1980 was the result of trickery, that Zapu had been robbed of its just reward. However, they had also been told firmly by the party's national leaders that the war was over, and that the new dispensation had to be accepted. As we have explored in our book, senior Zapu leaders in fact made great efforts to persuade their followers to accept the election results, and to begin the process of rebuilding. They toured the rural areas, holding meetings, delivering speeches and throwing their considerable influence as nationalist leaders behind the new dispensation. While there were many disaffected Zapu supporters, they for the most part fell into line, and sought to return their regions to civil order, to promote reconciliation between opposing sides, and to engage with and participate in the new state's institutions.

This brief period of transition was not, however, to last. Some groups of Zipra guerrillas had refused to disarm during the ceasefire, seeing the ceasefire itself as a sellout by their leaders. These groups created considerable disruption but the challenges they posed were minor compared to those that the arrival of a new generation of armed Zipra guerrillas was to bring. These began to arrive in the rural areas not because of objections to the new dispensation but because they were increasingly threatened by it. The deterioration in political relations between Zanu-PF and Zapu was paralleled by a breakdown of relations between the former liberation armies (Alexander 1998). The outbreak of violence in 1980 and 1981 between units of the two former guerrilla armies garrisoned side by side within the cities was one aspect of this. There was also a systematic persecution of Zipra guerrillas who had joined the newly integrated national army (made up of Zanla, Zipra and Rhodesian forces). With the open rejection of the political alliance with Zapu in 1982, the Zanu-PF government turned its attention to the newly defined threat which Zipra guerrillas were claimed to pose, and the label of dissident came into widespread usage (Alexander and McGregor 1999). There followed an increased persecution of Zipra guerrillas outside the army, whether they were in the cities or in the rural areas. They were now considered, by definition, a danger to the new government.

Zipra guerrillas responded in a variety of ways to this process of escalating persecution. Some protested publicly, others fled to Botswana or South Africa, some sought to disguise their past, and a small minority decided to take up arms once again. Those who took up arms began to call on Zapu party leaders in the rural areas for support akin to that which they had received in the liberation war. Some party leaders responded with sympathy, at least initially. But many were unsure. They consulted senior party leaders, who told them that they were to report the presence of armed men, and they debated amongst themselves whether another war could be justified in nationalist terms. Many decided it could not, concluding that the dissidents were wrong to take up arms again.

The ambivalent and at times hostile reaction of rural Zapu leaders created a new dynamic. So did the actions of government security forces. As has now been widely documented, the deployment of the notorious Fifth Brigade in 1983 marked the beginning of the most extreme period of repression: Rhodesian tactics paled by comparison.[5] The operations of the Fifth Brigade, alongside those of other army, paramilitary and intelligence units, created a situation in which party leaders were unable to respond to this new threat with any coherence. The Fifth Brigade in particular also introduced an ethnic dimension to the conflict, attacking 'Zapu' as 'Ndebele'. Those in the rural areas found their lives placed at risk, and found themselves lumped into the same category as dissidents by the Zanu-PF government. Senior Zapu leaders fled into exile or were detained, along with senior Zipra leaders. Zapu was unable to exert control over the developing situation. Rural Zapu leaders felt abandoned, without guidance, thrust into a murky world of tribal conflict in which their nationalist precepts no longer applied.

In this situation, interactions with dissidents took on a very different slant to the interactions between civilians and guerrillas during the liberation war. Civilians and party leaders described dissidents as a fighting force that lacked any of the redeeming characteristics of Zipra. Certainly they had once been guerrillas – people remembered particular dissidents from the liberation war – but they did not behave as guerrillas. Civilians reached this conclusion through comparison with a partly romanticised version of the 1970s war (see Alexander *et al.* 2000a). Zipra had leaders, dissidents did not. Zipra respected elders and women, dissidents did not. Zipra had a political programme, dissidents did not. And perhaps above all, Zipra made reasonable requests for food, but dissidents did not. In the memories of civilians, this aspect of dissident behaviour stands out starkly. The names by which dissidents were commonly known in the Shangani hinged on their relationship with food: they were called 'Silambe Over', meaning roughly 'we are over hungry', or 'Ozitshwala', a name that underlined their central concern with *isitshwhala*, the staple maize porridge.

In all the denunciations of dissident behaviour, their penchant for meat, for food better than that of those they were eating with, was denounced with the most consistency. Dissidents also stood accused of rape, of beatings, of grotesque atrocities, but the way in which they ate the food of civilians – their hunger – came to exemplify the loss of any sense of a common goal and shared struggle. It marked the loss of the political relationship that had characterised interactions with guerrillas in the liberation war. Dissidents, unlike Zipra, were not accountable to the people on whom they relied for material support. Support was thus given grudgingly, and it was resented. It was classified as more akin to theft than to the voluntary donations which people had made, often at great risk to themselves, during the 1970s war. In that war, the very process of sharing out food, which involved communication through the party ranks, negotiation with guerrilla commanders, and a symbolic equality in terms of the consumption of the same food as civilians, had acted to reinforce the sense of a shared purpose and struggle. Now, dissidents did not spread their demands among households – no mechanism existed whereby this might be accomplished. Now, they demanded that a chicken or goat be slaughtered, setting themselves above and outside the consumption patterns of their hosts. Such demands were particularly galling and onerous in the drought years of the mid-1980s.

The name 'Silambe Over' stood for what had gone wrong in the relations between armed men and civilians. The unreasonable demands for food symbolised a whole set of lost relationships which had been defined over the course of the liberation war, and which were now invoked as a critique of dissidents' very existence. Dissidents could not be guerrillas, could not be accepted as Zipra, even where they were the very same individuals who had visited homes only a few years earlier. The history of interactions with armed men and of political mobilisation formed the basis for a rejection of dissidents' claims to authority and allegiance as guerrillas.

Party leaders' accounts of their interactions with dissidents did not include the lengthy debates over morality and rules, over nationalist goals and strategy, as their memories of guerrillas had. Where party leaders said they had stood up to dissidents, they did so on the basis of their liberation war norms, but these were the exceptions, and to do so was to run the risk of brutal attack. On the whole, the ways in which some of the contentious debates of the liberation war years reappeared merely served to underline the change in relationship and context. Thus debates over sellouts had lost their political content. Witches were not targeted, as dissidents themselves did not claim the necessary authority to confront them: they knew they were in no position to address social evils. There was no question of dissidents 'proposing love' to young women – relationships were invariably described as 'forced', and uniformly condemned. Attacks on symbols of the government were likewise uniformly condemned. Such attacks were now unambiguously harming civilians, with no legitimate purpose in nationalist terms. Descriptions of dissident behaviour were not couched in terms of a failure of mediation or negotiation, but of a failure of political relationship altogether. Some rural party leaders went so far as to suggest that dissidents were in fact sent by the government as a means of justifying the clampdown on Zapu: not only were they no longer considered as Zipra, they were classified as sellouts. (There certainly were government agents posing as dissidents, but they were on the whole easily identified as such, and the vast majority of dissidents were not agents but former Zipra guerrillas.)

Not surprisingly, dissidents resented this characterisation by civilians, and particularly the name Silambe Over. Though they did not generally discuss relations with civilians unprompted, focusing instead on the military difficulties that they faced and on the cruelty and illegitimacy of the government forces and political situation (Alexander 1998), they defended themselves when asked directly. Two former dissidents discussed the reasons for the name Silambe Over:

> MS: It was common amongst us when we got to a home to say 'we are over hungry' and 'we are over many', can you cook for us?

LN: There was very little time for rest. Most of the time was spent walking, carrying material, and you were definitely going to be 'over hungry' because you 'over travelled'. . . . When someone doesn't like you, he will call you names. The fact that most of us were Zipras, we knew how to live among the masses. . . . The enemy was really bent on destroying Zapu so they would use all means of destroying it. So they could send pseudo dissidents who would claim to be us. . . . He would be the one demanding meat all the time. So the collective name would come to us of Silambe Over, meat over. But we were pure Zipra. . . . In the dissident activity, we were Zipra and stayed Zipra – we were not forming a new party – until the people of Zimbabwe united. We ignored insults like Silambe Over because we were clear who we were. They were trying to destroy us but they failed, we know that these Silambe Over were the agents of the government.[6]

The former dissidents' contention that one could not be both true to Zipra and 'Silambe Over' was in fact in accord with civilian assessments. Both agreed that such unreasonable demands for food were unacceptable. The difference was that dissidents maintained that they were not responsible for such behaviour, that others – government agents, the untrained – carried out such abuses. Some former dissidents were, however, more straightforward, at least in terms of the way in which they comandeered food: 'Food, everything, had to be taken by force.'[7]

While former dissidents maintained that they were 'pure Zipra', they admitted that they were unable to fight in the same way as before. Rather, they spoke of a quixotic attempt to re-create the 'professionalism' of Zipra: 'The fact is we were not dissidents, but we were ex-Zipra.'[8] Dissidents struggled to establish a command structure that mirrored that of the 1970s Zipra; they sought to employ similar operational tactics such as establishing Gathering Points, using war names and the like (see Alexander 1998). But they were quick to admit that it was near impossible to achieve anything like the operational success of Zipra.

Everything had changed. From dissidents' point of view, civilians were now too afraid to support them. The extent of the Zanu-PF government's targeting of civilians far outdid that of the Rhodesian government. And Zapu was an easy target. They were above ground, some were serving as elected councilors or as civil servants. How could they support dissidents as they had supported guerrillas?

The problem was people were harassed by the army, the Fifth Brigade. . . . It was so hard to get support because people were so frightened and we had limited arms. It was very difficult for the party chairmen. Even when we went to those people the Fifth Brigade would come and harass or kill them. . . . Support was minimal.[9]

Dissidents lamented their loss of supply lines and leadership; they did not have ammunition, some did not have guns. Some were willing to admit that they had lost discipline, that there were lapses in their treatment of civilians. But this was due to the type of war they were forced to fight, to the corruption of the goals of war by the Zanu-PF government – or due to the 'untrained' people fighting with them. Nationalism was no longer the motivating ideology: 'We fought (A) Partyism, (B) Regionalism, (C) Racism or I can say tribalism'; 'It was two tribes fighting.'[10] Dissidents fought in a conflict in which liberation war goals no longer made sense. They were merely fighting for survival, for an end to their own persecution and the persecution of their leaders, their friends and neighbours: 'we were fighting because some people were just being taken and cut, parents were just being killed. Friends were taken at night by CIO [the Central Intelligence Organisation]. So that's why we were fighting.'[11]

Nonetheless, former dissidents clung to their sense of being professional soldiers. Many cited the way in which they had turned themselves in in ordered fashion, after meetings among their several operational regions, when their political leaders in Zapu called on them to do so under the Presidential Amnesty offered in 1988 (Alexander 1998). They may have looked like an ill-armed, rag-tag gang but, in their own eyes, they had maintained the Zipra tradition as best they could, and were proud of their continued allegiance to Zapu, both essential to distinguishing themselves from mere thugs. The end of the war provided an opportunity to reclaim their Zipra mantle in the eyes of those they saw as their leaders, and the communities in which they lived. Now they would have to demonstrate their Zipra character in new circumstances. One former dissident remembered the call of Joshua Nkomo, Zapu's President, for just this: 'Josh held a rally at Gwelutshena and said it's time to stop being Silambe Over, time for Sebenza [work] Over.'[12] But this was to be no easy task.

Aftermaths of war

In the aftermath of the 1980s war, those dissidents who had turned themselves in under the Amnesty were distributed to police stations throughout the western regions. There was intense debate as to what, if any, special treatment they should receive. In the end, and under criticism from some leading Zapu figures, those interested were helped to establish three co-operatives (many former dissidents simply left the country or made their own way to their rural homes or to the cities). Here we focus on one such co-operative, optimistically and revealingly named Isifiso Sikazulu, 'the wish of the people'.

Isifiso Sikazulu was established on the outskirts of Nkayi town in late 1988. It had about forty members at the outset and was located on land designated for the purpose by the Nkayi Council and District Administrator. It received material support from the NGO Zimbabwe Project. The co-operative enjoyed early successes, even winning a prize for conservation from the Natural Resources Board. But it fell apart in the end, for a complex set of reasons. Former members of the co-operative cited the attractions of the town itself, of beer and *dagga* and women. Others complained that the inclusion of some civilians and 'untrained people' amongst their number undermined any sense of unity of purpose and discipline on the co-operative – such was possible only if membership was restricted to 'real Zipra'. The inclusion of these people had made it impossible to maintain the military command structure established during the war, as some had hoped to do. Certain members of the co-operative left when they found jobs; others simply did not like farming. Some criticised the material and technical support they were given in establishing the co-operative.

Former dissidents were not in agreement as to the reasons for the co-operative's demise, but they did agree that it had undermined their standing as 'real guerrillas', and their attempt to be rid of the label Silambe Over. As one explained in 1995:

> We are guerrillas so we are people's green light. Whatever we do people are watching because we are freedom fighters. Everything we do requires patience. We should be showing an example . . ., since we are people sent by the nation of Zimbabwe. If we demonstrate such things like destroying that life at Isifiso, I'm so much afraid. . . . I'm thinking of this term used against us 'Silambe Over' – this word isn't from government, everyone here is saying it, saying look at that mess at Isifiso. Mainly, on establishing that co-operative, it wasn't meant for wealth, but to teach the people what co-operatives are supposed to be like because before we could engage in co-operative activities, we had to be co-operative in our minds. . . . Given the money that was poured into Isifiso, you'd think it would prosper but you are greeted by starvation when you walk into that place.[13]

If the co-operative failed as a demonstration of an alternative route to well-being, as a way to escape the label 'Silambe Over', it also failed to create a consensus on the necessity for cleansing and the best way to re-establish the dissidents' relationship to the ancestors, and to their political leaders. Dissidents were in a difficult position in this regard. They claimed the Zipra mantle, so it was as Zipra that they should be accepted by their leaders and be cleansed. Cleansing for soldiers was understood to mean the cleansing of the army as a whole from the violence of specifically war, an idea that drew on the nineteenth-century practices of the Ndebele state.[14] This in turn necessitated the cooperation of their military and political leaders. But these leaders were not willing to help the dissidents, seeing them as an issue best forgotten, as a compromising constituency, and certainly not as anything approximating an army. Dissidents were thus unable to gain the backing they needed for 'proper' cleansing, and had to seek alternatives that proved less than successful. They felt abandoned by the very leaders for whom they considered themselves to have been fighting (see Alexander 1998).

The question of the propitiation of the spirits was also a source of bitter division within the co-operative. One former dissident who claimed spiritual authority had designated a tree within the co-operative's confines as a shrine, on the advice of one of the shrine-keepers at Njelele, the main spiritual centre of the region. Two snakes were found coiled at the top of the tree, a propitious sign. However, some members of the co-operative believed that the tree harboured insects that damaged their crops, 'So the tree and snakes were destroyed and a new tree selected.'[15] But this act produced division, and some members of the co-operative left, believing the destruction of the tree to be a harbinger of the failure of Isifiso Sikazulu.

In 1995, one former dissident reflected on the fate of the co-operative, of the former dissidents, and of the people on whom they had relied through two wars:

> Food is in the process of revolution, we were fighting for shelter, for clothing, and for food also. And now people here are 'Silambe Over'. We were labelled 'Silambe Over', but now everyone is Silambe Over – we're the same, today we're all too hungry.[16]

The droughts and structural adjustment, the misrule of Zanu-PF in many people's eyes, had seen to that. But this was not the end of the story, at least as far as the former dissidents were concerned.

The neglect which dissidents suffered did not apply only to them amongst the greater group of former guerrillas. Guerrillas as a whole felt they had not been given the necessary attention – material and otherwise – in the aftermath of the liberation war (see Barnes 1995). As guerrillas of both armies began to flex their collective political muscle in the late 1990s, dissidents sought to fall under their umbrella, and in fact many dissidents participated in cleansing ceremonies organised for guerrillas as a whole at the Njelele shrine. Many dissidents went on to benefit from the government's eventual payment of compensation and pensions – Z$50,000 as a lump sum and Z$2,000 per month – to all former guerrillas (see Alexander et al. 2000, Kriger 1995, Werbner 1998). Through their reabsorption into the body of guerrillas at large many former dissidents were able to escape from their endless cycle of being 'too hungry'.

The great irony is that those few former dissidents who still maintained their residence on the Nkayi co-operative (though it no longer functioned as a co-operative) in the late 1990s were suddenly wealthier than many of their neighbours. From the dissidents' point of view, they were now able to begin their lives, so long disrupted by war: they could buy cattle, they could build good homes, they could marry properly. Eighteen years after the end of the liberation war, and ten years since they turned themselves in under the government's Amnesty, they had overcome, at least for the moment, their hunger. Such was not the case for the civilians who fed and clothed the dissidents, and Zipra before them, and there was a heated debate in Zimbabwean society over the justice of compensation to guerrillas (including dissidents) alone when so many other groups also suffered during the liberation war. The question of compensation or even acknowledgement for the sufferings, deaths and losses of the 1980s war remained even more contentious (Alexander et al. 2000a).

Conclusion

Perceptions of the meaning of violence, of the relations between civilians and armed men more widely in wartime, need to be explored historically. The meanings attributed to violence and to material sacrifices are shaped by the understandings of political goals and the mediation of military and political organisations. In the Shangani region of Zimbabwe, wartime violence was not meaningless or natural, and was not beyond moral judgement, though it may often have been beyond the control of those subjected to it. The basis on which civilians interpreted the actions and agenda of dissidents was firmly rooted in their experience of the liberation war, and the norms and rules elaborated in the course of that war. Dissidents suffered in the comparison: they were judged to have fallen outside the bounds of the nationalist project, to have fallen outside the category of guerrilla, precisely because they failed to observe the norms of the liberation war. The name 'Silambe Over' encapsulated the range of wrongs for which they were responsible, and signified the extent to which their authority and their claims to allegiance had been rejected. The political relationship which party leaders had fought so hard to forge during the liberation war no longer existed, and without that relationship, violence and material sacrifice were understood in entirely different ways.

For dissidents, the liberation war was also a touchstone, if one that was beyond their grasp. Despite the manifest extent to which they had been unable to recreate their previous success, they still clung to their notions of themselves as professional soldiers. After the 1980s' war, they struggled to shed the label Silambe Over, to end the hunger with which they were associated, and to provide an example worthy of 'pure Zipra'. Isifiso Sikazulu failed in this but, ironically, their stubborn refusal to give up their liberation war credentials was to pay off, quite literally, in the end.

Epilogue

Since we conducted the research on which this chapter is based, many of the former dissidents and Zipra combatants discussed here have re-entered Zimbabwean politics in ways that were difficult to anticipate. This new politics underlined once again the importance of re-evaluations of the liberation war in debates over violence, identity and access to food. The payouts made to veterans in the late 1990s signalled the birth of a new alliance between an increasingly embattled Zanu-PF and the Zimbabwe National Liberation War Veterans' Association. Veterans subsequently became key agents in Zanu-PF's strategy and rhetoric of on-going revolution, in which a reworked history of the guerrilla war took centre stage, and the struggle for national liberation was narrowed to the goal of wresting the land from the hands of whites and those construed as their neo-colonial allies. In this context, veterans assumed a crucial role, leading often violent occupations of white-owned commercial farms, and policing the rural areas for 'enemies' of the revolution (see Alexander and McGregor 2001).

For the communities of the Shangani, the role assumed by veterans was particularly ironic and sinister. Many former dissidents and Zipra guerrillas had been persecuted by the Zanu-PF government, along with civilians, in the 1980s, but now they worked hand in hand with that same government as agents of repression. Many veterans – though it should be stressed by no means all – adopted the language of 'revolution' and 'enemies' promulgated by Zanu-PF and veteran leaders, and used it to justify violent attacks on those identified with political opposition, driving them from their jobs and homes. People subjected to this onslaught of violence saw it as a travesty of the long history of political relationships that they had built in the name of a shared nationalism. In 2002, ongoing political conflict coincided with an extreme food shortage brought about by a combination of drought, the disruptions to agricultural production on the commercial farms, and wider economic decline. Veterans allied to Zanu-PF now acted as gate-keepers to drought relief and food sales. They defined the right to food in terms of political allegiance to Zanu-PF, and justified such an extreme narrowing of the state's obligations to its citizens in the name of defending the goals of the liberation war.[17] Food once again stood at the centre of political and moral rela-tionships. But veterans' new role, and the version of history that went with it, could not have been more different from the nationalist ideals and moral economy of war developed and defended at such great cost in previous decades.

Notes

1 The research on which this chapter is based was funded by the Leverhulme Trust in the case of J. Alexander and T. Ranger, and ESRC grant R00023 527601 in the case of J. McGregor. Particularly in the interviewing of former dissidents, the help of Nicholas Nkomo was invaluable, and we are very grateful to him.
2 See Brickhill (1995), Dabengwa (1995), and Bhebe's recent study (1999), for Zipra's history and military strategy.
3 We use the term witch because the English term is widely known and used in Zimbabwe's rural areas (unlike the term sorcerer). In an area of immigration and complex ethnicity such as the Shangani, there are many different local names for witches, and a range of different practices associated with them, which it is beyond the scope of this article to discuss.
4 Interview, PN, Mjena, 8 December 1995.
5 The most comprehensive treatment of the abuses of government security forces is in CCJP/LRF (1997). For academic analyses, see Alexander, McGregor and Ranger (2000a, 2000b); Alexander (1998); Lindgren, forthcoming; Yap (1996); Werbner (1991).
6 Interview, MS and LN, 10 October 1995.
7 Interview, GN, 5 December 1994.
8 MS, Autobiography, December 1994.
9 Interview, LN, 30 August 1995.
10 MS, Autobiography, December 1994; interview, SN, 26 September 1995.
11 Interview, GN, 5 December 1994.
12 Interview, LN, 10 October 1995.
13 Interview, LN, 10 October 1995.
14 The cleansing of an army was seen as distinct ritually and ideologically from concerns

about the consequences of individual wrongs and acts of violence in other contexts, or concerns about witchcraft. See Alexander, McGregor and Ranger (2000a, chapter 10).
15 Interview, MS, 10 October 1995.
16 Interview, LN, 10 October 1995.
17 The reports of the Zimbabwe Human Rights NGO Forum [www.hrforumzim.com] detail the political uses of food in 2002. Reports from opposition activists in the Shangani in the authors' possession confirm the explicit denial of access to both food sales and aid to those associated with the opposition on political grounds. There are precedents for the denial of food on political grounds by the Zanu-PF government, most extensively and horrifically in Matabeleland South in the mid-1980s. See Ranger (1999); CCJP/LRF (1997). In the droughts of the 1990s, the Zanu-PF government used the distribution of food to shore up its legitimacy in the context of severe disaffection over the implementation of a structural adjustment programme.

References

Alexander, J. 1998. 'Dissident perspectives on Zimbabwe's post-independence war', *Africa* 68(2): 151–82.
Alexander, J. and McGregor, J. 1999. 'Representing violence in Matabeleland, Zimbabwe: press and Internet debates', in T. Allen and J. Seaton (eds) *The Media of Conflict: War Reporting and Representations of Ethnic Violence*, London: Zed Books.
—— 2001. 'Elections, land and the politics of opposition in Matabeleland', *Journal of Agrarian Change* 1(4): 510–534.
Alexander, J., McGregor, J. and Ranger, T. 2000a. *Violence and Memory: One Hundred Years in the 'Dark Forests' of Matabeleland*, Oxford: James Currey.
—— 2000b. 'Ethnicity and the politics of conflict: the case of Matabeleland', in E.W. Nafziger, F. Stewart and R. Vayrynen (eds) *The Origins of Humanitarian Emergencies: War and Displacement in Developing Countries*, Oxford: Oxford University Press.
Barnes, T. 1995. 'The heroes' struggle: life after the Liberation War for four ex-combatants', in N. Bhebe and T. Ranger (eds) *Soldiers in Zimbabwe's Liberation War*, London: James Currey.
Bhebe, N. 1999. *The Zapu and Zanu Guerrilla Warfare and the Evangelical Lutheran Church in Zimbabwe*, Gweru: Mambo Press.
Bhebe, N. and Ranger, T. 1996. 'Introduction', *Society in Zimbabwe's Liberation War*, London: James Currey.
Brickhill, J. 1992–1993. 'Zimbabwe's poisoned legacy: secret war in Southern Africa', *Covert Action* 43: 4–59.
—— 1995. 'Daring to storm the heavens: the military strategy of Zapu, 1976–1979,' in N. Bhebe and T. Ranger (eds) *Soldiers in Zimbabwe's Liberation War*, London: James Currey.
Catholic Commission for Justice and Peace and Legal Resources Foundation 1997. *Breaking the Silence, Building True Peace: A Report on the Disturbances in Matabeleland and the Midlands, 1980–1988*, Harare: CCJP/LRF.
Dabengwa, D. 1995. 'Zipra in the Zimbabwe War of National Liberation', in N. Bhebe and T. Ranger (eds) *Soldiers in Zimbabwe's Liberation War*, London: James Currey.
Kriger, N. 1992. *Zimbabwe's Guerrilla War. Peasant Voices*, Cambridge: Cambridge University Press.
—— 1995. 'The politics of creating national heroes', in N. Bhebe and T. Ranger (eds) *Soldiers in Zimbabwe's Liberation War*, London: James Currey.

Lan, D. 1985. *Guns and Rain. Guerrillas and Spirit Mediums in Zimbabwe*, London: James Currey.

Lindgren, B. forthcoming. 'Fighting for the nation, achieving ethnification: the Fifth Brigade and Ndebele identity in post-colonial Zimbabwe', in P. Richards and B. Helander (eds) *No War, No Peace*, Athens, O.H.: Ohio University Press.

McGregor, J. 1999. 'Containing violence: poisoning and guerrilla/civilian relations in memories of Zimbabwe's liberation war', in K. Lacy Rogers, S. Leydesdorff and G. Dawson (eds) *Trauma and Life Stories: International Perspectives*, London, Routledge, pp. 131–159.

Maxwell, D. 1999. *Christians and Chiefs in Zimbabwe. A Social History of the Hwesa People, c. 1870s–1990s*, Edinburgh: Edinburgh University Press.

Ranger, T. 1985. *Peasant Consciousness and Guerrilla War in Zimbabwe*, London: James Currey.

—— 1999. *Voices from the Rocks: Nature, Culture and History in the Matopos Hills of Zimbabwe*, Oxford: James Currey.

Werbner, R. 1991. *Tears of the Dead: The Social Biography of an African Family*, Edinburgh: Edinburgh University Press.

—— 1998. 'Smoke from the barrel of a gun: postwars of the dead, memory and reinscription', in R. Werbner (ed.) *Memory and the Postcolony*, London: Zed Books.

Yap, K. 1996. 'Voices from the Matabeleland conflict: perceptions on violence, ethnicity and the disruption of national integration', Britain Zimbabwe Research Day, Oxford, 8 June 1996.

—— 1996. 'Arrested resolution: democracy, national integration and the politicization of ethnic identity with regards to the Matabeleland conflict (1981–1987)', paper presented to the International Conference on Historical Dimensions of Democracy and Human Rights in Zimbabwe, University of Zimbabwe, 9–14 September 1996.

Chapter 5

Violence and the boundaries of belonging

Comparing two border disputes in the South African lowveld[1]

Isak Niehaus

In 1984 fierce fighting erupted over the demarcation of the border between two villages in the Bushbuckridge area of the South African lowveld. The conflict was overtly ethnic. Northern Sotho residents of Buffelshoek – in the Bantustan of Lebowa – fought the Shangaan residents of Okkernootboom – in the Bantustan of Gazankulu.[2] Armed with spears, sjamboks (a type of whip) and knobkerries (a type of stick), groups of men crossed the border from either side to attack their ethnic enemies. A week of sustained fighting left forty-five homesteads burnt, fifteen people killed and hundreds injured.

In 1997, thirteen years later, these villagers were again involved in a border dispute. But the very basis on which they were mobilised, the nature of the border and the violence that they engaged in was of a different kind. This time Basotho and Shangaans fought as regional allies rather than ethnic foes. When provinces replaced ethnic Bantustans at the end of Apartheid, Buffelshoek and Okkernootboom both became part of the single Bushbuckridge magisterial district of the newly constituted Northern Province. Villagers celebrated the demise of the Bantustans, but were furious that Bushbuckridge was not included in the province, Mpumalanga. For three months violent skirmishes occurred between Bushbuckridge residents and the police. Youths burnt the homes of Northern Province supporters and symbols of the new government such as official buildings, ANC (African National Congress) flags and schools. They also stoned vehicles with Northern Province number plates, tourist buses and post office vans.

This chapter seeks to compare these border disputes, and to investigate how they cast light upon the interface between local identities and broader changes and transformations in South Africa. Theoretically, I concur with Wilson and Donnan (1998) that despite the growing significance of non-places (Auge 1995) and deterritorialised, transnational identities such as ethnicity and gender, we have not seen the withering away of the state as the 'pre-eminent political structure of modernity', nor of the physical structures of government and territory (p. 1). Wilson and Donnan (1998) argue that borders mark the extremities of state power: politically and legally borders regulate and constrain movements, symbolically they construct the meanings of national identities. Hence borders are at the frontier of anthropological knowledge. A focus on borders shows the changing definitions of peripheries and their relationships to centres, processes of state centralisation and homogenisation, and the manner in which those living at borders negotiate state-imposed identities.

Borders and boundaries have defined, divided and given shape to South Africa in multiple ways.[3] Yet Thornton (1996) argues that whilst South Africa's external borders have been remarkably stable,[4] there has been an important shift in the country's internal borders. He suggests that as a modernist condition Apartheid was synonymous with the meticulous making and marking of racial, cultural and spatial differences according to a master plan. This plan aimed to enforce a vision of rational clarity and was instituted in bureaucratic practice. By contrast, post-Apartheid is post-modern. The logic of difference is still pervasive and all borders and boundaries still raise questions about who is inside and who is outside, who is an enemy and who is a friend. But the master plan is gone and confusion is chronic. Identities previously believed to be immutable are now open to negotiation and there is uncertainty about virtually all kinds of boundaries. However, following Gluckman (1960), Thornton suggests that the pervasiveness of boundaries, which crosscut each other in multiple ways, create different allegiances that never polarise sufficiently to permit devastating conflict. 'They are either too fragmented or too solid to permit the sort of bi-polar conflict that would destroy it' (ibid.: 160).

Thornton draws the contrasts between the modernism of Apartheid and the post-modernism of post-Apartheid too starkly. Indeed, the metanarratives of modernity and post-modernity may well conceal more than they reveal (Englund and Leach 2000). His focus on the aesthetics of power detracts from a consideration of the political economy of borders. The idea of borders as an image of cultural juxtaposition underplays the material consequences of borders as markers of the unequal distribution of wealth and resources (Wilson and Donnan 1998: 6). There are important continuities between the four provinces and ten Bantustans of Grand Apartheid, and the nine provinces of the new South Africa. South Africa's new provincial boundaries too are an outcome of rational bureaucratic planning: their demarcation was guided by the imperative of striking a balance between the centralisation and devolution of power. Moreover, the provincial boundaries were modelled upon the nine 'development regions' that were introduced during late Apartheid to facilitate 'confederalism' and to protect the coherence of the ethnic groups (Ramutsindela 1998, Ramutsindela and Simon 1999).

My analysis of the border disputes draws upon three main sources: ethnographic fieldwork that I have conducted in the village of Green Valley since 1990; Ritchken's (1994) superbly detailed, but yet unpublished, work on the political history of Bushbuckridge; and upon newspaper reports of these events. Green Valley is a multi-ethnic village formerly located in the Mapulaneng district of Lebowa, and now forms part of Bushbuckridge. First, I sketch the historical contexts of these disputes. I show how, since 1864, diverse Northern Sotho and Tsonga-speaking groups settled in the lowveld and accommodated themselves in a moiety-like social landscape. Northern Sotho chiefs made formal political alliances with leaders of refugees from Portuguese East Africa (now Mozambique). Broader, more embracing, Basotho and Shangaan identities emerged from the standardisation of languages by missionaries, segregated settlement patterns, and from experiences of solidarity amongst migrant mine workers. Ethnically based native reserves and Bantustans were established from 1936 to 1994. During this period inter-ethnic tensions became marked among Bantustan bureaucrats and among neo-traditional chiefs. The border dispute of 1984 erupted over the discriminatory allocation of land, and Basotho attacked Shangaans whom they perceived as beneficiaries of apartheid. However, social integration and cultural assimilation among commoners – as evident in the joint attendance of initiation lodges and in inter-ethnic marriages – contributed to the cessation of hostilities. These crosscutting ties of allegiance crystallised into a strong popular regional identity during the troubles on Bushbuckridge border. Villagers used violence to communicate their discontent about unfulfilled aspirations, the poor delivery of services, and their humiliating experience of abjection from the centres of power and wealth. Coercive violence is used rationally to achieve social objectives. Appealing violence is a cry for help by desperate people, unable to achieve social aims unaided by others.[5] These episodes show how concerns about boundaries are intimately connected to the political and economic constraints and opportunities that borders imply.

Towards the politics of ethnic nationalism, 1964–1984

The earliest oral traditions refer to the immigration of the Northern Sotho Pulana from their 'homeland' near the present-day Waterval Boven into Bushbuckridge. Here they assimilated the members of other Northern Sotho groups such as the Bakone and Baroka. In 1864 the Northern Sotho defeated Swazi invaders of the lowveld in the battle of Moholoholo (Ziervogel 1954: 195). Hereafter, their leader, Maripe, established a powerful chiefdom at the foot of the mountain.

The first Tsonga-speaking immigrants from Portuguese East Africa (now Mozambique) came to work on white-owned farms and on the gold mines of Pilgrim's Rest (Bonner and Shapiro 1993). Later subjects of king Gungunyane also fled into the South African lowveld to escape the devastating effects of the Luzo-Gaza war. After the final defeat of Gungunyane by the Portuguese in 1895, chief Maripe welcomed his father's brother, Mpisane, and gave him permission to settle in an unoccupied area towards the southeast (Hartman 1978: 51–52, Ritchken 1994: 37).

With the passage of the 1913 Land Act all territory in Bushbuckridge was scheduled as 'released areas' and was reserved for exclusive occupation by Africans. Whilst the Land Act outlawed rent tenancy on all white-owned farms, subjects of the chiefs in the released areas could continue to pay taxes to private land-holding companies for residential, cultivation and stock-holding rights.

Despite the alliances between Northern Sotho and Tsonga-speaking chiefs, the relations between commoners remained distant. Separate identities were fostered by the Lutheran mission that laid an exclusive claim to proselytising amongst the Northern Sotho, and by the Swiss Romande mission which worked exclusively amongst Mozambican immigrants. Moreover, the Swiss missionaries created a standardised Tsonga language, which was actually a written version of one of the numerous language forms spoken by the refugees (Harries 1989: 86). A 'nascent form of worker consciousness' also linked Mozambican migrants who travelled to the South African gold mines in batches where they did dangerous underground labour (Harries 1994). It is on the mines that Mozambican migrants were first called Shangaans – a term previously applied only to the subjects of chief Soshangane, who fled to Southern Mozambique from Natal with the growth of the Zulu state in the early 1820s.

The implementation of the 1936 Natives Trust and Land Act solidified these ethnic identities. This Act required African labour tenants on the white-owned farms to perform six months' labour service and stated that all other Africans had to be resettled on land purchased by the Native Trust. At the same time the aforestation of large tracts of land on the slopes of Mount Moholoholo scattered thousands of Africans throughout the lowveld. Since hardly any Trust Land was available, many dislocated households illegally moved into the 'released areas'.[6] Most people merely settled where land was available, and in any specific area people displayed loyalty to different chiefs (Ritchken 1994: 223). In the 1940s the South African government recognised only one chief per settlement and sought to divide land purchased by the Native Trust into Basotho and Shangaan spheres of influence. Six chiefs were recognised: Mnisi, Khosa and Nxumalo (Shangaan) and Mathibela, Chiloane and Mogane (Basotho). However, great tensions arose when the Basotho chiefs, Anias Chiloane, who resided on the white-owned farm of Bedford, and Matsikitsane Mashile, the leader of tenant struggles against the use of child labour at Welverdient, were not accommodated on the Trust (Ritchken 1994: 292–297).

Despite these tensions between chiefs, the relations between Basotho and Shangaan commoners actually became more accommodative. A huge expansion of schooling occurred with the introduction of Bantu Education in 1953. Bilingualism now became commonplace. Moreover, the Chamber of Mines also began to recruit Basotho men from Bushbuckridge. They were housed in the same compounds as Shangaan workers and were incorporated into the same networks of solidarity. Young Shangaan men, especially those resident under Basotho chiefs, also began to attend Sotho initiation lodges and became part of the same age regiments as Basotho youngsters. The above-mentioned processes facilitated inter-ethnic marriages. Indeed, eight (13 per cent) of the sixty recorded marriages that occurred before 1960 in Green Valley were inter-ethnic: five Basotho men had married Shangaan wives, and three Shangaan men had married Basotho wives.

In the 1960s the three-tier system of Bantu Authorities were established in Bushbuckridge. The Tribal Authorities in Bushbuckridge were grouped into the

Mhala Regional Authority for Shangaans in the east and the Mapulaneng Regional Authority for Basotho in the west. There were important discrepancies, however. Mhala included the Northern Sotho chief, Mathibela, and a substantial 'Basotho island' at Welverdient. The Mapulaneng Regional Authority was even more ethnically heterogeneous and five of its twelve councillors were Shangaans. Mhala immediately affiliated to the Mashangana Territorial Authority in Giyane, and Mapulaneng was forced to affiliate to the Northern Sotho Territorial Authority in 1967, much to the dismay of its Shangaan councillors. The allocation of land to the respective Regional Authorities was blatantly unfair. In 1970 Mhala, with a population of 59,498 people under four chiefs, had been allocated forty-one farms, and Mapulaneng with a population of 62,942 people who fell under nine chiefs, had been granted only twenty-three farms (Ritchken 1994: 227) (see Map 5.1).

Such discrimination ignited tensions between Basotho and Shangaan elites. Matsikitsane Mashile, who was popularly recognised as the Sotho chief of Welverdient, incited his followers to 'rise up' against the Shangaan chiefs. In 1963 Matsikitsane Mashile and his younger brother Segopela were banished from Bushbuckridge. Five years later Hudson Ntsan'wisi, head of the Mashangana Territorial Authority, proclaimed that the entire lowveld belongs to Gungunyane's children and that all Basotho 'should return to the mountains'. In 1973 the Mashangana Territorial Authority became the Gazankulu Legislative Assembly. In Gazankulu the cultural movement Ximoko Xa Ri Xaka (Smoke of the Nation) embarked upon a campaign to popularise Tsonga. Gazankulu also protested over the presence of thirty thousand Shangaans in areas that had been allocated to Lebowa. The Lebowa Legislative Assembly too was established in 1973. The Mashile brothers returned from banishment and were both elected to the Assembly.

At the same time as chiefs deployed the exclusionist 'tribal paradigm', a number of processes actually facilitated ethnic integration among commoners. Foremost among these was the very rapid growth of multi-ethnic Zionist-type churches. These churches were cohesive moral communities in the wake of the disintegration of domestic units wrought by villagisation and labour migration (Sundkler 1961, Comaroff 1985, Niehaus 2001).[7]

Through time many cultural practices had become so blurred that they were no longer marks of Basotho and Shangaan difference. Basotho incorporated items in the Shangaan diet, such as ground nuts, and Shangaans adopted Basotho practices, such as circumcision. Ethnic boundaries also became permeable. At the most basic level changing one's ethnic identity involved changing the language one prefers to speak. This was easiest in the case of surnames which were not specific to any particular ethnic identity. (Surnames such as Mnisi, Manzini and Nyathi were recognised as Swazi or Shangaan; Selinda as either Zulu, Swazi or Shangaan; and Mokoena as either Sotho, Swazi or Shangaan.) But surnames too could be changed. A Sotho man could adopt the Shangaan equivalent of his clan name. (For example, the clan of the Northern Sotho surname Mohlala is buffalo – Nyathi is Tsonga.) Children whose parents were not married could also choose to use

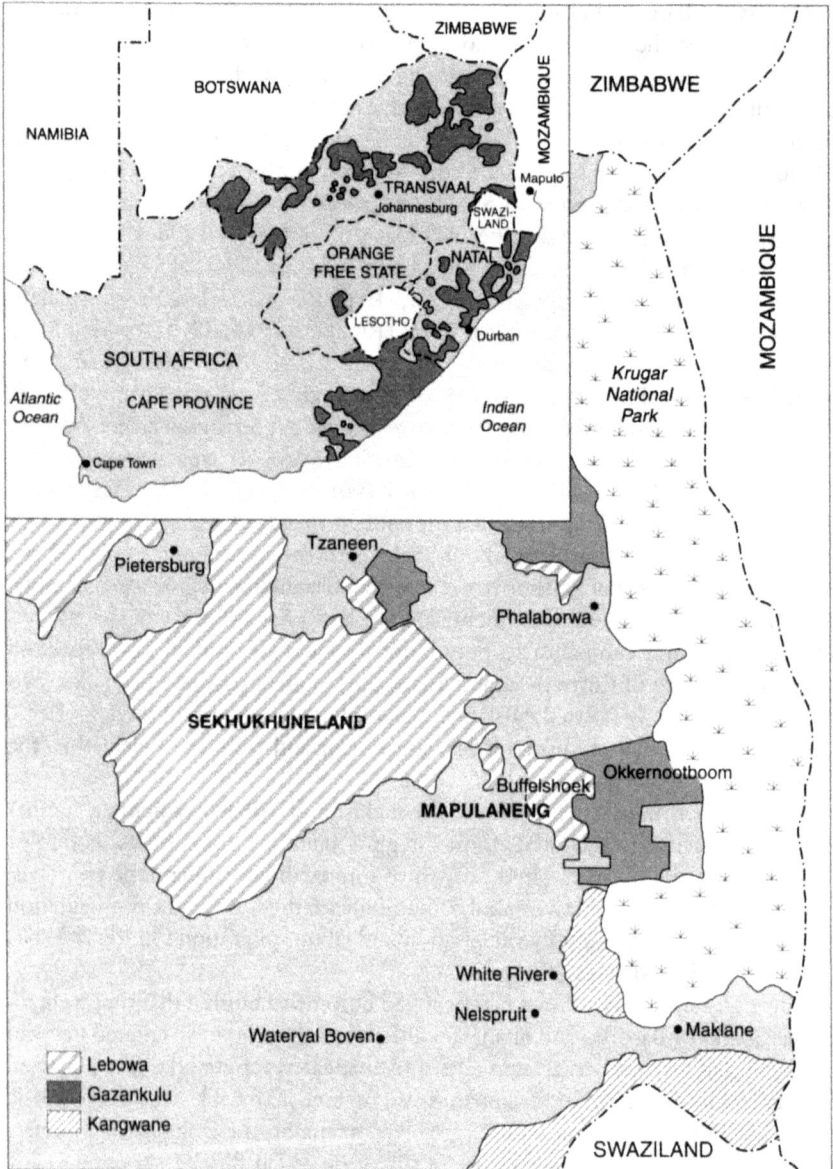

Map 5.1 North-eastern South Africa, indicating former Bantustan territories

either the surnames of their fathers, mothers or caretakers. If all else failed, people could 'pass': conceal their past, change their ethnic identity and hope not to raise too much suspicion (Goffman 1979).

The persons who chose to become Basotho included Shangaan scholars who studied in Lebowa's schools, a Zulu man who married a Sotho wife, and a teacher called Masingiyane (Tsonga) who adopted her mother's surname, Shokane (Northern Sotho) because her mother's kin had raised her. A Malawian called Mbebe who passed for Basotho changed his surname to Mpebe. However, it was more common for villagers to become Shangaan. This is partly because Setswati, isiZulu and some Malawian languages are closer to Tsonga. Many of the most well-known Shangaans in Green Valley – such as Manzini, Mnisi and Dlamini – were actually of Swazi origin. For them passing as Shangaans was a strategy to gain acceptance. Basotho became Shangaans to disguise the fact that they or their relatives had been accused of witchcraft, or because they discovered that their progenitors were really Shangaans.

On closer examination the cultural traits, or customs, that informants considered to be markers of a Shangaan identity – *muchongolo* dancing, marriage customs and divination – can actually be seen as mechanisms for social integration. Throughout Bushbuckridge Shangaan *muchongolo* dances replaced Northern Sotho *dinaka* dances as the basic form of public entertainment.[8] Shangaan women have also progressively replaced Basotho men as healers. Whereas Basotho men healed with the assistance of their own ancestors, Shangaan women healed with the assistance of alien spirits. In Bushbuckridge spirit possession involved culpability and reconciliation and was an important metaphor for ethnic assimilation. The healers identified three categories of spirits: the Malopo, who were Sotho spirits; the Ngoni (derived from the word Nguni); and the fierce Ndau who came from Musapa in Mozambique. The Ngoni spirits were primarily those of Swazi warriors and possessed the descendants of those Sotho warriors who had slain them in the battle of Moholoholo in 1864. The Ndau, in turn, possessed the descendants of the Gaza soldiers who had killed them and taken their wives. Possessed women aimed to appease these antagonistic spirits, to reconcile them with each other, and to build them small round thatched-roofed houses called *ndumba*. Once converted from a hostile to a benevolent force the spirits assisted their mediums. The Malopo assisted in diagnosing and treating venereal diseases and sick children, the Ngoni assisted in healing paralysis of the limbs and red spots, and the Ndau bestowed the powers of clairvoyance and the ability to detect witchcraft. As the mediators between lineages, women were more likely than men to succeed in this role. Spirit possession enabled women to perceive alternative ethnic identities[9] and the mystical world of spirits structured perceptions of society (Boddy 1989).

Whereas cross-cousin marriage had been preferred among Basotho, Shangaan marriage was strictly exogamous. No man was permitted to marry any of his cousins, nor any person who even had the same surname as any of his four grandparents. Transgressions of this prohibition were believed to generate a fatal affliction, causing women to bear crippled children. By the 1990s very few Basotho still married their cross-cousins, but exogamy continued to be extremely important to Shangaans. Forty of the 101 recorded marriages which occurred in Green Valley since 1960 were inter-ethnic. These included twenty-four Basotho men who married Shangaan wives, and sixteen Shangaan men who married Basotho wives. Some argued that they could only avoid serious afflictions by marrying a spouse from another ethnic group. Basotho men perceived Shangaan women – whom they stereotyped as more respectful, subservient and introverted than their Basotho counterparts – as preferred marriage partners. Indeed, the perceived dignity of the Shangaan wife accounted for higher bride price.[10]

Foregrounding ethnicity: the battle at Buffelshoek, 1984

The most important precursor to ethnic conflict at Buffelshoek was the discriminatory allocation of land. Basotho residents of Welverdient were extremely irate about the inclusion of their area into the Shangaan area, Mhala. The subjects of Anias Chiloane, head of the Moletele chiefdom, were similarly outraged. Though the capital (*mosate*) of chief Anias was located on the white-owned farm, Bedford, he was widely perceived as the paramount chief of all Pulana. Only in 1971, after Anias Chiloane had died and the entire labour force had been evicted from Bedford, did the South African government recognise the Moletele chiefdom and resettled the capital at Buffelshoek, in Mapulaneng. In contrast to the nine farms of the less prestigious Mnisi chiefdom, Moletele was granted only one farm. Moreover, the Consolidation Commission proposed that Buffelshoek would lose 100 hectares of land that lay between the railway line and the main road (Ritchken 1994: 230).

In response to such discrimination Lebowa's Minister of Education banned Tsonga as a medium of instruction and as a subject from Mapulaneng's schools in 1984. This measure affected at least ten thousand Tsonga-speaking pupils in Mapulaneng, and infuriated their parents who had contributed money for the erection of these schools. In protest, Shangaans attacked four schools, damaging furniture and breaking two hundred window-panes (Hiemstra 1985: 10).

Quarrels arose between the residents of Buffelshoek and Okkernootboom (in the Mnisi chiefdom of Gazankulu) whenever people crossed the border to collect water and firewood. These tensions came to a head in 1984, when the Lebowa government built the offices of the Moletele Tribal Authority on the contested territory, and the Gazankulu government marked out stands on the same land. After Basotho men burnt down the stakes, a group of Shangaans armed themselves with clubs and spears, and attacked those Basotho who had congregated at the offices of the Moletele Tribal Authority. Many men were injured in the attack. The following day groups of Basotho and Shangaans crossed the border to burn the homesteads of their ethnic enemies.

For the next week the fighting escalated. Skirmishes occurred all along the Mhala and Mapulaneng border. The fighters on both sides were predominantly young men who had been transported to the border from schools in Mhala and Mapulaneng by chiefs or Bantustan bureaucrats. About forty-five houses were burnt, fifteen people were killed and hundreds injured. Informants recalled how Basotho youths speared a Gazankulu policeman to death and killed a Shangaan elder with a 'tomahawk' axe. In Gazankulu cars with LEB5 number plates and in Lebowa cars with GH number plates were also stoned.

The South African police brought a brutally efficient end to the conflict. One evening seventeen police Land-Rovers parked at the Acornhoek Technical College and the next morning a large contingent of police attacked fighters on both sides of the border indiscriminately lashing anyone who stood near the railway line. They even lashed some of the local police who merely stood by watching as the houses burnt. One Land-Rover arrived at the capital of the Moletele chief, dispersed all those who had gathered there and ruthlessly pursued those who fled. A councillor of chief Exom Moletele remarked that when the police left everyone was too intimidated to continue fighting, 'There was only fear on both sides.'

The experience of these events in multi-ethnic villages such as Green Valley provide deeper insight into their significance. They point to contestation between the narrow tribal paradigm propagated by ethnic elites and a more inclusive popular version of ethnic difference. Whereas officials of the ethnically based Bantu Authorities were the most active participants in the conflict, many commoners strongly opposed the fighting. Moreover, even the most ardent Basotho supporters of chief Exom Moletele did not resent Shangaans nearly as much as they opposed ethnic discrimination.

In Green Valley councillors of the Setlhare chief campaigned for the removal of all Shangaans from Mapulaneng, and distributed pamphlets demanding that all Shangaan headmen and employees at the Dingleydale citrus farms be dismissed (see Appendix 5.1 on page 109). The movement was led by the son of a former regent and by a headman. Their campaign received a lukewarm response. When the councillors asked a school principal to dismiss all Shangaan teachers, he obstinately replied that he could only do so on instructions from Lebowa's government. They also asked a local Shangaan businessman to sell his general dealer stores and to move to Gazankulu. The businessman said he would gladly oblige if they paid him R4 million. Eventually the leader of the anti-Shangaan movement stole R1,700 from the magistrate's building fund and was dismissed. Ironically, he went to live in Lulekane – a Shangaan area near Phalaborwa.

During the dispute Matsikitsane Mashile, the Lebowa Legislative Assembly member, parked a large bus outside the Maripe High School. Dressed in what was described to me as 'traditional Pulana fighting gear', he shouted, 'Come! Help! The Shangaans are taking our land!' Basotho boys from the lower school classes boarded the bus, were handed weapons and were then offloaded in Acornhoek. From here they marched across the bridge to houses in Gazankulu.

There was much confusion in Green Valley. Former subjects of the Moletele chief complained that the Mnisi chiefdom had been allocated too much land and supported the struggle. Others strongly condemned the violence. The son of a Sotho father and Shangaan mother asked me, 'How could I kill my mother and my uncles?' Another Mosotho remarked, 'We were very surprised when we learnt that all they had fought for was a small piece of useless land.' Shangaans described the violence as foolish. A resident of Green Valley remarked: 'We have stayed here for over a century and we chose to be ruled over by chief Setlhare. The Basotho are our sons-in-law, our brothers and our cousins. How could we hate each other?' He recalled that youths cut the water pipes leading to the Acornhoek hospital. 'They could not even understand the Red Cross.' The dominant response was fear. During the fighting several Basotho and Shangaans fled into the mountains and only returned once the police had restored order.

Towards a new South Africa, 1984–1997

After the conflict at Buffelshoek, the tribal paradigm swiftly receded. Political attention now focused on the anti-Apartheid struggle. In 1986 the United Democratic Front (UDF) was established in Mapulaneng. The Mashile brothers and teachers from the Witwatersrand founded a Mapulaneng Crisis Committee, youth organisations and student representative councils. Young men known as Comrades assumed the lead in these struggles. They challenged corruption in Lebowa's schools, boycotted white-owned businesses, forced all Tribal Authorities to close and conducted vigorous anti-witchcraft campaigns in nearly all villages (Ritchken 1994, Niehaus 2001). In Mhala the struggle against the Bantustans reached its zenith when a three-month-long school boycott was launched in 1990. Mhala's Comrades demanded the resignation of Hudson Ntsan'wisi (Gazankulu's chief minister) and the disbanding of Ximoko Xa Ri Xaka. They too sought to eradicate witchcraft (Stadler 1994: 2–14, 179–209).

At the CODESA[11] negotiations, which preceded South Africa's first democratic elections of 1994, provincial borders were framed as part of the interim constitution. All Bantustans were dismantled and Lebowa and Gazankulu became part of the newly constituted Northern Province (now Limpopo). Mhala and Mapulaneng merged into the common district of Bushbuckridge. Local residents welcomed the end of Apartheid, but were outraged that Bushbuckridge was not included into Mpumalanga. Residents immediately submitted that Bushbuckridge be defined as an 'affected area'. This meant that the region would belong to the Northern Province for purposes of the elections, but that its votes could be transferred to Mpumalanga if the legislature of both provinces agreed. If there was a dispute about the border alteration the Secretary of Parliament could still be petitioned within six months of the elections (*Sunday Times* 6 July 1997).

Discontent about the border receded during the excitement of the elections. As the only effectively organised political party in Bushbuckridge the ANC enjoyed overwhelming support. ANC election meetings were regularly held and maroela trees were decorated with colourful ANC posters promising, 'Rights for Women' and 'Jobs, Peace and Freedom'. On 16 March 1993, Nelson Mandela himself addressed a packed stadium at Thulumahashe. He said that for eighty years the ANC had fought tribalism, and he made a passionate plea for national unity:

> We preach the idea that we are not Sothos. We are Africans – black people of a powerful nation. We succeed. But there are people in Thulumahashe who preach tribalism. Some people say the Sothos or Tsonga. They are enemies of the ANC. The Sotho and Shangaan are equal in everything we respect and admire. There is a right thing to do! Do it here and now! End tribalism![12]

Prospective voters heeded Mandela's call and strongly rejected ethnically based political parties. E.E. Nxumalo resigned as the leader of the Ximoko Progressive Party, joined the ANC and called on Gazankulu's civil servants to do likewise. The ANC won a dramatic victory, gaining 92 per cent of all votes cast for the provincial parliament of the Northern Province (*Weekend Star* 7–8 May). ANC support was even larger in Bushbuckridge.

After the elections people's attention refocused on the border. In May 1994 a Bushbuckridge Referendum Facilitation Committee was formed and several meetings were held. Joe Phaahla (Deputy Chair of the ANC in the Northern Province) and Mathews Phosa (Mpumalanga's premier) met with local organisations and promised to 'implement the will of the people'. But nothing further was done (*City Press* 15 June 1997). Because the Secretary of Parliament had not been petitioned the concept of an 'affected area' fell away. Now the constitution had to be changed before the provincial boundary could be altered, and this required the approval of at least two-thirds of the members of the National Assembly. In August 1994 Ngoako Ramahlodi, premier of the Northern Province, denied any knowledge about the border transfer at a meeting in Mkhuhlu. Militant Comrades took Ramahlodi 'hostage' until Mathews Phosa arrived in a helicopter to rescue him (*Weekly Mail and Guardian* 12 May 1995).

In November 1995 the two premiers brokered an agreement, involving a *quid pro quo* trade, whereby Bushbuckridge would be transferred to Mpumalanga, and Mpumalanga would cede the town of Groblersdal to the Northern Province (*The Citizen* 29 November 1995). In August 1996 Mathews Phosa announced that Mpumalanga had already set aside funds for servicing Bushbuckridge and would soon occupy provincial offices in the district (*African Sun* 8–21 August 1996). Though an enabling bill was submitted to cabinet in July 1996, the portfolio committee failed to debate the bill during the parliamentary session.

A confusing situation now prevailed. Whilst the Northern Province handled the administration and the delivery of services in Bushbuckridge, the area was 'politically managed' by Mpumalanga. The most prominent local activists – Jacques Modipane and Luckson Mathebula – were appointed as Members of the Executive Councils (MECs) for Finance and Public Works, respectively, in Mpumalanga. Other ANC leaders such as Matsikitsane Mashile, Patrick Mogale, Edgar Musoane and Sheila Sithole represented the Northern Province. Conflict soon arose between local supporters of the Mpumalanga and those of the Northern Province.

Before the local government elections in 1995, supporters of the Northern Province elected an interim local government and launched the Northern Province ANC Women's League in Acornhoek. Mathews Phosa castigated them for undermining incorporation into Mpumalanga and called Sheila Sithole *mapanyula* ('arsehole of an animal' in Tsonga). (She later laid a R300,000 defamation suit against him.) During the elections for Transitional Local Councils (TLCs) all candidates who supported the Northern Province were heavily defeated. Yet officials from both provinces continued to address business forums, schools and church meetings in Bushbuckridge.

The first formal protests against the Northern Province concerned ethnic discrimination. By now the language issue had been resolved successfully. Whenever a school committee decided that it was appropriate a school would offer multilingual education. However, Basotho alleged that the regional government of the Northern Province in Giyane (Gazankulu's former capital) favoured Shangaans. Fourteen of the fifteen school inspectors in Bushbuckridge were Shangaans and advertisements for teaching posts only reached Sotho schools once the deadlines for applications had expired. Schools in the former Mhala area were also better equipped with textbooks, clerks, cleaners and security guards. Official communications from the Department of Education were printed in Tsonga, English and Afrikaans, but not in Northern Sotho. The Traffic Department transferred all vehicle registration facilities to Thulamahashe (in former Mhala), and the Shangaan man who ran the Home Affairs office in Bushbuckridge issued official documents stamped 'Mhala'.

The Mashile brothers and Basotho chiefs claimed half of Mpumalanga's territory (*African Sun* 6–20 February 1996). They also lodged a complaint at the Traffic headquarters in Pietersburg and took over the running of the Home Affairs office. On 12 February 1997 Basotho chiefs, teachers, traffic officials and students marched to the Acornhoek police station, demanding an end to ethnic discrimination. The participants carried placards reading: 'This is the start of the second ethnic war', 'Away with Mhala', 'Viva Bushbuckridge', and 'Let's fight Homeland Apartheid'.

Foregrounding region: the Bushbuckridge border dispute, 1997

On 15 April 1997 Deputy President Thabo Mbeki announced that Bushbuckridge would no longer be transferred to Mpumalanga. This announcement ignited fury everywhere. Informants complained that the delivery of services in the Northern Province was extremely poor. They mentioned that Bushbuckridge is about 400 kilometres from Pietersburg (the capital of the Northern Province) and only 90 kilometres from Nelspruit (the capital of Mpumalanga). People of Bushbuckridge worked, did their shopping and paid taxes in Nelspruit; and could exploit their networks of political patronage with Luckson Mathebula and Jacques Modipane, who held prominent positions in the Mpumalanga government.

Moreover, informants perceived their incorporation into the Northern Province as a perpetuation of the situation that prevailed during Apartheid, when Mhala and Mapulaneng were ruled by ethnic Bantustans in the north.[13]

The nature of the protest soon changed from opposition to ethnic discrimination to a dramatic expression of regional solidarity against the Northern Province. The protest actions that followed asserted Shangaan and Basotho unity and spatial connectedness of Bushbuckridge. On 20 April residents elected a Border Crisis Committee of nine members, comprising Basotho and Shangaan men representing the ANC, PAC, taxi associations, teachers unions, student organisations and Tribal Authorities. Sub-committees were also elected in each village (see Map 5.2).

On 1 May the Border Crisis Committee held four simultaneous protest marches to different police stations in Bushbuckridge, submitting memorandums to demand its incorporation into Mpumalanga. At these rallies the protesters resolved to start a 'rolling mass action' campaign. They decided to remove all Northern Province number plates from their vehicles, close all shops except supermarkets, and to embark upon a protracted school boycott and work stoppage until their demands had been met. Hereafter, the Border Crisis Committee convened a mass rally in Thulumahashe. They decided to organise a 'one million march', to submit a memorandum to President Mandela, send a thousand women to stage a 'sit-in' at the president's office, and to hire lawyers to contest the government's decision in court (Mokgope 1998: 97–109).

On 23 May 1997 20,000 people attended the 'one million march' at the Pauliana stadium in Bushbuckridge. The protesters carried banners proclaiming 'Take out incompetent Deputy President Mbeki' and 'When standard three geography was taught Mbeki learnt that east was north'. Comrades burnt ANC flags inside the stadium, and carried a cardboard coffin, with the message 'Ngoako [premier of the Northern Province] Rest in Peace!' They burnt the coffin in front of the police station.

Five days later an even larger crowd assembled at the stadium. Some heard on radio that Valli Moosa (Minister of Provincial Affairs) would address the meeting and relay President Mandela's message to them. Their hopes were shattered when Valli Moosa failed to arrive. The Border Committee merely read out a letter saying that Charles Nqgakula from the ANC headquarters would address their problems. Comrades shouted slogans against Mandela and burnt ANC posters. Outside the stadium they burnt tyres, stoned cars and police vehicles, and hijacked cars to take them home. Police dispersed the crowd with teargas and rubber bullets. Two protesters died: a youngster who threw stones at a police vehicle and a seven-year-old girl who was struck by a stray bullet.

From May until July 1997 violence erupted throughout Bushbuckridge. Its targets were supporters of the Northern Province and government symbols. In Green Valley workers at a local saw mill embarked upon a work stoppage. After Griffiths Mokgope was seen driving scab workers to the mill in a company truck, arsonists threw a petrol bomb through the window of his home. Griffiths, his wife and son died in the attack. Protesters also burnt down the offices of the local chief,

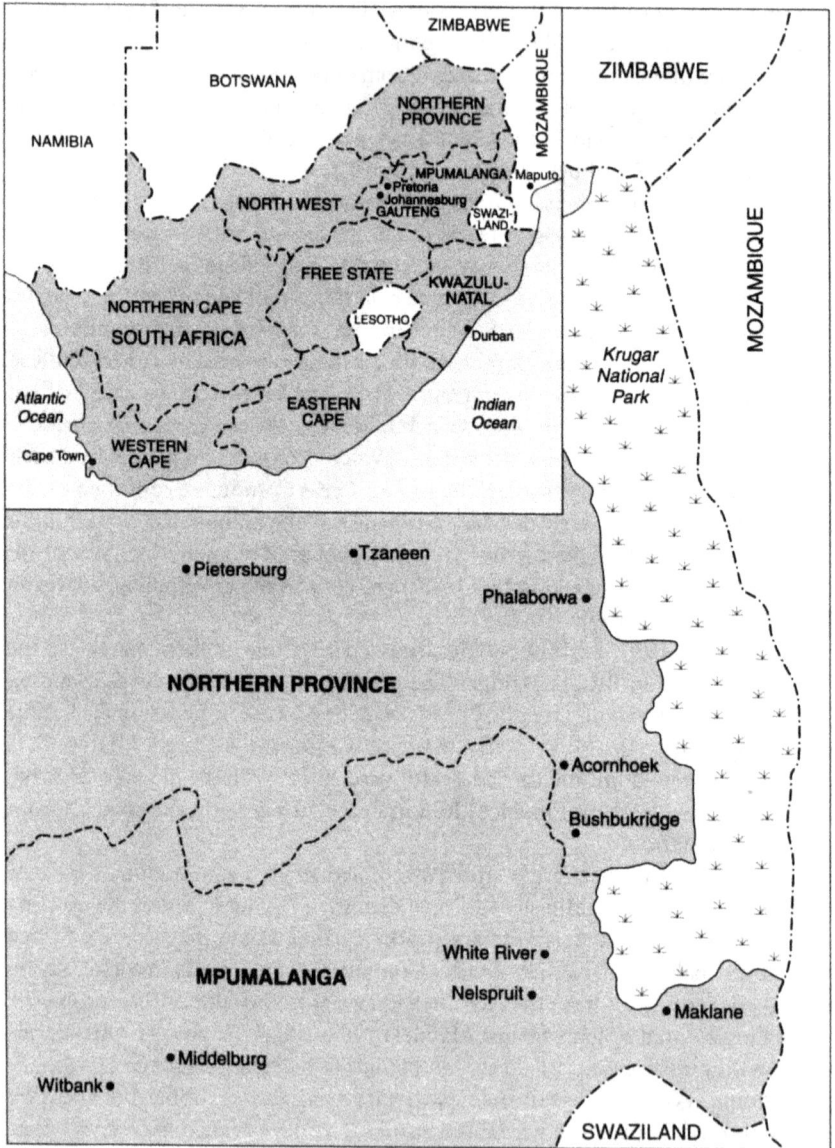

Map 5.2 North-eastern South Africa, indicating new provinces

a school circuit inspector, and of civic organisers, and stoned the BMW of Luckson Mathebula (he was MEC for Public Works in Mpumalanga, and the attack was possibly due to his lack of visible support for their struggle). Other targets were local government offices, vehicles with Northern Province number plates, freight trucks, a post office vehicle, three government complexes and nine schools (*City Press* 15 June 1997).

At another level public violence was used to force government into submission. There were barriers and burning tyres at the intersection of every road leading to Bushbuckridge and protesters caused millions rands worth of damage. It cost R600,000 to repair only one school and the Mpumalanga government paid R200,000 to tourists whose vehicles were wrecked (*City Press* 15 June 1997). One protester told a journalist, 'We are so far from the public eye that this is the only way to attract attention. This is the only language that government understands' (*Die Burger* 28 May 1997).

On 4 June the National Executive of the ANC sent Charles Nqgakula to address local ANC leaders in Nelspruit. At the meeting, which lasted for six hours, Nqgakula reiterated the government's standpoint, promising to maintain the *status quo*. He expressed doubt whether the ANC would get the required two-thirds majority to change the constitution, argued that changing the border could lead to the 'balkanisation' of South Africa, and promised that nobody would be disadvantaged by being a citizen of the Northern Province. On 10 June the Border Crisis Committee met with President Mandela in Pretoria. Nelson Mandela said that his government would not be intimidated by violence and that the border would remain as it is. But he appointed a task team to improve the delivery of services in Bushbuckridge.

Residents of Bushbuckridge were deeply disappointed. A local ANC official told me, 'When the Freedom Charter said the people shall govern, it left out the name of the NEC [National Executive Committee].' On 15 June the Border Committee suspended the work stoppage and school boycott and decided to use the R375,000 it had collected to take the national government to court. The Committee also asked representatives of other South African political parties to support their struggle. Though defeated both in court and in parliament, Bushbuckridge has continued to oppose its provincial government. Ngoako Ramahlodi's visits to the area – even to inaugurate housing projects – have been greeted by protesters, proclaiming, 'Mpumalanga First! Houses Last!'

Conclusions

A comparative analysis of the border disputes of 1984 and 1997 allow certain tentative generalisations about the significance of borders, changing social identities in the South African periphery and about the meanings of violence.

First, I found very little evidence to support the utility of the concept of a 'shifting margin' – which denotes pre-colonial African situations where there is governance of people rather than place (Kopytoff 1987). Despite their arbitrary nature, boundaries in the lowveld possess an almost sacred character (Thornton 1996: 148). Oral traditions about pre-colonial social units echo Schapera's (1956) comments about the importance of both people and territory in southern Africa. Elderly informants described how definite borders (*mollwane* or *monakatsela* in Northern Sotho) marked the limits of their fields, households and chiefdoms. Heaps of uncultivated soil were placed around the edges of their fields, high fences made from the branches of thorny trees surrounded each household, and rivers separated the territories governed by different chiefs. One had to request permission of the most senior man when entering the space of a household, and report to the local headman when entering the territory of another chiefdom. People resented any intruders. Hence people of Bushbuckridge were well accustomed to the meanings of territoriality, and borders were by no means a novel construct introduced by the creation of Bantustans and provinces.

My analysis of the border disputes of 1984 and 1994 does, however, suggest that there has been an important shift from ethnicity to region as the foremost basis for political mobilisation. These identities are not, and have never been, all embracing or mutually exclusive. Throughout this century there has been ongoing contestation between at least two versions of ethnic identities. On the one hand, headmen, councillors and chiefs have increasingly deployed the segregationist 'tribal paradigm' to mobilise a constituency in their struggles for land. On the other hand, non-royalists have adopted Northern Sotho and Shangaan identities as a mechanism to facilitate their incorporation into South African lowveld society. This has been most pronounced in multi-ethnic villages such as Green Valley. By adopting a Shangaan identity Mozambicans from diverse origins and also other Nguni-speakers have been able to assimilate into a single category.

In the lowveld ethnicity does not exclude 'the other'. Ethnic identities are not things per se. They are relational, and performances of ethnic identity implicate 'the other' (Comaroff 1996: 166, Bauman 1992). In the South African lowveld Northern Sotho and Shangaan identities have been forged in relation to each other. Even the ethnic confrontation at Buffelshoek, which was instigated by authorities of the Lebowa Bantustan, was not motivated by a utopic vision which excluded Shangaans. Basotho residents of Buffelshoek recognise Shangaans as an integral part of a moiety-like social landscape, but oppose Shangaan privilege.

Social conflict in the lowveld implies fission and well as fusion (Evans-Pritchard 1940, Gluckman 1960). During the conflict at Buffelshoek a Basotho segment opposed a Shangaan segment. But in the Bushbuckridge border dispute, the popular inclusive model of ethnicity prevailed, as Basotho and Shangaans united in a dramatic display of regional unity to oppose the South African state as a common outside adversary.

There is an important economic dimension to such conflict. Ethnic identities were foregrounded during the era of Apartheid when resources such as land were distributed along ethnic lines. Regional identities were foregrounded when resource distribution and political patronage shifted to the provinces. In this respect the 1997 border dispute was a revolt against ethnicity. Ramutsindela (1998: 295) writes:

> The attempt to transfer Bushbuckridge to Mpumalanga has great significance to the reconceptualisation of boundaries in South Africa because residents of the area [Bushbuckridge] want to be geographically dissociated from their ethnic group membership in the Northern Province.

Such foregrounding of region is also apparent in Malawi (Kaspin 1995).

We need to locate the different meanings of violence within these changing social contexts. In 1984 the violence of Buffelshoek was predominantly coercive. Violence was used instrumentally to achieve certain objectives and to transform people's social environment. The 'ethnic other' was both the primary victim and witness. The burning of homes and physical assaults were tests of power between Basotho and Shangaans, a means of establishing and sustaining a balance of fear, and a way of forcing one's opponents to give way in the competition for land and resources.[14] The violence that prevailed in the Bushbuckridge border dispute was appealing and was used to dramatise people's anger about mounting impoverishment and abjection (Ferguson 1999: 234–254). Supporters of the Northern Province were the primary victims, and the South African government the primary witness. The expressive potential of violence lies in its high visibility and in the probability that all involved are likely to draw basic common understandings of the acts and images concerned.[15] Protesters perceived South Africa's new government as more receptive to such messages than the Apartheid state had been.

Notes

1 I acknowledge the help of my field assistants, Eliazaar Mohlala and Kally Shokane, and of Santha Raju, subject librarian for Social Anthropology at the E.G. Malherbe Library at the University of Natal, Durban. My research was made possible by a generous research grant from the Research Office at the University of Natal. I am also indebted to Vigdis Broch-Due, Peta Katz, Henrietta Moore, Johan Pottier and Ellen Selvik for their assistance. As usual I bear sole responsibility for all errors and omissions in the chapter.

2 No term to describe the South African 'Bantustans', 'homelands', or 'national states' is politically neutral. I use the term Bantustans because it most clearly reflects rejection of the policy of creating separate political geographic entities for different categories of the South African population.

3 In this chapter I use the term border to denote a dividing line between geographic entities and boundary to refer to a division between different categories of persons. Following Thornton (1996) I see borders and boundaries as intimately interconnected. In the South African lowveld there is a strong correspondence between these phenomena.

4 Thornton (1996: 148) characterises South Africa as a country – 'a named area of land demarcated by international boundaries, but not necessarily possessing comprehensive state apparatus, full administrative or fiscal coverage of the area so named, or even a coherent self identity as such.'

5 My distinction between 'coercive' or 'instrumental' and 'appealing' or 'expressive' violence draws on the use of these concepts by Marx (1976) and Riches (1986: 11).

6 Native Affairs Department Circular, Restricting Movement of Natives, October 1932. Assistant Native Commissioner, Graskop, to Native Commissioner, Pilgrim's Rest, 13 March 1934, NTS 828/308 V3586.

7 In 1962 there were only four churches and a handful of Christians in Green Valley. But in 1992 the number of churches had grown to twenty-six with an estimated combined total of 5,557 adult members. At least 75 per cent of Green Valley's Christians belonged to the Zion Christian Church (ZCC) and to smaller Apostolic congregations.

8 In *dinaka* men and women dance separately in a circle around a drum (James 1999). *Muchongolo* dances involve both men and women who wear skin garments and carry umbrellas, knobkerries, sticks and shields. Large drums are beaten, kudu horns are blown and songs are sung, mainly about the prowess of the dancers.

9 Sharp (1993) shows how in the town on Ambanja in Madagascar outsider women become privileged insiders or *tera-tany* ('children of the soil') through possession by royal *tromba* spirits. There are similarities in the lowveld, though the transition effected is not nearly as dramatic.

10 Comaroff (1996: 166) argues that ethnic groups are usually gendered: 'women, their bodies, and their dress often being prime sites for the representation of ethnic difference'.

11 CODESA is an abbreviation for the Convention for a Democratic South Africa.

12 I wish to thank Peta Katz who ably recorded Nelson Mandela's speech in Thulumahashe and kindly allowed me to cite her field notes.

13 Ramutsindela (1998) argues that despite the geographic and economic links of Bushbuckridge with the Mpumalanga, Northern Sotho and Tsonga-speaking groups were assigned to the Northern Province (home to other members of their ethnic groups) to protect the geographic coherence of language groups.

13 See Marx (1976), Riches (1986: 1–32) and Steadman (1985).

14 Richards' (1996) analysis of the Sierra Leonean civil war informs the use of violence during the Bushbuckridge border dispute. Richards argues that the gruesome acts of violence perpetrated by Revolutionary United Front (RUF) rebels are indicative of the use of cultural resources in the absence of heavy weapons. In the context of a crisis in the 'patrimonial state' where peripheral regions are cut off or excluded from regular resource distribution, the RUF rebels use violence as an expressive resource to re-establish contact with the wider world.

Appendix 5.1 Anti-Shangaan propaganda
distributed in Green Valley, 1984

NOTICE: AWAY WITH MATSHAKANE AT MAPULANENG

It is time that ALL the Shangaans in Lebowa should quit our as soon as they possibly can – obviously to Maputo.

Steps are being taken to ensure that you people leave us in peace – for instance ALL the Shangaans working for Lebowa and in Lebowa must be sacked from their posts.

ALL SHANGAANS working with our chiefs, and or government, such as indunas, councillors, civil servants and school committee members must also be sacked with immediate effect – even if it means at all costs.

ALL SHANGAANS owning BUSINESSES in Lebowa should move to their own places provided by their so-called Gazankulu government. These people are SNAKES. Funny enough, some of them are busy expanding and improving businesses in Lebowa as though they are in Mozambique. Well, we pity these creatures because they may come out empty-handed. Carry your businesses to Maputo while you still have chance, otherwise. . . .

It is surprising that some Shangaans in Lebowa still use the GH number plates. These people must immediately because GH is stinking all over our place.

THE SO-CALLED GAZANKULU CITIZENS WHO COME TO LEBOWA FOR SHOPPING AT OUR WHOLESALERS, BANKING AT BUSH-BUCKRIDGE, RECEIVE MEDICAL TREATMENT AT MAPULANENG HOSPITAL, MUST GO ELSEWHERE IN GAZA. . . .

FINALLY, THE SO-CALLED GAZANKULU SHOULD DO SOMETHING FOR ITS OWN PEOPLE IN MOZAMBIQUE BECAUSE THERE IS NO PLACE FOR THEM HERE. WE HAVE STARTED ON A HIGH NOTE AND WE SHALL CONTINUE THAT WAY. SHANGAAN CHILDREN HAVE TO LEAVE OUR SCHOOLS, THUS THEIR PARENTS MUST FOLLOW AND LEAVE OUR LAND. FORWARD EVER, BACKWARD NEVER. . . .

THE STRUGGLE CONTINUES. . . .

References

Auge, Marc 1995. *Non-Places: Introduction to an Anthropology of Super-modernity*, London: Verso.

Bauman, Gerd 1992. 'Ritual implicates 'others': rereading Durkheim in a plural society', in D. de Coppet (ed.) *Understanding Rituals*, European Association of Social Anthropologists, London and New York: Routledge, pp. 97–116.

Boddy, Janice 1989. *Wombs and Alien Spirits: Women, Men and the Zâr cult in Northern Sudan*, Madison, Wis.: University of Wisconsin Press.

Bonner, Philip and Shapiro, Karen 1993. 'Company town, company estate: Pilgrim's Rest, 1910–1932', *Journal of Southern African Studies* 19(2): 171–200.

Comaroff, Jean 1985. *Body of Power, Spirit of Resistance: The Culture and History of a South African People*, Chicago, Ill.: University of Chicago Press.

Comaroff, John 1996. 'Ethnicity, nationalism, and the politics of difference in an age of revolution', in E.N. Wilmsen and P. McAllister (eds) *The Politics of Difference*, Chicago, Ill. and London: University of Chicago Press, pp. 198–214.

Englund, Harri and James Leach 2000. 'Ethnography and the meta-narratives of modernity', *Current Anthropology* (forthcoming).

Evans-Pritchard, E.E. 1940. *The Nuer*, Oxford: Clarendon Press.

Ferguson, James 1999. *Expectations of Modernity: Myths and Meanings of Urban Life on the Zambian Copperbelt*, Berkeley, Calif.: University of California Press.

Gluckman, Max 1960. *Custom and Conflict in Africa*, Oxford: Basil Blackwell.

Goffman, Erving 1979. *Stigma: Notes on the Management of Spoilt Identity*, Harmondsworth: Penguin.

Harries, Patrick 1989. 'Exclusion, classification and internal colonialism: the emergence of ethnicity among the Tsonga-speakers of South Africa', in L. Vail (ed.) *The Creation of Tribalism in Southern Africa*, London: James Currey, pp. 82–117.

—— 1994. *Work, Culture and Identity: Migrant Labourers in Mozambique and South Africa, c. 1860–1910*, Portsmouth, N.H., Johannesburg and London: Heinemann, Witwatersrand University Press and James Currey.

Hartman, Jan Barend 1978. 'Die samehang in die Privaatreg van die Changana/Tsonga van Mhala, Met Verwysing na die Administratiefregtelike en Prosesregtelike Funksionering', Ph.D. thesis, Departement Volkekunde, Universiteit van Pretoria.

Hiemstra, Judge V.G. 1985. 'Report on trans-border clashes between subjects of Gazankulu and Lebowa', unpublished report submitted to the Minister of Co-operation and Development, South African Government (mimeo).

James, Deborah 1999. '"*Bagageu* (those of my home)": women migrants, ethnicity and performance in South Africa', *American Ethnologist* 26(1): 69–89.

Kaspin, Deborah 1995. 'The politics of ethnicity in Malawi's democratic transition', *Journal of Modern African Studies* 33(4): 595–620.

Kopytoff, Ivor. 1987. 'The internal African frontier: the making of an African political culture', in I. Kopytoff (ed.) *The African Frontier*, Bloomington, Ind.: Indiana University Press, pp. 105–128.

Marx, Emanuel 1976. *The Social Context of Violent Behaviour*, London: Routledge and Kegan Paul.

Mokgope, Kgopotso 1998. 'Rural women and politics: a case of Rooiboklaagte B. Northern Province, South Africa', MA dissertation, Durban: Department of Social Anthropology, University of Durban-Westville.

Niehaus, Isak with Eliazaar Mohlala and Kally Shokane 2001. *Witchcraft, Power and Politics: Exploring the Occult in the South African Lowveld*, London: Pluto.

Ramutsindela, Maano F. 1998. 'The changing meanings of South Africa's internal boundaries', *Arena* 30(4): 291–299.

Ramutsindela, Maano F. and Simon, David 1999. 'The politics of territory and place in post-apartheid South Africa: the disputed area of Bushbuckridge', *Journal of Southern African Studies* 25(3): 479–498.

Richards, Paul 1996. *Fighting for the Rain Forest: War, Youth and Resources in Sierra Leone*, Oxford: James Currey, Portsmouth N.H.: Heinemann.

Riches, David 1986. 'The phenomenon of violence', in D. Riches (ed.) *The Social Anthropology of Violence*, Oxford: Basil Blackwell, pp. 1–32.

Ritchken, Edwin 1994. 'Leadership and conflict in Bushbuckridge: struggles to define moral economies in the context of rapidly transforming political economies', Ph.D. thesis, Johannesburg: University of the Witwatersrand.

Schapera, Izaac 1956. *Government and Politics in Tribal Society*, London: C.A. Watts.

Sharp, Lesley 1993. *The Possessed and the Dispossessed: Spirits, Identity and Power in a Madagascar Migrant Town*, Berkeley, Calif.: University of California Press.

Stadler, Jonathan 1994. 'Generational relationships in a lowveld village: questions of age, household and tradition', M.A. dissertation, Johannesburg: Department of Social Anthropology, University of the Witwatersrand.

Steadman, Lyle 1985. 'The killing of witches', *Oceania* 56(2): 106–123.

Sundkler, Bengt C.M. 1961. *Bantu Prophets in South Africa*, London: Oxford University Press.

Thornton, Robert 1996. 'The potentials of boundaries in South Africa: steps towards a theory of the social edge', in R. Werbner and T. Ranger (eds) *Postcolonial Identities in Africa*, London and New Jersey: Zed Books, pp. 136–161.

Wilson, Thomas and Donnan, Hastings 1998. 'Nation, state and identity at inter-national borders', in T. Wilson and H. Donnan (eds) *Border Identities: Nation and State at International Frontiers*, Cambridge: Cambridge University Press, pp. 1–30.

Ziervogel, D. 1954. *The Eastern Sotho*, Pretoria: Van Schaik.

Chapter 6

Fertile mortal links
Reconsidering Barabaig[1] violence

Astrid Blystad

Introduction

Violent encounters between East African pastoralists have been a popular topic in ethnographic accounts, but one that is poorly understood. Perhaps because it plays into Westerners' fear about the savage 'other' in a particular visceral way, *lilicht*, the so-called 'ritual murder' custom practised by Barabaig/Datoga herders of Tanzania, has received particularly biased reporting, both in terms of what motivates such a custom and the number of murders committed. In this chapter I shall reanalyse Barabaig violence by situating its different forms within a larger cultural framework in which there is an extensive focus on forces of life-giving and life-taking. I take my lead from a new wave of studies of violence in anthropology, replacing initial classifications of 'uncommonly violent' and 'uncommonly peaceful' societies, with a focus on continuity and discontinuity in violent forms and expressions as they unfold in concrete time and space (Lan 1985, Taussig 1987). Coronil and Skurski (1991: 289) sum up this new analytical locus:

> Whether treated as cause, function, or instrument, violence is generally assumed rather than examined in its concreteness. Little attention is paid to its specific manifestations, to the way its effects are inseparably related to the means through which it is exerted, and to the meanings that inform its deployment and interpretation.

In exploring the cultural workings of violence among Barabaig, I draw attention to two central Barabaig institutions in which violent conduct is integral, while embedding my analysis by discussing key violent events of the recent history. I will demonstrate how Barabaig perceptions of life-giving and life-taking are intimately connected, ideally making up a circle in which physical hurt, killing or death ritually facilitates transformation and growth. I shall argue that these concerns with the interrelations between life and death entail an explosive potential that may be violently acted out under particular political-economic circumstances. I will discuss the ambiguous issue of perpetrator and victim, demonstrating that it is far more complex than commonly understood. What ultimately emerges from this essay is that the forms and meanings of violent events are often partial and shifting – and this undecidability of violence is key to an enhanced understanding of how violent events have been produced, interpreted, reproduced and resisted in this area of Tanzania over the past forty years.

A fertile/mortal chain

The lands of Hanang and Mbulu districts are characterised by hilly highland areas and large low-lying plains, which are divided by the Rift Wall. In years of good rains this land becomes green, lush and fertile, and has until recent decades supplied herders and agriculturalists alike with ample opportunity for grazing cattle and cultivating crops. Normal seasonal variation transforms within days emerald green plains and valleys to brown, barren and dusty lands, and turns signs of blossoming and life into portents of death and dying. Natural processes of life and death thus make up a circle where the one depends upon the other for growth and continuation. The natural fluctuations both within and between years are, however, substantial. Too little rain, too much rain or too sporadic rain at critical times of the year may have devastating consequences for human and animal populations alike. This precariously balanced landscape generates a fundamental experience of vulnerability in its inhabitants, and in the same vein instigates immense concern with processes of fertility and related processes of mortality.

Preoccupation with procreation and the continuation of life, as well as with forces threatening such fertile processes, was a domain of great importance to my Barabaig informants. The connections between life and death, living and dying, birthing and killing were seemingly endlessly elaborated upon. Daily talk and action, ritual practice, myths, song and prayer were permeated with an underlying logic which weave fertility and mortality intimately together. An important domain of meaning, experience, and power was opened up through immediate fertile and mortal contexts engaging young and old, men and women alike in complex, partly complementary, partly contradictory ways (Blystad 2000). A brief review of two central institutions demonstrates how the life–death connection surfaces in Barabaig practice. The first institution is the much-discussed *lilicht*.

Ritual spearing (lilicht)

As far back as Barabaig can recall *lilicht* has engaged young men in hunting expeditions after the five dangerous mammals: lions, leopards, elephants, buffalo and rhinoceros, as well as human members of 'hostile' groups, all conceived as 'enemies' (*halooda*). The pre-hunt phase consists of youth meetings (*seyooda*) where promises and plans are exchanged between young men and women through prayers (*moshta ghawood*), riddles (*giighatta*, literally 'departure') and intimate oral competitions (*gharemanend dumeed*). The youth meetings take place in remote bush areas in 'the west'; the direction of danger, death and dying.

The hunt itself entails an arduous journey where thirst and hunger, pain and fear haunt the young men. The leader of the team and enticing chants (*bahew*) push the young men on. The climax of the hunt is reached in the dramatic encounters between hunter and prey where very real battles of life and death are fought. At the moment a Barabaig spear hits the prey, the young man calls out the names of his father, his spirit guardian and girlfriend. Bloodstain on the spear is sufficient to assure an honourable return home for the team, but the ultimate aim of a *lilicht* is to kill the prey. After a successful kill the men quickly remove their spears as well as a small part from the kill. Upon return the girls praise the deeds through gifts to the young hunters. The killer at this point placates his spear and a major clan grave with white butter, and experiences the rare exaltation of having butter plastered on to his head by women and girls – acts which create intimate relationships between the young and the spirits. The young man will also at this point tour Barabaig land together with his girlfriend(s) and request gifts of cattle, goats or sheep, although a man can today hardly count on substantial rewards due to the utter poverty of most Barabaig in the area. On these journeys the young killers perform the 'kill song' (*rang'deyda*) and the 'songs of the spear' (*salaneda ng'ut*) by means of which the listeners are brought along on perilous journeys through the landscape and into confrontations of life and death between young men and their dangerous prey. Girls reciprocate these performances with emotional signal-like calls. The songs create deep emotional engagement in the audience, and rather than being a celebration of killing, they invoke an aura which praises fertility and an unconstrained and vital life of Barabaig communities. The transition taking place in the *lilicht* is indeed regarded as 'fertile' to the extent that the young lion killers are hailed as 'women who have given birth'.

In Barabaig experience, the dramatic spearing or killing during the *lilicht* thus ritually transforms a young 'infertile' man into a fertile 'woman in post-natal confinement' (*udaghereega*). The transition gradually becomes visible in the young man's dress, decoration, and in behavioural and pollution-related restrictions, linking the deed closely to a woman who has given birth. Violent elements and ultimately killing thus appear as integral parts of a preoccupation ultimately aiming for growth and transition. This brings us to the second institution I wish to draw attention to: 'the meeting of married women'.

The 'meeting of married women' (girgweageeda gadeemg)

This institution has the mandate to address and act upon instances of male offence against what is considered to be a sacred female procreative domain. A concrete meeting may take many forms. A common scenario is a mass-mobilisation of women following events where a man has, among other things, beaten or talked harshly to a pregnant woman, has kicked or destroyed a vital material object located in a woman's kitchen/bedroom, or has treated improperly a woman who is engaged in sacred journeys (*ghadoweeda*). The three-day meetings consist of some main ingredients like litigation, lengthy hearing of similar and dissimilar cases, singing of lewd songs (*dumda gadeemg*), provocative dancing and playing (*dumda dumood*, literally 'the dance of the penis'), oral prayers (*moshta ghawood*) and solemn sung prayers (*dumda ghadoweeda*). During the mobilisation women stand up and cry out their messages of disgust, contempt and anger while waving wooden sticks ('the stick of the curse') in the air. Throughout the performance the participants communicate that their bodies and procreative potential (or rather 'birthing', *jeata*) have been violated, and that they now find themselves in 'near-death' states (*ghoghomnyeanda*). Women with close kinship affiliation to the male offender may try to intervene, but are silenced, and may be chased away and beaten by the women. Male intruders are also less than welcome, and may be chased away or beaten with sticks. Women's violent reprisals against anything interfering with their activity is in fact emphasised throughout the engagement, and stories of such companies of women who 'rape men to death' flourish. On the final day of the meeting the women move threateningly through the community. They approach the offender's compound, collect a black bull as fine, and with the assistance of men, beat and eventually choke the animal to death while singing 'we have given birth'. The meat is cooked and consumed jointly by the party of women, the offender and his male friends. Barabaig women and men talk of this activity as transforming infertility/barrenness to 'birthing' (*jeata*).

I will argue that the logics at work during the married women's meeting is parallel with what we saw during the *lilicht*. In this last case we saw how the participants attacked and beat their 'enemies' and eventually beat and killed a bull, the symbolic 'enemy'. The violence/death instigated a surge of fertility not only for the offended woman, but for the Barabaig community at large. In both cases the participants experience themselves to be in a near-death state linked to the precariousness of labor (*ghoghomnyeanda*) throughout the engagement, a condition which is eventually to turn into birthing (*jeata*) and an elevated state of post-natal convalescence (*ghereega*).

Enemies who 'nurse Barabaig blood'

To understand why the problem of fertility mobilises violent activity in the manner indicated above, we need to bring in aspects of the political-economic history of Barabaig: a history scattered by many lengthy and often violent conflicts. Four contextualised events are presented to serve as examples of how violence has taken form in Barabaig communities in the post-colonial period. Informants' discourse about their harsh history spoke of a series of adversities and enemies who were threatening pastoral life. An old woman made the point succinctly: 'Maasai took our cattle and warriors. Then came the colonialists and Nyerere and took our land and the houses of our spirits. Now our cultivating neighbours take what is left.' Another elderly informant said: 'You know, the colonialists and the present day leaders are all the same; they all nurse Barabaig blood.'

The wars between Barabaig and Maasai herders, which reached their peak during the 1880s, led to huge losses in both human and cattle populations (Jacobs 1979). A rich mythical repertoire indicates how the protective spearing ritual was among the means Barabaig peoples resorted to during this devastating conflict. Albeit eventually facilitating peace between Maasai and Barabaig, the colonial powers did not ensure fertile development of Barabaig communities. With reference to difficulties of administration in Barabaig areas as well as to Barabaig killing traditions, the colonial administration, and later the leadership of the independent Tanzanian state, produced images and policies with adverse consequences for Barabaig communities. Stigmatising stereotypes and a furnishing of the settlement of cultivators on to Barabaig land led to marginalisation and impoverishment. The post-colonial ambitious development measures in fact penetrated deeper into the land and livelihood of Barabaig pastoralists than did colonial policies. The rigorous and uncompromising manner of state intervention soon gave rise to distrust and fear far beyond the Barabaig community.

The concept of a nation with educated and healthy individuals was located at the core of President Nyerere's vision for the new state, and led to the development of national programmes entailing massive literacy campaigns and the construction of boarding schools for pastoral children. The policy was met with increasing scepticism and fear from Barabaig. This sets the context for the first of the violent events to be reviewed, notably the Barabaig killing of an Iramba teacher in 1968.[2]

The killing of an Iramba teacher, 1968

The Iramba teacher, who was travelling on his bicycle through the southern parts of what is today Hanang District, was found murdered in an area sparsely populated by Barabaig herders. The corpse lacked a finger when it was found, and both Barabaig and outsiders' accounts regard the murder as part of *lilicht*. The killing made headlines in the news, and government troops were sent into Barabaig dominated areas with the order to arrest every 'Barabaig' man they met to 'teach them a lesson'. The troops caught large numbers of adult men who were sent off to army camps or to Tanzanian prisons. The soldiers brutally entered houses, raped, stole household belongings and cattle. No trial was ever held in the case. According to informants, Nyerere after some time ordered that the arrested men were to be released. Barabaig call 1968 'the year of the soldiers' (*gwaida mutrass*).

It was envisaged that the 'Barabaig problem', as the government conceived it, could be effectively addressed by settling them in permanent villages where they could be more easily reached and controlled. This was part of a widespread measure aimed at a concentration of the country's scattered population through village formation (*Ujamaa*). 'Operation Barabaig', the most rigorous villagisation attempt among Barabaig, developed into a dramatic encounter where state employees forcefully removed Barabaig from their pastoral homesteads and relocated them in villages. While *Ujamaa* was implemented, the government declared that 'land is property' ('*ardhi ni mali*', Swahili), and argued that land should not 'lie idle', but should be farmed productively. The consequence was a new wave of cultivators moving into Barabaig grazing land. The next violent event I will bring attention to took place when the villagisation policy was at its height and Nyaturu cultivators had quickly expanded into the south-western corner of the land that had up to this point been utilised solely by Barabaig herders.[3]

The Kihonda murders, 1976

The pretext for the ethnic killing to follow was the murder of a newly married Barabaig woman (*sibeed*) earlier in 1976, a year referred to as 'the year of drought' by Barabaig. This prompted a series of killings of Barabaig including both adults and children. The killers were soon identified as Nyaturu. Barabaig community was terrified, and their 'call of vigil' quickly grew in strength as people prepared for more assaults. Everyone was talking of this evil people who long had taken their land, and who were now also killing their 'brides' and 'children'. A large group of young Barabaig men approached the Nyaturu village Kihonda. As they sat down and prayed during the early morning hours they heard noise nearby. Spies discovered that a Singida lorry that was bringing food aid was stuck in the mud caused by a sudden heavy rainfall, and that a crowd of Nyaturu were quickly carrying away large sacks of maize. Barabaig herders had been badly hit by the drought as well, but had never received food aid. Indeed, it was not unlikely that these sacks were intended to reach Barabaig communities. This was conceived as a new grave discovery of how the Nyaturu managed to cheat their way to increased wealth. The young men became enraged with fury, and decided to kill the betrayers while they were carrying out their mischievous acts. They encircled the crowd and killed everyone with their spears and sticks. It was reported that twenty-six people were killed. A couple of days later the Tanzanian Field Force Unit (FFU) moved into the area and started to arrest Barabaig men, and to confiscate cattle from Barabaig homesteads. Thousands of Barabaig soon filled up Tanzanian prisons. Most were eventually released, but twenty-two men, some of whom had taken part in the killings and some not, were eventually given sentences of twenty years' imprisonment. The ones who survived the harsh conditions of imprisonment, nine in all and less than half of the ones who had been imprisoned, were released in 1994 as 'Tanzanian prisons were filled up'.

Many of the farmers who had moved on to Barabaig land were eventually expelled with the coming of the large-scale national wheat scheme, the Tanzania Canada Wheat Project (TCWP). In 1970 the project initiated the clearing of woodland above the Rift Wall in Hanang District. With a total allocation of some 100,000 acres of land for large-scale wheat farming during the 1970s and 1980s, the problem of land shortage in the area was magnified (Lane 1996: 155). Adding to the impediment of land loss, the appropriation of Barabaig land took place in a manner that provoked reaction from both the national and the international community due to its gross violations of human rights.[4] This intervention sets the stage for a third example of violent conduct.

Violent confrontations at Gidabuygweargwa, 1973

Prior to the initiation of the Wheat Scheme, the Ghayroowa plains were the single most important grazing area for Barabaig herds. On these vast expanses of land the tree cover was completely removed, and Basotu Plantation, one of a total of seven TCWP wheat farms, was established. It was the clearing of Gidabuygweargwa, a sacred burial site located on the Ghayroowa plains, that to Barabaig became the most painful sight of all. At this site a large number of the characteristic 3-metre-high burial mounds are located. I shall return to the immense significance of these tombs below. Barabaig were bewildered by the sight of the graves that had been levelled to the ground, and the community became tense with aggression and fear. At one point in 1973 a tomb was destroyed on the same day as two Barabaig women were raped by TCWP employees. While the clearing of land continued, women started to mobilise at Gidabuygweargwa. To Barabaig it was beyond comprehension that graves and women were molested in the name of 'development' (*maendeleo*, Swahili).

The way in which the destruction of the tombs was perceived as demolition of the homes of their guardian spirits was elaborated upon throughout the meetings. The notion that the annihilation of the tombs implied a destruction of female wombs which ensured fertility and continuity of Barabaig communities moreover gradually appeared in women's distressed complaints. Prayer, fines, curses and magic remedies were in turn directed against the Tanzanian and Canadian staff with no result but more destruction. Female and male Barabaig leaders who were suspected of being central in the uprising were caught and imprisoned in Mbulu. When the demonstrations of up to a thousand Barabaig women still continued, the FFU was called from Moshi and Arusha and confronted the demonstrators with sticks, ropes, tear-gas and guns. Barabaig women's vengeance at this point became out of the ordinary; they cut open tractor tyres, set TCWP vehicles on fire and beat unarmed TCWP employees with their wooden sticks. The entire work force of Basotu Plantation eventually ran off. Upon their return however, more Barabaig bodies were molested, more cattle were confiscated or killed, more land was seized and more graves were destroyed.[5] For many Barabaig herders, the coming of the TCWP dealt the final blow to their pastoral adaptation in Hanang, and large-scale emigration of Barabaig out of Hanang and Mbulu was prompted. For the ones who remained, the hardships merely increased in terms of the continued harsh measures employed by TCWP in the seizure of traditional Barabaig pasture and large-scale immigration of Iraqw, Nyaturu and Iramba into Barabaig grazing land. During the mid-1980s the confrontation between Barabaig and their neighbours exploded.

The feuds of the mid-1980s

In Barabaig discourse the first stage of the conflict was seen as a traditional raiding feud between the Bureadiga sub-section of Datoga and Sukuma. But the initial conflict grew in scale as Iramba and Nyaturu joined Sukuma, and Barabaig and individuals of other Datoga sub-sections joined Bureadiga. The two sides were throughout the feud operating with very different means; the Barabaig utilised their traditional spears and sticks while the other side was armed with modern weaponry. Barabaig narratives reveal a turning point when a man referred to as 'Charlie' entered the war on the Sukuma side. With his advanced machine gun he initiated what informants talk of as mass killing of human beings and livestock. People, cattle and even calves that Charlie and his men were not able to take with them were brutally killed in front of people's eyes. The conflict also involved another peculiar feature: the raiders at times put confiscated Barabaig women's sacred leather skirts over their heads when the raiding took place, a move so frightening to Barabaig men and women that it threatened to paralyse their resistance completely. Whether the raiders were Sukuma, Nyaturu or Iramba varied in different accounts. The conflict gradually moved out of the bush, and killings and harassment eventually took place on the roads, at market places, in schools, at hospitals and in offices. Barabaig elders told their men that without entering the war with all their skills and strength, both human and cattle populations would disappear completely. It was at this point that Barabaig swore revenge and attacked a group of Sukuma who had gathered in a homestead across the Singida border. Barabaig men ambushed them and killed everyone present. The only killings that seem to have been established as 'true' in this conflict, and which have received media attention, are the murders of the forty-eight Sukuma men who were killed by Barabaig on 3 May 1985 (Ndagala 1991: 79).

Shifting forms, sustained meanings

In this last part of the chapter we shall take a fresh look at the violent conduct that has been presented above with some central questions in mind. What is the prime motivation for Barabaig violent conduct? Can we talk of continuities in motivation in recent violent events, and to what extent is form and meaning of concepts and practices modulated or transformed in response to changing historical and political conditions? How can the above events contribute to enhancing our understanding of how violent action is produced, understood, and opposed?

How do pain and killing become rites of fertility and renewal?

Returning for a moment to the meanings of the *lilicht* and the *girgweageeda gadeemg* we saw that the violent elements which were located at the heart of the activity of the two institutions were part of a preoccupation ultimately aiming for growth and transition. The crux in understanding this logic is a recognition of the way Barabaig perceive their world as consisting of both living human beings and dead human beings, or rather, of living spirits. During grand funerals lasting for some nine months Barabaig rituals transform deceased elders' bodies to living foetuses and eventually through birth-giving to living guardian spirits on whom they depend for prosperity and life. The transition is made visible with the expanding earthen burial mound, the metaphoric female womb, which is daily fed milk and honey mead to ensure growth. Small trees are planted in the fertile soil of the mound, and with time the grave turns into a sacred grove of trees sought for gift-giving and prayer. Eventually the trees die and merge with the natural landscape, creating potential for renewal of life. In this manner the continuous processes of life and death of the natural environment are inserted into human lives so to speak, creating a bond and identity between human processes of living and dying and natural processes of life and death.

The potential of the dramatic preoccupation with life bringing death is that it generates an excess that has the strength to transform infertility or barrenness, near-death or death into a condition experienced as life-bringing and fecund. The prototypical case of life-bringing pain is childbirth, where through immense pain, bleeding and sometimes even death, new life in a baby is brought into being, and a new identity is secured for the parents. This forceful logic of near-death or even death leading to birth and new life penetrates the logic of Barabaig mythical and ritual life. The physical pain inflicted upon the youngsters at the time of circumcision transforms young infertile boys to fertile men, and young infertile girls into women with procreative abilities. Fierce physical fighting between a bride to be and her future husband's companions prior to a wedding facilitates the transformation of an infertile unmarried girl to a fertile married woman. A funerary ritual transforms an infertile human corpse into a fertile living spirit through violent acts such as young men's wild penetration of the gate to the grave at the closing day of the burial, and the dramatic choking of numerous large black bulls in front of the grave. These rituals are said to boost the fecundity of all the Barabaig. Physical pain, bleeding or death taking place in sacred contexts thus become transforming techniques which ritually facilitate growth or shifts in identity or status at both individual and at communal level.

Modified violent forms

Can we talk of any continuation from such ritualised scenarios of life-giving pain and death to the many violent events that have characterised the recent history of Barabaig? Some features of continuity in form and content can immediately be discerned from the accounts. The killing of the teacher was conceived as a *lilicht* killing altogether. In the other two cases where young Barabaig men were involved, the killings were again carried out by groups of young men organised under a youth leader, spears and sticks were the sole weapons used, and song and prayer directed to God and spirits were performed. Traditional enemies, such as Iramba, Nyaturu and Sukuma, were targeted: peoples mythologically established by Barabaig as 'enemies'. Barabaig women's confrontation with TCWP farms likewise exhibited some similarity with the 'traditional' married women's meeting with its characteristic lengthy auditions, performance of lewd songs and dance as well as oral and sung prayers. The targets were also in this case 'men' who had violated their rights. Barabaig informants would in fact readily hold that the mobilisations against the TCWP farms was an activity of 'the married women's meeting'.

The discontinuities in both form and content do, however, appear to be as prominent as the continuities. Neither the killings of Nyaturu in 1976 nor the killings of Sukuma in 1985 can be characterised in *lilicht* terms. No cultural elaboration of the killings took place either before, during or after these killings; preparatory youth meetings did not take place, and no messages were exchanged between coming boy- and girlfriends either before or after the killings. There were no signs of removal of limbs from the corpses, nor were the murderers rewarded in terms of gifts from girlfriends, butter anointment or gifts of livestock. There were moreover, most importantly, no attempts at defining the murders of the Nyaturu or later the Sukuma within a *lilicht* framework.

The female mobilisation in response to the rapes and the destruction of graves carried out by TCWP employees were also surely of a different kind from that of a typical meeting of married women targeting an unruly male element within the population, not the least in the sense that on this particular occasion the women met an enemy consisting of a large undefined crowd of foreign males. The performances, enchantment, fines and curses presented by the leather-dressed women, highly meaningful to Barabaig, appeared bizarre to the male TCWP employees and the Canadian staff. The efficacy of the mobilisation against TCWP and the confrontation of the men was further impaired by a lack of will to listen, indeed by a lack of will to even translate Barabaig women's messages, and, most importantly, by the use of physical force with new and very serious proportions. Bulldozers, tractors, tear-gas, guns and the state's fully armed Field Force Units confronted women's prayer, song, fines, curses and small wooden sticks. In desperation Barabaig women during the last phase turned to new measures, cutting open car tyres and setting fire to vehicles. Indeed, not only in the mobilisation against TCWP, but in all the cases referred to above, the most radical modification from the established activity was that Barabaig men and women were confronted with an enemy of an entirely new kind. The consequence was mass arrests of Barabaig men, rapes of women, mass confiscation of cattle and destruction of sacred sites. The seriousness of the Barabaig losses indicated battle of a new array: battles wholly devoid of elements instigating fertile transitions and augmentation of life.

Violence as retaliation

Elements of fertile transformation were conspicuously absent from the violent events recollected above. The confrontations were rather perceived as retaliation for action taken against them, as acts of revenge. The purpose of the acts was to attack human beings who in the present historical and political context were not only humiliating them, but were violating their bodies and graves and were threatening their very existence by taking their land and cattle on a large scale.

Even the killing of the teacher, held to have been a *lilicht* kill, can at least partly be addressed in terms of retaliation and revenge. The prey was not an elephant, lion or Iramba predator in Barabaig lands, but a teacher on his bicycle. There was some confusion among Barabaig informants surrounding the fact that a man on a bicycle was not a traditional target in the *lilicht*. At my enquiry some asked what the difference was between an Iramba on a bike and an Iramba walking. Others held that the teacher was killed not despite the fact that he was a teacher, but because he was a teacher. It does not seem far-fetched to suggest that the killing of the teacher was at least partially motivated by Barabaig fear and frustration connected to the increasing negative impact government policy had on their lives, in this case, not the least the pitiless effort of taking away their children by sending them to boarding schools.

We saw that the colonial administration and the government of Tanzania's ideals of settled agriculture implied concrete political moves that agriculturalists took systematic advantage of (Rekdal and Blystad 1999). The serious border conflict between Nyaturu and Barabaig, which had started already in the 1940s, only developed over the years as the competition for land became increasingly fierce (see also Loiske 1990, Setréus 1991). The conflicts caused perpetuated hostility between the two groups that dramatically surfaced during the Kihonda confrontation. Barabaig accused Nyaturu farmers of systematically appropriating their land through cheating and clever manipulation of written words. Conventional notions of retaliation also became an increasingly apparent feature of the Barabaig women's action against TCWP as they understood that customary attempts at addressing the encroachment were futile. Aspects of regular inter-ethnic warfare with inherent features of revenge and retaliation moreover appeared strongly during the conflicts of the 1980s where Barabaig communities were so pressured that the elders told their young men to defend their survival with every means at hand.

A transition towards an increasing emphasis on 'retaliation' may in fact possibly also be reflected in an ongoing shift in terms. The *lilicht* term may in most contexts be replaced with the term *lugooda*, but *lugooda* commonly refers to contexts of somewhat less ritualised violent confrontations than *lilicht*, such as situations of raiding and warfare. Informants' insistence that the *lugooda* term increasingly takes over for *lilicht* as the term employed for men who go out to kill may be an indication of an ongoing transformation to more politicised violence in Barabaig communities.

But although the violent conduct represented above can be understood functionally as local response to political conditions characterised by a dwindling resource base in terms of depletion of grazing land and loss of cattle, or can be understood instrumentally as acts of coercion or resistance against mischievous acts, these understandings alone will lead us to miss their significance as genuinely new instances of recognisable social form. As has been argued (see e.g. Ross 1986, 1990, Taussig 1987) social structural models for conflict are not sufficiently specified, and fall short in articulating how the interests of social groups are transformed into organised political action. Concealed cultural presumptions indeed surfaced during each of the above events, but were recast by changing historical and political conditions.

Continuities: the killing of 'brides' (sibeed) and calves (muhoog)

Despite the overt elements of retaliation seen in the violent confrontations narrated above, we find that Barabaig discourse on these violent events speak less of anger against government policy on schooling, villagisation, appropriation of land, and cattle confiscation, and more of anger against 'Nyaturu', 'Iramba' and 'Sukuma' killing of Barabaig 'children' and 'calves', and of threats to the 'birthing' (*jeata*) of their communities. The Nyaturu killing of the Barabaig bride (*sibeed*), also talked of as 'the child' (*jeepta*) is of particular importance in the accounts the Barabaig tell themselves. The *sibeed* is the symbol par excellence of fertility among Barabaig. She is a young woman who has been transferred to her coming husband's homestead. The woman is commonly welcoming a number of lovers, men classified as her husband's 'brothers'. The pregnancy that often follows from this period is perceived as a manifestation of her husband's clan and lineage fertility, and ultimately of Barabaig fertility. The killing of the *sibeed* was as such not regarded solely as a killing of an individual woman, but was symbolically perceived as a kill meted out against the fertility potential of all Barabaig. The murder of the *sibeed* in 1976 shook Barabaig communities in a very fundamental way, and the response was also out of the ordinary. The corpse of the young woman was laid outside the home of her husband dressed only in the waist glass beads to communicate for everyone the magnitude of the crime that had taken place.[6] The murder was indeed considered as such a grave offensive act that several young Barabaig men immediately admitted having taken part in Kihonda killings as they believed they would be released when the facts surrounding the murder of the *sibeed* became known. The killing of the twenty-six Nyaturu was throughout referred to with reference to the *sibeed* killing, the killing of the 'child' in Barabaig accounts.

The manner in which Barabaig informants speak of the killing of the *sibeed* is analogous to the way they talk of the killing of 'the calves' (*muhoog*). As 'the child' is a key symbol of human fertility, female calves represent the parallel fecund potential of their herds, the only traditional source of wealth in Barabaig communities. The cruel killings of calves during the conflicts in the 1980s appeared completely meaningless to Barabaig. Nothing but immorality and perversion could in Barabaig understanding account for such evil acts, and the offence could thus be attributed to none but their despised neighbours Iramba, Nyaturu and Sukuma. Members of these ethnic groups have in Barabaig thought not been perceived as fully human, but as animal-like and degenerate. These notions are reciprocated by these neighbours' images of Barabaig. Ndagala's (1991) reference to the centrality of professional cattle raiders from the larger northern urban centers during the conflicts of the mid-1980s were never confirmed by Barabaig informants.

The mass mobilisation of women against TCWP may, as we saw above, be talked of in instrumental terms of retaliation for rapes of women and destruction of graves, but such an explanation alone would miss the significance of the event for the Barabaig. The central prose was cast throughout the meetings in a vernacular that accentuated the threat meted out by male offenders against female bodies threatening their fertile potency. The key concepts communicated thus remained the same as during the customary mobilisations of the *girgweageeda gadeemg*. The TCWP's employees' demolition of graves and the sexual abuse of Barabaig women were addressed in terms of 'destruction of female wombs'. Foreign male bodies were assaulting Barabaig land and tombs with bulldozers, and women's bodies with penises: tombs and wombs with the potential of giving birth to spirits and children. Predatory males were violating sacred female bodies harming their inherent respect and potency. During the meetings there was a dramatisation of the idea of the Canadian and the Tanzanian governments drawing its power from a notion of distorted violent male sexuality.

Despite substantial modifications both in form and content from the customary *lilicht* and *girgweageeda gadeemg*, we thus see that the response to recent violent events draws upon a highly meaningful vernacular of perceived threats to Barabaig fertility. The events are moreover confronted through culturally sanctioned conduct in a manner where mythologically established relations of friends and enemies surface, are confirmed and reconfirmed.

Perpetrator vs. victim revisited

The scenarios encountered in the stories above indicate that established truths about Barabaig as the sole perpetrators in the violent conflicts in the Hanang and Mbulu areas have to be reconsidered. Members of the Iramba, Nyaturu and Sukuma ethnic groups, TCWP employees, state guards and soldiers, and possibly professional cattle raiders from Arusha, have also been part of the conflicts. After the violent events in 1968, 1973 and 1976 government action implied the use of FFU which was responsible for throwing thousands of 'Barabaig' men in prison, for hearings of cases that were a mere fraud, for huge numbers of cattle being confiscated and never returned to their owners, and for the maltreatment and eventual death of Barabaig prisoners.

The severe show of state force against Barabaig must fundamentally be situated within the elaborate discourses on modernity and development that were launched during the colonial regimes and strengthened in the post-colonial period. The leadership was deeply troubled both by the apparent irrational inclination of pastoralists to roam about the country together with their livestock, and by the tendency of many Barabaig to remain illiterate, to wear leather dress, and to adhere to 'traditional' custom. The rhetoric on the 'Barabaig', which elaborated on the uncontrollable horrors of primitive man and the wickedness and danger associated with their way of life, was laid out in the many colonial credentials. Their very existence was considered to undermine the Tanzanian struggle to promote development and inter-ethnic brotherhood (cf. e.g. Lutwaza 1984). In the national game of politics 'the Barabaig' appeared as an assault against rationale and reason, and as a source to the nation's backwardness which made violence against them seem acceptable. On this basis, we can more readily comprehend why cattle thieves for the Tanzanian authorities became synonymous with 'Barabaig', why Barabaig youth without proof invariably became accused of murders in the area (Talle 1974: 68), and why punishment was meted out against Barabaig as a group (Kjærby 1979: 28) rather than against identified perpetrators.

The extreme show of force that followed the killing of the teacher is illustrating if understood in a context of state development discourse. 1968 was not the first time Barabaig had committed homicide. It does not appear to be the violence Barabaig carried out in itself therefore, but the specific pattern of violence on that day and in that place that made it especially open to moral and political appropriation as a symbol deployed in the political process. The extreme provocation that the killing of the school teacher on the bike represented can revealingly be understood in the context of an enormous positive emphasis on education and of a parallel glorification of the teacher (*mwalimu*, Swahili) in the newly independent state. Nyerere himself was in fact himself addressed *'Mwalimu'*. The killing of the teacher was therefore, I will suggest, not just any killing for the government of Tanzania, but was symbolically the killing of Nyerere himself and all that he represented. Just as Barabaig violence is not random in form and content, neither is violence carried out by the state. Coronil and Skurski (1991: 289) write:

> Just as riots are not direct response to hunger, state repression is not simply a means to control popular unrest. . . . The immediacy and apparent naturalness of moments of collective violence may conceal their intentionality and socially constructed significance.

Finally, the official discourse on the 'Barabaig' must also partly be related to the fundamental lack of knowledge of the other and lack of communication between the parties. The uncertainty and fear of the peculiar ritual activity and frightening traditional killings carried out by 'the Barabaig' could seemingly be elaborated upon indefinitely, Barabaig having no way in which to counter misleading Swahili statements. The state on their part surely never heard of the Barabaig elders' meetings which denounced the killing of human beings (Baynit 1981: 60, cited in Lane 1996, Blystad 1992: 87, Kjærby 1976, Wilson 1953: 45) and the songs and prayers that were increasingly filled with condemnation of murders.

Situating Barabaig violence in a pastoral context

In his review of Pokot–Turkana raiding, Bollig (1990) discusses characteristics commonly suggested to be motivating factors in connection with pastoral raiding and killing, and he particularly points out the scarce-resource problem, individual profit-making, emphasis on warrior traditions and age-set institutions. Except for the age-set institution these factors may all have some relevance in connection with Barabaig *lilicht* killing. The economic aspect of *lilicht* is of little significance in today's context of Barabaig impoverishment, but it has surely had some relevance in earlier times (Wilson 1952: 44). The activity may be linked to struggles for resources highlighted in situations of warfare (Blystad 1992: 87, Kjærby 1979: 10, Talle 1974: 13) such as during the conflicts with Maasai. The *lilicht* activity may moreover surely be partly accounted for in terms of gaining status, prestige and honour (Klima 1970: 60) although the concept of 'warrior traditions' may be somewhat misleading in connection with the Barabaig *lilicht* institution. Barabaig killing is connected to the aggressive exploitation of the fertility potential of the bush as among so many other pastoral peoples. This engagement characterised by killing, raiding and warfare is viewed in terms of its life-endorsing – rather than its life-taking – aspects (see e.g. Jacobson-Widding and van Beek 1990: 27). However, rather than patrilineages or patriclans engaged to boost their fertility through warrior activity, activity commonly portrayed as devoid of female influence, we find that the engagement in Barabaig *lilicht* brings gendered aspects to the forefront of attention.

I will argue that misleading statements about *lilicht* are often related to the fundamental misunderstanding of the gendered dimensions of the institution. The many sources that claim that the institution is a means for acquiring a wife, for example (Loiske 1990: 97, Lumley 1976: 80, Perham 1976: 103, Umesao 1969: 87), imply no 'oversimplification' (Kjærby 1979: 20, Setréus 1991: 20) but are simply wrong. While being no precondition for marriage, the institution is surely a most potent part of the process which socially transforms infertile boys and girls into procreative adults. I have argued elsewhere that *lilicht* is located at the heart of Barabaig construction of femininity and masculinity (Blystad 2000). Indeed, the recognition of the inherent potential implied in the excitement, the action, energy and force in the splicing of young men and women is a core theme in story/myth related to *lilicht*. The potential of the youthful engagement is highlighted through the employment of the most fertile of all symbols: birth-giving.

The attention given to the immense pastoral preoccupation with processes of 'fertility' has largely been focused through the preoccupation with the boosting of patriclan and patrilineage fertility, and through the elaboration of the pervasiveness of the interconnections between human and animal fertility.[7] A recognition of the pastoral focus on processes of procreation where the female and feminine is brought to the forefront of attention is, however, of more recent date. In ethnographically rich and theoretically informed studies such as those of Oboler (1994), Talle (1988), Broch-Due (1990a, 1990b, 1993, 1999), Hutchinson (1992a, 1992b, 1996), Ensminger (1987) and Hodgson (1995), the centrality of the female and the maternal in pastoral political-religious life has been established. Children and calves are the two critical sources of wealth and are crucial for pastoral survival, and the attention given to them and to the procreative processes which create and care for them is immense. 'Procreation is production,' Broch-Due revealingly writes of the Turkana pastoralists, and firmly situates the attention given to female procreative imagery in pastoral ways of life. The confused and anxious Barabaig response to the killing of their 'children' and 'calves' should be fundamentally located within such a scenario where procreation in a broad sense is emphasised as the very basis of life.

Concluding remarks

I have tried to show the importance of exploring the cultural workings of violence through a discussion of material from pastoral Barabaig of Tanzania. I have indicated that it is crucial that we go beyond mere explanation of violence and rather attempt to reveal the meaning given to violence as it unfolds. Explanation of violence surely assists our understanding of violence in some ways, but it does not help us to sort out the continuities and discontinuities in concrete experiences of violence. This is what I hope to have achieved in this example, in creating the links between the long-established activity of the *lilicht* and the *girgweageeda gadeemg* and the diversity of meanings and motivations of the many violent confrontations taking place in recent Barabaig history. Surface similarity of events may obscure how the force of these violent expressions stems from their complex articulation with each other on diverging sociocultural, political and historical grounds. Violent action should be understood therefore as a set of practices and cultural forms whose meanings can only be made sense of through an understanding of the social and political relations and the historical memory in the society within which it appears, evolves and comes into effect. While shaped by historical circumstances and contemporary politics, the rationalisation for the violence needs to be understood with reference to culturally established motifs.

Notes

1   I have carried out some twenty-five months of fieldwork in Datoga communities of Hanang and Mbulu districts of Tanzania between October 1989 and December 1998.
2   The following case material consists of condensed versions of information informants gave many years after the incidents took place, and I do not hold that what is presented here is the whole 'truth'. These recollections merely represent attempts at reconstructing certain central aspects of and circumstances surrounding the events, and make up parts of Barabaig discourse about the most painful events in their fairly recent history.
3   The story of the Kihonda murders includes several detailed interviews with one of the men who was part of the killing and who had survived years of imprisonment.
4   See e.g. *Africa Watch* (12 March 1990: 1–9), *Urgent Action Bulletin* (January 1990), *Africa Events* (Nov. 1990: 31–33), *Africa Events* (Apr. 1993: 30–31), Lane (1990), Lane and Pretty (1990), Lane and Scoones (1991) and Kisanga *et al.* (1993).
5   The 'Report of the Commission on Violations of Human Rights in NAFCO wheat farms Hanang District' (Kisanga 1993) states that between 1970 and 1992 local people reported 83 rapes and the desecration of 38 sacred sites.

6   The leather skirt (*hanang'weend*), which is to be worn by every married Barabaig woman, is said to be handed to women by the female spirit Udameselgwa with promises of fertility if sewn and worn correctly. The skirt is never to expose a married woman's thighs. The act of undressing the deceased woman was thus a forceful illustration of how Barabaig perceived their fertile potential as damaged through her death.
7   Such as in the works of Evans-Pritchard (1940, 1950, 1953, 1956), Gulliver (1969), Klima (1970), Spencer (1988, 1998), Lienhardt (1961) as well as in the works of Llewelyn-Davis (1981) and Dahl (1979, 1987).

References

Baynit, W.M. 1981. 'Contradictions of pastoral development. The Barbaig case in Tanzania', B.A. dissertation, University of Dar es Salaam.

Blystad, A. 1992. 'The pastoral Barabaig: fertility, recycling and the social order', Cand. Polit. thesis, University of Bergen, Bergen.

—— 2000. 'Precarious procreation: Barabaig pastoralists at the late 20th century', Dr. Polit. thesis, University of Bergen, Bergen.

Bollig, M. 1990. 'Ethnic conflicts in northwest Kenya: Pokot-Turkana raiding 1969–1984', *Zeitschrift für Ethnologie* 115: 73–90.

Broch-Due, V. 1990a. 'Cattle are companions, goats are gifts: animals and people in Turkana thought', in G. Palsson (ed.) *From Water to Worldmaking*, Uppsala: Scandinavian Institute of African Studies.

—— 1990b. 'The bodies within the body. Journeys in Turkana thought and practice', Dr. Philos. thesis, University of Bergen, Bergen.

—— 1993. 'Making meaning out of matter: perceptions of sex, gender and bodies among the Turkana', in V. Broch-Due, I. Rudie and T. Bleie (eds) *Carved Flesh/Cast Selves: Gendered Symbols and Social Practices*, Oxford and Providence, R.I.: Berg, pp. 53–82.

—— 1999. 'Creation and the multiple female body: Turkana perspectives on gender and cosmos', in H.L. Moore, T. Sanders and B. Kaare (eds) *Those Who Play with Fire: Gender, Fertility and Transformation in East and Southern Africa*, London: The Athlone Press, pp. 153–184.

Coronil, F. and Skurski, J. 1991. 'Dismembering and remembering the nation: the semantics of political violence in Venezuela', *Comparative Studies in Society and History* 33: 288–337.

Dahl, G. 1979. *Suffering Grass: Subsistence and Society of Waso Borana*, Stockholm: Department of Anthropology, University of Stockholm.

—— 1987. 'The realm of pastoral women: an introduction', *Ethnos* 52(1–2): 5–7.

Ensminger, J.E. 1987. 'Economic and political differentiation among Galole Orma women', *Ethnos* 52(1–2): 28–49.

Evans-Pritchard, E.E. 1940. *The Nuer*, Oxford: Oxford University Press.

—— 1950. *Kinship and Marriage Among the Nuer*, Oxford: Oxford University Press.

—— 1953. 'The sacrificial role of cattle among the Nuer', *Africa* 23: 181–198.

—— 1956. *Nuer Religion*, Oxford: Clarendon Press.

Gulliver, P.H. 1969. 'The conservative commitment in northern Tanzania: the Arusha and the Masai', in P.H. Gulliver (ed.) *Tradition and Transition in East Africa*, London: Routledge and Kegan Paul, pp. 223–242.

Hodgson, D. 1995. 'The politics of gender, ethnicity and "development": images, interventions, and the reconfiguration of Maasai identities, 1916–1993', Ph.D. thesis, University of Michigan.

Hutchinson, S.E. 1992a. 'The cattle of money and the cattle of girls among the Nuer, 1930–83', *American Ethnologist* 19: 294–316.

—— 1992b. ' "Dangerous to eat": rethinking pollution states among the Nuer of Sudan', *Africa* 62: 490–503.

—— 1996. *Nuer Dilemmas: Coping with Money, War, and the State*, Berkeley, Calif.: University of California Press.

Jacobs, A.H. 1979. 'Maasai inter-tribal relations: belligerent herdsmen or peaceable pastoralists?', *Senri Ethnological Studies* 3: 33–52.

Jacobson-Widding, A. and van Beek, W. 1990. 'Introduction: chaos, order and communion in the creation and sustenance of life', in A. Jacobson-Widding and W. van Beek (eds) *The Creative Communion: African Folk Models of Fertility and the Regeneration of Life*, Uppsala: Almqvist and Wiksell International, pp. 15–43.

Kisanga, C. *et al.* 1993. 'Report of the commission on violations of human rights in NAFCO wheat farms Hanang District', Dar es Salaam, mimeo.

Kjærby, F. 1976. 'Agrarian and economic change in Tanzania. A study of the pastoral Barabaig and agropastoral Iraqw of Hanang District, Arusha Region', M.A. thesis, Institute of Ethnology and Anthropology, University of Copenhagen.

—— 1979. 'The development of agropastoralism among the Barabaig in Hanang District', *BRALUP Research Paper* 56: University of Dar es Salaam.

Klima, G. 1970. *The Barabaig, East African Cattle-herders*, New York: Holt.

Lan, D. 1985. *Guns and Rain. Guerillas and Spirit Mediums in Zimbabwe*, London: James Currey.

Lane, C.R. 1990. *Barabaig Natural Resource Management: Sustainable Land Use under Threat of Destruction*, Geneva: United Nations Institute for Social Development.

—— 1996. *Pastures Lost: Barabaig Economy, Resource Tenure, and the Alienation of Their Land in Tanzania*, Nairobi: Initiatives Publishers.

Lane, C.R. and Pretty, J. 1990. *Displaced Pastoralists and Transferred Wheat Technology in Tanzania*, London: International Institute for Environment and Development (IIED).

Lane, C.R. and Scoones, I. 1991. 'Barabaig natural resource management: implications for sustainable savanna landuse in pastoral areas of Africa', paper presented at UBS-UNESCO-UNEP-CEC International Symposium on Economic Driving Forces and Ecological Constraints in Savanna Land Use, Nairobi, January 1991.

Lienhardt, G. 1961. *Divinity and Experience: The Religion of the Dinka*, New York: Oxford University Press.

Llewelyn-Davis, M. 1981. 'Women, warriors and patriarchs', in S.B. Ortner and H. Whitehead (eds) *Sexual Meanings: The Cultural Construction of Gender and Sexuality*, Cambridge: Cambridge University Press, pp. 330–358.

Loiske, V.M. 1990. 'Political adaption: the case of the Wabarabaig in Hanang District, Tanzania', in M. Bovin and L. Manger (eds) *Adaptive Strategies in Arid Lands*, Uppsala: Scandinavian Institute of African Studies, pp. 77–90.

Lumley, E.K. 1976. *Forgotten Mandate: A British District Officer in Tanganyika*, London: C. Hurst & Company.

Lutwaza, G.N. 1984. 'Resettlement of pastoralists for development: Tanzania's "Operation Barabaig" ', Department of Urban and Rural Planning, Ardhi Institute, Dar es Salaam.

Ndagala, D.K. 1991. 'The unmaking of the Datoga: decreasing resources and increasing conflict in rural Tanzania', *Nomadic Peoples* 28: 71–82.

Oboler, R.S. 1994. 'House–property complex and African social organisation', *Africa* 64: 342–358.

Perham, M. 1976. *East African Journey. Kenya and Tanganyika, 1929–30*, London: Faber & Faber.

Rekdal, O.B. and Blystad, A. 1999. '"We are as sheep and goats": Iraqw and Datooga discourses on fortune, failure, and the future', in D.M. Anderson and V. Broch-Due (eds) '*The Poor Are Not Us': Poverty and Pastoralism in Eastern Africa*, Oxford: James Currey, pp. 125–146.

Ross, M.H. 1986. 'Limits to social structure: social structural and psychocultural explanations for political conflict and violence', *Anthropological Quarterly* 59: 171–176.

—— 1990. 'Culture of conflict and conflict management: linking societal and dispute level theories', *Zeitschrift für Ethnologie* 115: 91–109.

Setréus, J. 1991. 'Barabaig – warriors transgressing moral order', unpublished student paper, Uppsala University, Uppsala.

Spencer, P. 1988. *The Maasai of Mataputo: A Study of Rituals of Rebellion*, Manchester: Manchester University Press.

—— 1998. *The Pastoral Continuum: The Marginalisation of Tradition in East Africa*, Oxford: Clarendon Press.

Talle, A. 1974. 'Økonomiske dilemmaer i kombinasjon av buskapshold og økonomisk jordbruk', Mag. Art. thesis, University of Oslo, Oslo.

—— 1988. *Women at a Loss: Changes in Maasai Pastoralism and their Effects on Gender Relations*, Stockholm: University of Stockholm.

Taussig, M.T. 1987. *Shamanism, Colonialism, and the Wild Man: A Study in Terror and Healing*, Chicago, Ill.: University of Chicago Press.

Umesao, T. 1969. 'Hunting culture of the pastoral Datoga', *Kyoto University African Studies* 3: 77–92.

Wilson, G.M. 1952. 'The Tatoga of Tanganyika, Part I', *Tanganyika Notes and Records* 33: 34–47.

—— 1953. 'The Tatoga of Tanganyika, Part II', *Tanganyika Notes and Records* 35: 35–56.

Chapter 7

'Food itself is fighting with us'

A comparative analysis of the impact of Sudan's civil war on South Sudanese civilian populations located in the North and the South

Sharon Elaine Hutchinson

Sudan is a breeding ground of social pathologies common to many of the world's most intractable sectarian conflicts. At war with itself for thirty-six of the past forty-nine years, Sudan's civil strife is usually glossed as a clash between a majority population in the North, identifying itself as 'Arab' and 'Muslim', and a politically marginalised population in the South, identifying itself as 'black African' and, increasingly, 'Christian'. While there some truth in this view, this war is also fuelled by powerful economic forces – forces that have increasingly pitted a small, savvy business/ military/governmental elite centred in Khartoum against ever-growing numbers of war-displaced subsistence farmers, drought-stricken herders, impoverished shanty-town dwellers and other struggling civilians throughout the nation. Among the most important of these economic forces are competing regional and international interests in the vast southern oil reserves located primarily in Nuer and Dinka regions of the Upper Nile and Bahr-el-Ghazal, second, the abundant gold deposits located in the southern province of Equatoria and third, the strategically important headwaters of the White Nile. To these must be added the profiteering of thousands of politicians, soldiers, aid workers, international oil companies, merchants, gangsters and warlords, who have gradually transformed Sudan's war into a self-perpetuating industry.

Since the latest round of fighting erupted in 1983, more than two and a half million Sudanese have lost their lives to war-related causes. Hundreds of thousands of others have become international refugees. In addition, some four million southern Sudanese have been displaced internally, with more than a million of these currently struggling to survive in sprawling shanty towns on the outskirts of greater Khartoum.

This chapter concentrates on the two largest ethnic groups of the South, the Dinka (Jieng) and Nuer (Nei ti naadh/Nath), respectively. It compares and contrasts the immediate life circumstances of Dinka and Nuer civilians who have remained deep within the southern war-zone with those who have fled north to Khartoum. My aim is to document the most pressing constraints on these people's survival strategies, with special attention being devoted to the deepening vulnerabilities of Nuer and Dinka women, children and the elderly to both economic destitution and gross physical abuse at the hands of gun-toting northern and southern soldiers. This chapter shows that although southern Sudanese civilians in both regions have experienced unprecedented levels of poverty and community breakdown over the past twenty-one years, specific military, economic and social factors have made these experiences regionally unique.[1]

The view from the South

The causes and consequences of Sudan's North–South conflict have been extensively analysed from a wide variety of perspectives (Abdel Salam and de Waal 2001, Alier 1991, Burr and Collins 1995, Daly and Sikanga 1993, Deng 1995, Johnson 2001 and 2003, Kok 1992, Prendergast 1997, Ruay 1994). So, too, have the waves of ethnicised, South-on-South military violence triggered by a collapse of southern military unity during the 1991–2001 period (Amnesty International 2000, Human Rights Watch 1999 and 2003, Harir and Tvedt 1994, Hutchinson 1998, 2000 and 2004, Johnson 1998, 2001 and 2003, Jok and Hutchinson 1999, Nyaba 1997). These confrontations grew out of a tragic leadership split within the Sudan People's Liberation Movement/Army (SPLA/M) – the main opposition guerrilla movement. In August 1991, Dr Riek Machar, a Nuer, and other disgruntled SPLA officers staged an unsuccessful coup against their (Dinka) Commander-in-Chief, Dr John Garang. Unable to gain control of the movement, Riek Machar and several other non-Dinka field commanders broke away to form a rival rebel faction. Initially known as SPLA-Nasir, this faction evolved into a largely Nuer-led group later renamed the South Sudan Independence Movement/ Army (SSIM/A). As military clashes between the two factions intensified, Machar's faction forged an unholy alliance with the Sudan Army, from which it secretly received arms in order to continue fighting Garang's SPLA-Mainstream faction. The disastrous result was a decade of ethnicised violence that destroyed hundreds of Nuer and Dinka villages throughout the Upper Nile and Bahr el-Ghazal regions.

In 1996, Riek Machar made his allegiance by signing a separate Peace Charter with the central government, followed by a formal Peace Agreement in April 1997. However, these agreements brought anything but renewed peace to Nuer regions nominally under Machar's control. Instead, they provoked a wave of political fragmentation and in-fighting among Nuer themselves and, in the process, paved the way for the government to gain military control over the oil-rich Western Upper Nile. By August 1999, the Sudanese government, aided by Talisman Energy, Chinese National Petroleum and other international oil interests, had successfully completed construction of a 1,600 km pipeline to carry southern crude from the Western Upper Nile to newly created oil refineries and export depots located in the far North (Gagnon and Ryle 2001, Harker 2000, Human Rights Watch 2003, International Crisis Group 2002). Government troops, aided by various southern and northern militias, proceeded to embark on a scorched-earth military campaign to drive remaining Nuer and Dinka civilians away from expanding oil installations and exploratory well-digging. Between 1998 and 2001, an estimated 300,000 Nuer and Dinka civilians were driven from their homes in the Western Upper Nile and Bahr el-Ghazal by helicopter gunships and fighter jets newly purchased with the government's ballooning oil revenues (Human Rights Watch 2003). Finally, in January 2002, Riek Machar changed his faction's allegiance once again by rejoining Garang's SPLM/A in opposition to the government of Sudan. Renewed international efforts at fostering a negotiated peace settlement between the SPLM/A and the Sudanese government followed, spearheaded by the Bush administration and the US State Department. As of May 2004, intense negotiations continue but, as yet, no final peace agreement has been signed.

Although the January 2002 reunification of the SPLA promises a rapid in south-on-south violence as well as the prospect of a more easily negotiated North/South peace settlement, the scars formed by a decade of SPLA in-fighting remain deep. The preferred and traditional livelihood options of rural Nuer and Dinka men and women, consisting of a mixed agro-pastoralist economy supplemented by seasonal fishing, proved untenable for growing numbers of civilians during the 1991–2001 period, as more and more families became both destitute and displaced. As these people's survival efforts became increasingly individualistic and/or household-oriented, their abilities to sustain the community-wide institutions and practices that formerly restrained gross abuses of military power declined dramatically (Jok and Hutchinson 1999). The end result was a progressive marginalisation of Nuer and Dinka civilian leaders by what was then a deeply divided and increasingly predatory southern military elite.

Regional ethical codes of intra- and inter-ethnic warfare eroded precipitously during this period. Indeed, up until the collapse of SPLA unity, Nuer and Dinka fighters did not intentionally kill women, children or elderly persons encountered during violent confrontations among themselves. However, once Garang and Machar squared off, their troops – sometimes under orders, sometimes of their own initiative – began to slaughter Dinka and Nuer women, children and elderly persons encountered during their inter-ethnic military raids. Whereas before the split, Nuer and Dinka women and children were more likely to be kidnapped than killed, rival southern military factions gradually recast them from being mobile assets to being legitimate targets of ethnic annihilation. Elsewhere (Hutchinson 2000 and 2004), I discuss this tragedy in detail and show how women's more fluid and ambiguous position at the margins of ethnic unities and distinctions was gradually transformed during this war into a dual liability. On the one hand, women's status as independent agents in men's eyes declined in the face of SPLA's glorifications of the raw, masculine power of guns. On the other hand, women's inherent capacity to produce children of differing ethnicities was gradually overshadowed by externally imposed concepts of ethnic rigidity. Nuer fighters, in particular, appeared to abandon more performative concepts of ethnicity, based on conformity to certain behavioural norms, in favour of more primordialist – if not racialist – ways of thinking about their ethnic essence.

During this tumultous decade, local southern military leaders also succeeded in monopolising much of the region's cattle wealth, especially along the tense borderlands separating neighbouring Nuer and Dinka communities in the Upper Nile and Bahr el-Ghazal regions. Some civilian cattle were collected directly through court fines or through mandatory contributions to the war effort. The vast majority of such wealth, however, was acquired through tit-for-tat cattle raids and inter-community attacks orchestrated by rival southern military leaders and warlords. Although these raids were nominally carried out for the purpose of recapturing civilian-owned cattle lost to earlier raids by the opposing faction, recaptured cattle were not returned to their original owners but, rather, were declared 'military/government property' to be distributed as the local commander saw fit. The end result was a steady siphoning of civilian herds into the byres of their nominal military protectors. Furthermore, as the banditry of spin-off southern field commanders and warlords gained momentum after 1991, so, too, did the individual commandeering of civilian resources.

In Nuer regions of the Western Upper Nile, I often stumbled across southern soldiers eating in the homes of women I visited during the 1990s. Some women exhibited broken fingers or other signs of past fights with local soldiers over household goods. Indeed, just about every Nuer woman I encountered during my 1996 and 1998 field trips to the Western Upper Nile reported having experienced threatening demands for the immediate provision of food, portage services or sexual access by gun-wielding men. Satisfying these unpredictable and recurrent demands severely limited the energies these women could devote to their families.

Although nearly all Nuer and Dinka women encountered during parallel field research projects carried out by Dr Jok Madut Jok and myself between 1998 and 2000 remained committed to liberating South Sudan by force of arms, many were uncertain how to respond to escalating military demands for food, cattle and other scarce household resources. One Dinka widow, whose militarily active husband was killed by northern Baggara raiders in 1997, struggled on a daily basis to feed her four young children in spite of these never-ending demands for her hard-earned provisions by individual SPLA soldiers. With tears hanging from her eyes, Abuk explained to my colleague and research partner, Jok Madut Jok, why she felt her marriage to a soldier was doubly tragic:

'When [a soldier] is strong and fighting for his nation, everyone likes him and his wife is respected. He is then sent to distant fronts, where he is unable to provide for his children. But when he is killed or wounded, no one cares about his family. One day, I told my children that their father is no longer around to help us, that they will have to be patient with me, and that we will get by just fine on the little [income] I can make. So whenever I go to the market or to work for the Khawaja [white foreigners], the children are able to cope with their hunger in the hope that I will return with something to eat in the evening. But when I come home empty-handed because I have been robbed along the way, it breaks my heart to see the disappointment on their faces. I begin to wonder how to tell them that the same army that their father fought and died for is the same army that constantly deprives them of their meals. If I tell them the truth, they will probably be discouraged from continuing [to support] the cause that took away their father. They will begin to think of the SPLA as their enemy and I don't want that impression to grow in them. I would have failed my husband if the children of such a nationalist [were to] turn against their own cause.'

(Jok Madut Jok, personal communication)

The bottom line was that the military always took what it needed, regardless of the consequences for struggling civilians. While living in Ganyliel in 1998, I documented many of the obstacles Nuer civilian leaders faced in seeking to reserve the bulk of food aid delivered by the World Food Program (WPF) for needy civilian families. Whatever control local headmen exercised over such inputs was routinely trumped by local southern military leaders, who did not hesitate to use force when necessary. Local headmen would summon individual women to collect their family's grain allotments directly from World Food Program overseers only to have these allotments transported to a prearranged location determined by the local military elite. Once the WFP monitors departed, these women were summoned again to carry food to scattered regional military posts. In the case of one WFP airdrop I witnessed, more than half of the food aid was shunted to local military posts in this way. Any woman who resisted by attempting to deposit her family's grain allotment elsewhere was severely beaten by local military personnel.

Like military movements worldwide, the SPLA and spin-off factions inculcated a kind of ultra-masculinity in new recruits, equated with demonstrations of aggressiveness, competitiveness and the suppression of emotional expression. A sense of sexual entitlement also pervaded this 'hyper-masculinised' military world-view (Enloe 1995). Just as Dinka and Nuer soldiers took responsibility for maintaining the war front, so, too, many reasoned, women should be held responsible for keeping up 'the reproductive front'. Pressures for women to disregard the weaning taboo (prohibiting sexual relations during lactation) mounted steadily as husbands and lovers on short, unpredictable military leave returned home determined to conceive another child. Similarly, women were pressured to reduce the fallow period between births by weaning their infants earlier. Whereas during the 1980s infants were routinely nursed for eighteen months or more, many Nuer and Dinka men argued during the 1990s that nine months were sufficient. And because women could not refuse their husbands sexual access for fear of a beating, more and more women lost their lives as the result of botched abortion attempts (cf. Jok 1998). Rape, another obvious consequence of this masculine attitude, was surrounded by a protective wall of silence. Among the Nuer, for instance, I was told that a girl would even attempt to hide the fact that she had been raped from her own mother.

Nuer and Dinka women faced many other moral conundrums. One of the most common was discussed by a middle-aged Nuer woman named Nyaluak. Nyaluak's husband, a Dinka merchant, was caught 'off-sides' when the SPLA first split. After he was rounded up and marched off to an unknown fate by a local Nuer military officer, Nyaluak was left alone to fend for her two young daughters. Seven years later, in 1998, she was still uncertain whether or not her husband was alive. She was thus uncertain whether or not she was a widow (*ciek joka*) who might legitimately seek the support of another man to help raise her children and, perhaps, bear others in her late husband's name. Thousands of other Nuer and Dinka women shared Nyaluak's limbo-like status. Some sought to attach themselves to individual soldiers in the hope of helping to shield their families and households from robbery, rape and physical abuse. Nyaluak, however, rejected this strategy on moral grounds in the hope that her husband was alive.

For many Nuer and Dinka families, growing hunger was aggravated by a gnawing sense of promises broken between between men and women, husbands and wives, parents and children and young and old. Many rural women viewed their marriages as illusory, since they struggled so often alone to feed their children. Sharpening cleavages of value and perspective between older and younger generations were also lamented by many people. The few older men and women I encountered in Nuer communities during the late 1990s were invariably severely malnourished and often blind. The cultural knowledge and historical experience accumulated by the older generation was deemed irrelevant by growing numbers of youth, who were 'driven crazy by the smoke and roar of guns'. Instead of receiving the deference and 'retirement' support they believe they had earned, many older Nuer and Dinka women and men were reduced to rags and treated openly with disdain by their gun-wielding 'sons'.

Nowhere was this intergenerational breakdown of communications more apparent than with respect to surviving remnants of the so-called Red Army. During the latter 1980s, SPLA officers systematically rounded up tens of thousands of Nuer and Dinka boys between the ages of six and fourteen and marched them to south western Ethiopia for the avowed purpose of enrolling them in UNHCR-supplied schools. While some boys were forcibly collected on a regional quota basis, others were voluntarily released by their parents in hopes they would find both a solid education and safety from the war in Ethiopia. Hundreds of boys died on route or during their first months in Ethiopian camps. Most were inducted into the SPLA as soon as they grew strong enough to wield guns. What emerged was a socially isolated contingent of armed youths brutally trained not only to kill but, also, to torture whomever their military superiors designated.

When some of these heavily traumatised youths eventually made the long journey home after the mass exodus of South Sudanese refugees from Ethiopia following the fall of Mengistu in 1991, they often experienced grave difficulties in fitting back in. Some returned only to discover that their parents and siblings were dead or missing. Others bitterly rejected their families once found, much as they felt rejected by their parents in the past. Having been forced to survive by their wits from an early age, these youths risked becoming a lost generation with little faith in the future or themselves.

The continual conscription of underage boys also constrained the survival potential of many rural families. On Machar's side of the SPLA divide, local headmen were responsible for handing over a specific number of youths each year on pain of being drafted themselves. Faced with this threat, it is not surprising that headmen sometimes resorted to drafting underage boys. Young conscripts were expected to serve in the southern military 'until this war ends'. Consequently, recruits had little opportunity for acquiring any survival skills other than fighting.

The wartime conversion of hundreds of thousands of younger Nuer and Dinka men and women also drove an ideological wedge between them and their seniors. For many southerners, Christianity came to symbolise the possibility of political equality, community development and self-enhancement in the face of the increasingly vicious Islamic *jihad* being waged from the North. Christianity also appeared to offer a non-political basis for reinforcing southern nationalist sentiments and for countering the ethno-national impulses of rival southern military leaders. Civilian youths and women of all ages were especially attracted to Christianity's promise of more direct relations with a forgiving God, unmediated by the rigid age and gender hierarchies characterising indigenous religious practices. Older men, in contrast, showed greater reluctance toward adopting a faith that undermined their position as the sacrificial agents of their dependants' welfare. In recent years, these tensions have been aggravated by deepening over the rapid introduction of new Protestant denominations supported by southern Sudanese refugee populations in USA as well by growing numbers of expatriate church officials operating in South Sudan (cf. Hutchinson 2004).

Declining feeling of communal responsibility for the well-being of children also plagued the 1990s. Many men and women felt too poor to share their dwindling assets with those less fortunate than themselves, including, in some cases, starving orphans. Consider a court case I witnessed in 1998. A Nuer man sought restitution from the courts after three hungry children (ages 3–8), living in a neighbouring household with their widowed father, ventured on to his property to collect some fruits that had fallen from a *neem* tree. Their father was away from home when the incident occurred. Before this war began in 1983, this case would most certainly have been dismissed on the grounds of the premise, universally accepted up till then, that: 'Food [disputes] cannot be litigated.' The very idea of an individual laying claim to a *neem* tree, which normally grows wild, so as to deny its fruits to a group of hungry children would have been unacceptable at that time. To my dismay, however, the presiding sub-chief not only agreed to hear the case (for a fee) but also ruled in favour of the tree's 'owner'. Six attending headmen supported the sub-chief's decision, although several objected to the initial imposition of a five-cow fine and a six-month jail sentence on the widower as excessively punitive. After further deliberations, the chief decided to reduce the widower's fine to one cow and to eliminate the jail term.

While the remarkable degree of 'social disintegration' apparent in this court case could be unusual, everyone recognised that the bonds between parents and children and between relatives and neighbours were being seriously eroded by the war. Many parents had already lost confidence in the support their children could offer them in the future. Not only were children dying at previously unimaginable rates but few of those who survived could realise their full potential, owing to wartime shortages of livestock, seed, fishing equipment, agricultural tools and markets. A badly bruised bridewealth system skewed increasingly toward military monopolisation also meant that fewer parents secured bridewealth cattle for daughters. As one exasperated father exclaimed: 'First the soldiers steal your cattle and then try to marry your daughter with cattle stolen from you!'

A survey of seventy-four rural households carried out among the Nyuong Nuer, Western Upper Nile, during June 1998 reveals something of the magnitude of these losses. All five rural settlements included in my house-to-house survey lay along the Western Upper Nile/Bahr-el-Ghazal (Nuer/Dinka) boundary, which was very tense at that period. Two communities had experienced direct SPLA-Mainstream attacks during the previous three years, while the other three had escaped relatively unscathed. The combined population of these settlements was 412 people, consisting of 72 adult males, 131 adult females and 209 children. With the noteworthy exception of several households headed by men active in local military or civilian administrations, there was little cushion of food security evident in any of these households, despite a major WFP airdrop earlier that month. In fact, many houses lay empty, their members having scattered in search of food.

The devastating effects of the SPLA split were immediately apparent in the crippled family structures and skewed sex ratios of many households surveyed. On average, each household contained 1.8 female adults for every adult male. Twenty-four per cent of these households, however, had no resident adult male. Of the 131 women uncovered in this survey, twenty-one were elderly mothers living as dependants in the homes of married sons or married or widowed daughters. In contrast, the survey revealed the presence of only one elderly male resident. This striking absence of older men was lamented by many residents, who associated it with a more general decline in the arts of political persuasion and compromise in their communities. Many of the younger men residing in these communities had multiple wives, some of whom lived in non-surveyed settlements. The familial responsibilities of the seventy-two men included in the survey were thus divided across distant households. This, too, must be considered when assessing the impact of a severely skewed sex ratio on the security requirements of resident women and children.

Not unexpectedly, polygynous unions were reported far more often in my 1998 household survey than they were during a house-to-house survey I carried out in the Western Upper Nile immediately prior to the outbreak of full-scale civil war in 1983 (cf. Hutchinson 1996: 357–362). The 1983 survey encompassed twenty-two Leek Nuer women, of whom 70 per cent were currently married (including leviratic unions), 15 per cent were single or living as unmarried, adulterous or widowed concubines, 4 per cent were were divorcees and 11 per cent older women without mates (ibid.: 359). Of those women 'currently married' approximately

30 per cent (or 25/85) had at least one co-wife. In contrast, the 1998 Nyuong Nuer survey revealed that 62 per cent (81/131) of the women surveyed were 'currently married' (including leviratic unions), of whom 58 per cent (47/81) were married to polygynous husbands. Unlike the earlier survey, there were no divorcees uncovered in the 1998 survey. Considering that divorce required a return of bridewealth cattle, this was not an unexpected finding during an era of unprecedented impoverishment. Paralleling this rise in the percentage of 'currently married' women reporting polygynous unions from 30 per cent to 58 per cent in the 1983 and 1998 surveys, respectively, was a decline in the proportion of 'single women' uncovered in these surveys from 15 per cent to 7 per cent (9/131).

Approximately 31 per cent (41/131) of the Nyuong women covered in the 1998 survey stated that they were unattached widows (20) or elderly mothers without mates (41). Indeed, many of them complained that their late husbands' families provided them with little or no support. Others complained that local headmen overlooked them and their households when distributing food relief and other humanitarian inputs. This was because households composed entirely of women and children were not taxed and, hence, did not appear on the tax rolls routinely used by headmen in distributing food aid. Only households containing a resident adult male were listed. Consequently, some widows and abandoned wives with young children had lost all hope of recovery. Faced with the devastating prospect of watching their children starve to death, a small number of Nuer and Dinka mothers had chosen to burn themselves alive with their children inside their homes. Others simply abandoned their children as their search for food intensified.

Of the 209 children reported in the 1998 survey, only 126 (60 per cent) were living with both parents. The remaining 40 per cent (83) were locally defined as 'orphans' (*reet*) since they had lost either one (43) or both (36) parents to homicide, illness or abandonment. Of the thirty-six children who resided with neither parent, fourteen were being raised by a stepmother, six by a grandparent, and sixteen by more distant paternal (7) or maternal (9) relatives. Child mortality rates, gleaned from the procreative histories of all adult female residents, hovered around 50 per cent.

On an even bleaker note, the number of family members who were slain as a direct consequence of the post-1991 explosion of Nuer/Dinka violence was truly astounding. A total of eighty-two homicides occurred between 1991 and 1998 alone in the seventy-four households surveyed. Of the eighty-two reported homicide victims, 45 per cent (37) were children, 6 per cent (5) were elderly grandparents, 7 per cent (6) were women and 41 per cent (34) were men. In other words, 59 per cent of the civilians killed during this period of fratricidal violence were unarmed women, children and elderly grandparents.

Thus far this chapter has concentrated on social distortions and economic hardships generated by nearly two decades of unrelenting warfare with Nuer and Dinka civilian populations remaining deep within the southern war zone. In particular, women's attempts to participate in the war effort appeared to have been brutally turned against them. As the primary agents of familial and cultural continuity, women came under increasing pressure to conceive and procreate in situations that potentially threaten their own physical well-being and their abilities to care for their children. Uprooted by recurrent raids and harassed by rising military demands, Nuer women were largely denied the protections of their gun-toting male counterparts. Older women and men have also been robbed of their children's support through forced conscriptions, kidnappings and murder. A severely skewed sex ratio and rising polygyny rates further constrained women's reliance on the protective and economic support of their mates.

Nevertheless, women were more than the passive victims of these militarising trends. Many actively encouraged their husbands, brothers and sons to participate in cattle raids and vengeance attacks on neighbouring ethnic groups. But women could also band together to restrain inter-community violence (cf. Hutchinson and Jok 2002: 102–103). But since few women participated directly in the ethnicised violence that followed the SPLA split, there is hope that they may play a pivotal role in restoring an atmosphere of forgiveness and peace between Nuer and Dinka civilians following the 2002 reunification of the SPLA.

The view from the North

Since 1983, an estimated 1.8 million South Sudanese civilians have sought refuge from the war in Khartoum. Although reliable statistics about this influx do not exist, extensive interviews carried out in Khartoum with displaced Nuer and Dinka living during 1998 and 1999 indicate that up to 40 per cent of those who attempted the perilous journey northwards were lost on the way. Many families fleeing Northern Bahr el-Ghazal and Western Upper Nile faced a gauntlet of northern Baggara raiders, who freely kidnapped, raped, robbed and murdered anyone they wished – with the blessings of the national army. Those Southerners who actually reached Khartoum arrived doubly traumatised. After witnessing the destruction of their home communities, they were forced to adapt to an alien social environment that actively discriminated against them. Most arrived with little or no money. Initially, they settled on unoccupied plots and industrial wastelands scattered throughout the three cities comprising the capital (Omdurman, Khartoum North and Khartoum). The largest influx of displaced southerners occurred during 1988, when a war-provoked famine of catastrophic proportions killed some 250,000 Southern Sudanese civilians. A second influx occurred between 1991 and 1994, when the 'ethno-nationalist' armies of Garang and Machar first began turning their guns against each other's entire civilian populations. More recently, the number of war-displaced in Khartoum continued to expand, as the result of government efforts to depopulate the Western Upper Nile in order to make way for further oil exploration and exploitation (Human Rights Watch 2003).

The cumulative result was a radical shift in the sociocultural 'complexion' of the nation's capital. According to various UN sources, greater Khartoum's population grew from approximately 1.8 million in 1983 to 3.5 million in 1993. By 1998, it topped 4.4 million. Of the latter figure, approximately two million were war-displaced, with some 250,000 to 400,000 of these residing in four official camps for displaced civilians located between 5 and 25 km from the city's centre. From being a capital dominated overwhelming by an Arabised Muslim population in 1980, Khartoum became an increasingly multi-ethnic and 'Africanised' city. Vilified in the government press as a dangerous 'fifth column', displaced Southerners posed a major obstacle to the solidification of Islamic legislation. Fearful that their return to the South would facilitate SPLA recruitments, the Government of Sudan aimed at controlling their settlement patterns in Khartoum both by placing severe restrictions on their rights of tenancy and land ownership and by forcibly removing displaced populations that infringed on these. These policies gained momentum after the present National Islamic Front government, headed by Omar al-Bashir, seized power in a bloodless *coup d'état* in 1989.

Beginning in the mid-1980s, the government instituted a policy of forced removals aimed at banishing displaced South Sudanese populations to the desert peripheries of Khartoum and proceeded to bulldoze systematically all spontaneous settlements – normally with little advanced warning and no compensation. Security forces ruthlessly suppressed all resistance. Residents of demolished shantytowns were either left to fend for themselves or trucked off at gun-point to an unstable series of camps far from the economic heart of the capital. Local Christian churches and schools were also routinely destroyed in these raids. Moreover, the government often barred their reconstruction at new locations.

In 1991 an official housing plan was drawn up which sharply distinguished 'squatters/migrants' from internally 'displaced' persons. Whereas 'squatters/migrants' were to be allocated plots in newly developed areas, 'displaced' persons were proclaimed 'temporary' residents of Khartoum and were to be herded into four official 'displaced camps'. Newly promulgated laws denied them rights of permanent residency and tenancy in Khartoum. Officially declared 'second class residents', they were vulnerable to arbitrary arrest, imprisonment and forced conscription into the national army.

Fearing concentrations of potentially hostile residents, the government sought to dilute southern enclaves either by forcibly dividing and scattering their members or by moving Northerners in. These policies proved only partially successful. After eight years of continuous bulldozing, the government only managed to corral 250,000 to 400,000 people in official 'displaced' camps. The overwhelming majority of displaced Southerners struggled to retain some form of residence nearer to the economic centre of the city.

The transition from a rural life style to the urban environment of Khartoum was traumatic for many displaced Nuer and Dinka. 'Even if you are living under a tree in the South, you are still a human being!' remarked one Nuer woman. 'But here in Khartoum,' she continued, 'we are thrown away by the government like garbage!' Whereas the South was remembered as place of strong community spirit and multiple livelihood options, Khartoum's money-dominated economy and mixed-ethnic composition created an atmosphere, many southerners argued, of amorality, alienation and cultural degradation.

The social cohesion of Nuer and Dinka families was also under constant threat. Public transportation was expensive and scarce. Mothers employed in domestic service often remained away from home six nights a week. Many fathers and sons migrated to distant agricultural schemes around Damazin and Gedaref for half the year. And thousands of southern children spent their days in the streets, searching for food, money and small trade items.

During 1998 and 1999, I designed and participated in a major qualitative and quantitative study of the social and economic conditions faced by displaced populations in Khartoum. Carried out at the request of Save the Children – Denmark and supported by the research expertise of Jeremy Loveless (1999) and Dr Paul Wani. The final report was composed by Jeremy Loveless and entitled *Displaced Populations in Khartoum: A Study of Social and Economic Conditions.* The study sampled all four official displaced camps (Mayo, Jebel Awlia, Wad al Bashir and As Salaam) as well as three spontaneous shantytowns (Kartoun Kassala, Soba Arady and Shigla) located in greater Khartoum. All in all, some 350 in-depth interviews and 1,085 formal questionnaires were completed by a group of twenty trained Southern Sudanese research assistants. For the purposes of this chapter, I will concentrate on a subset of this data consisting of a total of 399 Nuer and Dinka households uncovered in the quantitative portion of this survey and two dozen in-depth surveys of Nuer households carried out by myself.

The combined resident population of the 399 Nuer and Dinka households totalled 2,972 persons: 845 women, 824 men and 1,303 children, 699 of whom were seven years old or younger. Average household size in this data set was 7.45 persons (2,972/399). This contrasts with an average of 5.6 persons per household (412/74) in the Nyuong Nuer survey carried out in the South in 1998. A majority (62 per cent) of the 399 Nuer and Dinka households sampled in Khartoum lived in one-room mud houses, 28 per cent lived in two-room houses, 8 per cent in three or four room houses and 2 per cent were presently homeless owing to recent demolitions by government bulldozers. A total of 84 per cent of the Nuer and Dinka households surveyed were located in the camps, with the remaining 26 per cent congregated in spontaneous settlements. Fifty-two per cent (208/399) of these households were currently living 'rent-free'.

The sex-ratio of resident adults was better balanced than in the southern survey. Only thirteen displaced households (3 per cent) had no resident adult female and forty-one households (10 per cent) had no resident adult male. Twenty per cent (80/399) of these households had no children sleeping regularly in them. Six per cent (26) of the 399 households contained one child, 13 per cent (52) contained two children, 18 per cent (71) three children, 15 per cent (61) four children, 12 per cent (46) five children, 7 per cent (27) six children, 2 per cent (8) seven children, 3 per cent (12) eight children, and the remaining 4 per cent (16) contained anywhere from nine to fifteen children each. The average number of children residing in these 399 households was thus 3.26. Subtracting for the moment the eighty households with no resident children, those households containing at least one child held an average of 4.1 children each (1,303/319).

When one considers that 16 per cent of these 399 households were struggling to feed anywhere from six to fifteen children, one gets a better sense of the extraordinarily high dependency ratios characterising many displaced households.

In contrast, only 9 per cent (7) of the seventy-four Nuer households encompassed in my southern survey had no resident children, with an average of 2.8 children residing in each household. Subtracting these seven childless households, there was an average of 3.1 children in households containing at least one child (209/67) in the Southern survey as compared to 4.1 in the northern survey. The proportion of child orphans in homes containing at least one child, however, was considerably lower in the northern survey, consisting of 19 per cent (202/1,058) of all resident children as opposed to 40 per cent (83/209) in the southern study. This difference may reflect the fact that many young orphans and other children residing in Khartoum have taken to the open streets. Significantly, 75 (19 per cent) of the 399 displaced families reported that one or more child had either run off or become lost during 1998: a very disturbing figure, considering it represents the losses of a single year.

In the northern survey, only 19 per cent (76) of the household members interviewed were men. The remaining 81 per cent (323) were women, of whom 11 per cent (37/323) were classified as 'older' women. This is significant because only the marital status of the person interviewed was requested in the Khartoum survey. Of those person interviewed, 72 per cent (288) were currently married, 17 per cent (66) widowed, 1 per cent (4) divorced, and the remaining 10 per cent (41) single. Of the married population, 84 per cent were presently living with their husband or wife. Of the 306 informants currently living with a spouse or a partner, 71 per cent (218/306) were involved in monogamous unions and the remaining 29 per cent (88/306) involved in polygynous unions. This contrasts with the 58 per cent of currently married women involved in polygynous unions that was uncovered in the 1998 southern Nuer survey discussed earlier. Arranging new marriages while living in Khartoum was extremely difficult, owing in part to an absence of cattle (the traditional exchange medium for both ethnic groups) and in part to the exorbitant monetary demands many impoverished fathers-in-law demanded instead. Informal unions, forged by individual men and women, were thus becoming the norm, with significant numbers of young women being abandoned by their lovers following pregnancy.

The extreme poverty of many displaced Nuer and Dinka in Khartoum was reflected in the fact that 49 per cent (197) of the 399 households sampled reported serving only meal per day, with some reporting hunger gaps of two or three days at a time. Forty-six per cent (183/399) reported eating two meals per day, with only 5 per cent (19) claiming to eat three per day. Estimates of total household income spent on food ranged as high as 70–80 per cent. People's health was also poor, with 61 per cent of displaced households reporting a member having fallen seriously ill during the previous month. In answer to the question of how many resident adults died in 1998, 11 per cent (45) reported the death of one adult, 3 per cent (11) two adult deaths and 1 per cent (3) three or more adult deaths.

Otherwise expressed: 15 per cent of these households had lost at least one adult to illness in a single year. Child mortality rates were equally appalling, with 20 per cent (78) of all households reporting one or more child deaths in 1998. Subtracting the 82 households with no resident children, 78 out of the remaining 317 households (or 25 per cent) lost one or more children to illness in a single year.

Government efforts at forceful containment were coupled with the brutal suppression of Khartoum's informal economy, which nevertheless consitutued the major income source for most displaced households. In a security operation locally known as 'kasha,' police would sweep through the camps, markets and streets on a daily basis, arresting anyone caught peddling beer, tea, cigarettes, peanuts or other small trade items and unable to satisfy immediate demands for a bribe. Those arrested were carted off to Public Order Courts, where they were lashed, fined and stripped of their wares. Those unable to pay the fine imposed by the court faced terms of imprisonment of three to six months. Displaced women and children were the principal victims of these raids, since they were disproportionately dependent on small-scale trading for survival.

A national ban on all forms of alcohol production and consumption was imposed, together with the Islamic Shari'a Law, in 1983. By 1998, women caught brewing or selling alcohol were subject both to fines of up to 300,000 Sudanese pounds and to prison terms of three to twelve months. Police officers routinely seized household furnishings and other possessions while making arrests. Despite governmental suppression, beer-brewing remained the most lucrative livelihood option available to displaced women, especially since it was compatible with childcare and isolated urban locations. Displaced Nuer and Dinka men, in contrast, generally turned to day-labour in the Khartoum construction industry (including members from 46 per cent of the 399 households surveyed). Failing that, men often undertook seasonal labour migration to agricultural zones far from the capital. But owing to the suppression of petty trade and beer-brewing, there really were no 'safe' livelihood options available to most women. Domestic service, which was resorted to by 26 per cent of the households groups surveyed, was legal. However, it often entailed forced sex or other forms of physical abuse: a fact which emerged through our qualitative interviews. Children added what household income they could by delivering water, polishing shoes, begging for money, scavenging for food and peddling small trade items. But in times of pressing domestic emergencies, beer-brewing remained the most lucrative and efficient way for displaced women to raise money.

The number of displaced Nuer and Dinka women arrested for beer-brewing or other petty sales was truly astounding. Two-thirds of those Nuer and Dinka women sampled had resorted to beer-brewing on occasion and that half of these had been arrested and imprisoned for this offence at least once. All in all, 19 per cent of these 399 households had experienced the arrest and/or imprisonment of a member during 1998 alone.

One of the most destructive aspects of the extended prison terms imposed for beer-brewing, drinking or sales was that it often resulted in minor children being left 'in the care of God'. Tales of the tragic aftermath of the arrest of mothers and fathers abounded. Unable to support themselves during their mothers' absence, many young girls were reduced to prostitution or other highly dangerous activities in order to sustain themselves and younger siblings. Other children sought refuge in the streets, where they survived on the food discarded at restaurants or by scavenging in city waste dumps. Nursing infants invariably accompanied their mothers to prison, where many would swiftly fall ill or die.

Having visited Omdurman's Women's Prison in October 1998, I can attest to the appalling conditions many displaced women endured there. Omdurman Prison was constructed to hold about 250 inmates but held at the time of my visit 1,163 women, along with 253 dependent children below the age of five. The vast majority of these women were serving terms of between three and six months for brewing or selling beer. Others were arrested for peddling tea, bread and other small commodities without the requisite health certificates and licences. The Public Order Courts that condemned them recognised neither their right to legal representation nor to an appeal. Nor were arrested women's motives for engaging in such risky activities investigated by the court. Women who were pregnant upon arrest often delivered in prison without any medical care. One Nuer woman reported that she was arrested while pregnant and after giving birth in a prison was severely beaten for removing her dress in an attempt to wash out the blood. She memorialised her experience by naming her new-born son 'Prison.'

Roughly half of the women inmates in Omdurman Prison lay on rags in the open air, with no shelter from the rain. Tattered blankets and old pieces of cloth were patched together and strung from the collapsing mud-brick walls of the prison in order to shelter themselves and their young children from the merciless sun. There were no facilities for these women to cook for themselves. And water supplies were rationed and of extremely unsafe quality. Prisoners accompanied by young children received no larger rations than those without children, and the ration consisted at that time of two pieces of flat bread and some watery soup twice a day. Sanitary precautions consisted of three unwalled and overflowing pit latrines with uncovered rectangular mouths of about 18 inches square. Food supplements could be delivered to the gate by concerned relatives. However, such gifts were heavily 'taxed' by the guards.

Despite these risks of arrest and imprisonment, alcohol was becoming an attractive escape for displaced men and women themselves, especially older, unemployed or otherwise frustrated men. The predictable results were increased domestic strife and violence. As one Dinka man explained: 'When a man is unable to support his wife and children, he will hear any criticism his wife makes as a criticism of his failure to provide for his family and become angry.' At times, female beer-brewers found themselves sliding into alcoholism.

Many displaced Nuer and Dinka living in Khartoum, like their counterparts in the South, feared that the younger generation was becoming trapped in a cultural limbo. Ignorant of the cultural traditions of their parents, they were nevertheless precluded from integrating fully into the dominant culture of the North. Resentful of their parents' inability to provide adequate food and shelter, many children in Khartoum eventually left for the streets. For those children who experienced physical abuse at home from stepparents or other relatives (a lamentably common occurrence judging from our qualitative interviews), this move to the streets was experienced as an assertion of personal dignity. Once on the streets, they usually clustered together in bands of five or six for companionship and mutual support. These groups often cut across diverse ethnic backgrounds. Bands of street children often developed complex social hierarchies, complete with differentiated role assignments, secret languages and internal procedures for dispute settlement. Children coming from more harmonious homes often turned to the streets in search of opportunities to contribute to their families' welfare. Life on the streets was extremely risky. All children lived in constant fear of being forcibly rounded up by the police and confined within an expanding network of government reformatories and labour camps, where they were subject to physical and sexual abuse as well as pressured into accepting Islam.

Although a full discussion of the 'criminalisation' of Khartoum's 'street children' cannot be attempted here, I offer a representative first-hand account of a Nuer street boy named Dak as evidence of the perils and freedoms such these children faced daily. Dak, who was fifteen years old in 1998, identified himself as Nuer even though he could no longer speak his mother-tongue. Despite the filthy state of his clothing, he appeared healthy.

> 'I was born in a place called Mayorno,' he began, 'near Kenana town. I came to Khartoum in 1995 after my parents died. My older brother, who is mentally retarded, and I were left in the care of a paternal uncle. But my uncle regularly mistreated us, beating me severely. One day I decided that I could no longer stand the beatings and ran away. I boarded a truck to Kosti. Since I knew no one there, I spent the spent the first few days wandering around the marketplace, hungry and scared. After sometime, I made friends with some other street boys and was allowed to join their team. We usually roamed around the market all day long, looking for leftover food from restaurant bins, begging for money and stealing from cars. Sometimes we were lucky and found a car with some money left in the glove compartment. This we divided, using it to go to the cinema, to buy glue, to gamble or buy whatever we wished.' Asked why he sniffs glue, the boy replied: 'It makes me brave so that I can steal without any fear. And if I am caught and beaten by the police, glue-sniffing numbs the pain and helps the time fly and makes the days more fun. . . . My friends and I used to sleep under a small bridge at night. One day the police staged a raid, capturing me and seventeen others. We were initially detained in a small police cell for three days, where we were beaten repeatedly. We were then taken to a town called Faw and put in a detention camp for about a week. From there we were bought to Khartoum and taken to Dar el Bashir, where we stayed for a long time before being moved to a camp called Hijre Abudoom in the desert north of Omdurman. Some of the older boys

were sent to the army. When we arrived there was no camp at all. We slept on the bare ground. The next day, tents were brought which we were told to erect ourselves. We were also ordered to erect a fence. Sleeping mats were eventually provided and water was trucked in and emptied into big drums. Life was tough and some boys became very sick. Others were bitten by scorpions. All of us were made to work hard every day. We were also taught to recite the Quran and given classes in Arabic. I was beaten a lot by the camp supervisor as well as by bigger boys. We were given very little food and sometimes we starved. After some time, I escaped by hiding in a vegetable truck that came to the camp. I jumped off in Khartoum, where I joined up with nine street boys, eventually settling in Amarat (a wealthier suburb of Khartoum). Amarat is safer than Khartoum centre – less competition and fewer police raids. Since the people who do business in Amarat are rich, they are more generous to beggars. Our group has a leader, who has his own ideas. There is no room for any differences among us because unity is our strength. We have even developed our own language to communicate with. The biggest difficulty we face is when one of us falls sick. During the cold season, we must huddle together for warmth at night. My biggest fear is being caught again by the police and thrown in camp or drafted into the army. Some day I hope to be a humanitarian worker, helping the poor and other street children.'

Over the past few years, the number of Southern Sudanese girls roaming the streets has increased noticeably, a clear indication of the increasing economic desperation of many displaced families. During the 1980s and early 1990s, parents generally kept their daughters at home, even when they encouraged sons to fend for themselves on the streets. Whereas children on the streets faced many daily risks, including arrest, kidnapping, rape and forced blood donations, street girls were especially vulnerable to sexual exploitation. Police officers often extorted sexual favours from them and young girls were sometimes forced into prostitution.

Despite the tremendous hardships street children experienced at the hands of police, several youths interviewed stated that they hoped to join their ranks some day. As one young boy remarked: 'When I grow up I want to become a policeman because in this country whoever has a gun is respected, no matter how old or young. The whole community fears you. The police are above power.' Such comments revealed how far Nuer and Dinka youths in the North as well as in the South had come to glorify the raw masculine power of guns.

Since the formation of 'Operation Lifeline Sudan' in 1989, numerous international humanitarian aid organisations have endeavoured to assist the war-displaced and other impoverished residents of Khartoum by providing emergency food relief, basic health services and other forms of aid. Government support for these humanitarian programmes has run hot and cold over the past decade. On the one hand, the central government's coffers have benefited greatly from such aid. On the other hand, the government sought to control the distribution of such aid both by restricting contacts between the displaced and international food monitors, human rights workers and the like and by channelling growing proportions of aid through state agencies and/or local NGOs supportive of the government's Islamist agenda. The most important of these NGOs was the *Da'wa Islamiyya* or the 'Islamic Call', an organisation that openly discriminated against non-Muslims in the distribution of humanitarian aid.

Owing to the dismal human rights record of the present government, most international aid organisations operating in the North considered Sudan to be a pariah state, unworthy of development assistance during the 1997–2001 period. Consequently, most international humanitarian organisations restricted themselves to the provision of emergency assistance. This policy was inherently biased in favour of the war-displaced, since they were, at least until 1999, legally defined as temporary residents of Khartoum. Consequently, it was easier for International NGOs to justify material assistance to them as emergency aid.

This dichotomy between emergency and development assistance adopted by international aid agencies dovetailed nicely with the government of Sudan's efforts to distinguish displaced persons residing in Khartoum from economic migrants and squatters. However, neither discourse impinged on the UN-recognised right of the Sudanese government to act as the final arbitrator of the needs of its citizens, however categorised. And the present government did not hesitate to exercise its 'sovereign right' in this regard in order to further its political agenda. And thus, when the government abruptly announced in 1997 that 'general food distributions' in displaced camps were no longer needed, all UN-affiliated, international NGOs operating in Khartoum were forced to comply, despite rising malnutrition rates among the displaced. As one Nuer summed up their predicament: 'Food itself is fighting with us.' Having suppressed the informal economy and curtailed general food distributions in the camps, the government, in conjunction with Islamic Call and other sympathetic NGOs, could exploit offers of food and other relief items as more effective inducements for Islamic conversion. This strategy, which was well documented by our qualitative interviews, was reflected in the fact that 9.5 per cent (38) of the 399 Nuer and Dinka households surveyed identified themselves as Muslim by the end of 1998.

For reasons that remain debated, the government of Sudan abruptly reversed its policy toward the displaced in late 1998. Having sought to isolate 'displaced' Southerners from other Khartoum residents since 1990, government administrators came out in favour of amalgamation. A sub-set of war displaced from the South were granted rights to purchase and own land in Khartoum in the hope that they would spearhead a more general process of cultural and religious assimilation among Southerners. The four official displaced camps were to be replanned as suburban areas. The systematic bulldozing of spontaneous displaced settlements, however, continued unabated.

For displaced persons who arrived in Khartoum before 1991 and who held valid marriage certificates and national identity cards, this was a very positive policy shift. Nevertheless, large numbers of displaced South Sudanese were excluded by these same legal requirements. According to our survey, 52 per cent of the 399 households included in this analysis claimed title to the land on which their homes were built, most having taken advantage of this 1998 policy shift. Nevertheless, 39 per cent of the Nuer households and 27 per cent of the Dinka households sampled were ineligible to apply for plot assignments simply because they had reached Khartoum 'too late'. Other families could not pay the rapidly escalating fees (and bribes) required or lacked the necessary documents.

On the positive side, this shift in government policy helped administrators to devise more rational urban plans than was previously possible. However, it also enhanced possibilities for diluting and scattering resident-based pockets of southern dissent in preparation for future elections and referendums. However motivated, this policy change certainly spurred international donors into reassessing their 'emergency-aid-only' policies and to reconsider the possibility of providing 'development assistance' to Sudan. After 11 September 2001, the US government has taken the lead in this reassessment, which necessarily entails a weakening of the priority claims on 'emergency aid' currently enjoyed by displaced populations in Khartoum.

Conclusion

This chapter has sketched many of the hardships and humiliations Dinka and Nuer civilians have endured during nearly twenty-one years of unrelenting civil war. The social and economic devastation experienced by Nuer and Dinka civilians living deep within the southern war-zone was magnified, as we have seen, by a brutal surge in South-on-South violence during the 1991–2001 period. This fratricidal violence provoked not only the rapid polarisation and militarisation of Nuer and Dinka ethnic identities but, even more tragically, the collapse of former restraints on the killing of unarmed women, children and elderly persons by both groups. Violence in this region thus simultaneously sharpened ethnic divisions and dulled gender and age distinctions for Nuer and Dinka combatants. In contrast, those Dinka and Nuer who fled North faced a full-scale, frontal assault on their cultural traditions and identities from an oil-flush government determined to ensure its vision of a unified Islamic state takes precedence over the extraordinary cultural and religious diversity of Sudan's 33 million citizens. Confronted with the unchecked predations of government and SPLA troops in the South and with the government's brutal suppression of the informal economy in the North, Nuer and Dinka civilians in both regions were reduced to previously unimaginable states of poverty. Intermittent and ineffectual aid disbursements by the international community did little to stop this slide into economic destitution.

Women, children and the elderly have suffered most intensely in both geographical contexts. With respect to the elderly, Nuer and Dinka civilians in the South as well as the North reported a significant erosion of the authority and status formerly enjoyed by the older generation during the course of this war. Young SPLA soldiers, for example, evinced little interest in the accumulated knowledge of a senior generation that had tried but failed to liberate the South from Northern domination during Sudan's first civil war (1955–1972). Nor was this knowledge a suitable guide for younger Nuer and Dinka men and women struggling with government bureaucracies or seeking a viable livelihood in the urban jungles of Khartoum.

Faced all too often with parental abandonment or inadequate protection and support, thousands of displaced Southern Sudanese children retreated to the streets, where they leaned on one another as well as on glue and other toxic substances to dull their fears and pains. Even displaced children who remained at home were not safe. For the risks of violent police raids, forced prostitution, kidnappings and theft were omnipresent – risks that made parent/child bonds of authority especially tenuous. As one displaced Dinka woman explained: 'When your child sees you running [from the police], he cannot respect you.'

We have further seen how there has been a progressive 'feminisation' of poverty in both contexts. Southern Dinka and Nuer women were handicapped both by heavily unbalanced sex and dependency ratios and by a hyper-masculinised military sub-culture that glorified the naked power of guns. Contracting employment opportunities and discriminatory administrative policies also produced insecure and overcrowded households in the North, where women were frequently forced to take primary responsibility for provisioning their families. Although many displaced Dinka and Nuer men in the North worked hard to support their families, few succeeded in fulfilling the expectations of their wives and children for effective protection and adequate financial support. In Khartoum, men's protective powers and responsibilities toward women and children were completely undercut. For displaced men were incapable of defending themselves – let alone their wives and children – from the destructive impact of government bulldozers or from the ever-present risks of arrest, robbery, forced conscription, physical abuse and imprisonment at the hands of the police. Some displaced men and women sought solace in alcohol and/or vented their frustrations through domestic violence. Gender relations in the South were similarly marred by rising rates of alcoholism, sexual abuse and domestic violence. However, rural Dinka and Nuer women in the South continued to depend daily on men's protective powers, however insufficient such protection sometimes proved in the face of intensifying attacks from government bombers and helicopter gun-ships.

The magnitude of displacement, destruction and death experienced by Nuer and Dinka civilians during the present war far exceeds anything experienced by them during Sudan's first civil war (1955–1972). Considering how far the day-to-day realities of these two population sets have drifted apart over the past twenty-one years, the successful reintegration of Nuer and Dinka civilians located in the North and the South will present major difficulties when this war ends.

Notes

1   This chapter draws on two bodies of ethnographic material. Information on conditions in the South was gathered during more than two years of intensive fieldwork carried

out in Nuer communities since 1980, with my most recent field trips having taken place during the 1998–2000 period. Since 1998, I have co-operated with Dr Jok Madut Jok, a fellow anthropologist and native Dinka speaker, in a joint field project on the militarisation of rural Nuer and Dinka community life. Our joint field projects have been generously funded by two grants from the Harry F. Guggenheim Foundation, for which we are deeply grateful. As a result of our continuing collaboration, I am confident that conclusions drawn in this chapter about contemporary conditions among contemporary Nuer groups in the Western Upper Nile are relevant to Dinka group in the Bahr-el-Ghazal as well. The other body of ethnographic materials on which this chapter draws grew out of another collaborative research project carried out among displaced South Sudanese civilians in Khartoum during 1998–1999. This project was funded by Save the Children – Denmark and Channel Research Ltd, and was undertaken in co-operation with Jeremy Loveless and Dr Paul Wani. Although I have said nothing about the numerous hardships I faced while carrying out wartime field research, I hope that readers will take such difficulties into account when assessing the results.

References

Abdel Salam, A.H and Waal, Alex (eds) 2001. *The Phoenix State: Civil Society and the Future of Sudan*, Lawrenceville, N.J.: Red Sea Press, Inc.

Alier, A. 1991. *Southern Sudan: Too Many Agreements Dishonoured*, Exeter: Ithaca Press.

Amnesty International 2000. *Sudan: The Human Price of Oil*, London: Amnesty International Press.

Burr, J.M. and Collins, R.O. 1995. *Requiem for Sudan: War Drought and Disaster Relief on the Nile*, Boulder, Colo.: Westview Press.

Daly, M.W. and Sikanga, Ahmad Alawad (eds) 1993. *Civil War in the Sudan*, London: British Academic Press.

Deng, F.M. 1995. *War of Visions*, Washington, D.C.: Brookings Institute.

Enloe, C. 1995. 'Feminism, nationalism and militarism: wariness without paralysis?', in C. Sutton (ed.) *Feminism, Nationalism and Militarism*, Washington, D.C.: Association of Feminist Anthropology and the American Anthropological Association.

Gagnon, G. and Ryle, J. 2001. 'Report of an investigation into oil development, conflict and displacement in Western Upper Nile, Sudan', commissioned by Canadian Auto Workers Union, Steelworkers Humanity Fund, The Simons Foundation, United Church of Canada, Division of World Outreach, World Vision Canada (<http://www.crimesofwar.org/sudan-mag/sudanlinks.html>).

Harir, Sharif and Tvedt, T. (eds) 1994. *Short-Cut to Decay: The Case of Sudan*, Uppsala: Nordiska Afrikainstitutet.

Harker, J. 2000. *Human Security in Sudan: The Report of A Canadian Assessment Mission*, Ottawa: Ministry of Foreign Affairs.

Human Rights Watch 1999. *Famine in Sudan, 1998: The Human Rights Causes*, New York: Human Rights Watch.

—— 2002. *Sudan, Oil and Human Rights*, New York: Human Rights Watch.

Hutchinson, S.E. 1996. *Nuer Dilemmas: Coping With Money, War and the State*, Berkeley, Calif.: University of California Press.

—— 1998. 'Death, memory and the politics of legitimation: Nuer experiences of the continuing second Sudanese Civil War', in R. Werbner (ed.) *Memory and the Postcolony: African Anthropology and the Critique of Power*, London: Zed Books.

—— 2000. 'Nuer ethnicity militarized', *Anthropology Today* 16(3): 6–13.

—— 2004. 'Spiritual fragments of an unfinished war', in N. Kastfeld (ed.) *Religion in African Civil Wars*, London: C. Hurst.

Hutchinson, S.E and Jok, J. 2002. 'Gendered violence and the militarization of ethnicity: a case study from South Sudan', in R. Werbner (ed.) *Postcolonial Subjectivities in Africa*, New York and London: Zed Books.

International Crisis Group 2002. *God, Oil and Country: Changing the Logic of War in Sudan*, Brussels: International Crisis Group (<http://www.crisisweb.org/projects/showreport.cfm?reportid=534>).

Johnson, D. 1998. 'The Sudan People's Liberation Army and the problem of factionalism', in C. Clapham (ed.) *African Guerrillas*, London: James Currey.

—— 2001. 'The Nuer Civil War', in Maj-Britt Johannsen and Niels Kastfelt (eds) *Sudanese Society in the Context of Civil War*, Copenhagen: University of Copenhagen – North–South Priority Research Area.

—— 2003. *The Root Causes of Sudan's Civil Wars*, Oxford: The International African Institute (in association with James Currey, Indiana University Press and Fountain Publishers).

Jok, J.M. 1998. *Militarization, Gender, and Reproductive Health in South Sudan*, Lewiston, N.Y.: Edwin Mellen Press.

Jok, J.M. and Hutchinson, S.E. 1999. 'Sudan's prolonged second Civil War and the militarization of Nuer and Dinka ethnic identities', *African Studies Review* 42(2): 125–145.

Kok, P.N. 1992. 'Adding fuel to the conflict: oil, water, and peace in Sudan', in M. Doornbos, L. Cliffe, A. Ghaffar M. Ahmed and J. Markakis (eds) *Beyond Conflict in the Horn: Prospects for Peace, Recovery, and Development in Ethiopia and the Sudan*, The Hague: Institute of Social Studies in association with James Currey.

Nyaba, P.A. 1997. *The Politics of Liberation in South Sudan: An Insider's View*, Kampala: Fountain Publishers.

Prendergast, J. 1997. *Crisis Response: Humanitarian Band-Aids in Sudan and Somalia*, Chicago and Washington, D.C.: Pluto Press with Center of Concern.

Ruay, D.A. 1994. *The Politics of Two Sudans: The South and the North*, Uppsala: Nordiska Afrikainstitutet.

Chapter 8

The politics of identity and the remembrance of violence

Ethnicity and gender at the installation of a female chief in Zimbabwe

Björn Lindgren

In December 1996, Miss Sinqobile Mabhena was installed as chief to rule over the Nswazi area of Umzingwane district in Matabeleland South. Twenty-three years old and the eldest of four sisters, Sinqobile Mabhena was the first female Ndebele chief in Zimbabwe. In 1995, she had been appointed by President Robert Mugabe to succeed her late father Howard Mabhena as chief, but her installation had been postponed for over a year because of protests from other chiefs in Matabeleland. When her installation finally took place, it caused a public outcry, and it was debated by intellectuals in the Bulawayo-based newspapers the *Chronicle* and the *Sunday News*. The appointment of a woman as chief was against Ndebele culture and tradition, the critics argued. It was unheard of for a woman to rule men.

Reactions to this installation may be described as a politics of identity in which people enacted various identities in order to control the office as chief. Of these identities, the most apparent were those built on ethnicity, gender and kinship. Having dealt briefly with gender (male and female identities) and kinship (succession rules) elsewhere (Lindgren 2001), I focus in this chapter on ethnicity and gender. In this setting, the politics of identity implies a certain degree of agency; actors used, negotiated and changed social identities. Identities are not, however, constructed *ex nihilo*. If identities are situational, as the critique of situational analysis claims, then these identities and the situations in which they are used must themselves be situated (e.g. Verdery 1996: 36).

There are two complementary ways to put the politics of identity into context. You may situate the use of identities either temporally, that is historically or in relation to the future, or spatially, for instance with reference to transforming structures. In this chapter, I try to put ethnicity into context historically by referring to pre-colonial, colonial and, not least, post-colonial political processes. I suggest that the installation of Sinqobile Mabhena triggered the enactment of ethnic identity due to the recent past of the young nation state Zimbabwe, especially the atrocities perpetrated by the Fifth Brigade in Matabeleland in the middle of the 1980s. In a succession crisis, the social conflict created by the installation of a female chief was thus strongly influenced by a previous armed conflict.

At the same time, however, the installation of Sinqobile Mabhena also led to the enactment of a dominant form of male identity, which may remind us of the risk of focusing on ethnic identity at the expense of other social identities. Although the use, negotiation and change of male and female identities are also historically formed, I here put the use of these identities into context more structurally. Drawing on the works of Robert Connell (1987, 1995 and 2000), I suggest that the installation of Sinqobile Mabhena challenged the gender order in Matabeleland and the gender regime of the traditional leadership system, and that it threatened a male identity built on hegemonic masculinity. Many of her critics' acts and words could be read as a defence of this order, regime and identity, while the people in Nswazi and elsewhere who supported Sinqobile Mabhena continued to challenge them.

In the following, I first briefly describe how subjects were formed as Ndebele in pre-colonial times, and how the category Ndebele is related to various categories of origin. Thereafter, I put Chief Sinqobile Mabhena and the Nswazi chieftaincy on the map, historically and geographically, before turning to how the British colonial administration and the independent Zanu-PF government have formed subjects as Ndebele in new and different ways. I then describe the events leading to the installation of Sinqobile Mabhena as chief, including the protests put forward by chiefs and intellectuals in meetings and the media, after which I describe and analyse these protests as expressions of ethnic identity vis-à-vis the president, the government and the 'Shona'.

In the next section, I outline the gender order in Matabeleland and the gender regime of the traditional leadership system, and how, as an anomaly, Sinqobile Mabhena, challenged this order and regime. I address the chiefs' and intellectuals' protests against the installation as a politics of identity, but this time interpreted in terms of how the actors enacted male identity in order to defend existing gender relations. Thereafter I discuss the theme of bravery as an ingredient in the protests and how it was used both ethnically vis-à-vis the Shona and in gendered terms vis-à-vis women. I then describe the counter-critique put forward by people in Nswazi and how this critique transforms the gender order and regime. In conclusion, I sum up my findings and suggestions with reference to the need for studying ethnicity in relation to other identities as constructed, situated and subject to change, while at the same time putting these identities into a broader context.

The construction of Ndebele ethnicity and origins

There has been some debate whether ethnicities in southern Africa are colonial constructs or not. Terence Ranger has argued that Ndebele and Shona ethnicities were 'invented' (Ranger 1985) or 'imagined' (Ranger 1993, 1994) during colonialism, first by Europeans and then by Africans (see, e.g., Ranger 1999: 99ff.). Carolyn Hamilton (1998) has taken another stance regarding Zulu ethnicity, however, seeing it as a longer process in which indigenous people have been active agents from the beginning. While Ranger's emphasis is on the difference between the Ndebele, the colonial and the Zimbabwean states, and the way these states have influenced how people categorise themselves and others, Hamilton (1998) wants to draw our attention to 'the limits of historical invention' by, if I may borrow a phrase from Marshall Sahlins (1999: 408), focusing on the 'inventiveness of tradition' rather than the 'invention of tradition'.

There are indeed differences between the Ndebele pre-colonial state, the British colonial state and the Zimbabwean post-colonial state, and also in how the elites within these states have formed subjects as Ndebele, but this formation has nevertheless occurred during all three periods with 'Africans', that is indigenous people, as active agents. The formation of Ndebele subjects was first carried out during the pre-colonial period (e.g., Cobbing 1976), and then, in various ways, during the colonial and post-colonial periods. From this perspective, the construction of Ndebele ethnicity began during Mzilikazi Khumalo's pre-colonial 'migrant kingdom' (Rasmussen 1978) in the nineteenth century. It was heavily re-constructed after the collapse of the Ndebele state in 1893, as Terence Ranger (e.g., 1985, 1993 and 1999) has convincingly shown, and again after independence in 1980, which Richard Werbner (e.g., 1991, 1995 and 1998) has described in terms of 'quasi-nationalism'.

Although historians differ in their representations of the Ndebele past, I will here give a short account of Ndebele origins. Mzilikazi Khumalo left Shaka Zulu's kingdom in eastern South Africa with a small group of Nguni-speaking people around 1820, and migrated west over the Drakensberg into northern South Africa and later north over eastern Botswana into south-western Zimbabwe (I refer here to the modern names of states). Like Shaka, Mzilikazi built a strong military state; during this migration, Nguni-speakers, Sotho-speakers and what today are referred to as Shona-speakers either followed Mzilikazi voluntarily or were incorporated into the Ndebele state as captives. The reason for this migration is debated. Some emphasise the Portuguese colonisation of Mozambique and the British colonisation of the Cape as underlying causes (see, e.g., Cobbing 1988, Wright 1995); others stress Shaka Zulu's expanding kingdom and internal politics as the main cause (e.g., Omer-Cooper 1966 and 1993).

John Comaroff (1987) has suggested that both totemism and ethnicity are ways to classify oneself collectively in relation to others, but while totemism only draws on cultural differences, ethnicity also draws on unequal relationships. Both those who followed Mzilikazi from the beginning and those who were incorporated later spoke different languages and came from various totemic 'clans'. However, with time these people were recognised as a 'people', both by themselves and by others. The name 'Ndebele' was probably given to them during the migration north by Sotho-speaking people who called them *Matebele* (Hughes and van Velsen 1954: 42), which in Nguni became *amaNdebele*. In early missionary writings they are referred to as *Matabele* (e.g., Moffat [1835] 1940, Livingstone 1857). These people, the Ndebele, were bound together in a state with Nguni leadership, language and customs as the norm, and, from 1840, by the territory called 'Matabeleland' in today's southern Zimbabwe.

From the beginning, however, the Ndebele were not only a heterogeneous but also a highly stratified people, leading to the establishment of a hierarchy of belonging among themselves. According to Comaroff (1987), ethnicity has its origins in just this kind of asymmetric incorporation of dissimilar groupings into a single political economy, regardless of whether this happened in pre-capitalist Africa or during the colonial era (see also Comaroff 1991, 1995). The Nguni-speakers who joined Mzilikazi from emerging Zululand were accepted as more or less equal, but Sotho-speakers who were incorporated later on formed a second stratum, and various 'Shona'-speakers, who were incorporated still later, formed a third grouping. These three castes, as A.J.B. Hughes (1956: 53ff.) terms them, came to be known as Zanzi (*abeZanzi*), Enhla (*abEnhla*) and Lozwi (*abaLozwi*) or, pejoratively, Holi (*amaHoli*, 'slaves'), and are still recognised in Matabeleland today. Although people of Nguni origin often are regarded as 'pure' Ndebele, people of Shona origin are not (Lindgren 2004).

The construction of Ndebele ethnicity and various categories of origin began through the asymmetric incorporation of dissimilar groupings into a pre-colonial politico-economic system and into the Ndebele state. Very superficially described, this system involved political alliances established through marriage and with cattle as an important measure of wealth (see Kuper 1982). Colonialists may have indirectly influenced the politico-economic landscape and thereby the migration from emerging Zululand, but it would take until 1893 before British colonialists introduced British law and a market economy (which to a great degree, but far from entirely, has also today replaced cattle with money). From then on, not only indigenous people, but also Europeans were directly involved as actors in a continuous construction and re-construction of Ndebele ethnicity.

Chief Mabhena and the Nswazi chieftaincy

Sinqobile Mabhena, her family and the people living within her chieftaincy, Nswazi, are part of these pre-colonial, colonial and post-colonial political processes. The Mabhena settled at Umzingwane river together with one of Mzilikazi Khumalo's regiments, the *amatshetshe* regiment. This regiment (*ibutho*) was led by the Masuku. However, the area in which the *amatshetshe* regiment settled became too vast to rule. In 1910, Ndamoya Mabhena was asked to take over the Nswazi part of it as the first Mabhena chief.[1] Although Umzingwane and Nswazi belonged to the Ndebele inner state (Cobbing 1976), its inhabitants were of various origins. While some were 'Nguni' or 'Sotho', many were 'Shona' (especially 'Karanga' and 'Kalanga') who had inhabited the land long before the Ndebele arrived.

Today, Umzingwane is a district in Matabeleland South, which is one of Zimbabwe's eight provinces. The district has a population of 65,000 inhabitants, including Nswazi which has about 10,000 people (Census 1992). Apart from Ndebele-speakers of various origin, such as Nguni, Sotho, Tswana, Venda, Karanga or Kalanga, there are also 'Whites', 'Malawians' and other people living in the district. The 'Whites' are often referred to as *amakiwa* or *abalungu*, and many of them are of British or Greek descent. The district is administratively divided into wards, which in turn are divided into a number of villages. These villages may consist of over a hundred homesteads (*umuzi*, pl. *imizi*) spread over rather large areas with maize fields, bush and small mountains between them. The Mabhena chieftaincy, Nswazi, follows the borders of wards six and seven, which contain five and four villages, respectively

In rural Matabeleland today, political power is held in two different leadership systems: the 'traditional' leadership system and the post-colonial leadership system. The traditional system of three hierarchically ordered levels consists almost exclusively of male leaders, who all inherit their positions: the chief (*induna*), the headman (*umlisa*) and the kraal head (*usobhuku*). The post-colonial leadership consists of elected, predominately male, councillors at ward level. At district level, the systems overlap, since both chiefs and councillors sit in the district council.

Until recently, chiefs were above all responsible for 'traditional' matters, while elected politicians were to deal with development (Chiefs and Headmen Act 1982). However, this has never worked in practice, and chiefs and other traditional leaders have also been involved in the construction of dams, roads and schools. As a consequence, a new Act has given traditional leaders more political power than before (Traditional Leaders Act 1998, implemented 1 January 2000). One of the key issues addressed in this act is the right to distribute land. Until recently, the councillors have been responsible for the allocation of land, but due to corruption and other problems chiefs and other traditional leaders are now to assume part of this task. The position of chief, already an important political post, has thus been vested with more power.

Situating the installation: reconstruction of Ndebele ethnicity

When the British administration took over the Ndebele kingdom after having defeated it in 1893 and then putting down a rebellion in 1896–1897, they formed subjects as Ndebele by equating them with the 'Zulu', and distinguishing them from the 'Shona' (e.g. Ranger 1985). In rural Matabeleland, the British practised indirect rule by using chiefs and other traditional leaders as subordinate authorities, both during the time of Cecil Rhodes' British South African Company and after Southern Rhodesia became a British colony in 1923 (Hughes 1956). These chiefs were mainly Nguni, as they in the opinion of many of the administrators should be. When administrators removed unruly chiefs and appointed new ones, they chose men of Nguni origin. Some British administrators even tried to establish 'Ndebele' laws based on 'Zulu' laws from the Natal Code of 1891 (Ranger 1999: 101).

In the 1960s, Ndebele ethnicity became more strongly connected to Zimbabwean nationalism. Joshua Nkomo was central to this process as, in Terence Ranger's (1993: 98) words, a 'culture-broker'. He was 'Kalanga' by birth, was regarded as a Ndebele leader, and worked to liberate the country from colonial rule. There were, however, also other national movements rising in Southern Rhodesia. In 1965, when Ian Smith declared Rhodesia an independent state, the liberation movement was carried out on two fronts. Joshua Nkomo's Zapu (with its military wing Zipra) which was established in 1961 had now split into two movements, the other led by Robert Mugabe and named Zanu (with its armed forced Zanla).[2]

In the same way that people's identities were open to question after the collapse of the Ndebele state in 1893 and 1896 (Ranger 1999: 99f.), we may perceive the period after independence in 1980 as a period in which people's identities were, and still are, open to question. But the political struggles between Robert Mugabe and Joshua Nkomo, between Zanu and Zapu, and between Zanla and Zipra turned the politics of identity in a specific direction. With voting following ethnic and regional lines, Robert Mugabe and Zanu-PF won overwhelmingly in the elections of 1980 (Cliffe *et al.* 1980). Soon thereafter, Mugabe and the government started to blame Joshua Nkomo and Zapu for 'dissident' activities, including attacks on state institutions and the murder of White farmers.

At this stage, Mugabe and the Zanu-PF government could have built on national unity rather than on ethnic difference, and sent a peace-keeping national army to Matabeleland composed of ex-Zanla, ex-Zipra and ex-Rhodesian soldiers. Instead, they created the infamous Fifth Brigade, consisting of Shona-speaking ex-Zanla soldiers, whom they sent to Matabeleland in 1983 and 1984 with the order to 'plough and reconstruct' (Alexander 1998: 158). They did this by torturing, raping and killing not dissidents, who were very few in number, but Zapu officials, ex-Zipra guerrillas, and other, mainly Ndebele-speaking, civilians (see, e.g., CCJP/LRF 1997, Alexander *et al.* 2000, and Yap 2001).

As a result, people in Matabeleland responded by accusing Mugabe, the government and the 'Shona' in general of killing Ndebele. That is, the period after independence, and especially the atrocities carried out by the Fifth Brigade, heightened the victims' awareness of being Ndebele at the cost of being Zimbabwean (or, for that matter, of being of Nguni or any other origin). Further, since the publication in 1997 of the Catholic Commission for Justice and Peace's report on the atrocities (CCJP/LRF 1997), the discourse on the Fifth Brigade's violence has been publicly voiced in Zimbabwe to new generations of Zimbabweans, which has both strengthened and spread feelings of Ndebeleness in southern Zimbabwe.

Meetings and media: the installation of Sinqobile Mabhena

Originally, Sinqobile Mabhena was supposed to have been installed as chief in 1995, but due to protests from other chiefs the installation was postponed for over a year. The former chief, Howard, died in September 1993, and the Mabhena family recommended Sinqobile as his successor to the D.A. (District Administrator) in August 1994. After formal enquiries, the D.A. forwarded this recommendation to the P.A. (Provincial Administrator) in June 1995. The president approved the recommendation the same month, and the official installation was scheduled to be held in November 1995.

A few weeks before the scheduled installation the chiefs protested. A meeting was held at which chiefs Nyangazonke Ndiweni and Veza Maduna said that in 'the Nguni sub-tribe', to which they ascribed the Mabhena clan, there is no history of a female chief. The two chiefs argued that, instead of Sinqobile, her grandfather's younger half-brothers, all born to different mothers, should have been considered for the chieftaincy. Chief Augustin Masuku, whose forefather left Nswazi for Gwanda after handing over Nswazi to the first Mabhena chief in 1910, also expressed his disappointment over how the situation had been handled. The meeting concluded that the Mabhena family should discuss the matter with Chief Masuku and that Sinqobile should be suspended until they had agreed upon a successor.[3]

However, the D.A. never suspended Sinqobile. 'I don't get instructions from meetings,' he explained. 'I get instructions from the Minister of Local Government, comrade [John] Nkomo, through the secretary, through the Provincial Administrator. So I refused.'[4] But, despite letters to his superiors, the D.A. did not get instructions on how to proceed. The core of the Mabhena family then formed a committee and wrote to the D.A., stating that they still regarded Sinqobile as the rightful successor and that the chiefs were 'talking against the people'.[5] Included in this core were Howard's father and Sinqobile's grandfather, Makheyi Mabhena, who had lost his position as chief during the colonial period because of misappropriation of public funds. Makheyi felt too old to take up the position of chief again, even if allowed to do so, and strongly supported the appointment of his granddaughter as chief rather than letting one of his half-brothers take over the position.

In May 1996, the chiefs held a second meeting in Nswazi with some members of the Mabhena family. This meeting, which included chiefs Khayisa Ndiweni, Nyangazonke Ndiweni, Veza Maduna and Augustin Masuku, agreed that Sinqobile's grandfather's half-brothers Anderson Mabhena and Kefazi Mabhena were the next in line of succession. Since the Mabhena committee was excluded from the meeting, they wrote a letter directly to the minister and complained about the interference of the chiefs. The committee also contacted the press and an article was published in the *Chronicle* on 16 May 1996. After this, the *Chronicle* and the *Sunday News* carried several articles on the subject, including one in which the local Zanu-PF women's league supported Sinqobile as chief (*Sunday News*, 30 June 1996a).[6]

Finally, Minister John Nkomo decided the issue after three meetings with the chiefs and the Mabhena committee in November 1996. Although Chief Nyangazonke Ndiweni walked out in the middle of one of these meetings and many of the other chiefs were upset, it was decided that Sinqobile Mabhena was to be installed as chief on 21 December 1996. After this, some thought that the public debate had come to an end; however, the discussions were intensified and chiefs and intellectuals protested louder than ever, both by their actions and in the daily press (including a public debate on the issue held in City Hall in Bulawayo, see the *Chronicle*, 1 March 1997 and 12 March 1997).

Chief Khayisa Ndiweni, the most senior chief in Matabeleland, and chiefs Nyangazonke Ndiweni and Veza Maduna stood by their earlier claim that it is against 'Ndebele culture and tradition' to have a woman as chief and did not attend the installation ceremony (*Chronicle*, 27 December 1996, *Sunday News*, 22 December 1996). Governor Welshman Mabhena of Matabeleland North argued that the case might be taken to High Court, adding that: 'As Ndebeles we are not going to allow our culture to be abused by anyone. Whatever has so far taken place is a mockery of our culture, which we will fight to the bitter end' (*Sunday News*, 19 January 1997). And secretary-general Agrippa Ngwenya of the Vukani Mahlabezulu Cultural Society wanted to nullify the installation since it was carried out despite objections by 'Ndebele traditional leaders' (*Sunday News*, 26 January 1997).

Memories and ethnicity: blaming the government

Many of the chiefs and intellectuals who opposed Sinqobile Mabhena as chief were not only critical towards the Mabhena family for choosing a woman as chief within the ruling lineage of the family, they also blamed President Robert Mugabe, the Zanu-PF government and the 'Shona' for imposing a female chief upon them. In Umzingwane district, 'traditional' leaders are regarded as *Ndebele* leaders, in contrast to elected politicians, who have often been seen as representatives of Mugabe's 'Shona'-based Zanu-PF party. This has especially been the case after the Fifth Brigade's atrocities led to the dissolution of Joshua Nkomo's 'Ndebele'-based Zapu party in 1987, and before Morgan Tsvangirai and the opposition party MDC (Movement for Democratic Change) entered the political scene in the parliamentary elections of 2000.

Since independence in 1980, many people in Matabeleland have felt that they have been prevented from participating in Zimbabwe's nation-building project, and the Fifth Brigade's atrocities are often cited as the ultimate proof of this. Memories of these atrocities are a strong undercurrent in Ndebele ethnicity today, and they certainly influenced the way in which some reacted to the installation of Sinqobile Mabhena as chief. In these people's eyes, the central Zanu-PF government had yet again decided issues that were regarded as strictly local, and in response they argued that 'Ndebele culture and tradition' had been violated.

Although traditional leaders such as chiefs may be superior to politicians locally, they are subordinated to them nationally. When a chiefly family has made their choice of successor, their recommendation is taken upwards in the state bureaucracy, first to the District Administrator, then to the Provincial Administrator, then to the Minister of Local Government, and finally to the President, who officially appoints the chief. The critics claimed that at one point or another during this process, senior chiefs should have been consulted about the appropriateness of appointing Sinqobile Mabhena as chief (see, e.g., Welshman Mabhena in the *Sunday News*, 19 January 1997, Agrippa Ngwenya in the *Sunday News*, 26 January 1997, and Pathisa Nyathi in the *Sunday News*, 30 June 1996b).

Chief Khayisa Ndiweni, for instance, blamed the Zanu-PF government, and the Shona in general, for imposing a female chief upon the Ndebele.

> I have been chief since 1941. This has not happened before. It is not within our custom at all. The politicians want her to be chief. Just to make the Ndebele unhappy. I am talking about the people of Mzilikazi. We have our own rules which should not be broken by the government. There is a house of chiefs in this country. Ten of us are in Parliament. If there is something which goes against tradition, we discuss it. Why did they by-pass the house of chiefs? This was done purposely by the present government. Why is it done in Matabeleland when it is not done in Mashonaland? It is not done in Manicaland. We know it is a defeat of the Ndebele people by the Shona people.[7]

President Mugabe and the customary principles of succession

The legal argument the critics cited to justify the chiefs' interference in the installation of Sinqobile Mabhena is found in the Chiefs and Headmen Act of 1982. According to this Act, 'The president shall appoint chiefs to preside over communities'; however, when doing so 'the President shall give due consideration to the customary principles of succession, if any, applicable to the community over which such chief is to preside' (Chiefs and Headmen Act 1982, 3: 1, 2, repeated in the Traditional Leaders Act 1998, 3: 1, 2, which replaces the former). The critics claimed that such consideration should have been taken regardless of whether you favour or disfavour a female chief. Agrippa Ngwenya, for instance, held that:

> It is not a matter of what I think, but of what culture says. It is taboo that a woman becomes a chief in our culture. Let's suppose she gets married to a Shona man. That means that the chieftainship would be removed from the Mabhenas and transferred . . . to another tribe. But here we are. A woman chief has been imposed against our culture.[8]

And Pathisa Nyathi, a locally renowned Ndebele historian, held:

> The tradition according to which the chief is appointed must be stated. Ndebele tradition is very clear on that, whether it is progressive or counter-progressive is neither here, nor there. It is always a male line, and even then it is not smooth. There are contentions because the seniority of houses differs.[9]

Khayisa Ndiweni's, Agrippa Ngwenya's, and Pathisa Nyathi's protests, among others, are understandable if one takes into consideration their memories of how then Prime Minister Robert Mugabe and the Zanu-PF government ordered the Shona-speaking ex-Zanla soldiers of the Fifth Brigade to 'plough and reconstruct' in Matabeleland. For instance, E.D., a farmer in his fifties, explained: 'If it was a war between the government and the dissidents, they shouldn't have sent the *gukura* [Fifth Brigade] to kill everyone.' His grown-up daughter added: 'The *gukurahundi* wasn't a dissident war. It was a war between the Shona and the Ndebele.'[10] Such views are often also expressed in relation to the unity accord of 1987 when Zapu was dissolved, as M.N., an elderly teacher, said about Nkomo's signing of the accord: 'It was a good thing, because if he hadn't done it we would not have been living. He knew his people were suffering, that they were eliminated, that they were killed.'[11]

In the case of Sinqobile Mabhena, both President Mugabe and the Zanu-PF government, as well as the 'Shona' in general, were seen to be making decisions over the heads of the Ndebele without regard to what Ndebele spokespersons said or did. From the critics' point of view, the President did not 'give due consideration to the customary principles of succession', and when Ndebele chiefs and intellectuals tried to put things straight in meetings and the media they were ignored. The argument that it is 'against Ndebele culture and tradition' to have a female chief was in this context directed towards the politicians' decision and the administrators' work to appoint and install her. However, the installation of Sinqobile Mabhena also challenged the established gender order in Matabeleland.

Challenging the gender order: Chief Mabhena as an anomaly

Shortly after Sinqobile Mabhena was installed as chief, her subjects Phineas, Jairos and Lavert Dube jokingly claimed that the dictionaries must now be rewritten. Linguistically, the term *induna* is connected to maleness and men. The adjective *duna* means male; the prefix *in* turns it into the noun 'chief, officer, captain' (Pelling 1971). As a chief, they explained, Sinqobile Mabhena is an anomaly, something that does not fit the linguistic categories in *isiNdebele*. A new word with the feminine suffix *-kazi* has therefore to be added to the dictionaries: *indunakazi*, meaning female chief.[12]

Likewise, the installation ceremony is structured to install a man as chief, and the chief's regalia are meant for a man. This is in accordance with the belief in ancestral spirits in which the paternal line of chiefly spirits is of importance for the whole community. At the installation ceremony, Sinqobile Mabhena wore, as her predecessors had, the skin of a leopard around her waist, but, as a woman, in addition to this she wore a bra. She also received the usual regalia from the government: a British colonial-style helmet, a red robe and a knobkerrie. However, women do not wear helmets, and at public meetings Sinqobile wears a scarf around her head, as married women do, together with the red robe and the knobkerrie.

The installation of Sinqobile Mabhena as chief challenged the gender order in Matabeleland in general, and the gender regime of the traditional leadership system in particular. If we apply the theoretical framework of Robert Connell (1987, 1995 and 2000) to the conditions in southern Zimbabwe, we may focus on the three structures of power, 'marriage', and labour when studying this order and regime. These structures are far from static, but transform according to people's acts. In the debate about Chief Mabhena as a female chief, some defended this order, and thereby the privileges of men embedded in it, while others challenged and thereby changed it.

As stated, political power is held at various levels in two different leadership systems. Apart from Sinqobile Mabhena, all other traditional leaders in Umzingwane district and their advisors are men. Among the elected leaders, men occupy most, but not all, positions. The district has Mrs Khumalo as its representative in Parliament, and Mrs Harriet Sibanda is councillor in ward six. However, power is not just political power. Men also often dominate women in a rather unconscious way in everyday life. For instance, when a man greets a woman he places himself in a higher position, while she bows curtseys to him and avoids his gaze. If they are in a homestead, the man sits on a bench or a stool, while the woman sits on a goatskin or a mat placed on the floor or the ground. While some people explicitly explain this behaviour as expressing power relations, others do not. A typical example of the latter is the statement of Mrs Mloyi: 'I sit more comfortably on the ground,' she said. 'I have always done it and I'm used to it.'[13]

Power is also strongly interwoven with 'marriage', but not in the same way as in Connell's empirical studies in Australia, the United States and England. In general, people in Matabeleland follow a patrilineal principle regarding descent, succession and inheritance; the *isibongo* (the totem or clan name), social positions and property are reckoned and inherited in the male line. They also follow a patrilocal principle regarding residence; a new couple moves to the husband's and his male relatives' area of living. These two principles support each other in that goods inherited from father to son include cattle, which together with money is used for *lobola* (bride wealth) in exchange for one or several wives and the children they bear. In addition to this, men and women may have extramarital relationships. However, while it is more or less accepted that men have lovers, if women are discovered to have lovers they are usually condemned.

Power and marriage also often go hand in hand with the division of labour in the rural areas. Men or boys herd cattle and goats while women take care of children. Men slaughter cows, women slaughter chickens. Both men and women farm, but women prepare, cook and serve food. When eating within the family, men and women often sit apart, again with men on stools and women on the floor. Men may collect firewood, but this is mainly a woman's task. She also collects water, washes clothes and does the dishes. Both men and women may attend public meetings, but there are almost always more men than women at such meetings. Men are also very over-represented at the local beer halls, where traditional as well as bottled beer is served. If anyone in the family works in 'town' (Bulawayo) or 'down south' (South Africa), it is most often a man.

With the gender order in Matabeleland and the gender regime of the traditional leadership in mind, it is not odd if the installation of Sinqobile Mabhena as chief upset people. How should one behave towards this *indunakazi*? As one would towards a chief or as one would towards a woman? Should one greet her as a superior or as an inferior? Should one eat with her, which is normally a great honour if the chief is a man, or should one refuse, since men normally do not eat with women, at least not in public settings? And what happens if she marries? Is she superior or inferior to her husband? And who will succeed her? In meetings, should one talk after her as her subject, or should one talk before her as a man? The installation of Sinqobile Mabhena as chief caused a lot of anxieties. It challenged the established gender order in Matabeleland, as well as a gender regime of a traditional leadership system totally controlled by men, and it brought deeply held values about a dominant form of male identity to the fore.

Hegemonic masculinity and the alleged bravery of men

When chief Khayisa Ndiweni and others argued that it is against 'Ndebele culture and tradition' to have a woman as chief, when Welshman Mabhena threatened to take the issue to High Court and when Agrippa Ngwenya wished to nullify the installation, this had not only to do with Ndebele ethnicity and relations to the Zanu-PF government, but also with gender relations and men's privileges. While chiefs and intellectuals enacted Ndebele ethnicity vis-à-vis the president, the government and the 'Shona' for political ends on the national level, they also enacted a dominant form of male identity for other political and personal ends on a more regional level: to defend the existing gender order in Matabeleland and the gender regime of the traditional leadership system.

The chiefs' and intellectuals' statements uphold something akin to what Robert Connell (1987: 183, 1995, 2000) refers to as 'hegemonic masculinity', which is defined with reference to 'Western' societies as a stylised ideal masculinity that is often made public in the media and does not necessarily correspond to actual behaviour of the majority of men. According to Connell, hegemonic masculinity is based on heterosexuality in connection to the institution of marriage. It is always constructed in contrast to subordinated femininities, as well as to various subordinated masculinities. Connell terms the world-wide most common femininity 'emphasised femininity' – a femininity which is adapted to men's power and is organised around compliance rather than resistance. Hegemonic masculinity and emphasised femininity are thus what many people support ideologically in different ways, although they are not necessarily what they themselves represent.

With some alterations, these concepts make sense in relation to the chiefs' and intellectuals' reactions to the installation of a woman as chief. The dominant form of male identity in Matabeleland may be perceived as built, on the one hand, on social interaction (structured by power, marriage and labour), and, on the other hand, on cultural values (in the form of hegemonic masculinity). This masculinity is based on the idea of a heterosexual 'marriage', but in this case following the principles of patrilineality, patrilocality and *lobola*. It is constructed in contrast to specific kinds of subordinated femininities, both 'emphasised' and 'resistant' (the former exemplified by Mrs Mloyi sitting comfortable on the ground, the latter by Sinqobile Mabhena herself), as well as in contrast to subordinated masculinities (related to, for instance, young unmarried men).

According to the critics, since men rule over women in politics, marriage and labour, and since chiefly succession follows the principles of patrilineality, patri- locality and *lobola*, a chief should thus be a man. Some critics also took up the issue of bravery, which often is discussed in connection to warfare in the past, both in indigenous literature (Lindgren 2002) and in memories of lived experience. This trait is ideologically ascribed by Ndebele men to themselves, often in contrast to Shona men. Chief Khayisa Ndiweni, for instance, referring to pre-colonial times, argued: 'I can't find any Shona man fighting a White man like a Ndebele'.[14] And Councillor Joti Ndlovu in the Nswazi chieftaincy referred to the liberation war and claimed: 'The Ndebele are so brave [in comparison to the Shona]. You could even see it in the [Shona-dominated] Zanla forces. They were fleeing, shooting backwards while they were running.'[15]

This bravery is ascribed to and allegedly only held by Ndebele men, and not by women (despite the participation of women in the liberation war). Some people have therefore argued that Sinqobile Mabhena would not be able to lead a war, which is a role they still ascribe to a chief. Others have analysed the situation along the same lines, but not in connection with warfare as such. 'A chief must not only be respected, it is a certain element of fear in it,' explained Mark Ncube. 'That's African culture. I can't be afraid of a woman. There is nothing legally wrong with it, but culturally it has certain implications.'[16] Here then, arguments based on ethnicity and gender are again put forward together, since Ndebele bravery is contrasted both to the 'Shona' as a feminised 'Other', and to Ndebele women, or, for that matter, to any woman.

However, in Nswazi many people defended their chief and in so doing contested the gender order and the gender regime, as well as hegemonic masculinity. They claimed either that culture had indeed been followed since Sinqobile Mabhena is the firstborn within the first 'house' (Lindgren 2001), or that culture changes, sometimes with reference to other female leaders such as ministers. Mrs. Harriet Sibanda, the councillor of ward six, argued for instance: 'I don't know exactly about our culture, but in my opinion it is a step forward. I see it as a good thing that women are promoted so they can show that they are capable of leading men.'[17] And Lavert Dube, one of the men who suggested that the dictionaries must be rewritten, said: 'It is a bit reactionary to scream at the top of the voice that she should not be chief because she is a woman. It is not progressive language. Being a chief is relatively easier than being a minister, so how can she fail?'[18]

Some people also referred to Sinqobile's education as a teacher and to equal rights between men and women to legitimise their new chief. 'Yes, I know it is against our culture,' said Mrs Ndlovu, 'but today we have equal rights, and we are now educated. Women could also have that position.'[19] Likewise: 'Our tradition is not fully practised,' explained Mrs Ngwenya. 'Long back it was not good to have a woman as chief, [but] the law has given women rights, so it's okay.'[20] And:

'We, the people of Nswazi, like that girl,' said Mr Ndlovu, an elderly teacher who also bears the rather common *isibongo* (totem or clan name) Ndlovu. 'We have had the Mabhenas. Men, men, men. Let's try her. Perhaps she will do better than the other Mabhenas.'[21]

And who's next? The never-ending question of succession

Although the debate about the installation of Sinqobile Mabhena as chief is not yet over, it seems that Sinqobile has control of the situation. 'Her name speaks,' as a neighbouring headman commented, referring to the meaning of the name Sinqobile: 'we have conquered.'[22] The issue has not yet been taken to High Court, or to any other court, and it is doubtful that it will be. The critics have already been dismissed by minister John Nkomo, and the Mabhena family as a whole, and the people of Nswazi in general, seem to support her. The only two within the Mabhena family who would be able to take the issue to court are the two proposed alternative chiefs, Sinqobile Mabhena's grandfather's two half-brothers: Anderson Mabhena and Kefazi Mabhena.

However, Anderson (who told me that Sinqobile was not supposed to have been chief, but that he didn't want to talk about it) is known as a cattle-rustler and would probably have difficulty being appointed chief.[23] And Kefazi seemed to be happy with how things had turned out: 'To me it is nothing wrong as we have decided she should take over, but her children cannot take over, just because the chieftainship belong to the Mabhena family.'[24] One solution to the recurrent question of who will succeed Sinqobile is that she be given a son from the Mabhena family as her firstborn. She could then marry whomever she wishes and have as many children she likes. In that case, both Anderson's and Kefazi's sons and grandsons may be considered.[25]

Who will succeed Sinqobile Mabhena is thus still an open question, but some people at least seem ready to have a second female chief in Nswazi. 'When she steps down, the Mabhenas will sit down and choose a boy within the family,' explained elderly kraal head Pahle Ndlovu, who then added: 'For myself, I see no problem if they choose another girl.'[26] Moreover, Sinqobile Mabhena is young, while Khayisa Ndiweni and other critics are old. Fifty years from now, things may appear very different, as Mabhena spokesperson Agrippa Ndlovu optimistically argued:

> Some people are still very bitter about it. That's why you see all these stories in the news papers, [but] in any revolutionary situation, once anything starts moving, it doesn't stop. You can't go against a revolution. You can't go the other way, it is like trying to swim against the tide. Once a revolution starts moving, it doesn't stop until it's finished.[27]

Indeed, in October 1997 Sinqobile Mabhena married Regiment Sibanda, a teacher in Nswazi, and in January 1998 she gave birth to their first child – a daughter named Nobulelo. From their perspective, Nobulelo could very well take over after her mother as chief. In that case, Nobulelo would simply be referred to as chief Mabhena when acting as such, although she bears her father's *isibongo* Sibanda.[28] However, others are more sceptical about such a development. '[The] chieftainship was given to a family, the Mabhena family, by the Masukus, and not to a Sibanda family,' Pathisa Nyathi said and continued:

> She is the last Mabhena person, and therefore will be the last chief. I mean, her son or daughter can't [take over] because that becomes a Sibanda person. It will be a transfer of the chieftainship to the Sibanda clan, and I don't foresee the Mabhenas accepting that one. It won't be easy at all for her offspring, any of them, to claim it. They have no basis at all, unless we change the laws, the rules, the traditions.[29]

Conclusion: the use of social identities put into context

In this chapter I have tried to address two related problems in dealing with the politics of identity in social conflict: that of treating social identities in the plural, and that of putting identities into context. In other words, I have tried to treat not one, but several identities as constructed, situational and subject to change, while at the same time 'situating' these identities and the situations in which they occur. The politics of identity in relation to the installation of Sinqobile Mabhena as chief involved the enactment of many identities based on ethnicity, nationality, origin, caste, gender and kinship. Among these identities, I focused on those built on ethnicity and gender, which together with identities based on kinship were the most salient ones. While ethnic identity was expressed in relation to President Mugabe, the Zanu-PF government, and the 'Shona', in attempts to decide the issue locally, a dominant form of male identity was enacted in order to defend the privileges of men embedded in the existing gender order and in the gender regime of the traditional leadership system.

Richard Fardon has stated that

> the achievement of a previous generation of Africanists was to demonstrate that ethnic identities were not primordial, that they had histories of invention or construction that belonged, just as much as their counterparts elsewhere, to the conditions under which the contemporary world came to be what it is (Ranger 1993).
>
> (Fardon 1999: 74)

Ndebele ethnicity, I have suggested, has surely been constructed, and, in my terms, re-constructed over time, but the conditions under which this occurred were pre-colonial, colonial and, not least, post-colonial, rather than an invention or imagining during colonialism first by the British and then by Africans. 'Where this [constructed character of ethnicity] is not understood,' Fardon (ibid.) continues, 'it needs repeating' for only then 'it is possible to address more nuanced problems.'

The more nuanced problems Fardon (1999: 74ff.) wishes to address are twofold: 'the diversity of grounds, other than ethnic, for differing', and 'the realisation of the diversity of ethnic situations across Africa'. One of several ways to address these problems is to study the political use of identity in social conflict, rather than studying ethnicity per se. In any situation of conflict or crisis, people are inclined to defend values and resources by playing on identities. With this analytical approach, you may or may not end up studying the politics of ethnic identity. Moreover, since a conflict concerns several people or groups of people, you have to deal not only with several identities, but also with how these identities are related to each other.

In the case of Sinqobile Mabhena, identities based on ethnicity and gender are related in at least two ways. First, in line with Fredrik Barth's (1969) argument in *Ethnic Groups and Boundaries*, in this conflict people drew a boundary between themselves as Ndebele, on the one hand, and the president, the Zanu-PF government, and the 'Shona', on the other. However, they did this with reference to their alleged 'culture and tradition', that is to the 'cultural stuff' that Barth and his colleagues downplayed in their analyses of ethnicity. This culture and tradition includes succession rules related to the system of patrilineality, patrilocality and *lobola*. Second, Ndebele ethnic identity is partly fashioned with Ndebele male identity as a blueprint. There is a claim that Ndebele are brave and Shona are cowards, in the same way that Ndebele men are brave and Ndebele women are not.

With regard to the diversity of ethnic situations across Africa, it seems to me to be a problem of context. The more you 'situate' the enactment of an ethnic or any other identity, the more difficult it is to compare one ethnic identity with another, or, by the same token, one male or female identity with another. In this chapter I have put ethnic identity into context historically, since I believe that the installation of Sinqobile Mabhena triggered the expression of ethnic identity largely due to an earlier armed conflict: the Fifth Brigade's atrocities in Matabeleland. I situated male and female identities structurally, however, since the expression of male identity, although historically formed and in a constant state of change, was strongly related to the existing gender order in Matabeleland and the current gender regime of the traditional leadership system.

Notes

1 Umzingwane district's administrative archive, Sinqobile Mabhena, Personal File 5.
2 Zapu stands for the Zimbabwe Africa Peoples Union, and its armed wing Zipra for the Zimbabwe Peoples Revolutionary Army. Zanu stands for the Zimbabwe African National Union, and its armed force Zanla for the Zimbabwe African National Liberation Army.
3 Umzingwane district's administrative archive, Sinqobile Mabhena, Personal File 5.
4 Interview with the District Administrator, Mr Dlamini, at his office in Esigodini 10 June 1997.

5 Umzingwane district's administrative archive, Sinqobile Mabhena, Personal File 5.
6 *The Chronicle*, 16 May 1996, 18 May 1996a, b, 24 May 1996, 3 June 1996, 6 June 1996, 9 September 1996, 27 December 1996, 21 January 1997, 6 February 1997, 1 March 1997, 5 March 1997, 12 March 1997. *The Sunday News*, 26 May 1996, 30 June 1996a, b, 24 October 1996, 22 December 1996, 19 January 1997, 26 January 1997, 2 February 1997.
7 Interview with Chief Khayisa Ndiweni at his home in Ntabazinduna 10 February 1997.
8 Interview with Agrippa Ngwenya at his office in Bulawayo 10 February 1997.
9 Interview with Pathisa Nyathi at his home in Bulawayo 29 March 1997.
10 Discussion with E.D. and his daughter in Umzingwane district 20 May 1997.
11 Discussion with M.N. in Umzingwane district 17 June 1997.
12 Discussion with Phineas, Jairos and Lavert Dube, Nswazi, 27 February 1997.
13 Discussion with Mrs Mloyi at her homestead in Nkayi district 30 June 1995.
14 Interview with Chief Khayisa Ndiweni at his home in Ntabazinduna 10 February 1997.
15 Discussion with Councillor Joti Ndlovu at his homestead in ward seven, Nswazi 11 June 1997.
16 Discussion with Mark Ncube during travels in Matabeleland South 6 March 1997.
17 Interview with Councillor Harriet Sibanda at her homestead in ward six, Nswazi, 1 March 1997.
18 Discussion with Lavert Dube at Sezhube business centre, Nswazi, 27 February 1997.
19 Discussion with Mrs Ndlovu at her homestead, Nswazi, 12 February 1997.
20 Discussion with Mrs Ngwenya at her homestead, Nswazi, 13 February 1997.
21 Discussion with Mr Ndlovu at Sezhube business centre, Nswazi, 28 February 1997.
22 Sinqobile is built from the verb (*uku*)*nqoba*: (to) conquer, (to) defeat. See Pelling 1971, Doke *et al.* 1990.
23 Interview with Anderson Mabhena at his homestead, Nswazi, 12 March 1997. D.A.'s letter to the P.A., 4 May 1996. Personal File 5, Sinqobile Mabhena, Umzingwane district's administrative archive.
24 Interview with Kefazi Mabhena at his homestead, Nswazi, 12 March 1997.
25 Discussion with Joel Ndlovu, chairman of the Mabhena committee that worked to put Sinqobile into office, at his homestead, Nswazi, 28 February 1997.
26 Interview with Pahle Ndlovu at his homestead, Nswazi, 14 February 1997.
27 Discussion with Agrippa Ndlovu at Joel Ndlovu's homestead, Nswazi, 28 February 1997.
28 Interview with Sinqobile Mabhena and Regiment Sibanda, Lueve, Bulawayo, 7 March 2000.
29 Interview with Pathisa Nyathi, Ministry of Education and Culture, Bulawayo, 15 March 2000.

References

Alexander, J. 1998. 'Dissident perspectives on Zimbabwe's post-independence war', *Africa* 68(2): 151–182.

Alexander, J., McGregor, J. and Ranger, T. 2000. *Violence and Memory: One Hundred Years in the 'Dark Forests' of Matabeleland*, Oxford: James Currey.

Barth, F. 1969. 'Introduction', in F. Barth (ed.) *Ethnic Groups and Boundaries: The Social Organization of Culture Difference*, Oslo: Universitetsforlaget.

CCJP/LRF 1997. *Breaking the Silence, Building True Peace: A Report on the Disturbances in Matabeleland and the Midlands 1980–1988*, Harare: The Catholic Comission for Justice and Peace and the Legal Resources Foundation of Zimbabwe.

Census 1992. Provincial Profile Matabeleland South, Harare: Central Statistical Office (published in 1994).

Chiefs and Headmen Act 1982, Harare: Government of Zimbabwe.

Cliffe, L., Mpofu, J. and Munslow, B. 1980. 'Nationalist politics in Zimbabwe: the 1980 elections and beyond', *Review of African Political Economy* 18: 44–67.

Cobbing, J. 1976. 'The Ndebele under the Khumalos 1820–1896', Ph.D. diss., Lancaster University.

—— 1988. 'The Mfecane as alibi: thoughts on Dithakong and Mbolompo', *Journal of African History* 29(3): 487–519.

Comaroff, J. 1987. 'Of totemism and ethnicity: consciousness, practice and the signs of inequality', *Ethnos* 52: 69–86.

Comaroff, J. 1991. 'Humanity, ethnicity, nationality: conceptual and comparative perspectives on the U.S.S.R', *Theory and Society* 20: 661–687.

Comaroff, J. 1995. 'Ethnicity, nationalism and the politics of difference in an age of revolution', in J. Comaroff and P. Stern (eds) *Perspectives on Nationalism and War*, Amsterdam: Gordon and Breach Publishers.

Connell, R. 1987. *Gender and Power*, Cambridge: Cambridge University Press.

—— 1995. *Masculinities*, Cambridge: Cambridge University Press.

—— 2000. *The Men and the Boys*, Berkeley, Calif.: University of California Press.

Doke, C.M., Malcom, D.M., Sikakana, J.M.A. and Vilakazi, B.W. 1990. *English–Zulu, Zulu–English Dictionary*, Johannesburg: Witwatersrand University Press.

Fardon, R. 1999. 'Ethnic pervasion', in T. Allen (ed.) *The Media of Conflict: War Reporting and Representations of Ethnic Violence*, London: Zed Books.

Hamilton, C. 1998. *Terrific Majesty: The Power of Shaka Zulu and the Limits of Historical Imagination*, Cambridge, Mass.: Harvard University Press.

Hughes, A.J.B. 1956. *Kin, Caste and Nation among the Rhodesian Ndebele*, Lusaka: The Rhodes–Livingstone Institute.

Hughes, A.J.B. and van Velsen, J. 1954. 'The Ndebele', in H. Kuper, A.J.B. Hughes and J. van Velsen (eds) *The Shona and Ndebele in Southern Rhodesia*, London: International African Institute.

Kuper, A. 1982. *Wives for Cattle: Bridewealth and Marriage in Southern Africa*, London: Routledge and Kegan Paul.

Lindgren, B. 2001. 'Men rule, but blood speaks: gender, identity, and kinship at the installation of a female chief in Matabeleland, Zimbabwe', in R. Morrell (ed.) *Changing Men in Southern Africa*, London: Zed Books.

—— 2002. 'Power, education, and identity in post-colonial Zimbabwe: representations of the fate of King Lobengula of Matabeleland', *African Sociological Review* 6(1).

—— 2004. 'The internal dynamics of ethnicity: clan names, origins, and castes in Southern Zimbabwe', *Africa* in press.

Livingstone, D. 1857. *Missionary Travels and Researches in South Africa*, London: John Murray.

Moffat, R. [1835] 1940. *Robert Moffat's Visit to Mzilikazi in 1835*, Bantu Studies Monograph series, no. 1, Witwatersrand: Witwatersrand University Press.

Mudimbe, V. 1991. *Parables and Fables: Exegesis, Textuality, and Politics in Central Africa*, Madison, Wis.: University of Wisconsin Press.

Omer-Cooper, J.D. 1966. *The Zulu Aftermath*, London: Longman.

—— 1993. 'Has the Mfecane a future: a response to the Cobbing critique', *Journal of Southern African Studies* 23: 2.

Pelling, J. 1971. *A Practical Ndebele Dictionary*, Harare: Longman.

Ranger, T. 1985. *The Invention of Tribalism in Zimbabwe*, Gweru: Mambo Press.

—— 1993. 'The invention of tradition revisted: the case of colonial Africa', in T. Ranger and O. Vaughan (eds) *Legitimacy and the State in Twentieth Century Africa*, London: Macmillan.

—— 1994. 'African identities: ethnicity, nationality and history. The case of Matabeleland, 1893–1993', in J. Heidrich (ed.) *Changing Identities: The Transformation of Asian and African Societies Under Colonialism*, Berlin: Verlag Das Arabische Buch.

—— 1999. *Voices from the Rocks: Nature, Culture and History in the Matopos Hills of Zimbabwe*, Bloomington and Indianapolis, Ind.: Indiana University Press.

Rasmussen, K. 1978. *Migrant Kingdom: Mzilikazi's Ndebele in South Africa*, London: Rex Collings.

Sahlins, M. 1999. 'Two or three things that I know about culture', *Journal of the Royal Anthropological Institute* 5(3): 399–421.

Traditional Leaders Act 1998, The Governor of Zimbabwe.

Verdery, K. 1996. 'Ethnicity, nationalism, and state-making', in H. Vermeulen and C. Govers (eds) *The Anthropology of Ethnicity: Beyond Ethnic Groups and Boundaries*, Amsterdam: Het Spinhuis.

Werbner, R. 1991. *Tears of the Dead: The Social Biography of an African Family*, Harare: Baobab.

Werbner, R. 1995. 'In memory: a heritage of war in southwestern Zimbabwe', in N. Bhebe and T. Ranger (eds) *Society in Zimbabwe's Liberation War*, Harare: University of Zimbabwe Publications.

—— 1998. 'Smoke from the barrel of a gun: postwars of the dead, memory and reinscription in Zimbabwe', in R. Werbner (ed.) *Memory and the Postcolony*, London: Zed Books.

Wright, J. 1995. 'Beyond the concept of the "Zulu explosion": comments on the current debate', in C. Hamilton (ed.) *The Mfecane Aftermath: Reconstructive Debates in Southern African History*, Johannesburg: Witwatersrand University Press.

Yap, Pohjolainen K. 2001. 'Uprooting the weeds: power, ethnicity and violence in the Matabeleland conflict 1980–1987', Ph.D. diss., University of Amsterdam.

News articles in the *Chronicle* and the *Sunday News*

16 May 1996. Female chief sparks row. The *Chronicle*.

18 May 1996a. Woman chief hits back at critical men. The *Chronicle*.

18 May 1996b. Row over chief deepens. The *Chronicle*.

24 May 1996. Chieftainship row: Nkomo steers clear. The *Chronicle*.

26 May 1996. Denying Mabhena chieftainship a travesty of justice. The *Sunday News*.

3 June 1996. Why is Sinqobile's grandfather quiet? The *Chronicle*.

6 June 1996. Nswazi chieftainship row rages on. The *Chronicle*.

30 June 1996a. Women join chieftainess row. The *Sunday News*.

30 June 1996b. Chieftainship row side-tracks reality. The *Sunday News*.

9 September 1996. Woman chief to stay. The *Chronicle*.

24 October 1996. Nswazi chief to be installed. The *Sunday News*.

22 December 1996. Mabhena installed. The *Sunday News*.

27 December 1996. Coronation sparks row: woman chief out to conquer critics. The *Chronicle*.

19 January 1997. Discontent over chief resurfaces. The *Sunday News*.

21 January 1997. Equality for all. The *Chronicle*.
26 January 1997. More want chief to go. The *Sunday News*.
2 February 1997. MP defends woman chief. The *Sunday News*.
6 February 1997. Arguments against woman chief invalid. The *Chronicle*.
1 March 1997. Nguni scholars back Nswazi chief's appointment. The *Chronicle*.
5 March 1997. Give Mabhena a chance. The *Chronicle*.
12 March 1997. Nguni history was distorted. The *Chronicle*.

Chapter 9

Double-voiced violence in Kenya

John G. Galaty

> The object is always entangled in someone else's discourse about it, it is already present with qualifications, an object of dispute that is conceptualised and evaluated variously.
>
> (M.M. Bakhtin, *The Dialogic Imagination*, 1981: 330)

Introduction

Like a newsreel, violence is daily splattered against the minds of Kenyans in short bursts of light, sound and script, at seemingly increasing speeds. In recent years, Kenya has witnessed civil war in five of its northern and western neighbours (Somalia, Ethiopia, Sudan, Uganda, Rwanda) and served as host to many of their political exiles and refugees. But, although Kenya has itself been spared such grim events, during the decade of the 1990s it experienced two forms of structured violence that, though traumatic, fall below the threshold of overt warfare: first, an increase in conflicts between remote, borderland communities, that resemble cattle raids made virulent by the addition of automatic weapons (Galaty 1999a); second, sporadic episodes of civil strife in which a volatile mixture of electoral machinations and land conflicts took on the appearance of ethnic clashes (Galaty 1999b). With this backdrop in mind, I discuss here the less dramatic, almost routinised forms of violence that seem to have pervaded Kenyan public life. As an introduction to the topic, I present here discourse on several episodes, somewhat randomly selected from *Kenya Daily Nation* articles in 1998 and 1999, along with brief commentary.

HERDSMAN JAILED FOR KILLING ANOTHER

A herdsman who speared another to death during a circumcision ceremony in Samburu was yesterday jailed for four years. Josephat Lenewan Lekimenju killed Mr Lemash Leturchirit at Bahawa Location in Samburu District on December 13, 1996. Lekimenju was said to have repeatedly speared Mr Leturchirit when the two disagreed during a beer party hosted after the circumcision of the accused's nephew. Sentencing the accused, Nyahururu Principal Magistrate Wanjiru Karanja noted that he had been in custody for two years but said the offence was serious as somebody had lost his life. She dismissed his defence as a sham before convicting him.

(*Daily Nation*, Friday, 4 December 1998)

It is noteworthy that the magistrate felt it necessary to point out that the offence was serious; clearly – given the sentence – neither she nor the participants felt that it really was serious, and the reason may be inferred by the journalist naming the culprit by ethnicity and occupation: 'A Samburu herdsman'.

VIGILANTES CAUSE MAYHEM IN KURIA

A suspect, hands tied behind his back, stood terrified in front of the village 'court'. Rioba Nyasobe shivered as he laboured to answer questions from the crowd. 'Did you steal the cows? Do you own a gun? Who are your accomplices and where are the animals?' thundered a middle-aged man, the 'commandant' of the dreaded vigilante group calling itself 'Sungu sungu'. Its members had violently arrested the suspect from his home three days previously.

. . . Nyasongo was severely tortured to confess to the crime and could hardly walk. Two days later, he died of his injuries. In their quest to rid Kuria of the decades-old cattle-rustling menace and other petty crimes, they have literally taken over the role of the police and the law courts.

Suspects are arrested, put in cells at chiefs' camps, tried by the 'iritoongo' and made to pay hefty fines. Although they are credited with the reduction of crime in the district, their style has raised concern.

The Kuria DC, Mr Japheth Serem, who had earlier supported the formation of the vigilante groups, saying they were helping combat crime, last Thursday made an about turn after listening to cases of atrocities they had committed. Only a month ago, his boss, Nyanza PC, Mr Peter Raburu had commended the work by the vigilantes, perhaps unaware of the complaints against them. While addressing a public *baraza*, the PC told the youths to apprehend, discipline and fine the suspects.

(*Daily Nation*, Wednesday, 17 February 1999)

The public responds to an epidemic of local crime by forming a 'sungu-sungu' vigilante or community-defence unit, an innovation in self-reliance that came over the border from Tanzania. Administrative officials seeing the direction the crowd is marching rushes to the front, calling for 'youths' to carry on. Embarrassed by the predictable excesses committed by the vigilantes, officials reconsider.

SOMALI BANDITS STEAL 46 HEAD OF CATTLE IN NIGHT RAID

Armed bandits stole 46 head of cattle and four donkeys during a raid at a village in Tharaka-Nithi District on Wednesday night. The bandits raided Kathangachini sub-location at about 10 pm and escaped with the animals.

(*Daily Nation*, Friday, 15 January 1999)

A routine story: rustling in not extraordinary numbers. But how did they know the armed bandits were Somalis?

ONLY THE MILITARY CAN CURB RUSTLING

Friday's announcement that the Kenya Army intends to step in to end the cattle-rustling menace in some parts of the country is very good news indeed. This is because there is a war going on out there but the majority of Kenyans do not know about it because they are not affected.

For years, regular forays by contingents of regular and paramilitary police have failed to curb or even reduce the menace, mainly because rustling happens in areas that are not easily accessible. As Lt-Gen Daniel Opande explained, soldiers are trained to defend the country from external aggression, but cattle-rustling has become a threat to security in the affected areas. Although he did not say so, one can assume he specifically meant North-Eastern Province which is closest to neighbouring countries that have known nothing but civil war for years.

(*Daily Nation*, Sunday, 4 April 1999)

In an exercise in innuendo, the Kenyan Army states it will move against cattle-rustlers 'in some (unstated) parts of the country', 'areas not easily accessible', where rustling has become 'a threat to security'. Perhaps security forces have 'failed to curb or even reduce the menace' because most Kenyans 'are not affected', those, that is, who do not live in the not-to-be-mentioned areas of northern Kenya and who are not among those who are not to be explicitly identified. Informed journalists and readers draw their own conclusions about which agents of disorder, from the north-eastern part of Kenya adjacent to Somalia, are under discussion.

ALARM OVER TOURIST VAN ATTACK

The government should move fast to curb banditry, tourist organisations at the Coast have said in response to the weekend attack on a tourist van near Isiolo. 'While this may have been an isolated incident, it is a reminder to both the industry and the government that all is not well,' the three main tourist trade associations said yesterday in a statement.

The Mombasa and Coast Tourist Association, the Kenya Association of Hotel Keepers and Caterers and the Kenya Association of Tour Operators said the attack, which reportedly took place at around 6 pm near Isiolo Town, 'is deplorable and duly regrettable'.

In the attack, seven tourists were confronted by four bandits, who relieved them of cash, cameras, binoculars and clothes. The tourists were forced to cut short their safari and two have since left for home. The other five are continuing with their Kenyan holiday.

(*Daily Nation*, Thursday, 9 November 1998)

Who is alarmed and why? One might assume officials and inhabitants near or in Isiolo would be most upset by the attack. But two tourist associations were most alarmed, given that the attack represented a threat to an already weakened tourist trade, their commercial well-being and the Kenyan economy.

Murder of a relative by a drunk Samburu, murder of an accused thief by Kuria vigilantes, livestock theft by presumed Somalis, announcement of military action against 'rustlers' in the presumed north-east (thus presumably against Somalis), an attack on a tourist van in Isiolo, are reports chosen randomly which represent a reasonable selection of violent events that Kenyans read about in newspapers, hear on the radio, see on their television news programmes, and hear about through the reliable grapevine which they rely upon for all the news politically not fit to print. In each of these cases, the report focuses on 'the event' of violence, but includes quotes, commentaries and inferences that a discourse-wise public can interpret.

Most acts of violence gain chilling force by being inserted into some form of narrative, which lends them a 'told' character; the narrative serves to situate acts within a framework of legitimacy or illegitimacy (Smith 1997: 94) or to establish less what is true than what can reasonably be said about it (Van Der Veer 1997). Commonly, someone tells about what someone told him, and it is this third person whose vantage lends the events their memorable character. If someone tells us what he or she heard (the usual reversionary process in anthropology), our accounts will then resonate with at least two voices, one overlaying the other with its own interpretations, interests and opinions. Bakhtin (1981: 330) described the distinctive problem of prose as its 'double-voiced' quality, expressing both the intentions of the character speaking and the 'refracted' intention of the author. But it is in the complex character of action that it takes place in the shadows of an indistinct body of cultural precedent, making it unclear just which level of intentionality – whether of the individual or culture – is direct and which refracted. Asked differently, when do individuals voice intentions authored by customary expectations and cultural experience, and when do they in fact use customary forms to express their own authored intents? Leaving open the likelihood of both alternatives, let us consider how enactments of violence are expressed through double-voicing, in such a way that, like prose, in the words cited to introduce the paper, 'the object is always entangled in someone else's discourse about it' (ibid.).

I hesitate to assert the obvious, that over the last ten years Kenya has become a more violent society, only because this might reinforce current received wisdom regarding an African continent set apart from the world by increasing poverty and social disorder, which is not so much wrong as inadequate. True, it is my impression that many Africans feel poorer than they once did – which is also the case today in most western countries apart from the United States – and somewhat less physically secure – which is so even in the United States, outside of a socially renewed and safer New York City. What World Bank statistics, tales of corruption, accounts of civil upheaval, stories of violence do not convey is that many people in communities in Africa give every appearance of leading 'normal' lives, do not walk the streets and paths in fear, mostly pursue daily routines of farming or wage employment, raise families, enjoy social life, feel AIDS is something someone else will contract, aspire to goals, meet some, fail to meet others, and so on. Most violence, like traffic, water shortages, rising prices, illness and daily aggravation, has come to seem part of 'routine reality', routine precisely because, like pollution, though increasingly pervasive, it is usually absorbed in small quantities, and, like gossip, conveys experiences at second- or third-hand through words and images that mainly refer not to oneself but to others. Yet Africans with whom I have discussed the matter are not unaware of how their continent is globally viewed (that their worlds have 'already bespoke quality'). They variously respond with resigned concurrence, ambivalence, or ironic resentment at how their routine realities are, but only in part, refracted in diverse, globalised images.

This chapter concerns increasingly routinisation of several new forms of violence in Kenya today, carried out in novel settings by old actors: on-the-ground struggles over land titles and politics in the Maasai districts of southern Kenya, largely carried out by young men. Reporting results of research on property and development and on borderland violence in East Africa, I have elsewhere discussed the Maasai experience of land loss as an outcome of changing systems of rangeland tenure, where corruption and political intervention have occurred in the complex process of enclosure and privatisation of land (Galaty 1994, Galaty and Munei 1999). I have also examined the resurgence of large-scale pastoral violence in northern Kenya, old forms of local raiding revived with the influx of modern weaponry, the attraction of a market for livestock booty, and tacit collaboration of raiders with security forces (Galaty 1999a). Here, I am joining the issue of upheaval in Maasai land and politics with the question of violence in southern Kenya, violence that though increasingly pervasive and routinised is less traumatic and widespread than that occurring in the northern Kenyan borderlands. Only in my last example, developed at greater length elsewhere (Galaty 1999b), will I briefly allude to the eruption of the Rift Valley clashes associated with competitive politics, which involve ethnic violence that in scale and brutality begins to resemble conflicts occurring in the north.

In many respects, the reasons behind conflict seem self-evident: seizing land or preventing land from being seized, by individuals or collectivities; advancing the interests of politicians whom one's group or faction supports, or the opposite, deterring their opponents; and stealing others' livestock, preventing the theft of one's own, or, conversely, retaliating for the prior loss of livestock to theft. But especially when differences over land and politics coincide, reasons hide behind reasons: specifically, it becomes unclear who wishes to hide political motives under clashes for land, and who wishes to hide conflict over land under overtly political combat. If politicians use local squabbles for political purposes, locals use political clashes to acquire land, and intentions and refractions of intentions are melded together.

Teleologically, material ends can come to represent efficient causes, as people do construe acts to achieve intended aims. Just as often, however, it is the intentions of others that are refracted in their actions. Yet 'intention' is perhaps too definitive a notion for the complex motives and motivations that give rise to practices. An intention is often evoked retrospectively to make sense of what has already been accomplished or to lend clarity to the often vague, uncertain, inchoate or shifting aims that were its antecedents. So it might be more apt to say that in actions are refracted diverse emotions and practices, or social solidarities and ruptures, and that in these reverberate internalised sources of perceptual or cognitive affinity, regarding 'tradition' or leadership, group differences or identities, memories or anticipations, to mention a few instances. But insofar as individuals often draw their actions from pools filled by others with suggestions, commands, incentives and precedents, even the more diffuse notion of intentionality described above expresses a second-hand relation. Here, I focus less on causes and consequences or means–end relations of action and more on patterns of sense and processes of explanation and justification – through articulated or implicit discourse – that surround acts of violence. In this, my assumption is that violence – like its spectre war – is one part force to many parts anticipation, threat, negotiation, manoeuvre, self-justification, explanation, recollection, all of which lie in the verbal imaginary. How something is said, implied or inferred is often as important as what. Accordingly, I will explore here whether aesthetic and poetic dimensions of the discourse surrounding violence – most notably its double-voiced qualities – prove helpful in understanding why violence continues to be pursued and perpetuated in contexts where its explanation by apparent causes falls short. Several traditions of theory have developed important reservations about the adequacy of explaining action instrumentally, through reconstructing either the underlying rationality or private intentions of actors (Weber 1978, Winch 1958, Wittgenstein 1958), or by relying on propositional language, given that contextual variation and traces of past usage lend its interpretation an essential semantic indeterminacy (Derrida 1973). Here, two elements of indeterminacy in forms of narrative-in-violence will be explored: poetic aspects of multiple 'voicing', and its pragmatic use in asserting political 'presence'.

Land, politics, violence: 1952–1992

Finally convinced that 'development' is a goal worth pursuing, the Maasai community of Kenya has seen the possibility of attaining that state of grace rapidly recede during the recent years of political liberalisation and democratisation, when it has experienced land loss through enclosure and privatisation, and faces imminent exclusion from the modest proximity to national political power it has enjoyed during the Moi years. Though Maasai are now avidly involved in the machinations of privatisation and multi-party democracy, their case illustrates how illusory the belief has been that by adopting liberal political and economic policies prosperity and transparent governance would follow; rather than 'good for all', the way political pluralism and privatisation have been pursued in Kenya during the decade of the 1990s has, at least for Maasai, rather proved a 'free for all' in the desperate scramble for local land and power. To situate current strife in historical context, I will present a brief sketch of how questions of ethnicity, land rights and constitutional order have interacted in the evolution of political structure and power in Kenya from the immediate pre-independence period to the present.

The pre-independence jockeying to construct a political order that would replace the British colonial government took place in the shadow of the Mau Mau rebellion of 1952–1956. In Mau Mau, elements of class and ethnicity were intertwined as Kikuyu grievances over land were expressed in rural violence both against white settlers and the colonial government and against elements of the Kikuyu administration and rural middle class (Kanogo 1987, Berman 1990, Berman and Lonsdale 1992). Although in Lonsdale's (Berman and Lonsdale 1992: 451) terms, Mau Mau 'defeated two sets of hawks' (white settlers and forest fighters) and brought administrative loyalists and African politicians to the fore of independence negotiations, its legacy was not just to make majority rule inevitable in Kenya but to inextricably link nationalism to ethnicity.

In doing so, I will use the relatively unselfconscious ethnic labels around which political discourse is currently structured in Kenya today. In anthropology, a more sophisticated understanding of 'multiplicity' in the content, structure and usage of 'ethnic' symbolism has emerged, which emphasises 'shifting' in the contextual use of ethnic classification, mutability in the way identities straddle conventional differences, and the creative colonial and post-colonial manufacture of ethnic entities to accord with administrative divisions or conveniences (Galaty 1982, Comaroff 1987). Today, in the setting of national political contention, a 'new ethnicity' is being constructed out of conceptual elements refashioned and new affinities forged. 'Maasai', for instance, once a diacritical of internal social distinction, is now embraced as figure of collective affinity by all Maa-speakers, whether Maasai proper, Samburu, Chamus, Ariaal, Arusha or Laikipiak, as an intentional strategy of creating critical mass in national and regional political arenas (Galaty 1993). Rather than talking itself out of culturally constructed forms of ethnicity, the challenge to anthropology as a discipline is to talk itself into understanding the growing salience of identities, at once dissolving and being reconstituted, based on transparently 'ethnic' signifiers in states like Kenya where more encompassing affinities are increasingly being used to define inclusive and resilient entities in the face of national political strife and competition. One cannot understand political process without grasping something of the complex ethnic calculus that its proponents comprehend and reformulate to their own advantage.

Two axes of political affinity emerged in 1959–1960 with the formation of parties that participated in the Lancaster House Constitutional Conferences that preceded independence: an alliance between Kenya's two largest groups, the Kikuyu and Luo, lay at the heart of the Kenya African National Union (KANU), while a coalition of smaller groups, including Kamba, Luyia and Rift Valley pastoralists such as the Kalenjin and Maasai, formed the Kenya African Democratic Union (KADU). The latter feared domination by Kikuyu and Luo within a one-party state; Kalenjin and Maasai in particular were apprehensive that their historical claims to European settler lands in the Rift Valley would be superseded by Kikuyu claims, especially since administrative measures adopted during and after the Mau Mau Emergency had exacerbated the already pressing situation of the Kikuyu landless (Ogot 1995a: 64–67). The KADU coalition raised fears regarding discrimination between regions and groups that might occur in a centralised state dominated by the larger ethnic groups, to the detriment of smaller communities, and recommended that political rights should be assured through decentralising state power in a bicameral parliament and creating strong regional authorities. In its political philosophy, the KANU alliance supported an administratively centralised state, and the assurance of non-discrimination through guarantees on the security of persons, property and basic human rights (ibid.: 70–71).

Reading between the lines, KANU (composed of communities who during the colonial period had already begun to do so) sought to establish the right of citizens to move out of their home areas to live, work and own land throughout the nation, while KADU (composed of communities largely anchored to and dependent on traditional lands) sought through '*majimbo*' regionalism to protect and restore local land rights – transgressed through the process of white settlement – and to reinforce the cultural and economic prerogatives of smaller, resident groups. While in the nationalist context, KADU had been characterised as 'moderate', KANU as 'radical' (ibid.: 65), in fact their respective postures reflected the interests of their major constituencies: of Kikuyu, to legitimise their acquisition of land rights outside of their home districts, in particular on settler farms and ranches of the Rift Valley where as squatters they had provided labour, and of Kalenjin and Maasai, to defend against the definitive loss of Rift Valley lands they had ceded during the first decades of colonial rule for white settlement and to ensure retention of lands held for them in trust. During the transition to independence, in coalition with European and Asian members, KADU did form the first African-led government in 1961, when despite its electoral victory KANU refused to do so given the continued detention of Jomo Kenyatta (ibid.: 68). Due to its staunch nationalist posture and the leadership of Kenyatta, KANU won a strong electoral victory in 1963, formed a transitional government and assumed full power at independence, with KADU in opposition. Yet the two parties agreed on most policy issues associated with the achievement of independence, and in early 1964 KADU dissolved itself and was amalgamated into KANU, its leading figures assuming significant roles in the ruling party. For instance, Daniel Arap Moi and other founding member of KADU became ministers in Kenyatta's government and Moi was later installed as vice-president.

After the emergency, many Kikuyu insurgents and detainees found they had lost their land to loyalist landowners in programmes of land consolidation, and after independence over half of settler lands earmarked for squatter settlement schemes were in fact transferred intact, under private title, to more wealthy Africans who had organised themselves in partnerships or companies (ibid.: 64). So, although by 1970 more than 50,000 families held more than two-thirds of the mixed farms that had been owned by European settlers, and during the 1960s the rural economy grew four-fold bringing prosperity to many, numerous of the land-less were left out (Ochieng 1995: 88). The transfer of well over one million acres of former settler lands both to Kikuyu smallholders and to the wealthier African middle class realised the fears of Rift Valley pastoralists that at independence political rectification in land would be at their expense. During the first decade of independence, Nakuru District, Laikipia District and part of Uasin Gishu District, which prior to their appropriation for colonial settlement had been primarily inhabited by Maasai, were largely shifted from settler to Kikuyu hands through processes of land reform. The Kikuyu thus came to symbolise both the richest and poorest of Kenyans, a paradox that underlies much of the ambivalence felt by many Kenyans towards them in more recent post-colonial years.

Despite his presiding over an ethnically broad-based government, Kenyatta's presidency is often interpreted as a period of Kikuyu ascendency due to the strong influence of a coterie of ministers and advisors from Kiambu District and the progressive dominance of Kikuyu in civil service, trade and land acquisition. KANU's unity was fragmented with the withdrawal of Luo members from government who, in 1966, together with several prominent Kikuyu populists, formed the socialist-leaning Kenya People's Union (KPU), subsequently banned in 1969 (Ochieng 1995: 99–100). With Kenyatta's health failing, some Kikuyu colleagues attempted to change the constitution to prevent the interim succession to the presidency of the vice-president, which they feared would result in the loss of the presidency by their faction, but these efforts, and further political manoeuvres at Kenyatta's death in 1978, were met by the support Moi enjoyed within the party, including that of moderate Kikuyu (Ogot 1995b: 188–189). But, in part in response to an attempted coup by the Kenyan Air Force in 1982 and to attempts to overthrow him in a palace coup by the party's Kikuyu faction in 1983, Moi became increasingly intolerant of dissidence. The position of KANU was gradually rendered legally unassailable as the constitution was amended to declare Kenya a one-party state, to abolish the independence of the judiciary, to eliminate secrecy of voting in primary elections and to expand presidential powers of detention. But at the same time the base of KANU's popular support was narrowing, with numerous Kikuyu and Luo expressing disaffection, due in part to the abridgement of human rights in Kenya and in part to the consolidation of power in Kenya by a Kalenjin-centred alliance of Rift Valley peoples that, ironically, resembled the original KADU coalition (ibid.: 211–212).

Local calls to allow for registration of political parties in the 1980s were suppressed until the international tolerance for authoritarian government declined with the fall of the Berlin Wall in 1989 and the subsequent demise of Communism. The pro-democracy movement gained momentum in 1990, further energised by the call by two former Kikuyu ministers for a political rally at Kamakunji on 7 July (thus called 'saba-saba'/seven-seven), which, although its leaders were detained and the rally suppressed, turned out thousands of protesters. With the creation of a broad-based Forum for the Restoration of Democracy (FORD), which included prominent Kikuyu, Luo and Luyia leaders, the government renounced KANU's monopoly on political power in late 1991, amending the constitution to allow for multi-party democracy (Ayiemba-Omolo 1996, Mutunga 1996). When it came to a method of choosing a presidential candidate, however, the broad-based FORD splintered, with the Luo faction surrounding Oginga Odinga forming FORD-Kenya, the Kikuyu faction surrounding Martin Matiba FORD-ASILI (the 'pure' or 'original' FORD). Among numerous other parties formed at the same, the most significant was the Democratic Party led by the former Kikuyu vice-president, Mwai Kibaki (Wanjohi 1997). The high ground occupied by opposition parties during the campaign to allow multi-party democracy was to some extent lost by their retreat into ethnic particularism during the electoral campaign, allowing KANU to present itself as the only party with a truly national base of support (Chege 1994).

While international attention concentrated on realising the principles of democracy, human rights, and freedom of speech, press and assembly in Kenya, most local strategists – the most adept being President Moi – focused on what in the Kenyan context had always been most crucial: ethnicity, power, patronage and land. In this setting, despite the progressive stance of many Maasai concerning the principles of democratisation, the community's support for KANU was never in doubt. For Maasai, having seen the definitive loss of settler districts to Kikuyu resettlement and, since independence, substantial Kikuyu (and Kamba) migration into their home districts of Narok and Kajiado, the 1992 elections were about local self-determination, political control and security of land at home, both of which would be undermined were KANU defeated. Latent threats of violence had been instrumental, given the precedent of Mau Mau, in the acquisition of Rift Valley land by Kikuyu, violence had been used and threatened in attempts to topple Moi, violence had been used by Moi to suppress political dissidents and threatened in order to deter proponents of multi-party democracy, and the latent threat of violence had been used by the organisers of Saba-Saba, and was actually used in suppressing the event.

This brief account of the recent political history of Kenya demonstrates that at every juncture, political evolution has been advanced not just by principled argument and negotiation but by the willingness of advocates to establish a 'force-on-the-ground', with which their opponents have had to contend. This sort of 'presence' conveys both illocutionary and physical force: it 'says' something about political will, and 'portends' something about potential violence. What that will intends, what forms that violence might take, what that presence would achieve, and what is in fact at stake, is often conveyed in multiple sheaves of double-voiced meaning, regarding land, history, identity, power and loss.

The power of presence in land claims and politics

I wish to illustrate here not just that violence has underpinned transformations of land and democratic process, generally in Kenya and more particularly in the Maasai districts, but how in both instances 'force-on-the-ground' has become an important modality of political process. In some cases, on-the-ground 'presence' does anticipate or lead to violence, in other cases it does not, but, if not, still may be effective because of the sense conveyed, and the reality observed, that violence is indeed possible. Let me present a few illustrations from recent years of how a forceful presence can 'speak'.

In September 1992 a young community activist with his supporters went to protest in front of President Moi's house against the corrupt allocation of land from Lodariak, a site in northern Keekonyokie division. When the land had been registered in the early 1980s, 2,000 non-literate indigenous rights-holders were excluded from the register, since they did not offer bribes to corrupt officials, but at the same time 360 outsiders, with no rightful claim on the land, were registered and allocated titles; these included senior civil servants, politicians, businessmen and non-local Maasai. Ten years later, the number of landless had risen. Seeing their placards when he arrived, the president ordered his car to stop, and got out to speak with the group. One participant reported how the group addressed the president:

> We introduced ourselves first, where we came from and finally the long details of our problem, suffering and the struggle to return back what was taken away from us. Immediately after my long introduction of the matter, we handed over to him the prepared documents relating the latter and of course our Memorandum to him. He said, he was very sorry for what has taken place and since the time is running, i.e. it was late in the evening, we needed to appoint four people who will see him at State House at 8:00 a.m. the following day, on 9 September, 1992.

The President provided them funds for accommodation and return transport. But the day's drama had only begun, as intrigue ensued after their successful attempt to see the President.

> When we arrived in Kiserian (their home) we heard that some CID [Central Intelligence Division] officers were looking for us, to arrest us. We believed that what happened was that they got information immediately after we left that home of the President. The reason behind our [planned] arrest and detention was that they wanted the appointment to fail with the president. After spotting those fellows, we hired two taxi cars. We instructed one to be empty and it will follow us after 5 minutes or less. We took the direction of our homes. After a short time, we exchanged the cars. The first car proceeded with nobody to Kisamis, while the second car now proceeded towards Nairobi with us. The CID officers were chasing the first car believing and hoping that we were in that car. They chased the first car to Kisamis, but since the taxi car arrived at Kisamis shortly before them, thought we had alighted from that car, so we were just around. . . . It was too bad for them and very good luck for us. We spent our night very comfortable and after that,

the following day at 5:15 a.m. we started our journey to State House and at 6:00 a.m. were at the door.

Other security officers met them who 'were really friendly and sympathetic with our problem'. All believed that 'since the matter has been brought to the attention of the president, it will be a matter of history and it was going to be sorted out once and for all'.

I will leave the story of the meeting with the president for another time, but suffice it to say that eight years later the matter is still unresolved and the land has yet to be returned to its rightful owners. The titles that had been issued were, at one time, circulating through cycles of sale and purchase, but the illicit title-holders have yet to attempt to settle on the land they have theoretically been allotted, and an official survey was never made of the land, a fact which should technically invalidate the titling process. Later, when a title-holder attempted to visit Lodariak with a potential buyer, who knew little of the affair, they were intercepted by a party from the area who physically threatened them if they did not leave. Local dwellers have, indeed, threatened to resort to force if the illicit title-holders attempt to actually occupy the land. In the meantime, the value of 'owning' land in the area is assessed on the exchange value of a title deed, whether sold by fraud or used as collateral, not on the nature, the potential use or the market demand for the land (Galaty 1994, Galaty and Munei 1999).

I recount the above episode not because violence occurred in that instance but to demonstrate presence-on-the-ground and the ever-present tacit threat of violence that surrounds political affairs. Once contact had been made between the protesters and the president, how was it that unsympathetic CID officers were informed, such that they could attempt to intercept the party in order to prevent it meeting the president the next day? To come at the question from another angle, who would have sufficient access to the president to know what had happened, sufficient courage to intervene, or sufficient fear the land allocation would be reversed, to have planned the aborted interception? The vice-president was the MP for the riding in which the scandal occurred, was a close colleague of many who had received illicit allocations, and would the next morning be deeply embarrassed when called into the meeting between the Lodariak delegation and the president. On-the-ground presence occurred in several instances: by the delegation presenting themselves, without appointment, at the home of the president, making their case known in person; by the CID officers attempting to intercept the party directly, as it approached their home; by the delegation leaders, who used their wits to elude the officers who sought to arrest them; and by members of the community who confront potential buyers, and threaten anyone who would attempt to occupy the land taken from them.

In his discussion of enclosure in the 'Discourse on the Origin of Inequality' Rousseau (1755: 60) implicitly maintains that the very act of appropriating land as property entails violence ('You are lost if you forget that the fruits of the earth belong to all and the earth to no one!'), but nevertheless traced the origins of civil society to the assertion of private ownership, which required a state to secure. And Marx made his famous observation that 'property is theft' not as a generality but with reference to forced enclosures, as his chapter in *Capital* on 'Expropriation of the Agricultural Population from the Land' so pungently develops (Marx 1867: 717–733). In steps, Maasai land was in part appropriated for European settlement and in part secured by treaty as crown trust, during the first stages of British colonialism, in exchange for their ceding much of the central Rift Valley (in 1904) and Laikipia (in 1911) for white settlement; in return, Maasai gained treaty rights to the remainder of their lands in southern Kenya (Sorrenson 1968), a status only extinguished with independence when treaty responsibilities were devolved to the Kenyan Ministry of Local Government. After independence the portions reserved as trust were adjudicated into individual and group ranch holdings, in which community members were variously registered, these being issued with title deeds. Under private title, group ranches experienced pressure to sub-divide, both from the inside, initially by more educated members who sought individual land and later by non-educated members who saw their collective holdings diminished, and from the outside, by the president, who asserted that all Kenyans had the right to own their own land, and by a strong lobby of potential land-buyers, who saw in the southern rangelands potential land to purchase or otherwise acquire (Rutten 1992, Galaty 1994).

Throughout the colonial period, a drama had been played out between Maasai, colonial administrators and, most often, Kikuyu and Kipsigis settlers, who being landless sought to 'infiltrate' the Masai Reserve (in colonial parlance) to 'homestead', establishing farms in the higher, richer, wetter and more forested areas. Various colonial administrators tried in turn to prevent illegal infiltration, to discourage new Kikuyu settlers and to expel the old, and, as reported in the *Kenya Land Commission Report* (Kenya 1934), encouraged exchange of forest land in the Masai Reserve to be used for resettlement for grazing lands held by the colonial state (Galaty in press). Over time, Maasai responses to 'infiltration' evolved, as they successively assimilated Kikuyu settlers, accepted that some should be granted status as 'acceptees' in the reserve, tolerated their creation of agricultural settlements, resisted their incursions and, finally, supported their expulsion (Waller 1993).

Though close neighbours with and historically linked to Kikuyu, Maasai felt increasingly beleaguered over time, as the integrity of their land base and ultimately their continuing control over the districts created for them were threatened by in-migration. During the Kenyatta years, some Maasai areas were adjudicated and titles allocated to non-Maasai, but throughout Kajiado and Narok Districts spontaneous settlement occurred along rivers, in forests and highlands, and in towns, where cultivation or trade could be pursued. An obvious point of Maasai vulnerability lay in the apparent availability of lands seasonally utilised for pastures, periodically used for watering, or – in forests and mountains – exceptionally used for emergency grazing and watering.

By the 1990s, Maasai land was threatened in three ways. First, anticipating subdivision, the registration lists for some group holdings were corruptly amended, with outsiders added and insiders excluded. Second, when plots were surveyed and designated for members, very large amounts were allocated to more influential members, smaller amounts or nothing for the less influential. Third, anticipating their being allotted title deeds, some prospective title-holders were bribed to transfer their shares to outsiders, or upon their receiving titles were immediately pressured to sell; to their lasting shame, many non-educated Maasai title-holders, some under the influence of alcohol, sold portions of their land for risible amounts to speculators, some of whom represented land-buying companies (Péron 1995). And at a time when land transfers were subject to review by the District Land Board (with all family members theoretically to be present) and later officially frozen, land transactions continued to be registered under the signature of the Board's chair and the District Officer, who were reportedly bribed for each illicit transaction they approved. By the early 1990s, despite the fact that Maasai were already experiencing land shortages, it appeared as if major portions of the Maasai districts would pass out of their control. Given their lack of influence over the Ministry of Lands during the 1970s when some land was directly allocated to outsiders, few Maasai viewed as legitimate titles that had been acquired during that period. And numerous processes of subdivision were halted through appeal to the courts by members aware that land was being allocated to outsiders or in disproportionate shares to local elites (Galaty and Munei 1999). It was thus with a sense of crisis, if not desperation, that most Maasai watched events unfold that threatened the incumbent political coalition to which they belonged, which, if it were defeated in the elections, would (it was feared) further undermine Maasai security of tenure (Simel 1993, 1994).

Politics by other means: democratisation and violence in the 1992 General Elections

In the early 1990s, international pressure and brave displays of domestic pressure, described above, led the government of Kenya and the ruling party, KANU, to embark on a transition from one-party to multi-party democratic process. Accordingly, the General Elections of 1992 were held in the wake of a frenetic dual-track process: on the one hand, political parties were formed and registered, they engaged in soliciting, nominating and registering candidates, and they embarked on organised campaigns to contest the election; on the other hand, the Electoral Commission undertook to establish procedures for running complex and divisive elections, to educate the electorate, to register voters, to establish polling stations, to recruit returning officers and staff, to design and print ballots, to hold the ballot on election day, to carry out the counting of votes, to make judgements regarding the outcome and to announce results (Mutunga 1996). The government clearly resented being forced to diversify the electoral process, and warned, based on the experience of the late 1960s when the Luo-based Kenya People's Union (KPU) had been banned after it had apparently condoned violent demonstrations against President Kenyatta, that democratisation would lead to ethnic violence.

Violence did intervene when leaders tried to register parties, when opposition candidates attempted to hold public meetings (even after public assembly for political reasons was made legal), when opposition supporters attempted to register and then to vote in KANU-dominated areas, etc. (Wanjala 1996). How effective was 'presence-on-the-ground' during this transition?

In one Maasai riding, a contestant for the KANU nomination was opposed by the prevailing party leaders in the district. Using a well-known manoeuvre, his opponents attempted to block his motorcade from passing on its way to the party headquarters, where he was required to submit his nomination papers, with signatures and fee, on a certain date. It was not unprecedented that a prospective candidate's car would be sabotaged, his agents temporarily kidnapped or his nomination papers stolen. The Maasai contestant, anticipating problems, arranged for a large entourage of strong, young supporters to occupy the route, blocking the movement of vehicles driven by his opponents. He personally took a detour and was able to submit his papers. Not only did his action allow his nomination to proceed but it conveyed information about his strength, determination and support. Not only did he win the election but his action won him the attention of national leaders, leading initially to an assistant ministership and later a major ministership, the creation of his own district and leadership of the local party apparatus. His star has continued to rise.

Elsewhere in Maasailand, opposition parties fielded some candidates, who attempted to campaign. But the ruling party, KANU, with majority support in the district, pursued an effective strategy of both intimidating their opposition and demonstrating the latter's weakness to their constituents. In one case, local KANU activists tailed the vehicle of a certain opposition candidate, attending each of his meetings, watching each of his moves, and attempting to side-track his car whenever possible. Even thought the antagonists knew one another personally, the candidate was apprehensive about moving freely from place to place, and his appearances were curtailed. After the elections, I was told the story by both sides, not without humour, but during the elections the persistent presence of representatives of the ruling party clearly conveyed the latent threat of violence in pursuing the opposition candidate. Elsewhere, an opposition candidate was wildly chased by a set of Land-Rovers driven by KANU supporters, who threatened him. Near a trading centre, the vehicle was indeed forced off the road, where it rolled over. Hours after the candidate had walked away from the vehicle, it was burned, thus effectively ending his campaign, not to mention destroying his single most precious possession; the campaign now long forgotten, the loss of his vehicle remains a bitter memory.

The 1992 Elections are most famous for the declaration by the ruling party that certain areas represented 'KANU zones', where opposition parties would not be allowed to operate freely. In many districts in the Rift Valley Province, for instance, opposition parties were unable to register candidates, or if they registered candidates were unable to register voters, or if they registered voters were unable to ensure voters could vote, or if they voted could not ensure their votes would be legitimately counted. Anxiety about the presence of opposition voters in certain districts arose from electoral calculus, given the stipulation in the Kenyan Constitution that winning candidates for president were required to win 25 per cent of the vote in at least five provinces (Ayiemba-Omolo 1996).

The Rift Valley Province had been created in the late colonial period as an administrative entity where pastoral communities would predominate. The province was thus electorally critical in KANU's presidential politics, given its basis of support in pastoral communities, but within Rift Valley some districts contained internal migrant populations with opposition sympathies, whose presence threatened not only to tip the opposition balance over 25 per cent (had they all voted for the same party) but potentially to dislodge KANU candidates, if the latter lost supporters to several of the newly formed opposition parties (Ndegwa 1999). Ngong, a town south of Nairobi at the edge of Kajiado District in the Rift Valley, had become home to thousands of Kikuyu, some of whom had migrated there due to land shortage in Kiambu, others of whom were kept in colonial detention there in the 1950s during the Mau-Mau insurgency (Kanogo 1987), still others of whom had come to purchase land when it became the first area in the district to undergo adjudication. With Kikuyu representing a majority in Ngong, the Parliamentary riding in which it fell (Kajiado North) was considered a potential win by opposition parties. However, the incumbent Member of Parliament in the riding was the country's vice-president, whose complex ethnic background gave him claim to votes from both Maasai and Kikuyu. Nonetheless, since Kikuyu had largely deserted KANU, his own success clearly lay with the Maasai support he had worked hard to consolidate.

During one of the first major campaign meetings held by an opposition party, a large group of young Kikuyu, who supported FORD-Asili or DP, established a strong presence on the streets of Ngong and nearby Kiserian, chanting campaign slogans, taunting supporters of the ruling party, disparaging its candidates. A clearly well-organised group of young Maasai lined up against them, and attacked with clubs (*rungus*), stones and some swords, sending many of their opponents to hospital. The publicity they received was bad, as newspapers called them young barbarians. But their attack was effective in denying the opposition parties ready access to the public places near Ngong for their campaigns. Speaking to me later, one combatant expressed pride in the decisive action they had taken, which demonstrated to the Kikuyu that the Maasai were not to be taken for granted.

Another case in point was in Narok North, a constituency where the incumbent was William Ntimama, a Maasai leader and a KANU minister, but where a strong community of Kikuyu who supported opposition parties lived. Some had come into Narok District during the colonial period, through what was then called 'infiltration' or through resettlement (Waller 1993), and many had come during the Kenyatta years, when some areas occupied by squatters had been declared adjudication sections and their inhabitants issued with title deeds, with areas of gazetted forests being tacitly and informally ceded to new settlers. Still others had come more recently, to find relatives, to purchase land or to informally occupy land as 'squatters' that they not unreasonably hoped could be claimed by establishing on-the-ground presence through building houses, clearing forest and cultivating fields.

Narok North was a contentious site during the period leading up to the 1992 elections. In the highlands along the Mau Escarpment, large communities had been denied the right to register or, having been issued registration cards, were not entered on the register. When the elections occurred, many who were denied the right to vote on the grounds that their names had not been entered sat in silent protest on the grounds surrounding polling stations, demonstrations that I witnessed while serving as an international observer on the Scandinavian-Canadian Election Monitoring Team for the 1992 General Elections, representing the International Centre for Human Rights and Democratic Development in Montreal. Reportedly, some were killed on election day. It was in this region of Enoosopukia, during the two-year period after the elections, that hundreds of Kikuyu were expelled by armed gangs, called 'Maasai Moran' by journalists, who voiced the argument that the former had settled illegally on Maasai land and moreover had deforested and degraded the area, which was an environmentally valuable water catchment site, drying up streams on the plains below. Numerous people were killed at that time (Galaty 1999b).

Presence on-the-ground was demonstrated before and throughout the elections. At an earlier stage, claims to land were first asserted when Kikuyu established physical presence in the Masai Reserve, through 'infiltration' and 'squatting'; claims were made official when some eventually were formally given land in resettlement zones or were allocated letters of occupancy or even title deeds when the administration recognised facts on-the-ground by declaring the lands on which they squatted as adjudication sections. Not without precedent during the colonial period, in the 1992 elections a counter-presence was established by Maasai who attempted to discourage dissident candidates from arising within KANU, candidates from opposition parties from running, and Kikuyu, 'dissident' Maasai from acting on their rights as residents to take political action through the ballot box. In Trans-Mara, physical presence was used to intimidate a prospective KANU candidate, and counter-presence made his candidacy and eventual success possible. In Kajiado intimidation of candidates by following, harassing and threatening them occurred and in Ngong physical violence against opposition supporters served as a warning, while in Narok North deterrence was used to discourage opposition voters from considering themselves as legitimate residents of the region. Serious violence in fact followed the elections, with thousands being evicted from Enoosopukia, perhaps the most contentious area of Narok North, and thousands were later evicted from Trans-Mara, where they had squatted for years on Maasai group ranches (Land Rights Program 1996, Human Rights Watch 1997, Klopp 1999). These acts at once voiced several messages and achieved distinct aims: in electoral competition, in local conflicts over land, in struggles for local political ascendancy, in implicit debates over ethnic legitimacy, in environmental activism. In being voiced, aims can clarify the intentions of acting subjects but equally can hide them or make them seem what they are not. Similar events ensued during the 1997

General Elections, which, as in 1992, were won by KANU, but they fall beyond
the scope of this chapter (Rutten *et al.* 2001, Tostensen *et al.* 1998).

Speaking of an 'already qualified world'

I have tried to demonstrate, with reference to several episodes that occurred in
the two Maasai districts, that establishing an 'on-the-ground' presence is critical
in contemporary Kenyan political life. 'Law', 'justice', 'right' may be desirable
virtues of political life, but 'presence' is a necessary condition for it. Maasai may
have land rights in group ranches, but squatters have presence; Kikuyu may have
gained legal title in Lodariak, but, up to now, Maasai have had presence; Maasai
deserve justice in regaining their land, but, at some sites, current occupants have
presence; candidates have the legal right to compete for party nominations, but
unless they establish a strong 'presence', they will not even be considered;
candidates vie for votes, but the one with the strongest presence prevails. In short,
in Kenya, land and power may be fought with high-level planning but they are
won through the force of 'presence', not just at the polls but on-the-ground where
such matters are ultimately determined.

I suggest that presence itself represents a form of tacit violence that, directly
through force or indirectly through intimidation, marks, alters or moulds the
situation at hand. But, no matter how direct or brutal, the force of violence exceeds
the immediacy of the pain it causes and the coercion it invokes, since refracted in
it are forms of intent that exceed the individuality of the agent (such as ethnic will,
political ends, metaphysical anger) and elevate an action's particularity to a general
scale of significance. Achieving 'generality' is similar to Riches' (1996: 3) notion
that violence is usually a 'performance', as in both cases the instance draws its
power from conveying something behind it, larger and hidden. In this way,
violence that destroys something of metaphysical consequence is felt to be more
destructive than physical harm (Parkin 1986). When violence borrows force by
embodying some wider social, political or historical intent, it also undergoes a
doubling, tripling, a fragmentation, as its 'sense' is diffused through multiple forms
of discourse. Violence is involved in two dimensions of fragmentation, when it
embodies multiple aims, intents or emotions, and when it generates multiple
refractions conveyed along distinct trajectories as people speak of what they have
heard, many times over.

The implicit threats and overt acts of violence described here were in some sense
both 'observed' and 'reported'; in most cases we know that they were observed
only because they were reported, and most reports were by individuals who
conveyed what they were told by others who themselves observed, or had been
told by actual observers, what had happened. While the experience of violence
cannot be reduced to words, violence mainly lives through the telling. To think
that our understanding would be better had we only ourselves directly observed
the events concerned is, I think, to mistake experience for understanding. To
understand a single extended episode of violence between Maasai age-set regiments

that I observed in 1975 (Galaty 1981), I spent appreciable time immediately afterwards soliciting views not just on why it happened but even on what had happened, and I have returned to the issue many times over the last twenty years with those who took part. The complexity of overtly simple acts of violence does not make them incomprehensible, but should caution us that what we comprehend is the outcome of a particular overlay of voices, refracting only some intentions among the many possible.

In broader perspective, the subject-matter of double-voicing described here is not historically unique. The Maasai experience of enclosure has precedents both in colonial Africa and around the globe, as do the outcries and justifications that tend to accompany enclosure. Appeals and counter-appeals to justice often evoke different rights in order to support different sides of disputes, such as when claims based on precedents clash with claims based on presence. Advocates of democratisation who evoke pluralism as a method of pursuing group interests by other means participate in double-voicing. My aim here has been to situate the experience of violence side by side with some of the important projects pursued in Africa today, namely transformations in how land is held and in how political process is organised and governance is regulated. I have addressed an area of southern Kenya where overt violence is modest compared with that found in neighbouring countries, or even in northern Kenya, but where its increasing routinisation promises to define a corridor of political action running parallel to that defined by the institutions of legitimate governance and civil society and regrettably intersecting it when vital interests are at stake.

The propagation of violence-through-presence can in important respects be attributed to the power of the state to frustrate forces of political liberalisation, since Maasai disillusionment in land and politics can be attributed less to flaws in liberal theory than to the interested way liberal theory is applied (Joseph 1999). But, paradoxically, restraints placed on violence are due to the entrenchment of a complex state apparatus in the Maasai districts of southern Kenya and in the central Rift Valley, in contrast to the north where the state has never successfully implanted itself but still operates as a foreign body that in seeking to establish order increases disorder (Berman 1990, Chabal and Daloz 1999). If, as I propose, violence is invariably double-voiced, we should view explanations in terms of proximate causes and intentions with some caution, since it is an 'already qualified world', bearing the diverse hopes and hatreds of others, which is refracted in the violence we hear described and hope to understand.

Acknowledgements

Reseach support was provided by the Social Sciences and Humanities Research Council of Canada (SSHRC), Québec Fonds pour la Formation de Chercheurs et l'Aide à la Recherche (FCAR), National Science Foundation and McGill University. I am grateful for affiliation with the National Museums of Kenya and for co-operation with the Arid Lands and Resource Management Network in

Eastern Africa (ALARM), administered by the Centre for Basic Research and supported by the International Development Research Centre of Canada. For research assistance, I am indebted to J. Ole Simel and J. Ole Tumanka in Kenya and to J. Mitchell, J. Owiti and C. Archambault in Canada, and to the International Centre for Human Rights and Democratic Development, which I represented as an International Observer to the 1992 Kenyan General Elections.

References

Ayiemba-Omolo, 1996. 'Election monitoring and its constraints in Africa: lessons from the 1992 multi-party elections in Kenya', in J. Oloka-Onyango, K. Kibwana and C. Maina Peter (eds) *Law and the Struggle for Democracy in East Africa*, Nairobi: Claripress, pp. 607–624.

Bakhtin, M.M. 1981. *The Dialogic Imagination*, edited by M. Holquist, Austin, Tex.: University of Texas Press.

Berman, Bruce 1990. *Control and Crisis in Colonial Kenya: The Dialectic of Domination*, London: James Currey.

Berman, Bruce and Lonsdale, John 1992. *Unhappy Valley: Conflict in Kenya and Africa*, London: James Currey; Nairobi: Heinemann.

Chabal, Patrick and Daloz, Jean-Pascal 1999. *Africa Works: Disorder as Political Instrument*, Oxford: James Currey; Bloomington, Ind.: Indiana University Press.

Chege, Michael 1994. 'The return of multiparty politics', in J. Barkan (ed.) *Beyond Capitalism vs. Socialism in Kenya and Tanzania*, Nairobi: East African Educational Publishers, pp. 47–74.

Comaroff, John 1987. 'Of totemism and ethnicity: consciousness, practice, and the signs of inequality', *Ethnos* 3–4: 301–323.

Derrida, J. 1973. *Speech and Phenomena*, Evanston, Ill.: Northwestern University Press.

Galaty, J.G. 1981. 'Models and metaphors: on the semiotics of Maasai segmentary systems', in L. Holy and M. Stuchlik (eds) *The Structure of Folk Models*, London and New York: Academic Press (ASA Monograph No. 20), pp. 63–92.

—— 1993. '"The eye that wants a person, where can it not see?" Inclusion, exclusion and boundary shifters in Maasai identity', in T. Spear and R. Waller (eds) *Being Maasai: Ethnicity and Identity in East Africa*, London: James Curry; Nairobi: EAEP; Athens, O.H.: Ohio University Press: pp. 174–194.

—— 1994. 'Rangeland tenure and African pastoralism', in E. Fratkin, K. Galvin and E. Roth (eds) *African Pastoralist Systems: An Integrated Approach*. Boulder, Colo. and London: Lynne Rienner, pp. 185–204.

—— 1999a. 'Les frontières pastorales en Afrique de l'Est', *Horizons Nomades en Afrique Sahélienne: Sociétés, Développement et Démocratie*, sous la direction de André Bourgeot, Paris: Éditions Karthala: 241–261.

—— 1999b. 'Poetics and violence: competing narratives of justice underlying ethnic clashes in the Rift Valley, Kenya', presented in the Panel on Frontiers of Violence: Time, Conflict and Identity, American Anthropological Association Meetings, Chicago, 17–21 November.

—— In press. 'Environmental narratives and land policy in Africa', in S. Taylor, G. White and E. Fratkin (eds) *African Development in the 21st Century*, Rochester, N.Y.: University of Rochester Press.

Galaty, John G. and Munei, Kimpei Ole 1999. 'Maasai land, law, and dispossession', in J. Galaty (ed.) *Uprooted: Dispossession in Africa*, special issue of *Cultural Survival Quarterly* 22(4): 68–71.

Human Rights Watch 1997. *Failing the Internally Displaced: The UNDP Displaced Persons Program in Kenya*, New York: Human Rights Watch.

Joseph, Richard 1999. 'State, war and democracy in Africa: empirical and theoretical dilemmas", Symposium on African Development in the 21st Century, Smith College, September 24–26.

Kanogo, Tabitha 1987. *Squatters and the Roots of Mau Mau*, London: James Currey; Nairobi: Heinemann.

Kenya, Government of 1934. *Kenya Land Commission*, Report, Cmd. 4556, Vol. X, London: HMSO.

Klopp, J.M. 1999. 'Electoral despotism: ethnic cleansing and winning elections in Kenya', paper presented to the New York State Political Science Association, May 7–8.

Land Rights Program 1996. *Ours by Right, Theirs by Might: A Study on Land Clashes*, Nairobi: A Kenya Human Rights Commission Report.

Marx, Karl 1867/1967. *Capital: A Critique of Political Economy*, Vol. I, New York: International Publishers.

Mauss, Marcel 1925/1967. *The Gift: Forms and Functions of Exchange in Archaic Societies*, New York: W.W. Norton.

Mutunga, W. 1996. 'Building popular democracy in Africa: lessons from Kenya', in J. Oloka-Onyango, K. Kibwana and C. Maina Peter (eds) *Law and the Struggle for Democracy in East Africa*, Nairobi: Claripress, pp. 199–235.

Ndegwa, Stephen 1999. 'Democratization in Africa: work in progress', Symposium on African Development in the 21st Century, Smith College, September 24–26.

Ochieng, William R. 1995. 'Structural and political changes', in B.A. Ogot and W.R. Ochieng (eds) *Decolonization and Independence in Kenya, 1940–1993*, Nairobi: East African Educational Publishers; London: James Currey, pp. 83–109.

Ogot, B.A. 1995a. 'The decisive years, 1956–1963', in B.A. Ogot and W.R. Ochieng (eds) *Decolonization and Independence in Kenya, 1940–1993*, Nairobi: East African Educational Publishers; London: James Currey, pp. 48–79.

—— 1995b. 'The politics of populism', in B.A. Ogot and W.R. Ochieng (eds) *Decolonization and Independence in Kenya, 1940–1993*, Nairobi: East African Educational Publishers; London: James Currey, pp. 187–213.

Parkin, David 1986. 'Violence and will', in D. Riches (ed.) *The Anthropology of Violence*, Oxford: Basil Blackwell, pp. 204–223.

Péron, Xavier 1995. 'Land privatization and public appropriation of land among the Maasai in Kenya: a status of double deprivation', Working Paper No. 22, Nairobi: French Institute for Research in Africa.

Riches, David 1986. 'The phenomenon of violence', in D. Riches (ed.) *The Anthropology of Violence*, Oxford: Basil Blackwell, pp. 1–27.

Rousseau, Jean-Jacques 1755/1987. *Discourse on the Origin of Inequality*, Part Two, in *Jean-Jacques Rousseau: The Basic Political Writings*, Indianapolis, Ind./Cambridge, Mass.: Hackett Publishing Co.

Rutten, M.M. 1992. *Selling Wealth to Buy Poverty: The Process of Individualization of Landownership among the Maasai Pastoralists of Kajiado District, Kenya, 1890–1990*, Saarbrücken and Fort Lauderdale: Verlag Breitenbach.

Rutten, M.M., Mazruir, A. and Grignon, F. (eds) 2001 *Out for the Count: The 1997 General Elections and Prospects for Democracy in Kenya*, Kampala: Fountain Publishers.

Simel, J. Ole 1993. 'The history and the struggle of the Maasai community's land scandal – Loodariak', handwritten manuscript, 12 October.

—— 1994. 'Premature land subdivision, encroachment of rights and manipulation in Maasai Land – Keekonyokie Clan section', ALARM Working Paper, May 2.

Smith, Philip 1997. 'Civil society and violence: narrative forms and the regulation of social conflict', in J. Turpin and L. Kurtz (eds) *The Web of Violence from Interpersonal to Global*, Urbana and Chicago, Ill.: University of Illinois Press, pp. 91–116.

Sorrenson, M.P.K. 1968. *Origins of European Settlement in Kenya*, Nairobi: Oxford University Press.

Tostensen, Arne, Andreassen, Bård-Anders and Tronvoll, Kjetil 1998. *Kenya's Hobbled Democracy Revisited: The 1997 General Elections in Retrospect and Prospect*, Oslo: Norwegian Institute of Human Rights, Human Rights Report No. 2.

Van Der Veer, Peter 1997. 'The victim's tale: memory and forgetting in the story of violence', in H. De Vries and S. Weber (eds) *Violence, Identity, and Self-Determination*, Stanford, Calif.: Stanford University Press, pp. 186–200.

Waller, Richard 1993. 'Acceptees and aliens: Kikuyu settlement in Maasailand', in T. Spear and R. Waller (eds) *Being Maasai: Ethnicity and Identity in East Africa*, London: James Currey, pp. 226–257.

Wanjala, Smokin C. 1996. 'Presidentialism, ethnicity, militarism and democracy in Africa: the Kenyan example', in J. Oloka-Onyango, K. Kibwana and C. Maina Peter (eds) *Law and the Struggle for Democracy in East Africa*, Nairobi: Claripress, pp. 86–100.

Wanjohi, Nick 1997. *Political Parties in Kenya: Formation, Policies and Manifestoes*, Nairobi: Views Media, Lengo Press.

Weber, Max 1978. *Economy and Society: An Outline of Interpretive Sociology*, Berkeley, Calif.: University of California Press.

Winch, Peter 1958. *The Idea of a Social Science and its Relation to Philosophy*, London: Routledge and Kegan Paul.

Wittgenstein, L. 1958. *Philosophical Investigations*, New York: Macmillan.

Chapter 10

Escape from genocide

The politics of identity in Rwanda's massacres

Johan Pottier

Introduction

This chapter is based on an interview with Béatrice, a survivor of the Rwanda genocide, who recalls the story of her escape. The account of how she fled to safety, recorded in June 1994 by journalist Lindsey Hilsum, contains multiple references to the subject of identity or, more accurately, to the plurality of personae that came into play during the flight to safety. Besides being a personal, moving account, the value of Béatrice's testimony lies in the portrayal of complexity, in the revelation of subleties hardly detected at the time of the tragedy: subtleties, moreover, that do not appear in today's official Rwandan discourse on the 1994 genocide. Never broadcast nor used in any other way, the interview comes at the end of the chapter in order first to create a sense of how concerned westerners attempted but regularly failed to get a grip on the complex background to the Rwanda tragedy.

Media coverage of the Rwanda genocide: sticking to simple narratives

In the early days of the tragedy, concerned scholars wasted no time in informing the media of the multiple forces that had fused to set off the barbarous killings. Thus, Catharine and David Newbury (1994), researchers respected for their extensive knowledge of the Great Lakes region, commented that the initial killings in Kigali had been 'carried out principally by the Presidential Guard [which] . . . deliberately targetted those who were outspoken on human rights issues and those who were prominent participants in the multi-party initiatives'. With Kigali as its epicentre, the early fighting could not be portrayed as 'a case of instantaneous chaos, an "orgy" of ethnic violence throughout the country, as many early [press] reports implied' (*Raleigh News and Observer* 17 April 1994). Death lists in hand, the killers initially carried out their 'work' (as they euphemistically called the murders) without much interest in checking their victims' *ethnic* identity; sympathy with 'the enemy', the Rwandese Patriotic Front (RPF) invader, overrode ethnicity as such.

Alison Des Forges, an academic turned human rights activist, also used her past research experience in Rwanda to warn journalists that the lethal madness was not about centuries-old tribal warfare. In the second week of the genocide, Des Forges wrote:

> Politics, Not Tribalism, Is the Root of the Bloodletting. . . . As the piles of bodies mount in Rwanda, commentators are pulling out their generic analyses of violence in Africa: anarchy and/or tribal conflict. Content with ready-made explanations, they overlook the organised killings that opened the way to what has become chaos.
>
> (*Washington Post*, 17 April 1994)

The key word was 'plan': a nationwide killing machine had been engineered and set in place over the past two years. The signal required to make the machine grind into motion came with the downing of the plane which killed Juvénal Habyarimana, Rwanda's president. His death

> provided extremists within the ruling group with the long-sought pretext for wiping out their opponents. Within an hour of the announcement of Habyarimana's death, the elite presidential guard launched a search-and-destroy mission.
>
> One of those they sought was Prime Minister Agathe Uwilingiyimana, one of the first female heads of government in Africa. Soldiers were so set on eliminating her that they violated diplomatic convention to invade the home of a foreign diplomat where they thought she might be hiding; they did not hesitate to kill the United Nations guards who were protecting her. Her summary execution was anything but a random killing, outburst of anarchy or an instance of 'tribal conflict'. Uwilingiyimana was Hutu, one of the majority group, as were the soldiers who killed her. Key leaders as well as ordinary members of opposition political parties have been summarily executed or have disappeared.
>
> (*Washington Post*, 17 April 1994)

It was not long before the planned character of the killings became clear also to key journalists. Lindsey Hilsum, present in Kigali when the killings began, later reflected in *BBC Focus on Africa*:

> The most important thing I understand now, which I did not understand at first, is that none of [the killings] was spontaneous. It was all organised. It was a plan, the Final Solution, developed by Hutu extremists allied to the late President. They planned to exterminate the Tutsis, and all Hutu opposition. That was why the killing started immediately [the presidential plane was shot] and why the radio station had lists of targets.
>
> (*BBC Focus on Africa*, July–September 1994)

On 20 May 1994, Els De Temmerman, a Belgian journalist covering Rwanda, also commented on the systematic manner in which the genocide had been prepared and carried out. She wrote in her diary:

> The puzzle is increasingly clear. And increasingly ugly. What we are witnessing, it has become obvious, is a carefully prepared holocaust-scenario, a monster plan masterminded by a group of people bent on implementing a final solution for 'the Tutsi problem'.
>
> (De Temmerman 1994: 65–66; my translation)

But discovery of 'the plan', a plan about which much had been revealed already in early 1993,[1] did not mean that understanding the social parameters of the tragedy became easy. If it was clear that all thought of 'spontaneous tribal killing' had to be abandoned, it was less clear what should come in its place. Notions of class or cross-ethnic solidarity, for instance, were not easily brought into the frame; journalists faced an intellectual minefield they could hardly comprehend. Speaking at the London School of Economics on 1 July 1994, Richard Dowden (*The Independent*) admitted to being confused. He had been most puzzled, recently, when meeting Tutsi survivors in Benaco camp, Tanzania. Asked how they got away, they had replied referring to their Hutu friends. Dowden said:

> I asked how they could have Hutu friends and the reply was, 'we lived together. We are all friends.' These were the pictures I got. Trying to make some sort of coherent pattern from the fragments was exceedingly difficult.
>
> (Dowden 1995: 88)

Since then, Dowden has learnt that the unimaginable information he was presented with – Tutsi saved by Hutu friends, when all Hutu were supposed to be killers – *was* a piece of accurate information even though it came from the mouths of untrustworthy refugees who, in his opinion, did not deserve a voice (ibid.)[2] Heroic cross-ethnic solidarity in the face of death, it would later be revealed, had not been uncommon (African Rights 1994, Jefremovas 1995).

Despite the academic clarifications in the press early on in the genocide, 'tribe' became the term most habitually used for making sense of Rwanda's madness. Wholly inappropriate, 'tribe' just refused to go away. The way the term was used in the British press (e.g., Julian Bedford, *The Independent*, 5 July 1994, Julian Nundy, *The Independent*, 6 July 1994), and used over and again (Sam Kiley, *The Times*, April 1995), illustrated just how little journalists generally understood about the modern forces behind the plan. The term 'tribal killings' was still used as late as October 1996 when Rwanda invaded eastern Zaire (see Sam Kiley, *The Times*, 8 November 1996).

For those journalists who understood that 'tribalism' was not the correct term, bringing in other variables proved equally problematic. This could be seen, for instance, in the way Robert Block (*New York Review*, 20 October 1994) hinted at the importance of class via a quick reference to Rwanda's land problem. Block referred to the slaughter in Rwanda as 'not exclusively tribal' (but tribal nonetheless), stressing that 'a shortage of land had been at the core of the Hutu-Tutsi struggle'. As insufficient detail was given, readers ignorant about Rwanda may well have inferred that the minority Tutsi, as chief victim, must have controlled vast amounts of land despite their low numerical presence: a nonsensical assumption. Dangerously misleading, the suggestion that tribal/ethnic and class labels were interchangeable also appeared on British television. A good two years after the genocide, at the height of the refugee crisis in eastern Zaire, BBC1 (14 November 1996) ran the following visual:

Tutsi = cattle owners; rich elite; tall

Hutus = peasant farmers; lower class; small

(reported in Philo 1998: 36). The suggested dichotomy opposing 'rich Tutsi' and 'poor Hutu', a dichotomy imbued with racial overtones, was entirely inappropriate to contemporary Rwanda.

Reference to physical/racial characteristics also appeared elsewhere. In mid-July 1994, commenting on Rwanda's identity markers, William Pfaff (Los Angeles Times Syndicate) awkwardly brought back to life the long-discredited Hamitic hypothesis popularised under early Belgian rule. This hypothesis held that every trait of civilisation in Africa originated outside the continent. Pfaff resuscitated the Hamitic hypothesis and its essentialist stereotyping:

> The struggle between Hutu and Tutsi is not simply an ethnic rivalry. The spectacularly tall, cattle-raising Tutsis historically were the rulers of both [Rwanda and Burundi]. They are a Caucasoid people who arrived in the region four centuries ago, probably from Ethiopia, to subjugate the peasant Hutus.
>
> (*International Herald Tribune*, 15 July 1994)

No grasp here of how the pre-colonial history of Rwanda is packed with Tutsi elites fighting other Tutsi elites, nor of the spread of severe poverty among both Hutu and most Tutsi by the end of the nineteenth century. The image of centuries-old tribal warfare, which is what Pfaff held up despite using the term 'ethnic', was reinforced by other journalists. Seemingly unaware of any academic literature on Rwanda, Jennifer Parmelee of the *Washington Post Service* also wrote how the country had been 'wounded by recurrent tribal pogroms' (*International Herald Tribune*, 15 July 1994).

Rwanda's north–south divide, another key factor in the genocide, also received scant attention in early commentaries on the disaster, and was certainly not understood in its full historical context. Hilsum, however, provided a useful reference: 'The tensions in Rwandan politics were exacerbated. Being a Hutu was not enough, you had to be a Hutu from the president's northwestern region'

(*Africa Report*, May/June 1994: 15). Hilsum's message was very similar to Des Forges': the Rwanda killings were not about 'tribalism'.

With the exception of the Belgian press (Pottier 2002), most journalists struggled to comprehend the underlying causes of the genocide, as well as the various social identities at stake. But this lack of understanding was a problem about which the incoming RPF regime was not too concerned. If no one in the media fully understood the scene, then journalists could be turned into scribes, i.e. vehicles for transmitting the RPF's rendition of Rwandan society and history. The rewriting of history would become the RPF's development project par excellence (Jefremovas 1997). Some journalists proved so gullible they were prepared to rubbish all contemporary research and writings on ethnicity in Rwanda as 'fanciful nonsense, a carry over from the colonial era' (Keane 1996: 15). Fergal Keane's award-winning *Season of Blood* (Orwell Prize 1995) is an instructive example of how the pressures of war journalism (ignorance about the place, strict deadlines and trauma) may combine to produce and legitimate a most simplifying and distorting, but 'politically correct', version of history. Being alerted, rightly, to the racial fantasies found in certain colonial writings, Keane went on to reproduce and defend the RPF's take on Rwandan society and history, claiming that patronage, i.e. the cattle contract (and *only* the cattle contract), had shaped ethnic relations in pre-colonial times – *and done so with harmony*. The information was one-sided. While handy in relativising the importance of ethnicity in Rwanda, the exclusive focus on cattle obscured the highly complex, historical developments that had emerged in the wake of king Rwabugiri's military campaign and administrative expansion during the late nineteenth century (Newbury 1988).

Historical reality had been far more complex. As research in Rwanda in the 1960s and 1970s had brought to light, the infiltration of political appointees under Rwabugiri had eroded the autonomy of corporate kin groups (lineages) and the personal security of individuals. In terms of cultivators' access to land, the infiltration meant that land was appropriated by new, mostly Tutsi administrators, who then entered into personal relationships with cultivators, relationships without which cultivators could not survive. The various systems of clientship may have provided some benefit to the poor, but denied the vast majority of the population – Hutu and Tutsi – an independent, economically secure existence. This is the backdrop against which any claim regarding reciprocity and socio-economic mobility quickly loses its validity. As for cattle, the majority of Hutu had nothing to do with cattle. In some areas, including Central Rwanda, transfers of cattle from Tutsi to Hutu were simply unthinkable before 'les Blancs' arrived (Vidal 1991: 34). Pre-colonial reciprocity involving wealth (i.e. cattle) had been mostly an affair between elites already owning cattle (Vidal 1969). The cattle contract, moreover, was not a homogeneous institution found in the same form in all regions of pre-colonial Rwanda (Newbury 1988: 73).

Revolving mainly around the loss of rights in land and labour, the intricate patronage relationships of pre-colonial Rwanda were too complex for media consumption and would, in any case, not have been useful in getting across the message that the incoming RPF was not interested in the business of ethnicity. Only a strongly simplified narrative could convey such a message. Ignorant about Rwandan society and history, journalists like Keane willingly reproduced the RPF-functional, reductionist version of how Hutu–Tutsi–Twa relations had developed:

> What separated Tutsi and Hutu in the past was primarily a matter of occupation and wealth. Thus the Tutsi clan owned large herds of cattle, while their Hutu subjects farmed the land and the Twa subsisted on what they could gather in field and forest. As time progressed many Hutus bought cattle and were assimilated into the Tutsi aristocracy. Some Tutsis became poor and lost their privileged positions.
>
> (Keane 1996: 12)

Keane carefully avoided the trap of suggesting that the European colonists had invented Rwanda's ethnic distinctions, but then fell for an all too simplistic construction of social positions, resource use and social mobility. This also applies to Keane's handling of the significance of the ID cards introduced in 1933. By introducing these cards, the Belgian colonists took away the 'possibility of elevating oneself from the peasant classes to the aristocracy through the purchase of cattle ... [After] the introduction of the ID card system a Hutu was a Hutu for life' (1996: 17). While ID cards fixed and racialised the exclusionary system, which cannot be denied (see Survivor's Testimony, below), Keane exaggerates the ease with which poor peasants supposedly moved into the aristocracy. But it was what his RPF mentors wanted the world to believe.

The RPF used the services not only of journalists ignorant of the region, but also 'instant' academic experts. Eager to spread and legitimate the new 'politically correct' rhetoric on Rwandan society and history, partisan academics resuscitated the discarded, idealised representation of Rwanda's pre-colonial past (Maquet 1961). This model conjured up an idyllic, integrative pre-colonial society devoid of ethnic divisions and tensions, and originated in a functionalist anthropology nurtured by the colonial desire to justify indirect rule. Pre-colonial Rwanda had enjoyed harmony, or so the story ran, because its chief social institution – *ubuhake* cattle clientship – had permitted mobility across fluid occupational-cum-social categories. Hierarchy and status had been facts of life, but negotiable (for a full review of such post-genocide writings, see Pottier 2002).

Although westerners working in/on Rwanda after the genocide sometimes understood that Hutu and Tutsi were not 'tribes' but socially constructed ethnic categories, they rarely became *au fait* with Rwanda's socio-political complexity and regional (and historical) diversity. Rwanda was small, so how could there be complexity? Westerners were thus fed the line, popularised during late colonialism, that pre-colonial relations could be understood through recourse to a single institution, the *ubuhake* cattle contract (see Maquet 1961). Other contractual forms, that whole plethora of highly exploitative 'contracts' grounded in the appropriation of land by the ruling Tutsi central court, and among which *uburetwa* was the most hated, were of no importance (see e.g. Mullen 1995). Adopting the Maquet/Tutsi aristocratic view, Mullen believed that the advantages and disadvantages of the system were somehow in balance.

Right from the beginning of their military campaign, RPF spokesmen keenly emphasised the ease of social mobility in pre-colonial Rwanda, which, needless to add, carried the implied message that ethnicity was/is not worth making a fuss about. Ethnicity, RPF commanders told interested journalists time and again, was just a question of cows, a colonial mistake.

> 'If you have more than 10 cows you can become a Tutsi,' says Captain Diogène Mudenge, the RPF commander at the eastern Rwandan town of Gahini. 'Hutu simply means "servant" in our language. Somebody with lots of cows has the right to have servants. Tutsi just means rich. It was during the 1950s and the 1960s that the difference became politicised.'
>
> (*The Guardian*, 3 May 1994)

That the RPF should have wanted to simplify ethnic relations is perfectly under-standable: de-emphasising complexity can raise morale and hope for the future, might even persuade foreign diplomats and donors to have confidence in the new regime. Note, too, that Mudenge's reference to wealth (Tutsi = rich; Hutu = poor) trivialises not only the importance of ethnicity, but also that of class.

The Survivor's Testimony with which this chapter closes reveals a more complex entwining of ethnicity and class.

Power, class and 'ethnic strife'

Class hardly ever featured in journalistic accounts of the Rwanda genocide. I attribute this in part to the fact that the RPF itself refrained from bringing class into its explanations; doing so would have complicated matters (the RPF wanted simple narratives), and might have drawn attention to the persistence of sharp class divisions in post-genocide Rwanda. It would be quite some time, therefore, before the intricate interplay of the multiple forces underpinning the Rwanda tragedy would become evident, before it would be known that the crisis had roots in ethnicity (and the power of demagogues), class (acute impoverishment accelerated by unprecedented economic shocks), the country's north–south divide, and the RPF invasion and war begun in 1990.

One instructive demonstration of the class aspect to the genocide has come from Tim Longman (1995), who approached the topic ethnographically. On the basis of field research, Longman concluded that

> the massacres represented a calculated and systematic attempt by embattled elites to reassert their social, economic, and political dominance and to eliminate any challenges to their authority. . . . The disaster in Rwanda

indicates the extreme tenacity of authoritarian rulers and the great lengths to which their supporters will go to protect their privilege.

(Longman 1995: 20)

Given the cold-blooded preparations for genocide in Rwanda, its scale and the speed of its execution, it is important, even today, that the 'pattern' of the killings – and the role of class – be understood. I here refer to class as manifested in the incidence of land scarcity, a problem varying between regions and between communes (administrative units) within regions. Where disparities were wide and the frustration of the landless deep, the killings were carried out by locals who knew their victims well. The converse also applied. Longman highlights this by contrasting the socio-economic and political situation in two parishes in Kibuye: Kirinda and Biguhu. In Kirinda, where the disparity between rich and poor was marked, and the number of landless youth large, the killings were 'intimate'. Disparity in Biguhu was not so wide; in fact, Biguhu's elites had supported Rwanda's civil society movement and in 1992 sent a local peasant farmer to attend a seminar in civic education. Aware of his people's resistance to violence, Biguhu's *bourgmestre* brought in outsiders to do the killing. (It is 'small details' like this, acts of cross-ethnic solidarity, which would baffle outsiders who tried to make sense of the chaos that engulfed Rwanda, see Dowden above.)

When bringing class into the equation, however, one must take care not simply to substitute 'class' for 'ethnicity'. In his reflections on the Rwanda genocide, George Balandier, for example, drew too sharp a distinction between Hutu, as the oppressed masses, and Tutsi, as the privileged elite. Balandier's characterisation of the class issue is undoubtedly part of the 'collective memory of Hutu', and therefore important, but it is not an accurate summary of the importance of class oppression at the beginning of the 1990s. Highlighting Rwanda's economic problems and demographic explosion, Balandier concluded that

> more than an ethnic conflict in the strict sense of the term, the massacres represented first and foremost a clash between an aristocratic minority, the holder of privileges, and a mass of people traditionally subjugated. In a certain sense, this had been a class struggle which degenerated in terror.
>
> (*La Dernière Heure*, 30–31 July 1994; my translation)

What clouds the analysis here is Balandier's reference to an aristocratic minority, i.e. easily misconstrued as 'the Tutsi', whereas Rwanda's ruling elite of the late 1980s (early 1990s) had been a northern Hutu elite. Of course, deep-seated Hutu fears about the return of 'feudalism' (a slippery term) also played a part, but the more appropriate reference point, surely, was the domination by a northern Hutu elite, which was not aristocratic.

The more correct analysis, as Jean-François Bayart also argued, was to see Rwanda 1994 as an extreme yet typical case of how dictators threatened by democracy attempt to stay in power by resorting to a strategy whereby 'ethnic tensions' are artificially whipped up and blown out of proportion. Bayart:

> . . . the ethno-political conflict we are witnessing in Rwanda is not the leftover of some ancient Africa, but a political event which is part of modern Africa. The instigators of the massacres are politicised intellectuals, and not the peasant mass.
>
> (*Le Nouvel Observateur*, 2 June 1994; my translation)

It is important, though, to place the rise of Hutu extremism within the context of the acute impoverishment of the late 1980s; a process to which the 'international community' had contributed in such a significant way that one analyst has referred to the Rwanda genocide as being an 'economic genocide' (Chossudovsky 1997).

The class element in Rwanda's genocide has much to do with the gradual but persistent change towards smaller family farms. As Prioul remarked for the country as a whole,

> [i]n 1948 the typical peasant family lived on a hill which supported between 110 and 120 inhabitants per km²; in 1970, that same family [had] to make a living on a hill which support[ed] between 280 and 290 people per km².
>
> (Prioul 1976: 74)

The impact on food production was dramatic. In the words of Lydia Meschy: 'Compared with the average family of a generation ago, today's household harvests no more than half the customary amount of sorghum, beans and bananas' (Meschy 1974: 49). Despite efforts to intensify agriculture, this worrying trend continued and the statistics became alarming: 'From two million inhabitants in 1940, the population in 1991 . . . reached 7.15 million' (Waller 1993: 47). Waller concluded: 'If it increases at 3.1 per cent each year, the population of Rwanda will have reached 10 million by 2002 AD' (ibid.: 47). By now, the national average of people per km² had shot up to 422, with one northern commune reaching 820 people per sq km of usable land (ibid.: 18). This was the early 1990s: there was virtually no more arable land to be claimed.

Meanwhile, elites close to Habyarimana were busy *buying* land, particularly in the north-west. Researching a hill community in the north-west in 1988, and again between November 1992 and February 1994, Catherine André observed how land swiftly changed hands despite distress sales being outlawed (André 1995: 89). While a monetised market in land had existed for some decades, the incidence of land purchases rose sharply in the late 1980s. Many poor households now became landless. Importantly, those losing their entitlement to land included a range of 'social actors', such as individuals deemed illegitimate, divorcees and their children, and migrants who returned to their communes after long absences. The sudden boom of Rwanda's illegal land market originated in the growing disparity between rich and poor, a disparity widened with the arrival of multi-party 'democracy', i.e. Western-style democracy, in 1990.

At this point, many Rwandans felt victimised by international forces they could not control. Increasingly, they regarded their poverty as 'due to the structure of the world's economic and political systems' (Waller 1993: 60). The crash of the world coffee price was the proverbial last straw, although worse was to come. When multi-party politics, the policy prescription mistaken for democracy, was implemented as part of a Structural Adjustment Programme just months before the RPF invaded in October 1990, it became depressingly clear that 'as the different sides struggle[d] for supremacy, much of Rwanda's sovereignty [was] now invested in the Paris Club of creditor nations, in the European Community, and in the World Bank' (ibid.: 27). Following the RPF invasion, the scramble for resources and power became irreversible. From then on, '[a]ny group with aspirations to exert more influence in how Rwandese society should be run was . . . encouraged to make a move. The internal opposition was stimulated to become more active' (Pender 1997: 3). Rapidly, 'democratisation' became 'a dirty word' for most ordinary Rwandans, because the concept resulted in an increase in factional violence and further disruption of economic activities already badly affected by the war. The prescribed 'democracy' exacerbated inter-regional hostility – particularly between the north-western prefectures (Gisenyi, Ruhengeri), both privileged under Habyarimana, and the south-central prefecture of Gitarama, home of the largest internal opposition party, the Mouvement Démocratique Républicain, MDR (Mackintosh 1996: 44).

In 1994, south Rwanda paid the price for the inter-ethnic cohabitation it had fostered, when the mostly northern Presidential Guards and *interahamwe* ('those who attack together') death squads closed in on Butare. In *Libération*, Stephen Smith wrote:

> Tutsi were not the only victims who perished. After General Habyarimana's coup of 1973, southern Hutu, now also oppressed, had established a rapprochement with Tutsi. This made Butare the cradle of the country's internal political opposition, of 'moderates' who, between military dictatorship and armed rebellion, sought the median voice of democracy or, to put it more mundanely, sought a better sharing of power. Following the death of the president-general, 'progressive' Hutu, whom the nearly exclusively northern military now considered 'traitors of the race', were subjected to the wrath of the army and the militias the old regime had trained.
>
> (Stephen Smith, *Libération*, 27 May 1994; my translation)

The Rwanda tragedy must not be construed as a straightforward ethnic phenomenon. Besides deflecting from the class factor, a focus on 'pure' ethnic conflict also masks the deep, historically evolved rift *within* Rwanda's Hutu population.

The general failure by (most) journalists and 'instant academic experts' to probe beyond the simplistic, RPF-functional narrative on Rwandan society and history, needs to be put right: the complex interweaving of variables in the genocide – particularly the interplay of ethnic identity and class – must be better understood if the 'international community' is to have a way of monitoring future developments in the Great Lakes region. About these complexities, which the present RPF-led regime in Kigali prefers to ignore (Eltringham and Van Hoyweghen 2000), we can learn from Béatrice, the survivor of genocide whose story about her escape now follows.

Survivor's testimony

In her interview with Lindsey Hilsum, Béatrice Chika, a Tutsi from Kigali whose parents lived in Bukavu, Zaire, recalled the circumstances of her flight from Rwanda at the beginning of the genocide. The interview took place in Bujumbura in June 1994, in French, and was recorded on tape. (The translation into English is my own.) Although the tape has remained a 'family tape' up to now, its contents are too important not to be transcribed and circulated; all close to Béatrice, who sadly died in late 1998, share this conviction. Shortly after the interview, in August 1994, Béatrice returned to Kigali where I met her in an emotional reunion. From what she then told me about her escape from genocide, I can only deduce that the earlier, taped interview had been a 'sanitised' version of the escape; many graphic details were omitted. The interview, however, conducted in a more controlled, calmer atmosphere, sheds light on several identity-related aspects of the 1994 genocide, particularly on the complex interplay of ethnicity, nationality, class and gender.

The opening exchanges in the interview establish that Béatrice (B) lived near Bilyogo market in Nyamirambo, Kigali's Islamic quarter, where she headed her own household, caring for her two children, Denise (aged 10) and Hadija (aged 6). Béatrice had recently converted to Islam. At the time of the genocide, she traded in charcoal (*makala*), mostly in Bilyogo market. Lindsey (L) then asked about the night of the first killings.

L: When the situation exploded in Rwanda, when the president's plane was shot down, what happened in Nyamirambo?
B: That same night, by 3 a.m., we heard gunshots, they had started killing people. When we opened the door, we could see barricades everywhere; the CDR [Coalition pour la Défense du Rwanda] and *interahamwe* were already killing people. By 5 a.m. there were many dead bodies. Men, women and children.
L: Who was being killed? People you knew?
B: Yes, they were our neighbours.
L: And you, did anyone threaten you?
B: People came to tell me that I was Tutsi, and not a Zairean (*zaïroise*). We argued for a long time until some people [among the killer mob] recognised me and said: 'Leave her alone, she is *zaïroise*, and Zaireans are the friends of Rwanda.' That's what they said.[3]
L: Denise and Hadija, what did they do?

B: I tried very hard to hide Denise, because everyone said: 'Denise is Tutsi.' Denise hid under the bed. And later, we all slept in holes in the ground.

L: Did you know the people who attacked you? Were they from this area?

B: In Rwanda there are many people who bring '*les bagages*' to market [i.e. transporters], whom we call *abakalani*. They are like secretaries, but in reality they are house servants (*des 'boys'*), scoundrels (*des voyoux*) or bandits. Before the president's plane was shot, all these '*voyoux de Kigali*' had received weapons. Ah, they had grenades and guns with which to attack [the people of] Kigali. I knew them well the people who did this.

L: When those people came to kill you, how did you explain you were *zaïroise*?

B: I said I was *zaïroise* and not interested in politics. That I did not know the [political] parties of Rwanda, neither the RPF nor the others. I am *zaïroise*, I am a stranger here. This saved me, that's what I told them.

But then there was that man, Claude, who had once been '*mon "boy"*' [he had worked for me], and he came back afterwards at night and said he wanted to make love to me. So I said: '*Tiens!*, Claude, do you not know me?' He said he did, and that making love is what I am telling you ('*ce que je te dis*'). [Béatrice laughs on tape, sounding incredulous.] I went back home, then went to sleep elsewhere.

L: Was he a Hutu?

B: Yes, he was Hutu.

L: Were you frightened?

B: I was very, very, very frightened. Very frightened. What saved us then was that the RPF started bombing Kigali, the whole town. This gave us the opportunity to flee Kigali, everyone began to flee.

L: The moment you actually left the house, what did you do? What did you do with the children?

B: With Denise and Hadija, I began to run. But there was also Willy, my brother Willy, who was there with a car. He drove us to Mt Kigali and left us there. From here, I went on foot with the children, we walked across Mt Kigali until we reached the Nyabarongo [river]. But it's my brother who saved me.

L: When you were in the car with Willy, what happened at the barricades? There were so many barricades.

B: As bombs were being dropped on Kigali, there were no barricades; everyone had started to run. Even those who stood at the barricades, they ran too. It saved us. I was so scared.

[. . .]

L: What did Willy do after he dropped you off?

B: Willy could not leave Kigali. [On the radio] they had said that young men were not allowed to leave the town. But yes, when we were with Willy, they [the mob] attacked the car, saying he had to return to Kigali to fight. *Au combat!* There was no other way for him. He then told me: 'My sister, I know you will survive, you will save yourself and the children. I, too, will survive this. I'm a man, I can save myself.' Until now, I have no news from him, and he not from me.

L: You then continued on foot. Where did you go?

B: I left the Nyabarongo on foot with my children, we headed for Gitarama. It took a full week to reach there. At night we slept *en brousse* (in the bush), and each morning we saw that God had saved us.

L: How many were you?

B: I was with my neighbour from Nyamirambo, whose name is Laetitia [pseudonym]. She had a baby of 3 months, I took charge of them both. There were also other people, but I did not know them. . . . One night, Rwandan soldiers [of the Forces Armées Rwandaises] took Laetitia away, she stayed with them until the morning, so I was left with Laetitia's baby but did not have any milk to give. The following morning we sought out some neighbours (*des voisins*) at Gitarama, but with much fear. It was like this until the Prefect of Gitarama gave a bus to those refugees who wanted to reach Bukavu or Cyangugu.

L: When you were all walking, did you cross any barricades? Did you need to talk in order to pass?

B: They asked for ID papers (*les pièces*) to check whether you were Hutu or Tutsi. But, with luck on our side (*chance à nous*), because I was *zaïroise*, we passed. On Laetitia's ID card I had erased 'Tutsi' with methyl alcohol (*avec l'alcool*), and put 'Hutu' instead. Like this, Laetitia was lucky (*chance à Laetitia*), she was able to pass for a Hutu. But it did not stop the soldiers from raping her.

L: What about you, Béatrice, you do look Tutsi, you're elegant and slim?

B: At the barricades I was told I was a liar, that I was Tutsi and had changed my nationality. They often argued about that. [Note: Béatrice had a Zairean *carte consulaire*.] One day they took me out of the bus, took me aside. I gave money to continue the journey. Yes, I gave money.

L: What about the children?

B: Oh yes, they too, people said they were Tutsi. And always we palavered. When the *interahamwe* turned very nasty (*très grave*), each time I gave money.

L: How much money did you give?

B: Because Willy had given me $200 (US dollars), on leaving Kigali I changed $100 for 10,000RwF. So I had 20,000RwF. By the time I arrived at Gitarama, I remained with just 5,000RwF. In Gitarama I also met up with Xavier, my other brother, who lived in grandma's house. I went to see him at the house. Xavier said: 'my sister, leave now, leave quickly (*quitte vite, quitte vite*). You look Tutsi.' It's true, I take after my mother, I look Tutsi. Xavier also gave me 20,000RwF. But because of Laetitia, who had Rwandan nationality, at the barriers they always said she was Tutsi, she was Tutsi. So it was that I needed to give money for Laetitia to let her pass. Until we reached Ndendezi.

L: When the soldiers came, the soldiers who took away and raped Laetitia, did they find the two of you together?

B: In Gitarama, all the refugees from Kigali slept outside the shops. The soldiers came with a torch and called me, but I closed my ears. Then they turned to Laetitia, who said 'me?', so they took her and I remained.

L: How was Laetitia when she returned that morning? Did she cry? Did she cry a lot?

B: She cried and cried, very much. Because she had suffered a lot (*on lui a fait beaucoup de gaffes, beaucoup de gaffes*). I do not know how to say it, it was very very serious.

L: How did you get the bus to leave Gitarama?

B: You know, there were many women from Cyangugu, and because women were constantly being killed and raped they approached the Prefect to complain. The Prefect gave us three buses.

L: How many refugees left for Cyangugu on these buses?

B: A hundred and fifty women left, but only seventy made it to Cyangugu.

L: What happened to those who did not make it?

B: At each barricade we needed to get off the bus. Always they searched us, and always accused some women of being Tutsi. And everywhere, if you could not pay you were killed. They killed many people, everywhere, everywhere on the road.

L: And you?

B: Me too. When we reached the forest, at the place we call Kitabi, the 'chef' at the barricade took my ID card and pocketed it. He said: 'You, you must stay here, you must be my wife.' I said: 'no, I must not be your wife.' It was then 3p.m. We finally left at 10 a.m. the following morning, thanks to our bus driver who offered the chef money. After he gave a lot of money, the chef left us alone.

L: With that long wait, what did the others in the bus say?

B: They told the driver, 'Ah, why do you care about her? Is she your whore perhaps (*une putain à toi*)? Leave her and we continue.' But he refused. I do not know why, luck was on my side (*c'était ma chance*).

L: He was a good man.

B: Yes, because he saved us.

L: All in all, how long did the journey take?

B: Five days. From Gitarama to Cyangugu, we took five days. *Ha! 20 mètres, barrière; 20 mètres, barrière.* And each time we got out of the bus.

L: These people at the barricades, how were they? Did they have machetes?

B: At the barricades, they had knives, machetes, guns. Grenades too. And sticks and large stones. They often told women and men to lie down on the road, then they lifted the large stones and smashed their heads.

L: How were the faces of those who killed?

B: There was nothing in their faces. They were as they were, there was nothing in their faces.

L: Were they all men?

B: I saw women twice; once in Kigali, once at the Nyabarongo. They had guns. Even at Cyangugu, at the Kanembe barricade, I saw a woman with a gun.

L: The children were with you all this time?

B: Yes, they were with me. But then, after a dispute at some checkpoint, I gave Denise to a woman on the bus. Denise was always told she was Tutsi. I gave Denise to Mama Naima, so I was left with Hadija and Laetitia. But at Ndendenzi, the guards at the barricade were difficult; most of us were ordered off the bus . . . That's where Laetitia remained with her baby, they were killed.

L: They were killed.

B: Yes, with her baby Omar.

L: They made Laetitia get off the bus. What happened then?

B: Everyone and everything was taken off the bus. Then they began to look at the ID papers and our faces. And when they did not see anything in your face, they lifted your shirt and counted your ribs. And they looked at your feet and fingers. They looked at me too. I was lucky, *c'était ma chance*, my life was spared because of my fingers. They said no Tutsi could possibly have *des gros doigts comme ça* (such big fingers). They said: 'Your big fingers mean you work, you are *une vraie zaïroise* (a real zaïroise), so go.' It was there that Laetitia stayed with her baby.

L: Are you certain she was killed?

B: She did not come back on the bus. And then after they said we must continue, after a few minutes, we heard the gunfire. It was the beginning of the massacre. Guns that make a noise, they kill.

L: What did Laetitia do in Kigali? Did she work with you?

B: She was married to a garage mechanic, a Tutsi from Burundi. But he, he left Kigali and left behind his wife and baby. He went to save himself, that's why I stayed with Laetitia. They had already killed her father and mother, her entire family. Laetitia was my friend, so I said: 'Laetitia, you cannot stay here in Kigali by yourself. We'll stay together, sleep together, if I am saved you too must be saved.' But she died.

L: Did you find Denise when you reached Cyangugu?

B: Yes, I had just arrived in Cyangugu when I spotted Denise with Mama Naima on the road. Denise was so very thin, she had lost much weight. And Mama Naima, too, you know, she cried, she sobbed: 'You know, your daughter, everyone wanted to kill her, to kill her, to kill her. They said, "Ha, it is the *Inkotanyi* [i.e. the Rwandese Patriotic Front] who are leaving Kigali with their children".'

L: Mama Naima was Hutu?

B: Yes, she is a Hutu from Cyangugu, a friend. You know at Nyamirambo, Kigali's Islamic quarter, you know people there never distinguished Hutu from Tutsi, everyone there was the same.

L: What happened when you were reunited in Cyangugu?

B: I went to Laetitia's grandmother's place. There, everyone was frightened, everyone was very frightened. They said: 'Leave quickly, Béatrice, leave quickly. If they see you here, they will kill you, and all of us too.' I stayed for 18 hours, too frightened to cross [the bridge] to Bukavu. Then I said to Denise's grandma, the mother of her father: 'You know there is a boy, Babou, who lives here and sometimes stays with me in Kigali, I could stay with him.' The grandmother replied 'No, you must not stay here [in Cyangugu]'. With great fear I stayed till 5a.m., then woke and left for Bukavu. I was terrified. I thought I'd be killed at the border and thrown in the Ruzizi [river]. But it wasn't like that. On the other side, the soldiers told me: '*Félicitations maman, félicitations maman*! How did you manage to reach safety with your children? Everyone hugged me, saying '*Grand merci, grand merci*'.

L: And you said: 'I am *zaïroise*'?

B: In Bukavu we are all the same, whether Rwandan or Zairean. But the Zairean soldiers laughed and said: 'But you, you too, you are *Inkotanyi*, how did you pass?' So I laughed as well and said: 'But I, I am your sister.'

Conclusion: the interweaving of variables central to Rwanda's genocide

In the lived reality of Rwanda today, the survivor of genocide is all too often reduced to a singular identity, that of suspected collaborator with the *interahamwe*.[4] Béatrice's testimony tells us otherwise; it reveals a very complex world in which a survivor's multiple personae become manifest. The testimony makes reference to ethnicity (ID cards, racial stereotyping), class (the 'boy' out to humiliate Béatrice, the power of money), gender (rape, Willy's macho comment on the chances of survival, Laetitia's husband abandoning her), religion and cross-ethnic solidarity (among Muslim women), nationality (Zaire being perceived as a friend of Rwanda's Hutu), and of course '*la chance*' – a very Rwandan concept. Béatrice's testimony highlights how these variables are entwined within the person seeking escape from conflict and genocide. Unhindered by official agendas, Béatrice spoke not only as a Tutsi survivor, a category the RPF has now streamlined, but also as a single mother, a Zairean national, a poor urban trader (who nonetheless employed a 'boy'), a Muslim with close Hutu friends, a woman vulnerable to physical abuse. Béatrice spoke as a human being aware of the importance of her different personae.

Rwanda's official discourse on the events of 1994 recognises four social categories only: *rescapés* (Tutsi genocide survivors), old caseload refugees (Tutsi returned from exile), new caseload returnees (Hutu returned from the refugee camps that sprung up in 1994) and *génocidaires* (the Hutu perpetrators of that genocide). Anyone departing from this rigid typology, or offering a more nuanced reading of Rwanda's post-genocide social fabric, risks being accused of denying that genocide occurred, even risks being labelled *génocidaire* (Eltringham and Van Hoyweghen 2000, also Prunier 1997). Béatrice's story, however, recorded in an open, non-leading way, testifies to the need for a more detailed understanding of what it means to be a survivor of genocide, *une rescapée*. Béatrice did see herself as a Tutsi survivor, but her reconstruction of the escape from hell shows that identities other than 'Tutsi' also came into play. In the same way that ' "genocide" is shorthand for a complex country-specific tragedy' (Eltringham and Van Hoyweghen 2000), so *rescapé(e)* must be contextualised. As Béatrice escaped the killing fields, she drew upon multiple personae: sometimes passing the deadly barricades as *zaïroise*, sometimes as a person with money (payment leading to a social death), and always drawing strength from her Muslim identity and the cross-ethnic solidarity which accrued. Béatrice's testimony tells us not to fall for the lure of narratives grounded in simplistic, essentialist dichotomies – especially that of *Hutu génocidaire* versus *Tutsi rescapé*. The courage of Mama Naima, also not to be forgotten, should be a lever to help post-genocide Rwanda transcend the slippery but officially endorsed dichotomy in which collective Hutu guilt is pitted against collective Tutsi victimisation.

Acknowledgements

I am indebted to Lindsey Hilsum (Diplomatic Correspondent, Channel 4) for permission to use her June 1994 interview with Béatrice Chika. I also record my gratitude to the Leverhulme Trust for granting the fellowship and sabbatical year during which much of my research into journalistic coverage of Rwanda was undertaken.

Notes

1   Preparations for genocide, then dressed up as self-defence against the RPF invasion, began some two years before the actual genocide. Reyntjens recalled:

> the Rwandan state is an efficiently controlled system which runs from the highest level to the smallest *nyumba kumi* – the basic administrative cell of 10 houses. Two years ago, the general staff of the national army already decided to provide one gun for every *nyumba kumi*: 150,000 in total! This gives an immensely fast snowball effect: an instruction from the top needs just about a couple of hours to reach every prefecture, commune, sector and *nyumba kumi*. It takes just a few hours to mobilise some 100,000 and have them kill their neighbours (*Knack* 20 July 1994; my translation).

The whole of Rwanda was well and truly infiltrated by people ready to kill; Hutu in 99.9 per cent of cases. Identifying themselves as *interahamwe* ('those who attack together'), they were part of the extremists' masterplan for the extermination of political opponents and Tutsi; a plan already exposed by the Commission internationale d'enquête sur les violations des droits de l'homme au Rwanda (FIDH) in March 1993. The commission had obtained conclusive evidence that Habyarimana, or more precisely the 'little house' (*akazu*) of his in-laws, was planning to eradicate through violent means every form of opposition. From March 1993 onwards, details of the plan had circulated within the so-called 'international community'.

2   It is worth recalling here that when Tutsi fled the pogroms in Rwanda in 1959–1961, they too were sometimes accompanied by loyal Hutu servants. Also, some Hutu from northern Rwanda had joined the RPF in time for its 1990 invasion.

3 This was a reference to Mobutu supporting Habyarimana in his war against the RPF (see Prunier 1997, Kamukama 1997).
4 Similarly, the concept of 'the refugee' obscures the actual conditions and roles which individual refugees experience (Malkki 1995: 13, Pottier 1996).

References

African Rights 1994. *Rwanda: Death, Despair and Defiance*, London: African Rights.
André, Catherine 1995. 'Modes d'accès et d'occupation des terres: quelle justice sociale?', *Dialogue* 186: 83–94.
Chossudovsky, Michel 1997. 'Economic genocide in Rwanda', in *The Globalisation of Poverty: Impacts of IMF and World Bank Reforms*, Penang, Malaysia: Third World Network, pp. 111–124.
De Temmerman, Els 1994. *De Doden Zijn Niet Dood: Rwanda, Een Ooggetuigenverslag*, Groot-Bijgaarden, Belgium: Globe.
Dowden, Richard 1995. 'Media coverage: how I reported the genocide', in Obi Igwara (ed.) *Ethnic Hatred: Genocide in Rwanda*, London: ASEN Publication, pp. 85–92.
Eltringham, Nigel and Van Hoyweghen, Saskia 2000. 'Power and identity in post-genocide Rwanda', in Ruddy Doom and Jan Gorus (eds) *Politics of Identity and Economics of Conflict in the Great Lakes Region*, Brussels: Free University Press.
Jefremovas, Villia 1995. 'Acts of human kindness: Hutu, Tutsi and the genocide', *Issue: A Journal of Opinion* 23(2): 28–31.
—— 1997. 'Contested identities: power and the fictions of ethnicity, ethnography and history in Rwanda', *Anthropologica* 23: 1–14.
Kamukama, Dixon 1997. *Rwanda Conflict: Its Roots and Regional Implications*, Kampala: Fountain Publishers.
Keane, Fergal 1996. *Season of Blood: A Rwandan Journey*, Harmondsworth: Penguin.
Longman, Timothy 1995. 'Genocide and socio-political change: massacres in two Rwandan villages', *Issue: A Journal of Opinion* 23(2): 18–21.
Mackintosh, Anne 1996. 'International aid and the media', in Tim Allen, Kate Hudson and Jean Seaton (eds) *War, Ethnicity and the Media*, London: South Bank University, School of Education, pp. 37–56.
Malkki, Liisa 1995. *Purity and Exile: Violence, Memory and National Cosmology among Hutu Refugees in Tanzania*, Chicago, Ill.: University of Chicago Press.
Maquet, Jacques 1961. *The Premise of Inequality*, London: Oxford University Press, for the International African Institute.
Meschy, Lydia (misspelled as Meschi) 1974. 'Évolution des structures foncières au Rwanda: le cas d'un lignage hutu', *Cahiers d'Études Africaines* 14(1): 39–51.
Mullen, Joseph 1995. 'From colony to nation: the implosion of ethnic tolerance in Rwanda', in Obi Igwara (ed.) *Ethnic Hatred: Genocide in Rwanda*, London: ASEN Publication, pp. 21–34.
Newbury, M. Catharine 1988. *The Cohesion of Oppression: Clientship and Ethnicity in Rwanda, 1860–1960*, New York: Columbia University Press.
Newbury, Catharine and Newbury, David 1994. 'Rwanda: the politics of turmoil', *Raleigh News and Observer*, 17 April.
Pender, John 1997. 'Understanding Central Africa's crisis,' in Africa Direct (ed.) *Rwanda: The Great Genocide Debate. Conference Papers and Transcriptions*, 27 July 1997.

Philo, Greg (ed.) 1998. 'The Zaire rebellion and the British media. An analysis of the reporting of the Zaire crisis in November 1996 and 1997 by the Glasgow Media Group', London, background paper to the 'Dispatches from the Disaster Zone' conference, 28 May 1998.

Pottier, Johan 1996. 'Relief and repatriation: views by Rwandan refugees; lessons for humanitarian aid workers', *African Affairs* 95(380): 403–429.

—— 2002. *Re-Imagining Rwanda: Conflict, Survival and Disinformation in the late 20th Century*, Cambridge: Cambridge University Press.

Prioul, C. 1976. Pour une problématique de l'aménagement de l'espace rural au Rwanda', *L'informateur* 9.

Prunier, Gérard 1997. *The Rwanda Crisis, 1959–1994: History of a Genocide*, London: Hurst. Reprinted with an additional chapter.

Vidal, Claudine 1969. 'Le Rwanda des anthropologues ou le fétichisme de la vache', *Cahiers d'Études Africaines* 9(3): 384–401.

—— 1991. *Sociologie des Passions: Côte d'Ivoire, Rwanda*, Paris: Éditions Karthala.

Waller, David 1993. *Rwanda: Which Way Now?*, Oxford: An Oxfam Country Profile.

Chapter 11

Women and the politics of identity

Voices in the South African Truth and Reconciliation Commission

Fiona C. Ross

In observing the workings of the South African Truth and Reconciliation Commission, I have been struck by the formation and use of categories and their effects in understanding past violence. Here, I examine how, as a result of the tendency during the Commission's public hearings for women to describe men's suffering, 'women' emerged as a marked category in the Commission's work. I examine the consequences through close attention to the Commission's findings and then focus on one woman's testimony, showing how its complexity was filtered and reshaped in subsequent reports, including those of the media and the Commission. The final section of the chapter considers the Commission's findings about a site in which I conducted fieldwork. Here I show the difficulties of including subtle personal narratives in the crystallised forms generated by human rights discourses. The chapter illustrates the speed with which women's experiences, activities and identities are condensed, erased from or obscured in public recall.[1]

Giving voice to harm

A retrospective examination of gross violations of human rights committed between 1960 and 1994, the South African Truth and Reconciliation Commission (henceforth, the Commission) was an archival project. It was also something more: a specific, *public* form of bearing witness to violence and its consequences, a process of remembrance and a forum in which identities were articulated, negotiated and reformulated in the aftermath of institutionalised Apartheid. The Commission's tasks, established in law, were to document the nature, cause, patterns and extent of gross violations of human rights (defined in law as torture, abduction, killing or severe ill-treatment) committed inside South Africa and beyond its borders between 1960 and 1994. In order to achieve its goals, three committees dealt respectively with the tasks of offering amnesty to those who had committed crimes with political objectives, attending to testimonies and statements made by victims of gross violations of human rights and making recommendations regarding policies for redress.

The Commission represented an important mechanism through which some experiences and memories of violence and pain were given words. Victims were entitled in law 'to relate their own accounts of the violations of which they are victims' (Promotion of National Unity and Reconciliation Act, no. 34 of 1995). The measure was part of the Commission's task to 'restore the human and civil dignity . . . of victims' (ibid.). The Commission's work offered a particular discourse within which to place, describe and understand the violence of the past. In its work, violence was bifurcated into a concern with 'perpetrators' who committed acts of violence and 'victims' who suffered the consequences of violence: an approach criticised for obscuring the roles of beneficiaries (Mamdani 1996) and for failing to consider Apartheid's structural components (Submission by a coalition of NGOs 1997, Asmal *et al.* 1996). The Human Rights Violations Committee's definitions of violence and violation – laid down in law and predicated on ideas about the breaching of individual bodily boundaries – centred on 'the victim', defined as,

> (a) persons who, individually or together with one or more persons, suffered harm in the form of physical or mental injury, emotional suffering, pecuniary loss or a substantial impairment of human rights – (i) as a result of a gross violation of human rights; or (ii) as a result of an act associated with a political objective for which amnesty has been granted; (b) persons who, individually or together with one or more persons, suffered harm in the form of physical or mental injury, emotional suffering, pecuniary loss or a substantial impairment of human rights, as a result of such person intervening to assist persons contemplated in paragraph (a) who were in distress or to prevent victimisation of such persons; and (c) such relatives or dependants of victims as may be prescribed
> (Promotion of National Unity and Reconciliation Act, no. 34 of 1995)

Those who had suffered violations that fitted the legal criteria were invited to make statements to the Commission. By December 1997, the Commission's Committee on Human Rights Violations had received 21,298 statements concerning 37,672 violations (1998, Volume One: 166). Approximately 10 per cent of those who made statements during the Commission's process were invited to testify in seventy-six public hearings that began in April 1996 and continued throughout 1996 and part of 1997.

Seated on a stage facing a panel of Commissioners and committee members, accompanied by 'briefers', testifiers described the violations they and others had suffered. Behind them, flags proclaimed the Commission's mission: 'Truth, the road to reconciliation.' Hearings were widely broadcast in the print and electronic media. Accounts given before the public hearings on human rights violations were constructed by the rules of admission (such as the definitions of gross violations of human rights and of victims), the interpretation of these rules in process (see Buur 1999) and the narrative forms of testimonies (see Ross 2001 and 2003a). They were structured also by decisions made by individuals and by cultural patterns of expressing and acknowledging pain.

An imputation of passivity was built into the Commission's definitions and work. Testifiers were – by (self and legal) definition – victims. As such, they represented the locus of inflicted power. The Commission explicitly recognised this, stating,

> Victims are acted upon rather than acting, suffering rather than surviving. . . . [However, W]hen dealing with gross human rights violations committed by perpetrators, the person against whom that violation is committed can only be described as a victim, regardless of whether he or she emerged a survivor.
> (Report 1998, Volume One: 59)

Using the now defunct terminology of the Population Registration Act of 1953, the Commission reported that Africans made 89 per cent of statements (1998, Volume One: 168). No data is given on income levels, but the intersections of racial classification and class in South Africa are such that most testifiers were poor. Women gave approximately 50 per cent of the statements and African women gave 60 per cent of these (1998, Volume One: 169). 23,020 (61 per cent) of the reported violations were committed against men. The authors of the Commission Report argue that 'the violence of the past resulted in the deaths mainly of men' (1998, Volume One: 169). They continue (p. 171):

> Men were the most common victims of violations. Six times as many men died as women and twice as many survivors of violations were men. . . . Hence, although most people who told the Commission about violations were women, most of the testimony was about men.

Volume Four of the Report (p. 285) confirms the trend for women to testify about men (see also Ross 2001 and in press). Of female deponents, 43.9 per cent were identified as victims of gross violations of human rights (1998, Volume Four: 285), although the data presented shows marked differences by region. The most frequently reported gross violation of human rights suffered by women deponents recorded by the Commission falls into the category of 'severe ill-treatment' (1998, Volume Four: 286), a category that came under considerable debate and scrutiny within the Commission (see 1998, Volume One: 64–65 and 1998, Volume Five: 12–13, and Ross 2003b). No clear definition of 'severe ill-treatment', which included widely divergent experiences of violence, including beating, arson and solitary confinement, is provided in the volumes of the Report.

Prior to August 1996, few women deponents made statements concerning their own experiences of gross violations of human rights. Indeed, Commissioners often referred to women as 'secondary witnesses' because they made statements mainly about violations suffered by men. Some Commissioners and feminist activists expressed concern that women did not report violations, particularly those of a sexual nature. A position paper on gender (Goldblatt and Meintjies 1996) submitted to the Commission in March 1996, prior to the first hearings, seemed to have little effect on shaping how the Commission responded to deponents

(Owens 1996). Researchers and activists argued that women's silence about violation should not be read to mean that women had not suffered but rather to indicate that a different kind of social intervention was necessary to elicit stories of harm told by women about women. The gender submission pointed out that it was unlikely that women would easily come forward to share their experiences of pain, and argued that the Commission should

> reject a gender-neutral approach towards its analysis of evidence and in all other aspects of its brief. This means that gender must be incorporated into the TRC's policy framework for without this framework, gender issues, and women's voices in particular, will not be heard and accurately recorded.

The Commission was sensitive to the interpretation that it was not capturing what it called 'the complete story', more frequently glossed as 'the Truth'. The protocol used to record statements of human rights violations was refined throughout the two-year process of public hearings. By April 1997, it included a note to women deponents cautioning them: 'Don't forget to tell us what happened to you yourself if you were the victim of a gross human rights abuse' (Statement Concerning Gross Violations of Human Rights, Version 5, 1997: 3).

By mid-1996, the Human Rights Violations Committee devised a 'solution' to the 'problem' of the absence of women's stories of violation: 'Special Event Hearings' focusing on women's experiences. The hearings, held in Cape Town (8 August 1996), Durban (24 October 1996) and Johannesburg (29 July 1997), were aimed at eliciting descriptions of women's experiences of violation, particularly rape. A total of forty people testified or offered submissions to the Commission at these hearings. Two men testified about women's experiences; three women testified about the deaths of sons; four people presented three submissions to the Commission. Twenty-six women, most affiliated with liberation organisations or mass democratic movements, described violations committed against them, including horrific torture, rape, threats of rape or sexual violation, torture with electric shocks, separation from families and children. They stated that the lives of children and close kin were threatened. In Durban, young women who had been raped spoke anonymously from behind screens. A number of women who testified stated that other women they knew had been sexually violated, particularly during periods of detention and in the conflict between the ANC and IFP in KwaZulu-Natal. Most of the women identified the state and its agents as perpetrators of violations.

The women's hearings succeeded in drawing attention to particular forms of violence practised against women. However, few women who had been political activists testified to the Commission, whose record of the activities of women and youth in opposing Apartheid is scanty (Reynolds 1997). It was clear both during the Commission's work and from its subsequent Report that women's experiences are not easily translated into words for public consumption. When women did testify before the Commission, their words were not easily received (Goldblatt

1997, Ross in press). Below, I briefly describe the narrative forms of testimonies offered by women and explore the reformulation of testimony in a single case.

Speaking pain

I have described the diverse forms of women's testimonies elsewhere (Ross 2001 and in press). In general, most women testified about death of or injuries inflicted on their sons and, to a lesser extent, their husbands. Some spoke directly of violence, using plain language, frequently identifying representatives of the state as the cause of harm. A number of women showed horrid familiarity with the technologies of power that inflicted damage on bodies and relationships. Other women spoke more elliptically, drawing on metaphor, pause and gesture to create performances that carried their stories of harm. Many drew on domestic metaphor to tell the meanings of the harms wrought. Their descriptions show the intrusion of Apartheid at every level of life. They sometimes described their own violent responses to the intrusion of violence. A number implied their own political activism. Testifiers were often careful in describing the contexts within which violations were committed. Yet, few women initially testified directly about their own experiences of violation.

One woman who did describe her own experiences early in the Commission's process was Yvonne Khutwane, who had been an active member of mass democratic organisations in Zwelethemba, Worcester, Western Cape throughout the 1980s. On 24 June 1996 she testified at a Human Rights Violations Hearing in Worcester. She was sworn in at 3.10 p.m. before a panel consisting of four Commissioners (Denzil Potgieter, Wendy Orr, Alex Boraine and Mary Burton) and Pumla Gobodo-Madikizela, a young woman psychologist and member of the Human Rights Violations Committee. She spoke in Xhosa, assisted by Ms Gobodo-Madikizela. Her forty-minute testimony began with her warning to the panellists that her memory for dates was failing. She began by describing the funeral of four political activists – Mathew Goniwe, Fort Calata, Sparrow Mkonto and Sicelo Mhlawuli – who were killed by the police in 1985 in the Eastern Cape. A few minutes into her description, Ms Gobodo-Madikizela, interrupted her and asked, 'Are you trying to clarify how you got involved in politics?' Yvonne Khutwane replied,

> I started in 1960 to be involved in the ANC struggle. I was still a young girl. We worked underground, and it was very difficult for us even to hold meetings. I became prominent specifically when the Municipality offices were establishing community councillors, as you see this lady next to me on my left [a reference to her friend], we were the people who didn't like that.

Ms Gobodo-Madikizela intervened again and asked her to explain the events that led to her arrest and trial between 1985 and 1986. A founder member of the Zwelethemba Residents' Association, a grouping that stood in opposition to the state's local councils, Mrs Khutwane had been interrogated in 1984 about her involvement in protest activities designed to remove local councillors from power. She explained that when she had made a statement to the police, she realised that she may inadvertently have betrayed a comrade:

> It is then that I was affected severely, to the extent that, even today, I cannot explain [how it came] about that I should seem [to] have betrayed my friend. But fortunately . . . [he] won the case, he was acquitted.

Immediately after this description, Yvonne Khutwane embarked on a long and detailed explanation of her arrest in 1985 after the meeting to which she had alluded when she opened her testimony. The description was punctuated by questions from Ms Gobodo-Madikizela. On one occasion Ms Gobodo-Madikizela asked, 'In other words you are giving a statement in which you were degraded by the police: could you please just explain that?' Yvonne Khutwane described being interrogated about weapons possession and the burning of the municipal bar in Zwelethemba in June 1985 by progressives in Zwelethemba. She explained that she had been tricked into attending court: called there on the pretext that a charge she had laid concerning stolen property was receiving the court's attention, she had dressed smartly for her court appearance and had gone willingly, only to find that she had been duped. Instead of going to give evidence, she was taken to the police station for interrogation. During the interrogation, she was hit in the face and verbally abused by a white policeman 'young enough to be my son'. She fought back:

> When the fight continued, you could hear that there was somebody coming along and then they were ridiculing me and then saying I am a John Tait and a Gerrie Coetzee, the boxers. At the end I could see that they were also embarrassed because some of the black detectives came in. My shirt was in tatters and then one of them said, 'Are you fighting back, you kaffir?' Then they kept on insulting me.

In response to questions posed by Ms Gobodo-Madikizela, she explained that she had been pushed into a police van and driven to the township in leg irons and handcuffs. She was taken to her house which, she said, was 'infested' with policemen searching for weapons and the makings of petrol bombs. 'When we got there . . . there were still a lot of policemen around my place. You would think that a male person was arrested!' she told the panel.

The police did not find any weapons, but Yvonne Khutwane was arrested. At this point in the narration, Ms Gobodo-Madikizela intervened, prompting, 'Excuse me mama, can you please tell me what they did to you?' Yvonne Khutwane explained that she was locked in a cell:

> They [the police] said if I defy them I will be detained for years and I will never get out of prison again . . . I said I didn't care; they can do whatever

they liked. I was arrested and I was detained again. I was alone in the cell . . .
I was really in the solitary confinement. I was concerned about my child
because he was – I left [him] whilst I was taken to those offices. So I didn't
know where they have taken him.

She then explained that that night two policemen had taken her from the cell and
bundled her into a Hippo that drove out of Worcester and through Rawsonville,
a village a few kilometres away. As Mrs Khutwane embarked on a careful description
of the route, Ms Gobodo-Madikizela intervened: 'What were they doing to you,
as you are here?' In response to persistent questions posed by Ms Gobodo-
Madikizela, Mrs Khutwane described how two young white soldiers sexually
molested her.

> I was just alone at the back of the Hippo and they were just driving – it was
> pitch dark outside. They alighted from the Hippo and then they came to take
> me out of the Hippo. One of them said to me can I see what [situation] I
> have put myself in, and then they asked me when did I last sleep with a man.
> I was so embarrassed by this question. And I felt so humiliated. I informed
> them that I have nobody: I didn't have a partner. Then they asked me with
> whom am I staying. I informed them that I was with my family. The other
> question that they asked me is how do I feel when . . . I am having intercourse
> with a man. This was too much for me because they were repeating it time
> and again, asking me the same question, asking what do I like with the
> intercourse? Do I like the size of the penis? Or what do I enjoy most?
>
> So the other one was just putting his hand inside me [into] the vagina, I
> was crying because I was afraid. We had heard that the soldiers are very
> notorious for raping people. This one continued putting his finger right
> through [into] me, he kept on penetrating and I was asking for forgiveness
> and I was asking them, 'what have I done, I am old enough to be your mother.
> But why are you treating me like this?' This was very, very embarrassing.
>
> At the end . . . I think maybe God just came inside them and the other one
> said, 'Let's let her go', and then at the end they took me back to this police
> station and then they locked me up in the cell again. When I got inside there,
> I could see that there was one person inside the cell, I was afraid because this
> person was also – looked as if he is a male also, I was not trusting anybody
> now, I was suspicious of anything that was moving around.

A day later, Mrs Khutwane was interrogated by members of the Security Branch.
One, Geritt Nieuwoudt, emptied the breach of his gun of its bullets and hit
her repeatedly on the head with its butt as the other questioned her. Yvonne
Khutwane's description of the interrogation to the panel was interrupted again by
Ms Gobodo-Madikizela's questions about what information the police sought
from her. Yvonne Khutwane replied, with a hint of impatience, 'I am still saying
my story'. She continued by describing meetings held between blacks and whites

in Zwelethemba. Ms Godobo-Madikizela intervened once more, returning to the event of sexual violation. She asked Yvonne Khutwane to describe how she had felt about the experience of being molested by the policeman:

> I want to know and want to identify the situation that you were in while these people detained you. You have given us the – the other way that they treated you during that period and we got what you are trying to say and the way they treated you while you were in the van. . . . As I was sitting . . . listening [to your testimony] I couldn't take it, because our mothers are just the same age as yours and yet where there are people who . . . couldn't respect you – dishonour you as little [young] as [they] were.
>
> I just had the feeling that you could be my mother. That's where the pain is. We would like you to tell us, how were you feeling that time?

Yvonne Khutwane replied that the event had been painful and humiliating, not least because the men involved were young enough to be her children:

> It was so painful . . . because these kids were young and . . . they had all the powers [i.e. ought] to respect and honour me. They were just the same age as my children and what were they doing to me. I . . . think maybe they thought that I was just a black person . . . not knowing anything.

Ms Gobodo-Madikizela responded,

> Yes, it's like that, because like the one who slapped you hard on your face he was also a youngster. So I think they dishonoured you, humiliating you, lowered your dignity as much as they can. We would like to come to an end of this so that my colleagues [can] . . . ask you some questions. I would like to know how many children do you have? . . .

Mrs Khutwane replied that she now had four adult children, and, in response to further questions, revealed that she had been married but was now divorced and owned her own house (that is, was a woman of independent means). Ms Gobodo-Madikizela continued,

> I am just saying that you are also a mother. It's because I am imagining the way these children, these policemen . . . treated you. I had a picture in mind . . . [of] the way they were treating you.

Yvonne Khutwane described the appalling conditions of the jail, the lice in her cell and the brutal interrogation sessions in which she was repeatedly partially suffocated. She contracted meningitis and had been given wet blankets when she complained of the cold. She was refused medical attention until a lawyer intervened. Afterwards, she was sent back to prison. She was later released when a friend paid her bail. At the end of a trial in which she stood accused of inciting public violence, she was acquitted. During the trial, her house was bombed:

> During the period when I was detained, I was just in confused state. I didn't know what was happening to me. I didn't even know whether I was going to be acquitted or I was going to be kept for quite a long time. One of the people informed me that while I was detained my place was burnt down while I was in prison[2] and I was informed that . . . [a] petrol bomb was thrown at it. So, one of my children died because he had an epileptic attack.[3]

When she returned home after she was acquitted on all charges, she found herself alienated by her political community. Ms Gobodo-Madikizela asked Yvonne Khutwane to describe her feelings and the responses of residents in Zwelethemba:

> I had a picture in mind looking at the way they [i.e. the police] were treating you – even the people – the community people what were they feeling then. I . . . am wondering what was on your mind by the time they [the police] were moving with you in the van right around the location.

Mrs Khutwane answered,

> I thought that as I was one of the ANC members they wanted me to withdraw from the ANC not to hold meetings again because I would know what will be the treatment I will get, even now. . . .

Her response was not a clear answer to the question and Ms Gobodo-Madikizela asked, 'Were there people who said you betrayed others?' Mrs Khutwane replied by describing her feelings of alienation:

> I could see that even the community was ostracising me – I was being ridiculed by everybody because my house was destroyed through arson. But I have never turned my back against them. I am still an ANC member.

Ms Gobodo-Madikizela summarised Yvonne Khutwane's requests to the Commission: 'In your statement, you mentioned that we should find out why your house was burnt down . . . why you were degraded and why you were reported as an informer.' Mrs Khutwane agreed, asking that the case be investigated. Ms Gobodo-Madikizela then asked whether Mrs Khutwane knew the names of the policemen who had verbally abused and sexually molested her. She did not. Ms Gobodo-Madikizela asked what Mrs Khutwane would say to the young men if they were to ask for forgiveness. Yvonne Khutwane answered that she would tell them that, 'they should try to have manners'. At this point, her testimony came to an end. One-third of the time had been taken up with questions and answers about the event of sexual violation. The panellists did not pose questions. Dr Alex Boraine, the chairperson for the day, concluded,

You have been through a very hard time. Not only were you very badly molested and insulted, imprisoned, solitary confinement, charged, kept waiting for two years before your case was heard and found not guilty [but] then to find that your own friends and comrades suspected you of giving information and informing. You lost your house, your family has been unwell, you have suffered very, very deeply and we are very aware of the pain that you have experienced.

After thanking her, he asked her to step down from the stage and called the next witness. Yvonne Khutwane and her companion left the stage.

A diversity of harms becomes a story of sexual violation

In her testimony before the Commission, Mrs Khutwane described many experiences of harm and damage. They included the severe punishment meted out to political prisoners and the torture that women experienced. Her testimony described the connivance of the medical and legal systems in her ill-treatment, common complaints among the testifiers in the area. There is substantial evidence from public hearings of the Commission of collusion between state, police, and certain medical and legal practitioners throughout the country. (See 1998 Report, Volume Four: 109, 154, 155–157.) Mrs Khutwane told of the fragility of community relationships during violence: the apparent ease with which accusations of betrayal led to arson and ostracism, notwithstanding her claim to twenty-five years of work in the underground structures of the ANC. Her testimony linked several events into a continuous narrative of both tribulation and commitment. She described her experiences as a series of disasters that followed on from one another in rapid chronological and accumulative order and that were mediated by her self-conscious political knowledge. Carefully, she charted the intrusion of violence into her life: practices of violence that moved from her body's surface to its intimate spaces; a widening spiral of violence that once again impinged on the space of the domestic and destroyed her home. The descriptions presented her experiences as a seamless set of activities and relations in which she, as a political activist, was pitted against the state and as a consequence later came into – and appeared to have overcome – conflict within the community. Both Yvonne Khutwane and the Commission portrayed her story as emblematic of the experience of some activists: under surveillance by the police, detained or arrested, interrogated, tortured, her kin threatened, released, faced with community suspicion.

Yet, despite the diversity of harms that Mrs Khutwane described, many of which fell into the Commission's definition of gross violations of human rights, the print media and later the representations of her testimony in the Commission's Report depicted her as the victim of *sexual violation*. The South African Press Association (SAPA) reported the story as follows:

WORCESTER June 24 1996 – Sapa
WOMEN TELLS TRUTH BODY OF SEXUAL ABUSE
A Worcester mother of four on Monday told the Truth and Reconciliation
Commission how she was sexually molested and tortured by security force
members following her arrest in June 1985 for her involvement in African
National Congress activities. Testifying before the commission at its hearings
in Worcester, Yvonne Khutwane gave graphic details of the abuses she suffered
after two white soldiers removed her from her cell in the middle of the night
and drove her to a remote spot in a Hippo armoured vehicle. She was in her
mid-40s at the time of the attack.

'They asked me when I had last slept with a man. They asked how I felt
when I had intercourse with a man. I was so humiliated. I told them I did not
have a partner. One of them put his finger into my vagina. I was just crying.
He kept on penetrating me. I kept on asking for forgiveness and asking why
they were treating me like this. I said I was old enough to be their mother.
One of them then said "let her go". I think God came into him.'

Khutwane, a former member of the Western Cape Civic Association, said
she also suffered terrible injuries when she was interrogated by Paarl-based
security police. She named one of her alleged torturers as a Lt Gerhardt
Nieuwoudt, who she claimed sat on her chest. 'They also tried to suffocate
me with a towel. I was bleeding all over my body. My condition was very bad
and I was taken to hospital.'

During her detention her house was petrol-bombed after rumours spread
that she had become a police informer. In spite of being shunned by her
community, she had remained a loyal member of the ANC, Khutwane said.
(© South African Press Association, 1996
www.truth.org.za/SAPA/9606/S960624C.htm)

The report describes Mrs Khutwane as a mother of four, a middle-aged woman,
a person involved in ANC activities. She is not described as a political activist, and
her political 'involvement' in ANC 'activities' is secondary to the fact of her
motherhood. Her identities are described in almost the reverse order to her own
presentation of self in the hearing. The story highlights the sexual violation,
presenting the testimony as an uncomplicated story of sexual molestation and
torture. It is only in the last two sentences that the complexities of returning to
her community are described.

Yvonne Khutwane's testimony was also reported in the Cape Town daily
newspaper, the Cape Times, on Tuesday 25 June 1996 (p. 3):[4]

ANC VETERAN TELLS OF SEXUAL ABUSE
Soldiers the same age as her own children sexually assaulted African National
Congress veteran Mrs Yvonne Khotwane [sic].

Khotwane told the Truth and Reconciliation Commission yesterday her
involvement in the struggle went back to before 1960 – 'I was still a young

girl' – but it was in 1985 that she was made to suffer the greatest indignity of her life.

Accused of giving local youths petrol to make petrol bombs – she was prominent in the Zwelethemba township community's action against the community council system – Khotwane was arrested in June 1985 and held in Worcester.

Tortured, beaten and threatened continually after her arrest, Khotwane did not dream things could get worse. Then they did.

One night, two young soldiers loaded her into a car and drove about. Then they broached the subject of sex.

'They were asking me horrible things about intercourse. They wanted to know what I liked about intercourse, whether it was the size of the penis.'

One touched her.

'The other one was putting his hand inside me, on to my vagina. I was frightened because we had all heard how notorious the security forces were about raping people. He kept on penetrating me, and I was asking for forgiveness . . . I was old enough to be his mother, I was very frightened.'

'They were very young children. They were just the same age as my own children. I think maybe they just thought I was a black person . . . ' . '

When she cried, they threatened to shoot her.

Then they took her back to the police station. The threats and torture resumed.

After three months in detention, Khotwane was charged with public violence. The case dragged on for two years before she was acquitted. But her suffering was not over.

Some members of the Zwelethemba community thought she had cracked under the torture and passed information to the police.

Her house was burnt down.

'But I have never turned my back on them. I am still an ANC member.'

All of the newspaper articles focused on the event of sexual violation as *the primary event of harm*. Those that covered the story in some detail used extracts from Mrs Khutwane's testimony to describe the sexual violation but not any of the other violations. Two of the reports conclude with her assertion of political loyalty. In all the media representations, Yvonne Khutwane's story was presented as already intact: none of the reports showed how the testimony had been constructed, drawn from her through persistent questions and repetition. Rather, the event of sexual molestation was presented as though she had intended to speak of it all along and had done so without prompting.

The Commission's (1998) Report also describes her testimony in terms of sexual violation. Summaries of or direct quotes drawn from her public testimony are included in four places in the Report. In Volume Three (p. 448), quotations are included in a discussion of torture practices in the rural areas of the Western

Cape. Extracts from Yvonne Khutwane's description of sexual violation are quoted verbatim but the interventions by Ms Gobodo-Madikizela are erased from the narrative. In Volume Four (p. 298), Mrs Khutwane's description of the humiliation of being asked questions of a sexual nature by young men is included in a discussion of humiliations suffered by women. At no point in the Commission's Report is there a discussion of the possible humiliation of being asked questions about sexual violation by a young woman in public before an audience and in the knowledge that hearings were broadcast live on TV and radio and reported in the print media. A short description of the fight in which she was described as a 'Gerry Coetzee' is also included in the Chapter of the Report that deals with Women (Volume Four: 298). In Volume Five (pp. 352–353), in a section dealing with reconciliation and restoring the civil and human dignity of victims, extracts drawn from the section of Mrs Khutwane's testimony that described sexual violation are quoted in a discussion of the possibilities of healing offered through testimony. The author of the Volume states that Mrs Khutwane did not include the incident of sexual molestation in her statement concerning gross violations of human rights and states that the public hearing was the first time that Yvonne Khutwane had spoken about it.

The discussion continues by quoting her description of sexual humiliation and molestation. None of Ms Gobodo-Madikizela's interventions are included in the extract, which is presented as an intact and unmediated testimony. The author states,

> In her written statement, Ms Khutwane had made no mention of this sexual assault. In her debriefing session, she said that this was the first time she had spoken of it and that she felt tremendously relieved.

According to the Report, Yvonne Khutwane did not intend her public testimony to be concerned with sexual violation. The multiple facets of violence she described were displaced as her experience of sexual violence became the focal point of the panellist's interventions, and later, the media reports and the Commission's use of her testimony in its Report. The sexual violation was depicted in both the print media and the Commission's Report as the defining feature of Mrs Khutwane's testimony.

Recording violence and violation

'Women' emerged in the Commission's work as a category that sanctioned particular attention in the search for 'the Truth'. Women were not initially a focus for specific intervention, although the preponderance of women testifiers was noted early in the process of public hearings (Ross 1996). Gradually, as a pattern of testimonial practices in which women testified about sons emerged and solidified, their position was glossed as 'mothers' and then as 'secondary witnesses'. It was only later in the Commission's process that women were categorised and identified as potential 'victims' who had suffered a particular form of gross violations of human rights.

Of course, the knowledge that women had been subjected to specific forms of violence was not new. Documents published by the Detainees Parents' Support Committee in the mid-1980s described violence inflicted on women (see DPSC n.d.) as did 'alternative' newsletters such as *Crisis News*. The South African Institute of Race Relations' Annual Review of Race Relations has a limited record of women's experiences in detention (SAIRR 1960–1990, see Ross 2003b). Some of these materials are summarised in the gender submission (Goldblatt and Meintjies 1996). What I have described here however, is the emergence of 'woman' as a salient category within the Commission's workings. And, as Yvonne Khutwane's case illustrates, 'woman' was not a neutral category but a category that carried assumptions about the nature and severity of particular harms, particularly *sexual* violence. The focus owes something to the climate of violence against women and children in South Africa throughout the duration of the Commission's work and to increased media attention violence against women and minors in this period. In 1997, the South African Police Service estimated that a woman is raped every thirty-five seconds in South Africa (quoted in Shifman *et al.* 1997: 2).

The Commission did not offer a similar focus on sexual violation and rape inflicted on men. Few men described incidents of sexual violation. For the most part, rape and sexual violation were construed as acts of violence against women. As a result, it is not possible to examine the claims (such as those made by Diana Taylor for Argentina [Taylor 1997]) that military power works through (violent) feminisation of opponents.

Separate chapters in Volume Four of the Commission's (1998) Report deal with 'Women' and with 'Children'. There is no chapter on men. The chapter on Women (Chapter Five, pp. 282–316) presents data on the patterns of deposition that I have outlined above and describes the variety of harms to which women were subjected. It also points out (p. 286) the gender bias implicit in the Commission's mandate and interpretation of gross violations of human rights:

> The Commission's relative neglect of the effects of the 'ordinary' workings of Apartheid has a gender bias, as well as a racial one . . . The most direct measure of disadvantage is poverty, and there is a clear link between the distribution of poverty and Apartheid policies. Black women, in particular, are disadvantaged, and black women living in former homelands remain the most disadvantaged of all. It is also true that this type of abuse affected a far larger number of people, and usually with much longer-term consequences, than the types of violations on which the Commission was mandated to focus its attention.

The chapter's focus is on women as a particular category of victim of gross violations of human rights. Written by an independent consultant who specialises in research on women, it relies more heavily than others on testimonies and draws from critical analyses of the Commission's process and public hearings (Goldblatt 1997, Olkers 1996, Owens 1996, Ross 1996) to reflect on the data before the Commission. There is however, little other discussion of women's experiences and their diversity in the Report.

In the remainder of the chapter, I consider the findings concerning Zwelethemba – my fieldwork site and Yvonne Khutwane's home. As I show, it is difficult to insert the stories of women's experiences told to me into the Commission's chronology of violence and harm.

Zwelethemba was the site of sustained resistance to the state from the time of its formation in 1954. It was established to accommodate people classified as African who were forcibly removed from Worcester when the areas in which they lived were proclaimed residential areas for those classified White or Coloured. Residents consider the suburb to have been 'the spark that lit the fires of resistance in the Western Cape', and are justifiably proud of their role in opposing the Apartheid State.

Between 1997 and 1999, I have worked closely with women who were engaged in protest against the Apartheid State in Zwelethemba. We traced the many different expressions of women's political identities as these were manifest during the 1980s, particularly the period of the reimposition and annual renewal of the State of Emergency (1985 to 1990). In the discussion that follows, in order to reflect on the ways in which the past is described in the Commission's Report, I draw on the experiences of ten young women who were engaged to different degrees and with different consequences in youth protest and politics from 1979 to 1990.

In 1985, when the State of Emergency with its draconian measures was reimposed, the ten women varied in age from twelve to twenty-five years old. The women – Nowi Khomba, Nomeite Mfengu, Noluntu Zawukana, Nokwanda Tani, Noluthando Qaba, Ntsoake Phelane, Nokuzola Mtamo, Gertrude Siwangaza, Vuyelwa Xusa and Xoliswa Tyawana – were involved to varying degrees with formal structures of opposition to Apartheid. One was a trusted member of the ANC underground and a member of MK. She was one of two women in the focus group who had attempted leaving the country to join banned movements in exile: she was captured *en route* and severely tortured. Of the ten women, five had been detained for periods ranging from twenty-four hours to three months. All the women who were detained reported either having been tortured or having been present when their friends and comrades were tortured. Some were detained more than once. All of the women in the focus group reported having been beaten by police, or having witnessed the police beating others. Some had witnessed the deaths of comrades killed by the police or the deaths of suspected informers, burnt alive. All had attended funerals of young people killed in the violence that wracked Zwelethemba between 1985 and 1987. In every case, families were affected by violence. As I show below, it is difficult to connect their experiences with the chronology of violence that constituted the Commission's findings concerning Worcester (Report 1998, Volume Three: 428–30, 429, 444, 447–448).

In a section dealing with public order policing in rural areas in the Western Cape, the Commission Report (1998, Volume Three: 428–430) describes the escalation of violence in Zwelethemba in 1985. I have elaborated on the findings in italics to show the links between the events described in the Commission's Report and findings and the women with whom I worked and their kin. (Numbers in brackets refer to Commission case numbers and appear in the original text.)

Worcester

In Worcester, the spark was provided by the killing of Mr Nkosana Nation Bahume, after which a cycle of deaths and injuries took place until the end of the year.

On 16 August 1985, student activist Nkosana Nation Bahume (CT00547), aged twenty-one, was shot dead by the security forces. On 30 August, the local magistrate issued restriction orders on the funeral of Bahume, who was to be buried the following day. At the funeral, police fired on mourners, killing Mr Mbulelo Kenneth Mazula (CT00528), aged twenty. *[Vuyelwa's cousin, Brasilo Jacobs, went to assist Mazula when he fell. Jacobs was shot and injured. He fled to Cape Town where he was later shot and killed. It is believed that he was killed either by policemen or taxi-owners during a spate of violence between taxi-associations in the Western Cape. Many people accused the police of being complicit in 'taxi-violence'.]* An eyewitness testified that 'police dragged his body to the vehicle and took him to the mortuary'. People were assaulted, shot and detained by security forces in the uproar. *[Nokwanda and two other women were hiding from the police in an outside toilet at the time of the attack. The police saw them, captured them and told them to carry Mazula's body to the van. They were held in the van with the body for three hours before being released.]*

Mbulelo Mazula was buried on 8 September without incident. However, on 21 September 1985 Mr Andile Feni (CT08402) and two others were shot and injured by a policeman in Zwelethemba after a crowd had thrown a petrol bomb at a police officer's house after a mass meeting that had resolved to chase all police from the area following the killings.

On 1 October 1985, Mr Thomas Kolo (CT08400), age 18, was shot dead by security forces. *[Kolo was Ntsoake's cousin.]* He was buried on 11 October and the funeral was restricted by the magistrate. The following day, security forces shot Mr Zandesile Ntsomi (CT00320). Ntsomi's leg was amputated and he was discharged from hospital back into police custody the following day. . . . *[Nowi worked closely with Ntsomi in youth political structures. Together they were founder members of the Zwelethemba Youth Organisation, ZWEYO.]*

On 13 October, Douglas Ndzima (CT00821) was shot twice by police in Zwelethemba. That day Ms Martha Nomathamsanqa Mooi's house (CT03026) in Zwelethemba was petrol-bombed by UDF members. Mr Mpazamo Bethwell Mbani (Yiko) (CT03026), her brother-in-law, was shot dead and his body set alight. *[Mbani is widely believed to have assassinated Vuyelwa's uncle, Bubu Jacobs. The two men are buried alongside one another in the Zwelethemba graveyard.]*

On 2 November 1985, Mr Cecil Roos Tamsanqa van Staden (CT00132) *[another of Vuyelwa's cousins]* was shot by police and died two days later. The following day, Mr William Dyasi (CT00823) was shot dead by police in Zwelethemba. An inquest was held and Constable Michael Phillip Luff was found responsible for the murder but he was not prosecuted. At the intervention of the Commission the case was reopened, following which Luff applied to the Commission for amnesty (AM3814/96).

On 9 November, at the night vigil of one of the victims, Mr Buzile Fadana (CT00131) was shot dead after the police arrived and an 'armed encounter' resulted. His death marked an end to this cycle of killings and injuries that year.

By November 1985, an extreme environment of repression existed in Zwelethemba, which was declared out of bounds to all except residents. Roadblocks were set up and residents were only allowed to go to their homes on producing identity documents. There were twenty-four hour foot patrols, and searchlights swept the streets at night. Residents reported a heavy presence of Zulu speaking policemen. Funerals of unrest victims were restricted to only fifty people and the family of the deceased. In one instance, forty young people were detained whilst participating in a funeral vigil.

The Commission made the following finding about 'public order policing' in Zwelethemba:

> The Commission finds that the killing by police of Mr Nkosana Nation Bahume on 16 August 1985 triggered a sequence of violence in which numerous residents of Worcester were killed or injured by police and a number of persons or buildings were attacked in retaliation. The draconian response of the authorities, including curfews, roadblocks and sweeping detentions, only aggravated the situation.
>
> (Report 1998, Volume Three: 430)

There is scant focus on either the formal structures of protest or on attempts to halt violence. The chronology of men's deaths carries the weight of telling of the violence. Further description of events in Zwelethemba is provided in the section of the Report that describes violations in the Western Cape (Volume Three, Chapter Five).

[In] the early hours of 12 June 1986 with the declaration of a national state of emergency. Approximately 160 individuals were detained immediately and more over the next few weeks, including many of the people who had been detained in 1985. A non-governmental organisation (NGO) recorded 349 detentions in the urban Cape Town area over 1986. The majority of these detainees were released by the end of 1986. Among those detained were a Roman Catholic nun, an entire church congregation of 189 people in Elsies River, and Worcester UDF activist Christopher Tyawana, whose section 29 detention was brought about by a collaboration between the Security Branch and Allied Bank. *[Xoliswa Tyawana was detained three times for questioning about the whereabouts of her 'cousin-brother' Christopher. She was severely tortured. On one occasion she, Noluntu Zawukana and Ntsoake Phelane were detained on the same day. They were held overnight and the next day were blindfolded and, with some young men who had been detained with Noluntu, were taken away from the town to a deserted area. Noluntu and Xoliswa were tortured with electric shocks. Ntsoake heard them screaming in pain. The men were tortured too. Ntsoake said that it was nightfall that saved her from the same experience. As darkness fell, the policemen returned the detainees to their cells. Ntsoake, Noluntu and Xoliswa were released without charge.]*

It is difficult to place the experiences of the ten women within the narrative framework used by the Commission. They do not fit easily into the 'crystallised narratives' (Das 1995: 43) of gross violations of human rights. Young women in particular are less likely to appear in the chronology of violence or in the data collected by the Commission. Many did not testify or make statements. The Chapter on Women in the Commission's Report does not provide data on the ages of deponents at the time of the violation. Chapter Three of the Report (pp. 5–6) indicates that the majority of women who were victims of killings and torture fell between the ages of 13 and 36. Older women tended to report having been severely ill-treated: women between the ages of 37 and 48 were particularly affected.

Young women's stories are not widely documented elsewhere either (see Ross in press). For example, the Trauma Centre for Victims of Violence conducted research on detainees in Zwelethemba in 1995. None of the five women in my focus group who had been detained were interviewed in the process. The centre recorded only those who were detained for periods exceeding 48 hours. Yet, as Noluntu's detention and torture indicate, one cannot presume that those held for short periods were less badly treated than those whose detention periods were longer.

Conclusion

During the Commission's process, Pamela Reynolds and I wrote about the dangers of premature closure: 'It is dangerous to think that the truth has been excavated and reconciliation achieved and that therefore we can close the discussion on the past and, thus remembering, move forward' (Ross and Reynolds 1999: 7). We added a prediction: 'The Commission's work and final report run the risk of too simple a translation of the memory of pain from the intimate to the public, the risk of generating fixed positions' (ibid.).

A nuanced account of violence and the diverse ways in which it is (not) acknowledged is important for an understanding of the consequences of violence and forms of identity. There are tensions between the Commission's representation of pain and the perspectives that lie beyond its confines. These may be summarised as tensions between ideas of individual pain as a product of individualised violence, and ideas of 'the struggle' as a moral activity, collectively undertaken. It seems to me that in its focus on the violation of rights to bodily integrity, the Commission generated tensions at the same time as blurring distinctions between those who engaged in active opposition to the Apartheid State and those who, for many different reasons, did not.

Reviewing the work of truth commissions in Argentina and Uruguay in her provocative essay, 'Body memories: aides-memoires and collective amnesia in the wake of the Argentine terror', Julie Taylor suggests that the interrogatory and documentary practices that characterise truth commissions may produce forms of institutionalised forgetting. She argues that truth commissions reconfigure individuals, their collective struggle, ideals and political motivations into 'innocent or transgressing individuals with individual rights and obligations' (1994: 197). Writing of the *Nunca Mas* project in Argentina, she comments,

> Collective facts and sociopolitical identities underwent a profound transformation as they were denuded of the political language that had made them accessible to social actors in Argentina. The task of making sense of recent history had been assigned to an expert collectivity representing society. Truth was reached through methods of legal inquiry carried out by members of society other than those who had been the principal actors in the events.
>
> (1994: 197)

Her conclusion is that the precise practices of archiving represented by truth-garnering bodies are themselves intrinsically violent or violating – or minimally, misleading – both in what they purport to represent (human experience of violence and pain) and in their intention in so doing (to prevent future lapses into comparable violence). The efforts at documentation give rise to forms of genre, 'a collectively recognisable shape of accounts of lives and experiences', that, at the least, have a tendency to reproduce dominant modes of discourse and, like other genres, may 'share capacities to trivialise and exclude experience' (ibid.: 201). Taylor notes the consequent effect of transforming individuals from political activists to victims (ibid.: 198).

Taylor's is not the first account to recognise the propensity of human rights discourses, and indeed of much representation (especially that to do with violence, horror and pain), to elide individual experiences (see Schwartz 1997, Das 1997, Kleinman and Kleinman 1997) and cultural representation of harm and violence. Richard Wilson (1997), for instance, suggests that it is, perhaps, the function of human rights discourse to tame violence in this way: to remove it from the purview of harmed bodies and resistance practices to the domain of words and legalities.

The Commission's focus on 'women' permitted the expression of pain of a particular kind but also narrowed the focus, drawing attention away from women's multiple forms of political activism and strategies for coping with suffering. The category 'woman' emerged over time as a point of intervention for the Commission. The intervention crystallised around a set of narrative conventions and essentialist assumptions about women and the nature of particular kinds of harm.[5] I do not suggest that 'not-telling' is any less problematic, but rather draw attention to the exclusions and boundaries that some kinds of interventions in social life may generate.

Much current theoretical writing suggests that narrative is important in the work of restructuring individual and collective worlds shattered by violence (see Feldman 1991, Werbner 1998, Roth and Salas 2001). Yet, recounting harm is not simple. A growing literature indicates that pain, witnessing and language bear a complex relationship (see, for example, Agamben 1999, Scarry 1985, Langer 1991, 1995), suggesting that pain or horror cannot easily be recalled in language. Given this, processes of eliciting testimony are both fraught and admirable. But recording stories of harm through bureaucratic processes may 'fix' identities in particular ways, constraining the range of expression and acknowledgement and imposing narrower limits on an understanding of agency than might be possible, necessary or desirable. If, as seems to be the case, the model offered by the Commission is to be copied or adapted for use elsewhere, then 'rights of recountability' (Werbner 1998: 1), must be secured in ways that do not limit acknowledgement or harm or narrow the range of identities necessary for living in (the aftermath of) the raw life.

Notes

1 I am grateful to Pluto Press for permission to republish material which appears in my book *Bearing Witness: Women and the Truth and Reconciliation Commission in South Africa* (London and New York, 2003).
2 This appears to be a mistranslation. The house was attacked while she was on trial, having been released from prison on bail.
3 From her Commission testimony, it is not clear whether the child died of an epileptic attack triggered by the arson or in a separate incident. In fact the child's death was not linked to the arson attack.
4 I am grateful to the *Cape Times* for permission to reprint the article here.
5 I do not assume 'woman' or 'womanhood' to be a homogeneous category or even one that is meaningful at all times. Henrietta Moore (1994) has described identity as fragmented and ruptured. She suggests that 'experience . . . is not individual and fixed, but irredeemably social and processual' (1994: 3).

References

Agamben, Giorgio 1999. *Remnants of Auschwitz: The Witness and the Archive* (trans. Daniel Heller-Roazen), New York: Zone Books.
Asmal, Kader, Asmal, Louise and Roberts, Ronald Suresh 1996. *Reconcilation Through Truth: A Reckoning of Apartheid's Criminal Governance*, Cape Town: David Philip.

Buur, Lars 1999. 'Monumental history: visibility and invisibility in the work of the South African Truth and Reconciliation Commission', paper presented at the conference, *The TRC: Commissioning the Past*, University of the Witwatersrand, 11–14 June 1999.

Das, Veena 1994. 'Our work to cry, your work to listen', in Veena Das (ed.) *Mirrors of Violence: Communities, Riots and Survivors in South Asia*, Delhi: Oxford University Press, pp. 345–398.

—— 1995. *Critical Events: An Anthropological Perspective on India*, Delhi: Oxford University Press.

—— 1997. 'Language and body: transactions in the construction of pain', *Daedelus*, 125(1): 67–92.

Detainees Parents' Support Committee. n.d. *A Woman's Place is in the Struggle and Not Behind Bars*, Johannesburg: DPSC.

Feldman, A. 1991. *Formations of Violence*, Chicago, Ill.: University of Chicago Press.

Goldblatt, Beth 1997. 'Violence, gender and human rights: an examination of South Africa's Truth and Reconciliation Commission', paper presented to the annual meeting of the Law and Society Association, St. Louis, Missouri.

Goldblatt, Beth and Meintjies, Sheila 1996. *Submission on Gender to the Truth and Reconciliation Commission*, Johannesburg: University of the Witwatersrand.

Kleinman, Arthur and Kleinman, Joan 1997. 'The appeal of experience, the dismay of images: cultural appropriations of suffering in our times', *Daedelus* 125(1): 1–25.

Langer, Lawrence 1991. *Holocaust Testimonies: The Ruins of Memory*, New Haven: Yale University Press.

—— 1995. *Admitting the Holocaust: Collected Essays*, Oxford: Oxford University Press.

Mamdani, Mahmood 1996. 'Reconciliation without justice', *South African Review of Books* 46, November–December: 3–5.

Moore, Henrietta 1994. *A Passion for Difference*, Cambridge: Polity Press.

Olkers, Ilze 1996. 'Gender-neutral truth: a reality shamefully distorted', *AGENDA* 4: 61–67.

Owens, Ingrid 1996. 'Stories of silence: women, truth and reconciliation', *AGENDA* 5: 66–72.

Promotion of National Unity and Reconciliation Act, No. 35 of 1995, Cape Town: Government Printers.

Reynolds, Pamela 1997. Unpublished Inaugural Lecture, University of Cape Town.

Ross, Fiona 1996. 'Silence and secrecy', paper presented to the Faultlines Conference, Cape Town: Breakwater Lodge, University of Cape Town.

—— 2001. 'Speech and silence: women's testimony in the first five weeks of public hearings of the South African Truth and Reconciliation Commission', in Veena Das, Arthur Kleinman, Margaret Lock, Mamphela Ramphele and Pamela Reynolds (eds) *Remaking a World: Violence, Social Suffering and Recovery*, Berkeley, Calif.: University of California Press, pp. 250–279.

—— 2003a *Bearing Witness: Women and the Truth and Reconciliation Commission in South Africa*, London: Pluto.

—— 2003b. 'Measuring wrongs with rights: method and moral in the work of the South African Truth and Reconciliation Commission', in R. Wilson and J. Mitchell (eds) *Human Rights in Global Perspective*, London: Routledge, pp. 163–182.

Ross, Fiona and Reynolds, Pamela 1999. 'Wrapped in pain: moral economies and the South African Truth and Reconciliation Commission', *Context* 3(1): 1–9.

Roth, Michael and Salas, Charles (eds) 2001. *Disturbing Remains: Memory, History and*

Crisis in the Twentieth Century, Los Angeles, Calif.: Getty Research Institute.

SAIRR 1960–1990. *Annual Review of Race Relations*, Johannesburg: SAIRR.

Scarry, Elaine 1985. *The Body in Pain: The Making and Unmaking of the World*, New York: Oxford University Press.

Schwartz, Vera 1997. 'The pane of sorrow: public uses of personal grief in modern China', *Daedelus* 125(1): 119–148.

Shifman, P., Madlala-Routledge, N. and Smith, V. 1997. 'Women in Parliament caucus for action to end violence', *AGENDA* 36: 23–6.

Statement Concerning Gross Violations of Human Rights 1997. Truth and Reconciliation Commission, Cape Town.

Submission by a coalition of NGOs to the Commission, 1997. 'Submission to the Truth and Reconciliation Commission concerning the relevance of economic, social and cultural rights to the Commission's mandate', 18 March 1997. http://www.truth.org.za/submit/esc6.htm.

Taylor, Diana 1997. *Disappearing Acts: Spectacles of Gender and Nationalism in Argentina's 'Dirty War'*, Durham, N.C.: Duke University Press.

Taylor, Julie 1994. 'Body memories: aide memoires and collective amnesia in the wake of the Argentine terror', in Michael Ryan and Avery Gordon (eds) *Body Politics: Disease, Desire and the Family*, Boulder, Colo.: Westview Press, pp. 192–203.

Werbner, Richard 1998. 'Smoke from the barrel of a gun: postwars of the dead, memory and reinscription in Zimbabwe', in R. Werbner (ed.) *Memory and the Postcolony: African Anthropology and the Critique of Power*, London: Zed Books, pp. 71–102.

Wilson, Richard (ed.) 1997. *Human Rights, Culture and Context*, London: Pluto.

Chapter 12

Ambiguous identities

The notion of war and 'significant others' among the Tigreans of Ethiopia

Kjetil Tronvoll

Introduction

To understand the effect at the grassroots of modern warfare and armed conflict poses a great challenge to social sciences in general and social anthropology in particular. With anthropology's reliance on fieldwork, the methodological constraints imposed by warfare create obstacles to our study of micro-level social processes. Simons claims that

> with a few notable exceptions, anthropologists have barely studied modern wars, and when modern war is treated as a subject, it is the why behind the fighting and the aftermath of it – not the how or the process – that receives most attention.

> (1999: 74)[1]

The difficulties of data-gathering in contexts of war also have an influence on the development of anthropological theory.[2] This chapter aims to correct some of these shortcomings by highlighting one aspect of identity formation during war, exemplified by the case of the recent Eritrean–Ethiopian war (1998–2000): the chapter challenges the notion of a singular significant or relevant 'other' in the creation and maintenance of boundary mechanisms within theories of ethnicity and nationalism during conflict and war. The contention argued is that the notion of a significant 'other' related to ethnic and national boundary mechanisms during wartime has generally been viewed from a macro level with a 'top-down' approach, and has thus been too much influenced by the production of 'formal nationalism' (or ethno-nationalism) (Eriksen 1993a), blurring the actual empirical processes on the ground. Hence, the notion of a significant other is portrayed as a singularly understood, commonly perceived concept by all the members of the in-group. This is a simplification which, according to the Ethiopian material presented here, overlooks the individual creation of selfhood and the multivocal capacity of ethnicity and nationalism; a capacity which is increased during conflict and war due to the grave impact of violence which permeates all aspects of everyday life.

The situation at the local level in times of war is complex, contested and contradictory, creating an empirical flux that macro-level theories seldom manage to incorporate and reflect. During war, there are individuals attached to the military, the government or administration who work and argue in favour of warfare. Others, on the other hand, are desperately trying to avoid enemy attacks, recruitment to the army, or political mobilisation in favour of the politics of war. Some feel comfortable and identify with the nationalistic rhetoric, others reject it and give their loyalty to counter-nationalistic forces and feel at ease within sub-national or supra-national groups. At local, regional and national levels, processes of identity formation, negotiation and re-creation are taking place, involving a multitude of different actors; the state and government, military and party, intellectuals and NGOs, churches and community-based organisations, and so on. All these actors produce information that influences the formation of identities in place as well during times of war and conflict. However, the experience and perception of this flow of information is likely to vary from individual to individual, based on his or her subject positions and life histories. Hence, the formation of their identities during conflict also takes on different expressions.

War and the formation of identities

Theories of ethnicity and nationalism embed a notion of the 'other' as inextricably linked to the concepts of a collective ethnic or national identity. From the time of Fredrik Barth's seminal statement that 'ethnic distinctions do not depend on an absence of social interaction and acceptance, but are quite to the contrary often the very foundations on which embracing social systems are built' (1969: 10), and until today, the unambiguous position of a significant or relevant 'other' within the studies of identity has more or less been taken for granted. Generally, the notion of a significant other is cast in cultural, social or political terms, emphasising processes of dichotomisation and identifying distinctions – or boundary markers in Barth's terminology – where they exist, or the creation of new ones where none are to be found. The issue stressed is that a collective group 'identity' cannot be established without the presence of a singularly perceived significant other external to the group of concern.[3] Collectives, or rather individuals in leading positions within collectives, be that the ethnic group or nation, need to constantly re-create and demarcate the boundaries of identity towards the contrasting 'other'.[4]

During times of conflict and war, ethnicity and/or nationalism as political ideologies are generally understood to be at their peak and most powerful in influencing collective identities, establishing clear-cut distinctions between the 'in'-group and 'out'-group.[5] The 'cohesion' theory, as it has been labelled, advocates that:

> all internal group solidarity is a product of external armed conflict, or the imminent threat thereof. In a crisis, in the heat of battle, old divisions are laid aside, and the nationalist dream of ethnic fraternity becomes a momentary reality.
>
> (Smith 1981: 378)

In other words, war will enhance mechanisms of boundary creation and maintenance between the antagonistic factions. The strong force of nationalism during conflict will thus create a dichotomising process that helps to 'homogenise' the two warring factions, since, it is argued, few or no traits that may identify sub-groups or diverging views are displayed.[6] The classic formulation of this view is argued by Simmel (1964, first published in 1908), and it still has resonance among current researchers. Bourne writes, for instance, that 'identification of and mobilisation against external enemies is an effective means of creating loyalty, uniformity, and mystical attachment to the state' (Bourne in Sorensen 1993: 12).[7]

From the point of view of power-holders at a macrolevel, such theories might present an adequate argumentation of the formation of national and/or ethnic identities. Indeed, I have written elsewhere on how the recent Eritrea–Ethiopia conflict helped to demarcate and sustain a 'formal' national Eritrean identity, contrasted against an Ethiopian 'other' (see Tronvoll 1999). However, if we want to view conflict and war from the grassroots up, and analyse how violence impinges on the everyday life of individual citizens, such macro-oriented models might confuse more than they enlighten, and tend to blur or over-simplify the actual empirical processes on the ground.[8] Hence, this chapter seeks to challenge the assumption that during war collective identities, be they ethnic or national, are necessarily undergoing a homogenising process, streamlining a singularly understood concept of identity among the 'in'-group and cementing the image of only one significant other.

Anthropology's focus on person and self may form a contrast to the 'homogenising' tendencies of collective identity theories. Self-identity is something that has to be established socially through a set of discourses which are both discursive and practical, argues Henrietta Moore. She claims that these discourses establish the grounds for identities and the framework(s) within which identity becomes intelligible (1994: 37). Particular experiences and subject positions during individual life-histories shape people's reaction to and conceptualisation of war and violence, and consequently how they interpret the formation of collective identities such as ethnicity and nationalism.

Thus it is important to recognise that people differ in the way they imagine themselves – both as individuals and as members of a collective – and how they imagine others, both as individuals and members of other collectives. This requires attention to the individual and agency, particularly when it comes to analysing ethnicity and nationalism. Epstein claims that 'ethnic identity is always in some degree a product of the interaction of inner perception and outer response, of forces operating on the individual and group from within, and those impinging on them from without' (1978: 101–102). Thus, if we treat ethnicity and nationalism as a tactical posture only, we ignore the important aspects of self-consciousness and the symbolic expression of group identity. Anthony Cohen argues that 'when I consult myself about who I am this entails something more than the negative reflection on 'who I am *not*'. [. . .] It is the *symbolic* expression of ethnicity which renders it multivocal' (1994a: 61). To turn Cohen's words into mine, just because one identifies oneself as Tigrean rather than as Eritrean, it does not necessarily mean that one is just like every other Tigrean. One do not have to sublimate oneself in an anonymising 'Tigreanness' in order to suggest that Tigreans have something significant in common which distinguishes them from Eritreans. Moreover, Cohen argues further that 'because ethnic identity is expressed symbolically, it is possible for this internal diversity to be preserved, even while it is masked by common symbolic forms' (ibid.: 62). Thus, Cohen's assertion may at first sight appear similar to Barth's famous contention: ethnicity has a definite appearance, but rather indefinite substance. But, Cohen qualifies it by stressing that 'indefinite means just that, rather than 'insubstantial.' It is simultaneously indefinite and substantial because it is informed by self experience and self consciousness' (ibid.). Hence, we may find a variety of ethnic expressions within one 'ethnic group', reflecting *individual* life histories and experiences. And, from this it follows they we will also find a variety of significant others against which these identities are contrasted.

Tigray: a history of violence and the flux of identities

Violence is not something novel and unexperienced in the lives of the Tigrean population. Quite the contrary, violence forms a common thread in most people's life histories, and links one generation with the next through the common experiences of past, current and future violence. Few regions in the world are so war-torn as the Horn of Africa, where inter- or intra-state conflicts have been rampant during most decades in this century. This history made Sorensen say: 'Ethiopia became the emblem of disaster, a symbol of the nightmarish collapse of all order' (1993: 1).

In 1991, two major wars originating in the area came to an end: the thirty years of liberation war waged by the Eritrean People's Liberation Front (EPLF) who finally succeeded in ousting the Ethiopian army from Eritrean soil; and the 'seventeen-years-of-struggle' pursued by the Tigrean People's Liberation Front (TPLF) also against the Marxist Derg government in Ethiopia. The combined effect of these two wars led to the military defeat of the Derg government, and consequently the establishment of Eritrea as an independent state and the coming to power in Ethiopia of the Ethiopian People's Revolutionary Democratic Front (EPRDF), a TPLF-led coalition movement. Both these two movements – the EPLF and the TPLF – have as their core constituency the Tigrinya-speaking population dispersed in the highlands on both sides of the border between Eritrea and Tigray in Ethiopia (the trans-Mereb, named after the border river Mereb). During their struggle against the centralised and Amharised Derg regime, they were also exposed to the same policy of violence. A Tigrean social anthropologist who wrote on the formation of Tigrean and highland Eritrean (the trans-Mereb area) identities during the Derg period stated that:

the inhabitants of the trans-Mereb were treated as disposable and torturable. They were subjected to deportations, conscription and mass murder. Intellectuals and professional elites were being falsely implicated as members of the insurgent groups, arrested, tortured and/or killed.

(Alemseged Abbay 1998: xi).

Sadly, the wars continue in the trans-Mereb, and violence was once again infecting the area in the late 1990s, turning everyday life into turmoil with the outbreak of the Eritrean–Ethiopian war.[9] Present impressions of violence are thus affected by past histories and the prospects of future incidents of violence. The youngsters of the area understand their parents' stories of and reaction to past violence under the Derg regime based on their own experiences of the current violence, as it will form their behaviour towards their own children's participation in or victimisation under future violence.[10]

This continuous experience of violence during shifting political contexts radically impinge on local conceptions of allegiances and identities: yesterday's liberators become today's suppressors; friends and kin who once were considered to be unshakeably likeminded change their views and positions on vital matters; last year's brother-in-arms is your current enemy; today's confidants become next week's informers. There are shifts the other way around too; from bad to good. Past perpetrators may turn into present human rights defenders. Enemies become friends, superiors become equal. Individuals living in destitution and with lost illusions turn into determined citizens fighting for common goods. Old divisions and schisms are forgotten and new allegiances are established and friendships made. Thus, in such a context, to establish a common significant other for people to identify against might not be that easy. Haile Berhane,[11] an elder farmer from eastern Tigray, has somehow internalised this notion of shifting ethnic-based political alliances in his world, as he reflected upon the wars he has experienced.

Haile Berhane is 60 years and the father of eight children, of whom two have been TPLF fighters since 1985.

'Since I had contributed two of my children to the 17 years of struggle long ago, I was not asked for more. Indeed I feel proud for not being asked this time,' he states.

'Has the new conflict changed your daily life?' I inquire.

'Yes I'm strongly affected. I consider it as if someone is snatching or taking the food I was supposed to swallow. Moreover, my children are not beside me for support, because of the war. As a result I'm not getting the proper fatherly assistance that a father is supposed to get,' he says grudgingly. After a moment, he continues:

'We were very happy in the old days, though. Then we had one king and one crown for both people, and this is how it should be. Even a cow will not be sent alone to grass without a shepherd. But now we gave them [Eritrea] independence and allowed the cow to grass alone. However, it turned out to be unable to do that, and hence created a problem for us, leading to the present terrible situation.'

I am catching interest in his new line of thought, and asks:

'Is highland Eritrea [*kebessa*] historically part of Tigray?'

'Yes, the Eritrean highland is historically part of Tigray. Our children, sons and daughters, even when they quarrelled with the family, used to go to Eritrea and work there in order to come back later to a better position and with a good amount of money for the family. They did this because the highland was more of a kitchen for all of us to use. Today, however, even those who are gone are unable to come back and we don't know about their whereabouts.'[12]

'Tell me,' I ask, 'how has the historical, cultural and political relationship between the Tigrean and Amhara people been?'

'Well, the history of the Tigrean people and the Amhara was basically a history of political disobedience. Haile Selassie leading the Amhara people tried to impose Amhara domination over Tigray. We refused and revolted in 1943.[13] His successors had also tried to dominate their supremacy over us in the name of the Amhara people. We revolted and achieved what we are now, the second Woyane. Thus, to me there was no long and deep cordial cultural or historical relationship between the Tigreans and the Amhara.'

I become encouraged by his outspokenness, and I decide to challenge him further on the shifting ethnic allegiances.

'Today, the Amhara you used to consider as an enemy are behind you in the war against Eritrea. How do you see this?'

'The Eritreans like the Tigreans were heavily dominated and used to suffer under the yoke of the Amhara since the days of Haile Selassie,' responds Haile, continuing,' however, like us they took control over Asmara in 1991. Nevertheless, soon they caused the deportation of many Amhara from Eritrea. Not to mention the destructive and cruel inhumanity they inflicted on the Amhara soldiers, killing them, looting their property and even taking the gold out of the teeth of their dead corpses! Now the Amhara people are siding with us against the Eritreans just to revenge all this.'

Our discussion continues into a description of the relationship between Tigreans and other ethnic groups in Ethiopia, before we turn back to the issue at hand, and I explain to Haile:

'For me as a foreigner, even though I have read Ethiopian history, it is confusing to see the constant shift of allegiances. One day Eritrea and Tigray fight the Amhara, today the Tigrean and Amhara fight the Eritreans, and tomorrow we might have yet another change. Why is this so?'

'Although we have shifting allegiances, the people do not change. The Tigreans were fighting the Amharas, being supported by the Eritreans. Now the Tigreans are supported by the Amharas in our fight against Eritrea, and it's not surprising. Moreover, the reverse again might be true tomorrow! It is the same people, but passing through historical changes and shifting kings [i.e. political contexts]. When we were fighting with the Derg, that was the time the Amharas were killing us, making all kind of suffering on us, throwing all kind of bombs on our grassing and farming lands. We never used to think that the Derg would come to its demise, and that the torrential rain would stop. Nevertheless, God has shown us the death of the Derg and the defeat of the Amhara by us. Not sooner than this the Amhara who were our yesterdays' mortal foe and enemy are siding with us against the Eritreans. Therefore, who knows what tomorrow will bring? May be the Eritreans who are fighting and killing us today will come to us in peace tomorrow?'

It is obvious that a shifting political landscape in trans-Mereb has influenced the identification of a significant other to contrast a Tigrean – and/or an Ethiopian – identity against. Changing political elites have had different political agendas and have thus sought to establish different ethno-political alliances, which again have influenced the understanding of ethnic and national allegiances of their subjects. As for the story of Haile Berhane, it is futile to analyse his life history and conceptualisation of identity as a fixed and singular expression of identity. Rather, it can be seen instead as an identity based on a series of subject positions, some conflicting or mutually contradictory, that are offered by the different contexts and discourses that change the political landscape he is trapped in at infrequent intervals (cf. Moore 1994).

Throughout the various wars and conflicts, violence has recreated past impressions of significant others and formed future ones. Violence as such is perceived as an enduring social and political phenomenon, which manifests itself within all aspects of social life. Hence violence will have an 'essentialising' effect on the formation of identities (Povrzanovic 2000: 154). The Eritrean–Ethiopian war abruptly changed the formal presentation of official Ethiopian enemy-images, and the Ethiopian government changed EPLF from being an ally and friend into a collective enemy for the Tigrean group and the Ethiopian people at large. Consequently, political entrepreneurs (i.e. TPLF cadres) were encouraging the Tigreans to establish allegiances with other ethnicities, like the Amharas, Oromos and so on, in order to mobilise resources against the new enemy. However, since different wars have swept over the trans-Mereb during the last decades, individuals have been forced into different personal allegiances with the many warring factions operating in the area, be they TPLF, Derg, EPLF or some other movement.[14] These previously personal allegiances were influencing the positions and attitudes taken towards the formally designated significant other, the EPLF.

Who is the 'other'? Tigrean voices

Contemporary politics and present experiences bear heavily upon all Tigreans. Not one household was left untouched by the Eritrean–Ethiopian war, through recruitment to the army, economical constraints, family members injured or killed, displacement, political distress and so on. How does this form the perception of identities and the role of a significant other? Let us hear two more voices explaining their life in the midst of war and conflict, representing two different life histories within a wide range of individually situated positions.

Workilull is 42 years of age, and the chairman of the local branch of the Women's Association of Tigray (WAT), an organisation with a strong, although informal, bond to the TPLF. She has been responsible for her own household since she was 18 years old, when her newly married husband went 'to the jungles' (joining the TPLF) in the late 1970s, and she has given birth to and raised eight children from the age of 4 to 19 years. Her husband remained a TPLF frontline fighter throughout the struggle against the Derg regime. He was demobilised in 1995 and was starting to adapt to a civilian life for the first time in his adulthood when the new war erupted in 1998 and he immediately rejoined the army. Thus, Workilull is once again left alone with the children and the responsibilities of the household.

> 'Are you afraid that your elder son will be sent to the frontline?' I inquire.
>
> 'I don't have the slightest fear,' she responds. 'It's rather me who encouraged him to decide and he has made up his mind. In fact the first round of recruited youths is ready and will be sent off tomorrow. However, my son is allocated in the second batch that I hope will not be far away.'
>
> 'Why do you want your son to go to the frontline, your husband is already there?'
>
> 'Yes, it is true that his father is at the frontline, but our son is basically born to stand by for his mother country. Therefore, if he did not decide to defend the country, on whose soil can he then stand? I was three months pregnant with him when his father joined the Woyane [TPLF] nineteen years ago. It was only in 1987 that his father came and met him for the first time. Our son has an obligation to continue the struggle as his father does,' she explains calmly.

Her steadfastness and patriotic conviction that seemingly make her willing to sacrifice both her husband and eldest son at the warfront may not be that surprising, considering her life history and personal political conviction, to which she refers in order to interpret the ongoing war.

> 'Are you afraid for the well-being of your children and yourselves because of the war?'
>
> 'We know that a cruel and powerful enemy is in front of us. We know that the enemy could inflict all possible miseries on us. However, we are in a state of war and these things happen in wars. We [the women] are even insisting on going to the frontline to fight, being side by side with our brothers,' she says in a determined manner.

Workilull has seemingly no difficulties in accepting the new war and the need for Tigray to mobilise resources, both in manpower and in kind, to fight it. Her life history has inspired her support of the TPLF and the Tigrean revolution. She not only feels comfortable with the nationalistic rhetoric and the creation of EPLF as the significant other; she is also actively participating in the process herself. Being the local chairman of WAT she is touring the area visiting female-headed households for support and addressing public gatherings to encourage people to give donations to the warfront. However, when we ask her directly about her feelings towards the Eritrean people, she hesitates and states,

> They are our brothers. There is nothing wrong with them, but by snatching their children and throwing them to the burning fire, this man [Issaias Afwerki, president of Eritrea] has decided to see the two brothers destroy each other.

Modifying somehow her previous stand, Workilull narrows in on the significant other and instead of casting it in cultural or ethnic terms, identifying all Eritreans, she describes it in political terms as the EPLF and its leadership only. Thus, the cultural and kinship affinity to the Eritrean highlanders (*dekki kebessa*) is restored.

Let us move on and present another story, the one of Hiwut Hagos,[15] a woman in her middle age from a village just some few kilometres south of the main frontline at Zalambessa.

> 'You have a lot of experience and lived through various difficult times and wars. Could you share some of your experiences with us?' I ask.
>
> 'What is war?' she responds thoughtfully. 'I've seen many things in my life. I've seen and experienced a number of wars, but I've found them useless for me. In an earlier war I've lost one of my sons. I'm now left with one son only, and now they [TPLF] are pressuring me to give them the only son I'm left with. I'm spending the night praying and holding the "pillars" so they will not cave in on me. My husband is confined to his bed sick and blind. My daughter is changing her face and becoming bony. Not because she could not find something to eat, but they have denied us our single and only surviving son. He was a hope for "our face and the eye for us". He is forcefully recruited to go to the training centre and they will take him tomorrow!' she cries. 'We will surely miss him. This is a big devastation to the family.' Hiwut is all tears: 'We are seeing him off, weeping and crying. There is nowhere to fly. They're pressuring us and even those who were not willing to go will be forced. They argue that your country is invaded and there is no one to defend it other than you.'
>
> I have sympathy with the old lady and am uncomfortable with what she tells me about the political pressure she is under. 'How will this situation affect your household directly when your son is leaving?' I wonder.
>
> 'When he leaves, I will have several problems,' Hiwut explains. 'Who will be responsible to farm my lands? Who will look after me? I will be left like a "dry wood" [useless] with my blind husband. You see our physical bodies only, but they are mere containers. We are as living dead,' she says.

'Are you offered any help from the baito [local administration]', I inquire?

'Yes, the local community will afford me some assistance. But under any circumstances it could not be compared with what my son could do for me. His departure is a loss.'

'What kind of changes will this war bring to Tigray and you?'

'There is nothing we can gain from the war, except we are being destroyed and are dying like flies,' Hiwut answers.

I am curious about what happened to her oldest son. She looks at me with sad eyes and tells briefly.

'He was forcefully recruited to join the Derg army and served there for six years. He was killed in action in 1991 fighting the TPLF, only two months before the peace,' she explains with a sad voice.

Hearing this, I fell quiet once again and didn't know how to continue without being too intrusive into her personal grief. However, after a minute, she continues herself:

'It was only the last five days that I decided to collect money by serving as a daily labourer myself in the communal water and soil conservation scheme.[16] It used to be my oldest son who was looking after us. He was the breadwinner of the household. But then the Derg took him. Now the Woyane [TPLF] are taking my youngest son by force, darkening the household once again. I don't even have a single chicken in my house. They are neither making us benefit from the grain aid package. They are taking him and killing the household,' she utters bitterly.

'But households who contributed sons to the 17 years of struggle are excused,' I say.

'I have never contributed a son before in the armed struggle,' Hiwut explains. 'The only son I have left is this one. I cannot cut him into two pieces and give one piece to them before, and reserve the other piece for me now! It's unfortunate I happen to only have one son left', she resigns.

'But your oldest son died in the war too. What is the difference?' I try to argue.

'Yes, be it on the wrong or the right side, I have sacrificed a son in the struggle too. They should have considered and seen that. But who dares to speak out on that now?'

I cannot argue against her on that issue. It is of course impossible for her to raise such a question under the current circumstances. I try to get her to explain to me who the actors in the war are.

'Who is fighting with whom? Whose war is this?' I ask.

'What can I say?' she sighs. 'Both [EPLF and TPLF] are destroying for their own supremacy and I observe that we [the ordinary people] are being destroyed. The war is being fought between the two elephants, Meles [prime minister of Ethiopia] and that terrible man; I forgot his name [Issaias Afwerki, president of Eritrea]. While doing this they are finishing the people.'

'Is it a war between Eritrean and Ethiopian people or is it a war between the political leaders?' I follow up.

'The two leaders are the mechanics in this war, but they are using the people as firewood. This is the reality. I do not want to hide that, not to say the truth from the bottom of my heart.'

In Hiwut's view the TPLF is just as much an adversary to her survival as the EPLF is. The TPLF killed her oldest son and is now taking away her youngest son too. For her the current war does not concern some disputed territories and the national integrity of Ethiopia. It concerns her personal survival and the well-being of her family. So far, the TPLF has only brought her sorrow and there is no need for her to have a distant actor as the EPLF as a significant other, while the TPLF is so much closer at hand.

These and similar voices are heard throughout Tigray: some clear and positioned, supporting the government stand, some muted and indecisive, and others reluctant and protesting. As these individuals digest the flow of information reaching them, and observe local action taken by the authorities, they interpret the war and make up their impression on what this is about – who the significant other is for them. These are not individuals trapped in the trenches at the frontline, who have a clear and present 'other' just some few hundred metres away dug in at fortified positions, ready to kill. For the military personnel and the frontline fighters, few grey zones exist. They live in constant fear of combat and engagement with Eritrean troops. Hence, the possibility of interpreting the situation in varying degrees is limited. It is you against the enemy. Period. If you don't kill him, he will kill you. For the civilians living in the rural areas indirectly affected by the war, on the other hand, the landscape is somehow more confused and blurred. They are not eye to eye with the Eritrean soldiers. Their everyday experiences are not trench warfare and bombing, but the struggle to cope with agricultural activities when most of the men are mobilised, or to secure enough food for their children when the evening falls. They are not harassed by Eritrean shelling, but by the local TPLF administrators who are pressuring them to give their sons to the warfront, or some food to the soldiers, or money to the displaced. For the peasants in Tigray and elsewhere in Ethiopia, the war means that the state is intruding into their household and private sphere, prying for resources to confiscate on behalf of a war very few people really understand. Thus, some may perceive a significant other much closer to their everyday sphere than the Eritrean soldiers at the warfront, namely the state represented by the local administrator who is continuously harassing and pressuring them to contribute whatever meagre resources they have to the war effort.

The violent making and unmaking of identities

Violence is not expressed in a dichotomy between the perpetrators as active and victims as passive. Stereotypes of this kind blur the fluid, contested and negotiable manifestation of violence (cf. Nordstrom 1995), and hence how violence impinges on the formation of identities. National narratives of war are created with the intention of enhancing the willingness of the citizens to participate in and sacrifice for the war effort. However, since war and violence is perceived differently by individuals, so also are the national narratives. Povrzanovic writes from the Croatian war theatre that:

> The variety of experiences and responses of civilians who are not recognised as victims tends to be overlooked. Croatian war ethnographers have been trying to express that variety and reveal that the national narrative and personal narratives on the war differ considerably and in some cases are scarcely compatible.
>
> (2000: 153)

Moreover, Allen Feldman, in his seminal work on political violence in Northern Ireland (1991), explains that violence in itself is formative, in that it shapes people's perceptions of who they are and what they are fighting for across space and time – a continual dynamic that forges as well as affects identities. And, since each person's experience of war and violence is unique, and the expressions and characteristics of violence vary from village to village, from area to area, violence must necessarily form every person's identity individually. Thus, to concentrate only on the formation of a collective ethnic or national identity in response to 'collective violence' might obscure the actual empirical processes on a micro level.

The formation and negotiation of identity has been and still is a favoured subject within anthropology. In the classic Copperbelt studies anthropologists had already concluded that ethnicity and social identities in general are relative and to a certain degree situational. Whether or not ethnicity should be made relevant in an interactional context, or which 'identity' to communicate in specific social interactions, are questions that have been thoroughly studied in many anthropological cases. It is also well documented that the boundary markers which defines the 'we' group may expand and contract according to the specific situation. However, most of these studies have taken for granted that individual identities are being constructed in the images of their collective representations. Hence, the studies have been more concerned with analysing the boundaries of the collective, or a segment of the collective, rather than with individuals as autonomous agents. This is also the core of the critique raised by Anthony Cohen against anthropological constructs of collective boundaries of identity, such as ethnicity or nationalism. Cohen argues that:

> Rather than questioning their existence [collective boundaries], or questioning the extent to which they might reasonably be generalised (*whose* boundaries are they?) they [anthropologists] have been concerned almost exclusively with the ways in which boundaries are marked.
>
> (1994a: 64)

Anthropology (and social science in general) has been too concerned with 'making order out of chaos' and has used boundary mechanisms as a convenient analytical tool for that purpose. But by doing so, anthropologists have 'imputed boundary-consciousness to people without pausing to enquire quite what it is of which they are supposed to be conscious,' as Cohen explains it (ibid.: 65). In this chapter I have made an attempt to drive this argument further within an Ethiopian context, and shown how violence actually reinforces diversity in identity, rather than eliminating it. War and conflict impinge directly on every household, forcing all individuals to take a stand and to adapt to the changing circumstances created by warfare. Since political affiliation and loyalty build on individual experiences and life histories, and violence is unequally distributed and individually perceived, it is not a question of the creation of 'one' boundary demarcating a single collective identity against the enemy as the significant other. It is a matter of individuals forming their own consciousness of identity under, or parallel to, or outside the formation of a 'formal' or official collective identity, and hence the creation of multiple 'significant others'.

Teame Medhin[17] may serve as an illustration to the above point on violence and its impact on individual identity formation – or, in other words, the violent making and unmaking of identities. Today Teame is a farmer and a strong supporter of TPLF's war with Eritrea. However, some extracts of his intriguing life history tell us that he has not always been supportive of the TPLF, or hostile towards the Eritreans for that matter.

> Teame explains: 'During the hardships in the late 1970, my family and I had a difficult time to get enough food. At the same time there was political unrest in the area and Woyane and EPRP [Ethiopian People's Revolutionary Party] were fighting each other here in Tigray, simultaneously as they fought the Derg. I was struggling to acquire a living for my family, when I decided to join the army [Derg military]. At that time I did not have the slightest political conviction, know-how or understanding of the war,' he hurriedly excused himself, before continuing: 'I simply joined them on the basis of the wheat-salary we received as militia members. I believed we should stay in Ogaden to fight the Somali invasion of our motherland. After a while, however, in 1984 the Derg transferred us from Ogaden to Asmara [capital of Eritrea]. We spent only a day in Asmara before we were taken to the front to fight the Shabia [EPLF] under the Weqaw regiment. For one year I was fighting the Eritrean rebels before the Shabia captured me during combat.'
>
> Teame goes on to tell about the time as a prisoner of war, when he was kept in caves for almost five years. The conditions of imprisonment in the caves have ruined his lungs and he is constantly coughing and having difficulties to breathe. During this time, Teame tells, he gradually developed a Tigrean consciousness, since the EPLF treated them harsher than the Oromo prisoners.[18]
>
> 'The majority of the prisoners were Oromo and the Shabia [EPLF] was frequently taking Oromos out of the prison camps and gave them military

training in order to be integrated later into the Oromo Liberation Front,' Teame explains. 'As such the Oromo prisoners were treated cordially and well, while the Tigreans were under Shabia's strict control. The Shabia used to think that all Tigrean prisoners were Woyane.'

Teame tells how he was later released into the custody of the TPLF. We continue to talk about the reasons why the new war erupted and Teame reflects upon the Tigrean position.

'In a certain way the Woyane cannot escape from taking a historical responsibility of causing the war on itself. It was the Woyane that gave Eritrea its independence and created favourable conditions for its growth, making military contributions to Eritrea and paying all sorts of political price for it in Ethiopia. And still the Shabia invaded us! This has caused a deep anger and frustration among the Tigreans in particular. We know the Eritreans and we know each other [the other Ethiopian groups]. We don't need any military assistance from the Amhara, Oromo and other peoples. Tigrean heroism is sufficient for fighting the Eritreans, whom we know very well in fighting. We are, however, currently facing some unorthodox experiences at the battlefront where non-Tigrean fighters are captured by the Shabia and surrender voluntarily to them!'

I interrupt him and ask if he means that they are not good fighters and that Tigray can take care of this issue alone. Teame hesitates and rephrases his earlier explanation, accepting that non-Tigreans can go to the frontline.

'However, we Tigreans are nearer to the front and we have a profound history of struggle and heroism, thus we only need economical assistance from the others. Otherwise our fighting spirit and cult of heroism is much superior to the Eritreans and we don't need the issue to take a national dimension. The issue is very narrow and not too complicated, thus we can handle it ourselves,' he states self-confidently, and continues surprisingly by saying: 'Ethiopia can only get peace, liberty and territorial integrity if and only if the Tigreans and Eritreans are going to war. For Ethiopia to remain in peace the two people have to fight so that the political situation remains intact. Eritrea and Ethiopia can only live in peace if both of us are going to war. Because if we occupy Eritrean territory and continue the war in order to strive for more territory which is not ours, we will be defeated and destroyed. Likewise, if they dare to do the same, they will also face a similar fate,' concludes Teame with a Machiavellian attitude towards power balance and politics.

'Has the relationship always been like this between Eritrean and Tigray?' I wonder.

'No, no,' rejects Teame. 'This is due to a political confession we gave them recently. Since we gave them their independence just some years back, this problem is also new, something which has grown out of the current political situation. [. . .] What is puzzling us and became abnormal for us is the event of this year [i.e. the new war]. Otherwise there is no doubt that we [Tigreans and Eritreans] are one and the same people.'

During a three-hour conversation with Teame where he recalled his 'political life history', he projected several different identities with correspondingly different 'significant others' based on a series of subject positions. Starting with being 'an Ethiopian' during the Derg and serving in the national army against enemies of the state (i.e. first Somali, subsequently the resistance movements of the EPLF and the TPLF), he later recast his boundaries of identity more narrowly as a Tigrean nationalist, defining Eritrea/EPLF as the major significant other, with other Ethiopian groups, such as Amhara and Oromo, as minor 'significant others' to distinguish his Tigrean identity against. Finally, Teame ends up with modifying his narrow Tigrean consciousness, and defines his identity boundaries according to a trans-Mereb view, i.e. a greater Tigrinya identity within a greater Ethiopian identity sphere. This synthesised version of Teame's boundaries of identity clearly shows that the specific political and discursive contexts at particular times during his life have influenced his own understanding of identity. Thus, by adopting the collective as the main focus of analysis, one will overlook or neglect the continuous shifting positions of individuals in and out of that collective.

Conclusion: the ambiguity of identity

Anthropological studies have shown that social identities are segmentary in character, a model first described by Evans-Pritchard in his seminal study of the Nuer (1940). Thus, being a member of a lineage or clan does not preclude being a member of an ethnic group; and being a member of an ethnic group does not preclude that the same individual also may hold a national identity. However, for that more encompassing identity to exist, it must be socially relevant and attractive for its potential members to identify with. It must also have some goods to deliver for its potential members, be that material, political or symbolic: goods which are perceived as valuable by the target group (Eriksen 1993b: 76). The question will thus be whether being a 'Tigrean' or 'Ethiopian' is more socially relevant and attractive during this war than identifying with sub-ethnic and sub-national groups and identities. It is not necessarily the case that during conflict and war, ethnicity and nationalism, or other social categories as gender and age for that matter, are an obvious basis for solidarity.

Conventional ideologies of nationalism and/or ethnicity tend to over-emphasise the division of individuals into two mutually exclusive and fixed categories of 'insiders' and 'outsiders'. Moreover, such theories advocate that conflict and war with the out-group will reinforce and cement a 'black and white' stereotypification of the relationship between the in-group and out-group, at the same time as having a homogenising effect within the in-group. The Ethiopia material, on the other hand, indicates that identity-formation processes which take place during conflict are much more complex and ambiguous than previously argued. Rather than only stressing common denominators of inclusion or exclusion in identity formation and the drawing of national and/or ethnic boundaries, one should make allowances for individual subject positions and contradictory and conflicting aspects of identities. Fredrik Barth claims in a recent article that 'people's own experience of a cultural contrast to members of other groups is schematised by drawing an ethnic boundary, imposing a false conceptual order on a field of much more broadly distributed cultural variation' (2000: 30). But, Barth substantiates, at the same time as the boundary demarcates groups, it also connect groups. 'To draw a boundary is a cognitive act that lays down some premises; but it does not determine all the social forms that eventuate,' he explains, and continues:

> The affordances of a boundary set the scene for social activities, and in that sense, yes boundaries also connect. But the connections that emerge are the work of people who respond selectively and pragmatically to the affordances, spinning connections in forms that will be shaped by social and material processes, not by cognitive fiat as the drawing of the boundary was.
>
> (ibid.: 30)

During conflict and war, the socio-economic and political processes are at their most influential and impinge directly on every household in the conflict zone, and thus have the strongest potential to shape individual 'connections'. Hence, during conflict and war it might be beneficial for the study of identity formation to focus on the *individual* rather than on the collective. Individual experiences of terror and violence and material and social processes will influence people's understanding of the collective. Still, they might use collective forms to assert their identities, 'but we should not mistake these for *uni*formities', as Anthony Cohen argues (1994b: 178). The collective, be it the ethnic group or the nation, and its boundaries, signifies different things to different actors. An individual's loyalty to the group is never so pressed and challenged as in times of war. Thus, it is no wonder that the processes of recasting or reinventing the boundaries for the collective from the individual's point of view is also at its peak during war, as the ambiguity of identity is easily pliable. As anthropologists, with our advantage of qualitative methodology and fieldwork, we need to be perceptive towards the more complex and contradictory social processes which influence cognitive operations and people's conceptualisations of their own group and their significant others during conflict and war. These are processes which are blurred and over-looked when conflict and war are viewed and analysed on a macro level with a top-down approach.

Notes

1 The reference work *The Anthropology of War* edited by J. Haas (1990), for instance, only covers war in stateless societies. For examples of anthropological case studies of modern warfare, see, for instance, the monographs of Daniel (1996) and Nordstrom (1997), and the edited volume by Sluka (2000).

2 On fieldwork and data-gathering during conflict and war, see the seminal edited collection of Nordstrom and Robben (1995). See also Lee (1995).

3 See Triandafyllidou 1998 for an overview on the recent theoretical debates on this issue.

4 In recent years there have been an upsurge of studies on the 'anthropology of boundaries'. For further reading into this field, see Donnan and Wilson (1994), Michaelsen and Johnson (1997), Wilson and Donnan (1998), Conversi (1999) and Cohen (2000).
5 Some even go as far as to negate this contention, and claims that 'the lack of a common distinctive culture, which can promptly identify or mark a group, is likely to generate violence' (Conversi 1995: 80).
6 Within cognitive theory this is explained in the manner that the more emotionally aroused people become, the more narrowly are their concern focused and the fewer are the categories they use to interpret their experiences and surrounding social and political context. The implication, argue cognitive theorists, is that the more emotionally charged individuals are, as most people tend to become during conflict and war, the less finely tuned are the distinctions they make in categorising other people and the 'grey' zones of ambiguity vanish until one is left with a dichotomised division of only two categories: 'with us' or 'against us'.
7 Some argue that similar processes of 'homogenisation' also may occure in intra-state wars, where inter-ethnic/political coalitions are formed as a consequence of authoritarian policies by governments (see Afflitto 2000).
8 For a joint political science and social anthropological effort to address 'perspectives on nationalism and war', see the edited volume by Comaroff and Stern (1995).
9 For an introduction to and explanation of the 'second' Eritrean–Ethiopian war (1998–2000), see Negash and Tronvoll (2000).
10 A number of studies on the 'anthropology of violence' have been published in the recent years. For two illustrative volumes discussing various aspects of violence, war and identity, see Aijmer and Abbink (2000) and Schmidt and Schröder (2001).
11 Name altered.
12 Due to the outbreak of war, several thousands of Ethiopian 'guest-workers' in Eritrea were trapped on the other side of the frontline, unable to go back to their homes in Tigray or elsewhere in Ethiopia.
13 This uprising was called *Woyane*, today used as a popular term for the TPLF (see Gebru Tareke 1996 for an analysis of this uprising).
14 Several political/military resistance movements were operating in Tigray in the 1970s and into the 1980s, such as: Ethiopian People's Revolutionary Front (EPRP), Ethiopian Democratic Union (EDU), Tigray Liberation Front (TLF), Eritrean Liberation Front (ELF).
15 Name altered.
16 Peasants receive 7 birr (less than one USD) per day when they work on communal agricultural rehabilitation programmes.
17 Name altered.
18 Between 1985 and 1988 TPLF and EPLF had a breach of relations and were engaged in a fierce 'ideological warfare' against each other.

References

Abbay, A. 1998. *Identity Jilted or Re-Imagening Identity? The Divergent Paths of the Eritrean and Tigrayan Nationalistic Struggles*, Lawrenceville, N.J.: Red Sea Press.
Afflitto, F.M. 2000. 'The homogenizing effects of state-sponsored terrorism. The case of Guatemala', in *Death Squad. The Anthropology of State Terror*, Philadelphia, Penn.: University of Pennsylvania Press.
Aijmer, G. and Abbink, J. (eds) 2000. *Meanings of Violence. A Cross Cultural Perspective*, Oxford and New York: Berg.

Barth, F. 1969. 'Introduction', in F. Barth (ed.) *Ethnic Groups and Boundaries: The Social Organization of Cultural Difference*, Oslo: Universitetsforlaget.

—— 2000. 'Boundaries and connections', in A. P. Cohen (ed.) *Signifying Identities. Anthropological Perspectives on Boundaries and Contested Values*, London and New York: Routledge.

Cohen, A.P. 1994a. 'Boundaries of consciousness, consciousness of boundaries. Critical questions in anthropology', in H. Vermulen and C. Govers (eds) *The Anthropology of Ethnicity: Beyond Ethnic Groups and Boundaries*, Amsterdam: Het Spinhuis.

—— 1994b. *Self Consciousness: An Alternative Anthropology of Identity*, London and New York: Routledge.

—— (ed.) 2000. *Signifying Identities. Anthropological Perspectives on Boundaries and Contested Values*, London and New York: Routledge.

Comaroff, J.L. and Stern, P.C. 1995. *Perspectives on Nationalism and War*, Amsterdam: Gordon and Breach Science Publishers.

Conversi, D. 1995. 'Reassessing current theories of nationalism: nationalism as boundary maintenance and creation', *Nationalism and Ethnic Politics* 1: 73–85.

—— 1999. 'Nationalism, boundaries, and violence', *Millennium: Journal of International Studies* 28: 553–584.

Daniel, E.V. 1996. *Charred Lullabies: Chapters in an Anthropography of Violence*, Princeton, N.J.: Princeton University Press.

Donnan, H. and Wilson, T.M. (eds) 1994. *Border Approaches: Anthropological Perspectives on Frontiers*, Lanham, Md.: University Press of America.

Epstein, A.L. 1978. *Ethos and Identity*, London: Tavistock Publications and Chicago, Ill.: Aldine Publishing Company.

Eriksen, T.H. 1993a. 'Formal and informal nationalism', *Ethnic and Racial Studies* 16: 1–25.

—— 1993b. *Ethnicity and Nationalism: Anthropological Perspectives*, London and Boulder, Colo.: Pluto Press.

Evans-Pritchard, E.E. 1940. *The Nuer*, Oxford: Oxford University Press.

Feldman, A. 1991. *Formations of Violence: The Narrative of the Body and Political Terror in Northern Ireland*, Chicago, Ill. and London: University of Chicago Press.

Haas, J. (ed.) 1990. *The Anthropology of War*, Cambridge: Cambridge University Press.

Lee, R.M. 1995. *Dangerous Fieldwork*, Thousand Oaks, Calif.: Sage Publications.

Michaelsen, S. and Johnson, D.E. (eds) 1997. *Border Theory. The Limits of Cultural Politics*, Minneapolis, Minn. and London: University of Minnesota Press.

Moore, H.L. 1994. *A Passion for Difference*, Cambridge: Polity Press.

Negash, T. and Tronvoll, K. 2000. *Brothers at War: Making Sense of the Eritrean–Ethiopian War*, Oxford: James Currey.

Nordstrom, C. 1995. 'War on the front lines', in C. Nordstrom and A.C.G.M. Robben (eds) *Fieldwork Under Fire: Contemporary Studies of Violence and Survival*, Berkeley, Calif.: University of California Press.

—— 1997. *A Different Kind of War Story*, Philadelphia, Penn.: University of Pennsylvania Press.

Nordstrom, C. and Robben, A.C.G.M. (eds) 1995. *Fieldwork Under Fire. Contemporary Studies of Violence and Survival*, Berkeley, Calif.: University of California Press.

Povrzanovic, M. 2000. 'The imposed and the imagined as encountered by Croatian war ethnographers', *Current Anthropology* 41: 151–162.

Schmidt, B.E. and Schröder, I.W. (eds) 2001. *Anthropology of Violence and Conflict*, London and New York: Routledge.

Simmel, G. 1964. *Conflict and the Web of Group-Affiliations*, New York: Free Press.

Simons, A. 1999. 'WAR: back to the future', *Annual Review of Anthropology* 28: 73–108.

Sluka, J.A. (ed.) 2000. *Death Squad. The Anthropology of State Terror*, Philadelphia, Penn.: University of Pennsylvania Press.

Smith, A.D. 1981. 'War and ethnicity: the role of warfare in the formation, self-images and cohesion of ethnic communities', *Ethnic and Racial Studies* 4: 375–397.

Sorensen, J. 1993. *Imagining Ethiopia: Struggles for History and Identity in the Horn of Africa*, New Brunswick, N.J.: Rutgers University Press.

Tareke, G. 1996. *Ethiopia: Power and Protest. Peasant Revolts in the Twentieth Century*, Lawrenceville, N.J.: Red Sea Press.

Triandafyllidou, A. 1998. 'National identity and the "other"', *Ethnic and Racial Studies* 21: 593–612.

Tronvoll, K. 1999. 'Borders of violence – boundaries of identity: demarcating the Eritrean nation-state', *Ethnic and Racial Studies* 22: 1037–1060.

Wilson, T.M. and Donnan, H. 1998. *Border Identities. Nation and State at International Frontiers*, Cambridge: Cambridge University Press.

Index

For Product Safety Concerns and Information please contact our EU
representative GPSR@taylorandfrancis.com
Taylor & Francis Verlag GmbH, Kaufingerstraße 24, 80331 München, Germany

www.ingramcontent.com/pod-product-compliance
Lightning Source LLC
Chambersburg PA
CBHW070354270326
41926CB00014B/2551

9 7 8 0 4 1 5 2 9 0 0 7 4